MEMORY'S LIBRARY

MEMORY'S LIBRARY

Medieval Books
in Early Modern England

JENNIFER SUMMIT

THE UNIVERSITY OF CHICAGO PRESS

CHICAGO AND LONDON

Portions of chapter 1 were previously published as "'Stable in Study': Lydgate's *Fall of Princes* and Duke Humphrey's Library," in *John Lydgate: Poetry, Culture, and Lancastrian England*, edited by Larry Scanlon and James Simpson (Notre Dame, IN: University of Notre Dame Press, 2006). Portions of chapter 3 first appeared as "Monuments and Ruins: Spenser and the Problem of the English Library," *English Literary History* 70.1 (2003): 1–34.

The University of Chicago Press, Chicago 60637
The University of Chicago Press, Ltd., London
© 2008 by The University of Chicago
All rights reserved. Published 2008.
Paperback edition 2011
Printed in the United States of America

20 19 18 17 16 15 14 13 12 11   2 3 4 5 6

ISBN-13: 978-0-226-78171-6 (cloth)
ISBN-10: 0-226-78171-2 (cloth)
ISBN-13: 978-0-226-78170-9 (paper)
ISBN-10: 0-226-78170-4 (paper)

Library of Congress Cataloging-in-Publication Data
Summit, Jennifer.
Memory's library : medieval books in early modern England / Jennifer Summit.
    p. cm.
Includes bibliographical references and index.
ISBN-13: 978-0-226-78171-6 (alk. paper)
ISBN-10: 0-226-78171-2 (alk. paper)
    1. Libraries—England—History—1400–1600.   2. Libraries—England—History—17th century.   3. Books and reading—England—History—16th century.   4. Books and reading—England—History—17th century.   5. England—Intellectual life—16th century.   6. England—Intellectual life—17th century.   7. Reformation—England.   8. Book collecting—England—History.   I. Title.
Z791.E5S86 2008
027.042—dc22   2007044242

CONTENTS

ILLUSTRATIONS

ACKNOWLEDGMENTS

Given that this is a book about libraries, it is a special pleasure to acknowledge the libraries in which I researched and wrote it. I am grateful to the librarians and staff at the following institutions: the British Library; the Bodleian Library, Oxford University; Cambridge University Library; Folger Shakespeare Library; Hereford Cathedral Library; the Huntington Library; Lambeth Palace Library; Magdalene College, Cambridge; the Parker Library, Corpus Christi College, Cambridge; and Trinity College, Cambridge. I owe special thanks to the wonderful librarians at Green Library, Stanford University, especially John Mustain and my colleagues on the Parker Library on the Web project.

I am also grateful for fellowships I received from the National Endowment for the Humanities and the American Council for Learned Societies, as well as for research support from Stanford University, for which I owe thanks especially to Deans Keith Baker and Sharon Long.

I have had new reasons to recall with gratitude the contributions that my teachers made to my thinking about topics developed in this book: to Jonathan Goldberg, John Guillory, Daniel Kempton, Mary Poovey, and Winthrop Wetherbee I am pleased to extend my thanks.

I have been fortunate at Stanford to be able to pursue my work within a stimulating community of colleagues. Among them I thank especially Cécile Alduy, John Bender, George Brown, Terry Castle, Paula Findlen, Denise Gigante, Hans Ulrich Gumbrecht, Roland Greene, Nicholas Jenkins, Seth Lerer, Stephen Orgel, Patricia Parker, Rob Polhemus, David Riggs, Ramón Saldivar, and Michael Wyatt.

Opportunities to share my work at conferences and talks have helped shape this book in important ways. I am grateful to my hosts and audiences at U. C. Davis, Ohio State, U. C. Irvine, and the University of Pennsylvania, and I am also grateful to the organizers of conferences and sessions where I presented this work at various stages: Patricia Badir, Elizabeth Hageman, Chris Ivic, John King, Sarah Salih, and Grant Williams.

Among the many colleagues who have read this work or offered important guidance while it was in progress, I thank especially David Baker, James P. Carley, Joyce Coleman, Margreta de Grazia, A. S. G. Edwards, Margaret Ferguson, Angus Fletcher, Alexandra Gillespie, William Kuskin, Richard J. Palmer, Sara S. Poor, Catherine Sanok, Larry Scanlon, Colin G. C. Tite, and David Wallace. I couldn't have wished for more thoughtful responses than I received from William Sherman, James Simpson, and Peter Stallybrass, all of whom read the entire manuscript at a late stage. Jason Friedman and Kasey Mohammad offered editorial help at a crucial moment. And I am especially grateful for the contributions and help of Stanford graduate students past and present: including Janelle Fender, Karen Gross, Randy Johnson, Jenna Lay, and Ryan Zurowski. I am also grateful for the astute readers' reports I received from the University of Chicago Press, as I am for the help of Pamela J. Bruton, Randolph Petilos, and Alan Thomas.

For debts of a more personal nature I am happy to thank my family and friends. I thank Ruth Firth for her many kindnesses and remember with gratitude the conversations I had on antiquarian topics with the late Mike Firth. This book develops from a lifelong conversation I continue to enjoy with my father, Roger K. Summit; I am grateful to him for fostering my appreciation for libraries, as I am to my mother, Ginger Summit, who took me to my first ones.

While this work was in progress, the Summit-Firth household was joined by Ada and Michael, who have enriched it, and their mother's life, beyond measure. Simon Firth has supported this project and its author in every way possible: with loving gratitude, I dedicate this book to him.

Libraries of Memory

Memory is a library—or so it was conventionally figured by premodern writers. Cassiodorus praises the scholar who stores scriptures "in the library of his memory" (in memoriae suae bibliotheca), while St. Jerome recommends cultivating one's memory, through careful reading and meditation, into "a library for Christ."[1] The figure became a rich source for imaginative writers such as Edmund Spenser, whose *Faerie Queene* (1590) offers an allegory of human memory that takes the shape of a vast library. In 1626 popular sermons were still describing "Mans Memorie" as "Gods Library."[2] The metaphor encourages us to compare the interior of the library with the interior of the mind, the ordering of books and documents with the mental arrangement of memories and thought. Both memory and library, in this metaphor, are endowed with powers of storage but also with a surprising degree of plasticity; if our memories can be "Gods Library," they become so through active arrangement and even selective censorship. From the Middle Ages onward, memory's library not only contains written knowledge but manifests ways of knowing: thus, the seventeenth-century John Evelyn's "Method for a Library According to the Intellectual Powers" projects contemporary models of rationality onto the organization of an ideal library.[3] Today memory and the library continue to be joined in the idiom of computing, in which the term "memory library" commonly refers to the digital architecture of information storage.[4] The figure, along with its very persistence, can tell us much about the importance of libraries to our understandings of ourselves and our most intimate acts of cognition. The library, it tells us, is central to who we are.

The library is also central to who we were. As the figure of memory's library further tells us, libraries bear a privileged relation to our past, safeguarding our collective identity as communities, peoples, and nations by documenting our histories. This point is well known to students of the pre-modern periods, who depend on libraries to preserve and order the books and scraps that survive from, and come to define, our object of study. *Memory's Library* takes these libraries as its subject, exploring questions that today's readers of medieval books must continually ask themselves: How did this book, so far from its original place of production and reception, reach me in the present? And how have its original meanings changed in that trans-portation across time and place, from monastery to well-lighted and guarded modern reading room?[5]

To begin to address these questions, my study focuses on a pivotal two-hundred-year period in the history of libraries in England, from 1431 to 1631—a period that spans the initial collecting activities of Humfrey, Duke of Gloucester (1390–1447), whose foundational bequests to Oxford University are still commemorated in the Bodleian's Duke Humfrey's Library, to the death of Robert Cotton (1571–1631), whose library has been called "the most important collection of manuscripts ever assembled in Britain by a private individual."[6] At the beginning of this time span, England's most im-portant libraries belonged to its religious institutions; by its end, they had shifted into private hands, to be re-collected by scholars who envisioned the beginnings of "public" or "national" collections.[7] The English Middle Ages that we now study is the product of these Renaissance libraries, which be-came and remain the defining collections of the period today: they include the Parker Library in Cambridge (established 1575), the Cotton Library in London (begun in 1588), and the Bodleian Library in Oxford (opened in 1602). These collections and the individuals who made them, I argue, not only es-tablished the documentary sources of the medieval past but also generated new protocols for approaching medieval manuscripts as sources of histor-ical knowledge. Many of these protocols still survive in the catalogues, classificatory schemes, and notation systems through which Renaissance collectors, readers, and librarians arranged and left their mark—sometimes literally—on the medieval textual materials that they collected.[8] They also form the basis, I further argue, of the scholarly reading practices through which we continue to interpret the same materials. If we hope to under-stand the medieval manuscripts that we study and the manner in which we study them, we must begin by asking where they came from.

The pivotal event during the period of my focus was the English Ref-ormation, which transformed both libraries and the books that they com-bined.[9] With the dissolution of England's monasteries in the 1530s, religious libraries were closed and their contents scattered, destroyed, or lost. Writing in 1611, the historian John Speed describes how, in the dissolution, monastic buildings were "laid open to the generall deluge of Time, whose stream bore down the walles of all those foundations, carrying away the shrines of the dead, and defacing the Libraries of their ancient records."[10] Despite this apocalyptic vision, not all medieval texts were lost—as Speed himself knew, being a regular user of Robert Cotton's library. As well as preserving "ancient records" from the dissolved monastic libraries, Cotton supplied many to Speed, who incorporated them into his *History of Great Britaine*. In the process of establishing new libraries from the remnants of the old, collectors like Cotton reinvented the idea of the library by redefining the meanings and functions with which libraries were identified. In so doing, they made the library an institutional symbol of both the nation's self-conscious break from its past and its effort to rebuild a new national identity.

Where monastic libraries had upheld the authority of a church whose head was based in Rome, the major post-Reformation libraries that I examine became centers of national memory. But in keeping with medieval and early modern understandings of memory as library, those libraries were marked with a degree of plasticity that is surprising and even shocking to modern sensibilities.[11] The new libraries were not meant simply to contain and preserve the past; rather, the books and written materials that they contained were deliberately selected and in some cases literally remade in order to strengthen the king's supremacy and to support the cause of religious reform.[12] The makers of these libraries accomplished their goals not only through what they included but through what they left out. As scholars like Neil R. Ker remind us, their libraries' contents represent just a small percentage of the total holdings of medieval libraries, the bulk of which was lost through neglect or intentional destruction.[13]

Brian Stock observes that "the Renaissance invented the Middle Ages in order to define itself."[14] As institutions that contributed to the Renaissance invention of the medieval through its objects, libraries offer material examples of this self-definition in action. But those very objects—the books that Renaissance libraries collect, order, and reshape—also reveal how contingent and sometimes polydirectional this process was. Libraries do not "invent" the objects that they contain, but they do produce what cognitive theorists call "standards of coherence" by which those objects are used and understood.[15] In libraries, these standards are produced through, for example, the catalogues, shelf and desk systems, and practices of storage and retrieval by which books are presented to readers. Such systems of ordering, I argue in this book, reflect the expectations that post-Reformation readers brought to pre-Reformation books. We stand to learn much about those expectations when we determine whether, after the Reformation, a medieval saint's life was catalogued as a work of fiction or of history; whether a medieval miscellany was disassembled and re-bound with works of different genres and provenance; or whether the early modern collector of a medieval devotional book was Catholic or Protestant, sympathetic or hostile to its original meanings.

Details like these clarify the contexts of medieval books' interpretation; but they do not wholly determine them. Part of the story that this book tells concerns the uneven transactions of influence and denial that were carried out in libraries not only between early modern readers and medieval texts but also between Catholics and Protestants, political partisans, or friends who applied their readings of medieval texts to vastly different ends. As these examples show, the medieval textual past was an unruly legacy. If libraries reveal that the Middle Ages were a creation of the Renaissance, they also make it possible to see the Renaissance as a creation of the Middle Ages. The very survival of medieval books and materials in early modern libraries attests to their continued relevance and interest to later readers, who, in touching these earlier books, could not fail to be touched by them in turn.

The dynamism of libraries in the period of my focus mirrors medieval and early modern ideas about memory, to the extent that both libraries and memory were seen as creative, rather than static, entities, the products of selection rather than simple retention. As Mary Carruthers has shown in her foundational scholarship on the topic, medieval theorists of memory conceived it not as a passive vessel for storage but rather as an engaged process of sorting, selecting, preparing, and internalizing information gleaned from texts, directed toward making it available and useful to the reader.[16] Thus, in his treatise *De animae ratione*, Alcuin describes memory as a "fashioned image."[17] Similarly, in 1631 John Doddridge calls memory "the receptacle wherein is reposed and laid up what-soever thing the Understanding hath apprehended and judged worthy of receipt or entertainment," again stressing the active and conscious work of judgment, of which memory is the product.[18]

These early ideas about memory find parallels in recent models posed by neuroscientists. As Gerald M. Edelman and Giulio Tononi observe, "it is commonly assumed that memory involves the inscription and storage of information," but, they continue: "we see memory as the ability of a dynamic system that is molded by selection."[19] Similarly, Daniel C. Dennett and Marcel Kinsbourne compare memory to a "revisionist historian" whose interpretations rewrite the records of the past.[20] In the words of Tobias Wolff: "Memory is a storyteller, and like all storytellers it imposes form on the raw mass of experience. It creates shape and meaning by emphasizing some things and leaving others out. It finds connections between events, suggests cause and effect, makes each of us the central figure in an epic journey toward darkness or light."[21]

In addition to bringing us closer to medieval and early modern concepts of memory, Wolff's storyteller memory also recalls medieval and early modern conceptions of libraries, which, as I have been arguing, do not simply store but rather select and arrange their contents to make them meaningful in a changing world. The libraries from this period did not aspire to the totality or universality that is implied in the post-Enlightenment ideal of the "library without walls."[22] Indeed, as Michel Foucault observes, the idea of the library as "a place of all times that is itself outside of time and inaccessible to its ravages" is one that "belongs to our modernity," while "in the seventeenth century, even at the end of the century, museums and libraries were the expression of an individual choice."[23] The library makers I consider constructed libraries in the same way that authors construct books, through a purposeful selection of materials, directed toward specific interests. Recent work on the history of the book has demonstrated the need to preserve and study individual books as unique artifacts whose material features not only reflect but also shape their broader cultural uses and meanings.[24] As similarly constructed artifacts, libraries need to be studied not just as spaces for reading but as what Roger Chartier calls "readable space."[25]

Scholars of library history have long appreciated the fact that individual libraries, like books, are historical artifacts, and a number of landmark studies and ongoing projects in library history have been dedicated to reconstructing libraries of the past and rethinking their contexts.[26] Yet the implications of their findings and analyses have not registered widely outside the specific fields of library and book history. *Memory's Library* attempts to bridge the bibliographical disciplines, particularly that of library history, and the disciplines of the academic humanities, particularly that of literary history.[27] It is not a general survey of medieval and early modern libraries, of which many excellent examples already exist (and are cited in my notes). Rather, this project closely reads a necessarily select number of libraries and materials in order to trace a specific story about how early modern libraries remade the medieval past, along with the books and textual practices they inherited from it.

In researching and writing this book, I have continually benefited from the work of those outside my field, not only book historians but also those working in the histories of science, religion, jurisprudence, and knowledge in these periods. This wide range of scholarship befits the study of libraries, since libraries both precede and produce the very disciplinary categories in which we work today, while also making it possible to imagine bringing

them together in a single, interactive space.[28] Yet however necessarily mul-
tidisciplinary its topic, this project also stakes a claim for a distinctly literary
perspective on the events and institutions it considers. As I read them, libraries become foundational in the history of reading and writing. If, as
Diana Fuss has recently observed, "every act of composition takes place
somewhere," libraries demonstrate that reading and writing are embodied
activities, whose particular meanings are shaped by the material and history-
bound spaces and structures in which they take place.[29]

Numerous medieval and early modern writers bear witness to the generative role that libraries played in the conjoined histories of authorship and
literary culture. From the fifteenth through the seventeenth century, from
John Lydgate to John Weever, a number of literary authors researched or
wrote their works in the foremost libraries of their day; others observed the
making of flagship libraries from a distance, as did Edmund Spenser, who was
a Cambridge student when Archbishop Parker bequeathed his library to the
university, and Francis Bacon, whose friend Sir Thomas Bodley founded the
Bodleian Library at Oxford. When these and other writers make libraries
the settings of their works or evocative sites within them, they reveal that
libraries occupied a central role in contemporary cultures of books, literacy, and knowledge that was both material and symbolic. In the works of
Thomas More and his humanist contemporaries, for example, the library
presents an outward manifestation of the learned mind, a medium of cultural transmission, and a meeting place between the institutions of literacy
and the literate self. Thus, whether they are set in the monastery, the private
house, the chapel, or, figuratively, in the human brain, libraries are not only
places of literacy; they represent the place of literacy within the broader
social and political world.

Libraries also stage material encounters with the textual legacy of the
past. By focusing on the afterlives of medieval books in early modern libraries, I aim to counter a persistent assumption that the only past that
mattered in the early modern period was the classical one. The records
of early libraries show that medieval books continued to be handled and
read in early modern England, though not without controversy or contest.
By transmitting medieval books to early modern readers, libraries brought
those later readers into contact with medieval modes of reading that they
themselves actively disputed, contested, or selectively adapted: such as *lectio divina, allegoresis,* or *compilatio.*[30] As much as these practices and their
outward forms offended Protestant sensibilities, they were not obliterated
but adapted as the bases of new practices. If the early modern encounter
with medieval books left libraries as its material legacy, its literary legacy

was registered in the forms of reading and writing that issued from these libraries. In the chapters that follow, I find evidence of this encounter in a range of early modern literary practices. In the generation following the Reformation, early modern readers from the obscure (such as Stephen Batman) to the well known (such as Spenser) adapted the allegorical reading practices of medieval *lectio divina* to produce a reading practice marked by a judicious and selective approach to medieval texts, which I call in chapter 3 a *"lectio* of suspicion." This reading process features an "oscillat[ion] between demystification and restoration of meaning" comparable to processes that Paul Ricoeur ascribes to the "enlarged concept of exegesis" of a post-Freudian age.[31] But in the post-Reformation period, challenges to exegesis came from the deliberate rejection of monasticism and its defining literacies as well as the selective adaptation of its material sources, the books that were re-collected after the dissolution of the monasteries. The seventeenth century's suspicion of medieval texts fueled its production of new textual forms, as witnessed in a surge of nonfiction prose works that were written in connection with the library of Robert Cotton. Although Cotton's associates such as William Camden and John Speed have been identified with the emergence of positivism and objectivity—which posit the primary source as vehicle of historical truth—I find instead that their encounters with medieval manuscripts in Cotton's library forced them to confront the primary source as a vehicle of potential falsehood, as they reckoned with the Catholic contexts in which these texts were originally produced and read.[32]

The reading and writing practices that I associate with post-Reformation libraries and the textual communities they fostered emerged in opposition to monastic modes of reading that held sway in pre-Reformation libraries.[33] In the course of transforming medieval manuscripts into archival sources, these libraries and their early modern users prepare the ground for academic literacies of the present day—in particular, the "skeptical, wary, demystifying, critical, and even adversarial" reading practices that have been described by Catherine Gallagher and Stephen Greenblatt.[34] Critical reading has become "the folk ideology of a learned profession, so close to us that we seldom feel the need to explain it," as Michael Warner observes: it is characterized by an "aggressive defensiveness in relation to the object of criticism" as well as an "apparently boundless faith in the efficacy of exposure."[35] This unlikely dyad of skepticism and faith is evident in Gallagher and Greenblatt's account of historicist reading practices, which offset the literary text as "sacred, self-enclosed, and self-justifying miracle" by promoting "interpretation, as distinct from worship"; yet the same practices reserve another form of "piety" for what Gallagher and Greenblatt call "the archive itself."[36]

Where today's critical reading aims to demystify its objects, it retains the archive as an alternate source of positive knowledge ("the touch of the real") that is exempted from its demystifying program.[37] Yet the archive of the English Middle Ages as produced in the wake of the Reformation reflected a concerted program of demystification, which was directed at neutralizing monastic books' appeals to sacred and miraculous authority in ways that anticipate Gallagher and Greenblatt's neoreformist rhetoric. In Reformation-era libraries, such a literacy of demystification was not distinct from library making; rather, the two were mutually generative. The libraries' very project of redirecting medieval manuscripts from monks to antiquarians necessarily desacralized those manuscripts, thus allowing their transformation from objects of belief into sources for a history of belief. Examined in this light, libraries are revealed to function less as transparent containers of historical truth than as embodiments of historically specific ideas about what constitutes truth in its textual forms.

As guardians of the textual past, libraries supply both the material and the structure of our literary histories, by placing books in relation to one another following likenesses or distinctions between authors, subjects, and historical periods.[38] They also allow us to reexamine the foundations of our own literary-historical thinking. In England, the dissolution of the monasteries has become the defining boundary between medieval and early modern periods. To Andrew G. Watson, the dissolution's destruction of medieval books and libraries marks "nothing less than the end of the Middle Ages," a view that is echoed by some contemporaries who witnessed these events and clearly saw themselves living at the end of an era.[39] As Francis Trigge, a Lincolnshire cleric, reported in 1589, "Many do lament the pulling downe of abbayes. They say it was never merie world since."[40] Yet in other ways, the dissolution marks the start of the Middle Ages. By releasing monastic materials into the hands of collectors newly inspired by what Margaret Aston calls a "sense of the past," the dissolution enabled the Middle Ages to emerge as a distinct chapter in English history as well as an object of study.[41] In our own age, the terms "medieval" and "Renaissance" have come under increased scrutiny from scholars on both sides of what Judith Bennett calls "the great divide."[42] The analysis of books as destructible and collectible objects offers a material approach to this project of rethinking periodization.

As I have argued, the libraries of Parker, Cotton, and Bodley reveal that Renaissance collectors created versions of the Middle Ages by ordering and shaping its textual remains; they thus contributed to what we could call, following Stephanie Trigg, the "medievalization" of the Middle Ages.[43] At the same time, libraries reveal that many early modern readers experienced the

Reformation as less dramatic a break than we have. The Bodleian's librarian Thomas James saw the Reformation less as a chronological and periodizing dividing line than as one chapter in an ongoing struggle between representatives of truth and error.[44] The Cotton Library may be one of the premier medieval collections in our age; but it maintained a powerful cultural presence in the seventeenth century, attracting readers such as William Camden, John Donne, Ben Jonson, Fulke Greville, and Francis Bacon.[45] These readers' engagements with Cotton's medieval materials adapt them to the needs and concerns of their age, showing that they belonged as much to the Renaissance as they did to the Middle Ages. Against a view of the Reformation as a point of total and cataclysmic destruction of the medieval, then, libraries reveal that the Reformation converted medieval forms to create new objects and practices, subject to new modes of circulation and interpretation.[46] Where the recent work of scholars such as Helen Cooper and Andrew King explores medieval cultural influence that persisted in the genres and literary forms of the early modern period, I examine material evidence of that persistent influence in medieval books themselves, which survived, and continued to attract readers and readings, in post-Reformation libraries.[47]

Libraries offer a particularly rich vantage point from which to chart the effects of historical change and their institutional and literary manifestations. Across the late medieval and early modern periods of my focus, contemporary conflicts over the meanings, uses, and objects of literacy made libraries into ideological lightning rods. The dissolution of the monasteries, whose transformation of medieval books and libraries defines the center of my historical focus, was not an isolated or sui generis event. Indeed, to the extent that they targeted religious libraries directly, the agents of the Reformation did not introduce so much as they continued, and brought to a head, hostilities directed at monastic libraries that had been ongoing throughout the fourteenth and fifteenth centuries. As representatives of a perceived, and resented, ecclesiastical control over literacy and its privileges, monasteries and their collections of books and records had in fact been subject to attack long before the Reformation. In 1327, a mob of three thousand stormed the abbey at Bury St. Edmunds, sacking its archives with deliberate violence; similar attacks against the institutions of monastic literacy were repeated in 1381, attacks that confirmed the growing importance of monastic collections of books and writing to the material privileges they were perceived to confer.[48] The sense of being under attack pervades ecclesiastical bibliography from the volatile fourteenth century. Writing in 1345, England's most famous bibliophile, Richard de Bury, justifies his book-collecting efforts by invoking the climate of religious struggle in which they took place: "for behold how good and how pleasant it is to gather together the arms of the clerical warfare, that we may have the means to crush the attacks of heretics."[49] As de Bury shows, the love of books—which became the title of his manifesto, *Philobiblon*—was a powerful assertion of reading privileges at a time when these were deeply contested. By extension, libraries such as the one he assembled were not cloistered from but indeed lay at the center of the social, political, and religious conflicts of their time, conflicts that increasingly focused on the vexed problem of lay literacy.

Thus, Duke Humfrey of Gloucester, who gave his name to Oxford's famous library, made his reputation and a considerable fortune by putting down a popular rebellion by Wycliffite heretics in 1431.[50] With that fortune he initiated two library projects that I read as interrelated: his book collection and his sponsorship of John Lydgate's *Fall of Princes*, which incorporates and adapts material from Humfrey's library in order to commemorate his successes against the Lollards. Where Humfrey's library grew out of the pre-Reformation campaign against Wycliffites, in the early seventeenth century the Bodleian's ultra-Protestant librarian Thomas James took charge of Duke Humfrey's Library in post-Reformation Oxford and actively collected Wycliffite texts for its collection, which James celebrated as evidence of England's proto-Protestant past. Duke Humfrey's book collecting upholds a religio-political project that is diametrically opposed to that of the later James, but the two library makers were united in their view of the library as a place that not only stores the past but actively shapes its meanings and uses in response to present concerns. As English collectors from Richard de Bury to Robert Cotton recognized, those who made libraries made history.[51]

Memory's Library begins with Duke Humfrey's Library in the fifteenth century. Famous for his library no less than for his turbulent political career, Humfrey, Duke of Gloucester and younger brother of Henry V, maintained a shaping influence on fifteenth-century literary culture.[52] Where Shakespeare's Prospero asserts that "my library/was Dukedom large enough," Duke Humfrey conceived his library not as a retreat from political power but an instrument of it.[53] Following the model of the great seignorial libraries in Italy, Humfrey constructed his library as a manifestation of political power, a project that he enlisted Lydgate's *Fall of Princes* to support. While Humfrey has long been feted for bringing Italian humanism to England, I argue that his library originated in a particularly English circumstance: the perceived need to combat the Lollard threat to public order, particularly in the realm of literacy. In the 1431 rebellion that Humfrey quelled, Lollards publicized their subversive intentions in written bills and broadsides, which are mentioned in every contemporary account of the rebellion. I argue that

Humfrey's patronage of and involvement in *The Fall of Princes*, which reflects and amplifies the larger goals of his library, responded to the Lollard threat by asserting Humfrey's political and cultural might through monuments of literacy.[54] Lydgate, a monk of Bury St. Edmunds, also had access to one of the great monastic libraries of the late Middle Ages in England, which was consolidated in response to another popular threat, the 1327 mob attack that targeted the monastery's books and written records. Crossing between the monastic library of Bury and the secular library of Duke Humfrey, Lydgate shows how the aims of the two were unexpectedly aligned in their common response to late medieval popular uprisings.

In England, the fifteenth century has been called "the age of libraries," since it was during this time that book collections began to be consolidated into rooms or places set aside for them; thus, the word "library" shifted from meaning a collection of books to meaning a specific place.[55] In my second chapter, I reconsider the meanings of private libraries that proliferated in the early sixteenth century, which have often been linked to a rise in secular literacy and learning that is seen as the necessary correlative to the spread of humanism. In early Tudor England, however, humanism was incompletely and unevenly absorbed into traditional institutions, and libraries became emblems of a literacy that was divided in its aims and effects. By focusing my analysis on an exemplary early Tudor reader, Thomas More, I find that humanist ideals of worldly learning and monastic ideals of contemplative devotion met and clashed in libraries. An engaged observer of literacy and its practices, More chronicles the rise of lay literacy and secular learnedness in his fictional and instructional writings. But his own representations of private libraries also reveal the deep divisions between the institutional and ideological forces that competed to define lay literacy in early Tudor England. The spread of book ownership among the English laity was fostered on the one hand by the "pragmatic humanism" of a new secular class of lay administrators and bureaucrats and on the other hand by monastic orders such as the Carthusians and the Bridgettines, who actively promoted the transmission of devotional texts and monastic modes of reading from the cloister to the lay household. Where many of his humanist contemporaries uphold the essential compatibility of these two models of literacy, More continually plays pragmatic humanism and quasi-monastic devotion against one another. This chapter focuses on two of More's early works, *Life of Pico* (c. 1510) and *Utopia* (1516), both of which feature libraries as crucial settings for representing and exploring the spread of literacy to the laity; in those works, the private, lay library becomes a battleground on which an opposition between Erasmian humanist and Carthusian devotional literacy is played out. In representing libraries as ideological and religious battle-grounds, More anticipates the activities of Thomas Cromwell and the works of the English humanists whom Cromwell patronized, Thomas Starkey and Thomas Elyot. Where More reveals that the spread of English humanism occurred through conquest of formerly monastic spaces, Starkey and Elyot turned such conquest to the service of the English Reformation, as they helped convert libraries, including the very buildings that housed them, from monastic to patriotic aims.

The destruction of the monastic libraries during the English Reformation had the paradoxical effect not of eradicating but of heightening libraries' symbolic power in post-Reformation England. A new generation of book collectors, beginning with John Bale and Matthew Parker, continued the work of Starkey and Elyot and also reconceived the library's shape and purpose by redefining it from an ecclesiastical receptacle of written tradition to a state-sponsored center of national identity. In so doing, those collectors transformed the social meanings of the books and reading acts that libraries contained. As my third chapter argues, Henrician and Elizabethan library makers, in the process of recovering medieval books for new uses, reshaped the past through its written records, establishing new protocols of reading that stressed the value of history and national "posteryte" over the allegorical and contemplative literacies promoted in monastic libraries. This reading program continues to be reflected in the contents of post-Reformation libraries such as the Royal Library (now a core collection of the British Library) and the library of Matthew Parker, which was donated to Corpus Christi College and University Library, Cambridge, after the arch-bishop's death in 1579. Both libraries preserve large numbers of books that had formerly belonged to the dissolved monasteries; but these books were carefully selected and even, in some instances, selectively remade to support a reformist view of the English past.

As well as transforming the meanings of libraries and their contents, the work of collectors such as Parker had wide-scale cultural ramifica-tions, which are evident in post-Reformation literary works such as Edmund Spenser's *Faerie Queene*. In the second book of Spenser's epic, which alle-gorizes the human brain as a vast library filled with history books, Spenser extends the aims of the post-Reformation book collectors by making the li-brary into an imaginary center of Protestant nationhood, as well as a model for the nationalist poetics and reading practices that underpin *The Faerie Queene* more broadly.

My fourth chapter focuses on the early-seventeenth-century library of Sir Robert Cotton, which represents a later stage in the history of the post-

Reformation library and its response to the medieval textual past. Where Reformation era collectors built up libraries by selecting the individual books that went into them, Cotton acquired entire collections or parts of collections that he tirelessly rearranged, sometimes unbinding volumes in order to rebind them into compilations of his own making.[56] Cotton made these compilations by arranging medieval primary sources in rough groupings by chronological order, appropriating the *compilatio* techniques used by the medieval chronicles and hagiographies that he collected, while adapting those techniques to produce new models of the past. Cotton's library became a rich resource for seventeenth-century writers of nonfiction prose, who mined its holdings for manuscripts that they deployed as primary evidence, thereby demonstrating the correlation of literary and institutional forms. Fostering the use of manuscripts for the production of nonfiction prose, I argue, Cotton invents the modern documentary source by transforming the medieval texts in his collection from objects of belief into objects of historical knowledge. But even while privileging the "originall" record, Cotton radically transformed the original contexts in which those records were produced and read.[57]

Among the many contemporary writers who made use of the Cotton Library, William Camden, John Speed, and John Weever make abundant use of Cotton manuscripts in their works, especially those relating to the British past, which they signal with frequent marginal references: "Ex MS Bib. Cot." These works thereby establish the Cotton Library as a source of primary evidence and prefigure the archival investments of modern historical and historicist scholarship. But unlike modern, positivist forms of historicism that take the archive to be a source of transparent evidence or documentary truth, Cotton's seventeenth-century readers engage in active struggles with their sources, as they seek to generate new modes of historical truth and evidence that differ from those upheld in their medieval sources.

In my fifth and final chapter I turn to Francis Bacon, for whom the library became a frequent target of sometimes-vehement critique. In *The Advancement of Learning* (1605) Bacon writes, "Libraries are as the shrines, where all the Reliques of the ancient saints, full of true vertue, and that without delusion or imposture, are preserved, and reposed."[58] In this and other representations of libraries in his published work, as well as his private correspondence, Bacon made the library into the embodiment of past learning, which he contrasted with the new learning of experimental science that he championed throughout his work. Bacon's knowledge of contemporary libraries came from personal experience: he himself oversaw the foundation of the Lambeth Palace Library in 1610, and he maintained a close relationship

with Sir Thomas Bodley, founder of the Bodleian, whose library-based learning he contrasts with his own. Yet in attempting to define his scientific project against library-based models of literacy and knowledge, Bacon misrecognizes the actual work that took place in and around early modern libraries as
well as his own debt to the very textual models he disowns. Although Bodley
himself resisted Bacon's calls for intellectual reform, those calls found an
unexpected resonance with the practices of Bodley's first librarian, Thomas
James. Following in the model of earlier Protestant librarians and book collectors such as Matthew Parker, James sought out, edited, and acquired
books that supported his contention that the reformed Church of England
was grounded in unimpeachable authorities from the past, while the beliefs
and acts of the "Prelates, Pastors, and Pillars of the Church of Rome" were
founded on textual error.

As an editor as well as Bodley's librarian, James refined a method of collation in which "sundry good Manuscripts" were compared in order to uncover
the true meaning of texts that had been corrupted over time. James's theory
of collation recalls many of the historical principles that underpinned English Protestantism, including the central belief that Catholicism departed
from an original purity that only radical reform could recapture, while also
developing them into a textual practice.[59] Insisting that the library was a
place for "the libration of bookes," James conceived textual criticism in
line with proto-scientific models of observation, investigation, and verifica-
tion.[60] In so doing, I argue, James establishes a parallel to Bacon's scientific
project, despite Bacon's effort to distance himself from libraries such as the
Bodleian. As I contend in reference to James's collation practices, the modernity of Bacon's project took shape not by abandoning library-based methods
of textual analysis but rather by adapting them to new objects.

Bacon's efforts to contrast libraries with spaces of scientific investigation
anticipate modern disciplinary formations that separate the tradition-bound
humanities from the forward-looking sciences.[61] Bacon thus looks forward
to a time much like our own, when projections of an ideal "library without
walls" come too often at the expense of libraries with walls, which are contrastingly pictured as inefficient warehouses whose physical features hinder,
rather than advance, the production of knowledge.[62] Yet this is a misleading
view of library history, just as Bacon's denigration of library-based knowledge
as merely conservative misrepresents the actual library practices that were
taking place around him.

If medieval and early modern libraries were seats of memory, the "memory" they represent is not a static, passive, or simply retentive function—a
point that was understood by medieval and early modern theorists of memory

no less than it is by cognitive scientists today.[63] Nor were libraries merely static, passive, or retentive during the formative chapter in their history that I examine here. Rather, as their history in late medieval and early modern England shows, libraries were dynamic institutions that actively processed, shaped, and imposed meaning on the very materials they contained. In preserving the medieval past, the libraries of post-Reformation England also remade it into a body of evidence, while teaching readers how to approach the medieval manuscript as source. As users of the same libraries, we have inherited the legacy of not only their books but also their modes of reading.

CHAPTER ONE

Lydgate's Libraries:
Duke Humfrey, Bury St. Edmunds,
and *The Fall of Princes*

Reading Privileges

The fifteenth century has been called "an age of libraries."[1] But the period also confronts us with a most basic question: what is a library? Long before this period, religious institutions employed the term *"libraria"* to describe collections of books, which played a central role in their cultures of knowledge and literacy.[2] In the monasteries, these collections were held in *armaria*, portable boxes and cupboards, situated in places convenient to their various uses—in the choir, refectory, or cloister, reflecting the three kinds of reading (at services, at mealtimes, and during private meditation) stipulated in the Rule of St. Benedict.[3] In the fifteenth century many of these collections were consolidated into rooms set aside for the purpose of both storage and consultation, which came to be known by the term *libraria*.[4] Thus, in the middle decades of the fifteenth century, major religious houses such as Bury St. Edmunds and St. Albans constructed *librariae* in which they consolidated and stored their book collections, while library rooms were also introduced at the same time in the cathedrals of Durham, Lincoln, Salisbury, St. Paul's, Exeter, Hereford, and Wells.[5]

At the universities, several colleges housed or planned library rooms as early as 1338 (Merton College, Oxford) and 1350 (Trinity Hall, Cambridge), but the major period of development also came in the fifteenth century: at Cambridge, libraries were introduced in King's Hall in 1416–17, Michael House in 1425, Peterhouse in 1431, Gonville Hall in 1441, and Pembroke College in 1452, while at Oxford, libraries appeared in Balliol College in 1431, Lincoln College in 1437, and Oriel College in 1444.[6] In addition, central university libraries were established at Cambridge in the 1420s and at Oxford in 1444, when the university moved to place the books it received from Duke Humfrey of Gloucester in "a suitable chamber, separate from others," to be named after its benefactor.[7] When the narrator of the anonymous poem "Magnificencia ecclesie" (c. 1475) announces, "I wyll go in to Þe library/To serche & stody in bokes of auctoryte," he or she bears witness to the broad cultural visibility and authority that libraries had attained by the late fifteenth century, not simply as collections but as spaces set aside for reading and writing.[8] The fifteenth century can be called an "age of libraries," then, not because it was the first time books were systematically collected, but because it was during this time that the "library" became a place.

Although the consolidation and centralization of English book collections during the fifteenth century can be clearly traced, it is far less clear what this development meant to contemporaries and how its significance was registered in literary and textual culture. The development of libraries as places has generally been understood as both growing out of and further enabling a cluster of associated developments: rising rates of literacy, increasing demands for books, and a level of prosperity that enabled the expansion of book collections and the building or equipment of new rooms to house them.[9] Thus, C. L. Kingsford, the same scholar who proclaims the fifteenth century to be an "age of libraries," accounts for the increase in centralized libraries by linking it to "a general intellectual ferment" that included "the spread of education and the common writing of letters."[10] Not only the demographics but also the uses of literacy were broadened in the late Middle Ages; in the monasteries, which still housed England's richest and largest books collections, this broadening reflected the influence of the fraternal (or mendicant) orders, such as the Dominicans, Franciscans, and Carmelites, and their reading practices. While the Rule of St. Benedict required monasteries to own books to which monks could continually return for contemplative rumination in their *lectio divina*, the friars developed a scholarly approach that stressed the importance of reading widely in many books to construct learned arguments through comparison, collation, and exposition of sources.[11] This practice required a large number of books stored close together to allow for greater ease of consultation and cross-referencing.[12] As M. T. Clanchy observes, "Modern libraries really started with the friars."[13]

Yet these two parallel developments—the broadening of lay literacy and the growth of the fraternal orders—produced a fault line within English literacy that made libraries into particularly volatile institutions. Popular and learned antifraternalism focused with particular intensity on the friars' libraries, which were seen to be hoarding precious resources. The late-fourteenth-century Wycliffite text *Jack Upland* asks, "Frere, what charite is it to gadere up Þe bokis of Goddis lawe, many mo Þanne nediÞ ȝou, and putte hem in tresorie, and do prisone hem from secular preestis and curates?"[14] This complaint illustrates features of the antifraternal critique—particularly its focus on property, here underscored in the reference to books "in tresorie." Such accusations are extended to clerks and monks in a late-fourteenth- or early-fifteenth-century collection of pseudo-Wycliffite tracts now preserved as Corpus Christi College, Cambridge, MS 296.[15] "Comment on the Testament of St. Francis" charges friars with harming the "comune profit of cristen men" by hoarding "many costly bokis, & myche hid tresour biried in here houses fro Þe comunte of cristen men."[16] Likewise, "How Religious men should keep certain Articles" warns both mendicant and monastic orders to "drawen not noble bokis of holy writt & holy doctouris & oÞere needful sciences fro curates & clerkis in-to here owne cloistris, Þat ben as castellis or paleicis of kyngis & emperouris, & suffre hem be closed Þer & waxe rotyn."[17] "Of Clerkis Possessioners" similarly accuses the endowed clergy, who "suffren Þes noble bokes wexe rotten in here libraries."[18] These complaints reflect a sense that writing belongs to "the comunte" rather than to privileged religious institutions and their members—an assertion that is only possible once literacy too begins to be imagined as common currency.[19] According to these charges, the libraries of the religious orders do not advance popular literacy so much as they restrict it; in this regard, the holdings of libraries can be contrasted with the so-called common-profit books, which were communally owned and circulated among groups of readers in the fifteenth century.[20] If the common-profit book reflected and served the growing literacy of the laity and secular clergy, the new libraries of the religious institutions were seen in the opposite light, as enemies of the "comune profit of cristen men."

In response to Wycliffite criticism, William Woodford, of the Oxford Greyfriars, defended the exclusivity of the fraternal libraries, explaining that the libraries had to guard books "in safekeeping so that they are not exposed to theft": "For in some places where books have lain about in the open, and secular clerks had free access to them, the books frequently have been stealthily removed, in spite of their being sturdily chained.... So it behoved the friars to hold onto their books and to keep them more securely locked up, or they would have done without the books which they ought to study."[21]

Similar concerns run throughout library statutes in the fourteenth and fifteenth centuries. William of Wykeham's statutes for New College, Oxford, "de libris collegii" (1400), insist that "all the books of the college are to be *kept in some safe room*, to be assigned for the college library," a formulation that is repeated often enough to suggest that library security had become a major preoccupation.[22] For example, Abbot William Curteys, who centralized the abbey library at Bury St. Edmunds, devised draconian punishments against violators of its security, ordering that any secular person who took books from the abbey be excommunicated.[23] This development marked a shift from earlier practices at Bury, when, as Robert S. Gottfried notes, the abbey shared its books more generously: "[At Bury] as early as the twelfth century, select townsfolk were permitted to borrow books [from the abbey's collections]. By the fifteenth century, their numbers had grown to the point where records suggest that they used it more frequently than did the monks."[24] Some institutions cite growing numbers of readers as necessitating stricter security precautions in libraries, as does an Oxford statute of 1412.[25] If the complaints like those in *Jack Upland* respond to specific instances of library restrictions—and, in so doing, reflect an emerging sense among the laity that literacy and books should be common property—other instances of library restrictions, like those at Bury and Oxford, postdate those complaints and appear to respond to the growing incursions of the literate laity. In other words, the complaints against libraries and the formalization of restrictions in libraries were reciprocal and mutually generating developments.

Library restrictions applied not only to library users but also to the books that the libraries contained. The consolidation of book collections into library rooms brought awareness of the limitations of space, forcing librarians to adopt a selective, rather than inclusive, approach to library acquisitions. A long-held assumption that medieval libraries grew through careless accretion downplays the extent to which medieval librarians actively deaccessioned books in order to make room for new ones.[26] Many wrote restrictions into their acquisition and storage policies: the statutes of Corpus Christi College, Oxford, for example, insist: "No book is to be brought into the Library or chained there, unless it be of suitable value and utility"; "books which are of greater value" (libri qui sunt pretiosiores), which will be "stored up in the Library" (in Bibliotheca reponantur), are differentiated from "those which are not fit for the Library" (indignos Bibliotheca).[27] In these cases, libraries not only provided places of reading but determined what could be read and who could read it.

This chapter will present, and examine the implications of, the following argument: while the fifteenth-century "age of libraries" took place against the backdrop of expanded literacy in late medieval England, to both their founders and their critics, the new libraries represented an effort to restrict, rather than advance, popular literacy. This argument counters an assumption that the growth of libraries was a natural outcome of, or nec- essarily promoted, the spread of books and literacy, and it carries implica- tions for understanding the broader cultural significance of libraries. At a time when literacy could no longer be considered the exclusive domain and defining privilege of the clergy—because the rise of lay literacy untethered the formerly synonymous terms *"clericus"* and *"litteratus,"* *"laicus"* and *"illiteratus"*—the newly centralized libraries worked to safeguard literacy and its privileges by other means.[28]

I make this point by considering two of the most important libraries of the fifteenth century: the library of Bury St. Edmunds, established by Bishop William Curteys in the middle of the century, and that of Duke Humfrey of Gloucester, who would go on to endow the central university library at Oxford. While the two libraries represent two different—and, some have held, opposed—forms of literacy, monastic and humanist, they are joined and mediated through the work of John Lydgate, who was a monk at Bury under Curteys and who enjoyed Humfrey's patronage as well as access to his library while composing his monumental work *The Fall of Princes.*[29] Lydgate's work, I argue, provides exceptional insight into the cultural sig- nificance of the fifteenth-century English library. A compilation of multiple narratives from a panorama of classical, biblical, and medieval sources, the work represents a one-volume "library" in the traditional sense of a collec- tion of texts. But it also illustrates the emergence of a newer understanding of "library" as a distinct *place* by projecting its author-narrator into a library space in the model of "poetis," who, we are told, "sitte in ther librarie."[30] *The Fall of Princes*, I find, presents an extended meditation both on the library as a "place" of literacy and on the library as the embodiment of the symbolic "place" of literacy—its acts, objects, and meanings—in response to its historical dislocation. Adapting protocols of reading developed in the monastic library of Bury to the library of his aristocratic patron, Duke Hum- frey, Lydgate belies conventional distinctions between monastic and secular libraries by revealing their common concern: to safeguard literacy and its privileges from the threat of popular incursion. At a time when literacy was expanding to an ever-broader *"comunte,"* I will argue, Lydgate works to define the library precisely as a place that excludes the "common."

Bury St. Edmunds and the Archives of Authority

The abbey of Bury St. Edmunds, with its collection of over two thousand books, helped to define the institution of the monastic library for its time.[31]

The first reference to the Bury collection as a "library" was by William Curteys, Bury's abbot from 1429 to 1445, while Lydgate was a monk there.[32] Under Curteys, Bury's documentary culture flourished; the abbot drafted new regulations governing the library's administration, consolidated the abbey's key charters, and asserted the centrality of written records to the abbey's continued authority.[33] But Curteys's administrative fervor was precipitated by a series of crises in the fourteenth and fifteenth centuries in which the abbey's authority and, in particular, its control of books and documents were directly challenged. In 1327, a mob of townspeople stormed into the abbey and, according to a contemporary account ("Depredatio abbatie Sancti Edmundi"), "broke open the book chests and carried away the books and everything else in them" (armoriola fregerunt, et libros ac omnia in eis inventa similiter asportaverunt).[34] The result was the loss of "books of various disciplines in various volumes" (plures libros diuersarum scientiarum et voluminum), as one Bury register reports.[35] The 1327 rioters sought control of the abbey's charters, which were perceived to be manifestations of the abbey's unjust control over the town of Bury St. Edmunds. Forced by the riots into a desperate act of reconciliation, the abbot ordered a new charter that revoked some of the monastery's most controversial privileges: its power to dispose property, collect tolls, and levy taxes in the town.[36] Perhaps most importantly, possession of the charter was taken from the abbey and granted to the town's alderman and burgesses (this right was returned to the abbey in 1332), revealing how monastic privileges and properties hinged on the archival control of documents.

Following the destruction of the abbey's *armaria*, Bury monk Henry de Kirkestede inventoried the abbey's holdings of books in the 1340s and 1350s, producing a massive bibliography known as the *Catalogus de libris autenticis et apocrifis*, which pioneered the method of organizing book catalogues alphabetically by authors' names, often accompanied by brief biographies.[37] As Mary A. Rouse and Richard H. Rouse suggest, Kirkestede's intent was "to bring order out of confusion" following the archival disasters of 1327.[38] A similar effort to repair riot-inflicted damage to the abbey's trove of documents drove Brother John of Lakenheath to draw up a register of its archives in 1380; as he explains, "After our monastery was destroyed by fire and plunderers, and the abbot's registers and other muniments were thievishly abstracted without compensation, there hardly remained a meager grain or two from such an abundant harvest left behind by the reapers."[39] But in the rising of 1381 rebels again sacked Bury's archives and demanded a renewal of the charter of 1327, along with its removal from the abbey.[40] When the rebellion was suppressed, the 1327 charter was again repealed; but the attacks held lasting significance for contemporary and later observers. Accounts of the 1381 rebellion at Bury St. Edmunds cast the rebels' assault on the abbey's documents as an assault on the very institution of clerical literacy: as Thomas Walsingham recounts, "it was dangerous to be known a cleric; much more dangerous to be found with an inkwell."[41] In the wake of such attacks, efforts like Curteys's to consolidate the abbey's collection of books and records were attempts to defend clerical literacy itself at a time when it was perceived to be under threat. The abbey's library and archives were thus both the targets and the products of popular attacks throughout the fourteenth century; while the *armaria* and their contents were sacked and scattered by rioters, the book collection was organized and consolidated in response to these attacks.

As these accounts reveal, popular attacks on monastic collections targeted books and administrative writings together. These accounts remind us that the modern distinction between the library as a receptacle of books and the archive as a receptacle of records was not an absolute one in the Middle Ages. Books and muniments were routinely classified and stored together throughout the fourteenth and well into the fifteenth century—which is why the 1327 rioters, in search of charters, also destroyed "books of various disciplines in various volumes" (plures libros diuersarum scientiarum et voluminum) when they sacked the abbey's *armaria*.[42] After book collections were consolidated into *librariae*, some religious houses and colleges separated muniments into parallel, and sometimes contiguous, *thesauri*, "treasuries," which held charters, bulls, and other important documents together with money and plate, as appears to have been the case at Curteys's Bury.[43] But even when libraries and archives were separated, the two institutions continued to overlap and inform one another's modes of administration and use. Under Curteys's abbacy at Bury St. Edmunds, the organization of books and documents in the library and archive followed strikingly similar patterns: the same hand that transcribed the abbey's charters as part of Curteys's effort to centralize the archives also annotated the library books with *ex libris* notes, a fact that suggests that the archives and library were not only parallel but interlinked developments.[44] This point bears relevance to our assessment of the library's significance at Bury. As Mary A. Rouse and Richard H. Rouse observe, library catalogues began as "simple inventories of property, no different from the prior's list of the candles on the altars."[45] In the fifteenth century, libraries continue to safeguard property, which is the chief function of the archives, but the property they protect is immaterial as well as material—including not only land but also an array of cultural and political liberties secured by written texts and their uses. At Bury, the contiguity of the archives and the library reflects the alliance of these material and immaterial privileges.

Lydgate himself played a direct role in the development of the Bury library and archives by virtue of his close relationship with Abbot Curteys; indeed, when Curteys ordered new copies of the monastery's charters, these were translated into Middle English verse by Lydgate himself. The resulting *Cartae versificatae* reveals the interpenetration of administrative and literary genres at Curteys's Bury.[46] The *Cartae versificatae* was bound into one of Curteys's massive administrative registers, British Library, MS Add. 14848, which compiles letters, charters, and other documents important to the abbey's foundation such as the hagiographical "Vita et passio S. Edmundi abbreviata," which immediately precedes Lydgate's *Cartae* in the register.[47] Written between 1435 and 1440, the *Cartae versificatae* asserts the documentary bases of Bury's property holdings and legal privileges by translating a series of the abbey's royal charters, purportedly issued by Kings Cnute, Harthacnute, Edward the Confessor, William the Conqueror, and Henry I, into a single document.[48] By translating these founding charters into Middle English verse, Lydgate evinces what Emily Steiner calls the "documentary poetics" of the Middle Ages, which brought together without apparent contradiction categories that modernity would later divide: the poetic and the administrative, the literary and the historical, the cultural and the political.[49]

Charters, as scholars of medieval diplomatics and documentary culture have shown, came to play a foundational role in monastic archives in the later Middle Ages.[50] Copied and consolidated into cartularies, they provided a legal basis for monastic privileges and endowments as well as a written basis of institutional memory. Cartularies, these scholars show, need to be studied as more than administrative compilations—they are the result of selective and rhetorical efforts to construct a usable past.[51] Deploying topoi or authorial postures familiar from literary works, cartularies commonly open with prefaces meditating on the instability of human events and the utility of writing to protect against oblivion.[52] The cartulary is above all, as Patrick Geary observes, a genre of memory, showing that "for each institution the memory of its past was a key to its ability to meet the challenges of the present."[53] As just such a cartulary, Lydgate's *Cartae* writes small the larger purpose of Curteys's register, Add. 14848; by consolidating the abbey's vulnerable archives into a single document, it aims to create an institutional memory that can stabilize a crisis-ridden present.

"Memory" is a key term for Lydgate's *Cartae versificatae*; as a note that prefaces the text in Curteys's register discloses, Curteys ordered the charters translated in order to "restore them to memory" (ad memoriam reducens).[54]

Within its immediate context, memory is a highly charged category with practical applications. As the preface details, the abbey was embroiled in a series of disputes over its exemptions that involved Bishop Alnwick of Norwich, Archdeacon Denston of Sudbury, and local rector Nicholas Bagot; the preface compares these disputes to an earlier one between the abbot of Bury and Bishop Bateman of Norwich, which was resolved by an appeal to the charters.[55] Addressing this context, the charters themselves narrate their own successful application in the case of similar disputes: the charter of William the Conqueror, for example, recounts a dispute with Arfast, bishop of Elmham (later Thetford and Norwich), who hoped to move his episcopal see to St. Edmunds.[56] He lost the case, Lydgate recounts in his versified translation, because he lacked documentary support:

> Bishhope Arfast gan sore allege and crye
> By elloquence his cause to magnefie;
> But for he wanted witnesse and wrytyng,
> His cause was voyde and stood stede in no thyng.[57]

By insisting on the superiority of "wrytyng" over "elloquence," the charter creates an apologia for the literary culture of the monastic archive. Writing gains the force of material witness:[58]

> Ther charters bere witnesse,
> By Edmond, Knut, and Hardeknut, this thre,
> And by Seynt Edwardis grete auctorite. (235)

As the *Cartae versificatae* insists again and again, in a distinctly Lydgatean mode, the world is characterized by instability; yet charters achieve a permanent authority through the lasting value of writing.[59] Thus, while the charter of Harthacnute laments the instability of human temporality, by which "Al worldly thyngis be variable and unsure" (221), it also asserts that writing, in the form of the signed charter, carries perpetual authority, promising "that it shal laste unto the worldys ende" (228). Similarly, the charter of Edward the Confessor insists that the abbey shall "perpetually stonde in liberte" (229) and grants the monks "perpetually to be fre" (230). The abbey is as permanent as its charter, insists William the Conqueror: "lyke his charter, as ye have herd telle, / that monkys there perpetually schal dwelle" (233). Yet the corollary is also true: the abbey is only as strong as its archive, which is why the charters themselves must be constantly recopied and thereby "restored to memory" (ad memoriam reducens).

As a miniature archive, Lydgate's *Cartae versificatae* can help us grasp the memorial function of archives in late medieval institutional contexts. The *Cartae* both commemorates and renovates the documentary past.[60] It reproduces the physical features of the original documents in an archaizing hand, such as Anglo-Saxon characters in the case of the earlier charters, but, unlike the archives valued by modern researchers, the Lydgatean archive does not value the original over the copy.[61] As an example, following each charter the scribe copies the names and authenticating crosses of its signatories, suggesting that the document's authenticity is guaranteed less by the original signature than by the superior witness of God, attested by the cross.[62] Further, the archive—in the case of both Lydgate's *Cartae* and Curteys's register—values narrative coherence, produced by selective presentation of sources, over comprehensiveness.[63] Lydgate's *Cartae* shows how the archive is above all a constructed memory. The overall effect—heightened by the moralizing envois that Lydgate affixes to his translations—indicates that this document is meant, not simply to record, but to persuade. The intended reader, moreover, is clearly not Curteys himself—who keeps his records in bureaucratic Latin—but readers outside the abbey, who would find Middle English verse more perspicuous. These might be lay readers such as those who smashed into the *armaria* searching for the abbey's charters in 1327 and 1381. They might equally be the royal patrons and consumers of Lydgate's English verse—Henry VI, who visited Bury St. Edmunds in 1434 and for whom Lydgate produced *The Lives of St. Edmund and St. Fremund*, or Duke Humfrey himself, who was one of Curteys's most important allies and whose patronage of Lydgate's *Fall of Princes* from 1431 to 1439 was concurrent with Curteys's patronage of the *Cartae versificatae*.[64]

Lydgate's *Cartae* insists on the historically close relationship between the abbey and the Crown, recognizing that Bury owes its privileges, however "perpetual" they are said to be, to ongoing royal protection.[65] But the text also insists on the reciprocity of that relationship. In the series of patronage narratives presented in the charters, Lydgate's *Cartae* repackages its accounts of royal endowments within the literary conventions of advice to princes. Echoing *The Fall of Princes'* lesson that it is "onto pryncis gretli necessarie/To yiue exaumple how this world doth varie" and "To shewe thuntrust off al worldli thyng" (1.426–27, 429), the *Cartae versificatae* asserts:

> In many a place of devyne scripture
> It is remembryd by ful contemplatyf,
> al worldly thyngis be variable and unsure. (221)

This lesson of worldly instability, familiar from the monastic genres of cartularies and chronicles, owes its legibility to monastic literacy—and its performance of "contemplatyf" remembrance—which alone is able to extract
such lessons from "many a place of devyne scripture" and "the sentence of
seyntys [saints] and of clerkys" (224).[66] Through clerical reading practices,
the *Cartae* recalls,

> Holy seyntys that ha be byforn
> Han mevyd us by ther parfyt [perfect] doctrine,
> To voyde the chaf and chesyn oute the corne. (222)

As well as preserving the lives of these "holy seyntys" in the volumes of hagiography that were staples of its library (as Lydgate's own literary output attests), the abbey's monks produce "parfyt doctrine" from these texts through
their allegorical reading practices, which show how "to voyde the chaf and
chesyn oute the corne." In this passage, Lydgate cites Augustine's famous
model of allegorical reading as a process of separating "spiritual" corn from
"literal" chaff, by extracting "the mystery" that is "covered in the wrapping
of the letter."[67] If monarchs produce writing of perpetual authority, the *Cartae versificatae* insists on the parallel utility of the monk's literary labor.
Thus, the *Cartae* emphasizes rulers' debt to "holy chirche" and its institutions for the very "doctryn" that they themselves are expected to model:

> For of old custom it longith unto kynges
> First holy chirche to meyntene and governe
> And for ther sogetys [subjects] in al maner thynges
> for to prouyde and prudently discerne,
> to shewe themsylf lyk a clere lanterne,
> with lyght of verteu ther sogettys tenlumyne [subjects to illuminate]
> Both by example and vertuous doctryne. (223)

The relationship between abbey and ruler is perfectly symbiotic: where
rulers "maynteyne and governe" the church and its monasteries, those
monasteries in turn produce and maintain the "vertuous doctryne" through
which monarchs project and enforce their authority. The authoritative "wrytyng" of kings and "the sentence of seyntys and of clerkys" are mutually
supportive, just like the archive that contains the former and the library that
contains the latter—though, as Curteys's own register shows, by bringing
together the *Cartae versificatae* and the "Vita et passio S. Edmundi abbreviata," the two are overlapping entities. The effect is a literary culture that

binds the abbey's interests with those of the ruler for the sake of domestic harmony: "with lyght of verteu ther sogettys tenlumyne."

By stressing the long history of the abbey's relationship with, and service to, secular rulers, Lydgate's *Cartae versificatae* attempts to build royal alliances that might protect the abbey from challenges arising within the church hierarchy, such as those waged by the bishop of Norwich. But challenges to Bury's privileges also issued from outside the church. The event that precipitated the bishop of Norwich's encroachment on the abbey's privileges occurred when he learned of a pocket of Lollards in Bury St. Edmunds. In light of the history of popular uprisings in fourteenth-century Bury, Bishop Alnwick insisted on his right to try the suspected heretics himself, in violation of Bury's jurisdiction. Complaints by Curteys only succeeded in delaying the trials, which took place in Norwich from 1428 to 1431.[68]

Bishop Alnwick's investigations focus a particularly searching light on the literate practices of the laity, which, following restrictions on vernacular theology imposed by Archbishop Arundel's Constitutions of 1409, became a key index of heresy.[69] In a letter of 3 September 1428 preserved in Curteys's register, the bishop asserts his right to investigate lay individuals—even those dwelling within the Bury jurisdiction—suspected of possessing or reading "books in our vulgar English"[70] (libros . . . in vulgari nostro anglicano). Those suspects who were eventually named indicate an underground Lollard textual community apparently flourishing in Bury: a priest, Robert Berte, was charged with owning *Dives et Pauper*, a book that Alnwick claimed "contained many errors and heresies" (Ille liber continet in se plures erores et hereses quamplures).[71] Under examination, Berte revealed that he had lent the book to others, including a man from Hitchin, Hertfordshire, and Sir Andrew Boteler (or Butler), who ordered a copy of the book for himself from one Robert Dykkes, a Bury scribe already suspected of copying heretical books.[72] Together, Boteler, Dykkes, and Berte follow a pattern of book circulation that resembles that of the contemporary common-profit books, as well as a vernacular textual community like the "scoles of heresie" that the Norwich trials sought to unearth.[73]

The naming of *Dives et Pauper* as the linchpin of this community is telling; contrary to Bishop Alnwick's charge, the book, a long dialogue in English on the Ten Commandments between Pauper, "a lettryd man and a clerk," and the aristocratic layman Dives, cannot be considered Wycliffite, a point underscored by the fact that John Whethamstede, abbot of St. Albans, commissioned a copy of *Dives et Pauper* himself for his own house's library.[74] Whethamstede, a close ally of William Curteys and Duke Humfrey of Gloucester and a patron of Lydgate, was a vociferous critic of Lollards, whom he charged with attempting to be "wiser than the learned are wise" (Plus sapere quam dogmatici sapere) and thus usurping the literacy of the clergy.[75] A similar attempt to shore up the traditional privileges of the "learned" (dogmatici) seems to motivate Bishop Alnwick's charges against Berte's possession of *Dives et Pauper*. In this case, the book's content would appear to be less threatening than its context: the same book that was instructive and useful within the strictly monitored confines of the monastic library became dangerous once it fell into the hands of an unbeneficed chaplain who shared books with the literate laity.[76] The implication is that the Norwich Lollard trials, and the fear of Lollard literate communities from which they sprung, arose as an attempt not to restrict illicit books so much as to restrict illicit readers; if the same book could be licit in a monastic library but illicit when circulated like a common-profit book, the effect was to bolster a monastic literacy that was secured by its library.

Curteys's register reveals an ongoing anxiety about the possibility of Lollard uprisings and an eagerness on the part of the abbey's leadership to ally itself with secular rulers in order to suppress them. Among the documents preserved in the register is a 6 July 1431 letter from King Henry VI written in the wake of the Norwich heresy trials, warning against an assemblage of "heretiques in this oure Reaume, com[m]only called lollardis, the which now late by setting vp of cedicious billes, and o[ther]wise, treiturly exhorted, stired, and meued [th]e people of oure land, to assemble, gadre, and arise ayenst goddis pees and oures."[77] The letter refers to a conspiracy organized by one Jack Sharp, which was subdued in the same year by Duke Humfrey of Gloucester, who is identified in the letter as "our saide lieutenant and consail." Fears of Lollard uprisings continued in Bury and throughout the kingdom, as attested by another letter preserved in Curteys's register, written on 5 June 1438, which enlists the abbot's help in looking for "mysgou[r]ned men ... aswel lollards as other robbers & pillers of oure peple" who aim "to have subu[er]ted al the polletique reule of this oure land."[78] As these letters show, if Curteys helped establish Bury as a center of literacy by centralizing its archives and libraries, he did so in the face of, and I would argue in response to, threats to the stability of the abbey, town, and nation such as those described here. As I have argued, William Curteys's register, together with Lydgate's *Cartae versificatae*, represents an attempt to fortify the abbey's authority against threats from above, in the case of the bishop of Norwich, and from below, in the wake of the attacks that Bury sustained throughout the fourteenth century and continued to fear from Lollards in the fifteenth. By grounding the abbey's authority in its control of written documents, moreover, Lydgate's *Cartae* and Curteys's register both centralize the abbey's archives and present reasons for doing so.

Duke Humfrey's Library: "Stable in Study"

The library of Humfrey, Duke of Gloucester, has helped to define the English library for its own and successive ages. One of the first English libraries to include an extensive selection of works by classical and Italian humanist authors, and thus built explicitly on the model of the seignorial libraries in Italy, it has earned Humfrey a reputation as "the first Englishman to show a lively appreciation of humanism," a reputation secured by his book donations to the University of Oxford, which founded the university library that bears his name.[79] Yet Humfrey's library has more in common with a monastic library like that of Bury St. Edmund than is suggested by its humanist reputation.[80] One clear line of continuity is reflected in Humfrey's patronage of Bury's own John Lydgate; at Humfrey's request and with his ongoing support from 1431 to 1439, Lydgate wrote his massive work *The Fall of Princes*, which was based on Laurent de Premierfait's translation of Boccaccio's *De casibus virorum illustrium* (*On the Fall of Illustrious Men*).[81] Readers who have upheld Humfrey as a progressive humanist have found his patronage of Lydgate anomalous, imagining Humfrey and the monastic author of *The Fall of Princes* to be representatives of conflicting cultural forces and eras.[82] Yet Humfrey not only commissioned the work but actively involved himself in its production, lending Lydgate books from his library to use as sources and custom-ordering the envois that moralize the many stories the work compiles. Indeed, *The Fall of Princes* everywhere registers Humfrey's influence, as he repeatedly intervened in the writing process, playing the role less of distant patron than of collaborator.[83] But this collaboration cut both ways. Some of the most innovative recent work on Lydgate has begun to question traditional readings of the poet as a hireling writer of Lancastrian propaganda.[84] Evidence of Lydgate's active role in his collaborative relationship with Humfrey bears out this reassessment of his library labors.[85] Humfrey, I argue, called on and valued Lydgate as a clerical writer who honed his literate skills at Curteys's Bury St. Edmunds, skills that Humfrey hoped Lydgate would bring to bear on his own library. If the *Cartae versificatae* argues for the symbiosis of clerical literacy and secular authority, *The Fall of Princes*, I argue, shows how this symbiosis could be mobilized for political ends by applying clerical literate practices—particularly the production of commentary and allegorical reading—to produce a vision of social order and hierarchy.

Taken together, *Fall of Princes* and *Cartae versificatae* suggest that there is greater continuity between the two libraries with which Lydgate was closely connected—those of Bury St. Edmunds and of Duke Humfrey—than is appreciated when monastic and humanist libraries are strictly differentiated. Armando Petrucci and Pearl Kibre have found that Italian seignorial libraries during this time, while bearing a distinct humanist stamp, also maintained close ties to monastic libraries, which in many respects they attempted to emulate both in the scope of their holdings and in the institutional authority that they projected.[86] Similarly, Humfrey's library and that of Bury St. Edmunds are marked by a similar continuity in content. Although Humfrey was an assiduous collector of classical texts—a practice that has been seen as a sign of his humanism—the Bury library also included classical authors in great numbers, such as Cicero, Virgil, Horace, Ovid, and Juvenal.[87] It also contained a number of works by English Dominican friars such as Nicholas Trevet, Thomas Waleys, and Thomas Ringstead, whose presence in the collection indicates how the classics were read at Bury.[88] These authors were known for commentaries that extracted moralized fables from classical sources by submitting them to allegorical readings.[89] Producing such commentaries required a massive support system of indices and cross-references that might be compared to the sophisticated index systems fostered by late medieval library catalogues, particularly Kirkestede's *Catalogus*.[90] These "classicizing friars" (so called by Beryl Smalley) were frequent targets of attack by humanists such as Petrarch, Boccaccio, and Salutati, who charged them with submitting the classics to obfuscating glosses and willful misreadings, in opposition to which the humanists championed the historical fidelity of their own approaches to the ancient texts.[91] If humanists downplay the friars' contributions to classical learning, the "humanist" library of Duke Humfrey makes them manifest, revealing an unexpected consanguinity between Humfrey's classicism and that of the friars. Both rest on a program of virtuous reading, premised on the belief that "reedyng off bookis bryngith in vertu." Where friars' skills in allegorical exegesis, or *allegoresis*, allowed them to mine the classics for Christian lessons, Lydgate asserts that the same skills can serve the goals of the learned statesman.

In the reading that follows, Humfrey's library forms the general context for *The Fall of Princes*, which in turn supports—and even enables—the famous library's place in the world of fifteenth-century English thought and letters. If Humfrey brought humanist books into England, Lydgate's *Fall of Princes* adapted them to English circumstances by applying monastic protocols of literacy to secular subjects. The product of Lydgate's close association with his patron and his books, *The Fall of Princes* both reflects and reflects upon Humfrey's own ambitions for his library. It also allows us to revise one prevailing assumption about Humfrey as an intellectually disengaged Maecenas who "preferred to look at rather than read his books."[92] To the contrary, *The Fall of Princes* suggests that not only was Humfrey intimately familiar with the contents of his books—enough so to hand-select those he pressed on Lydgate as sources—but he was also deeply concerned with the politics of reading. From this perspective, Duke Humfrey's Library emerges as an institution whose founding purpose was not merely to accumulate books but actively to shape their uses and interpretations toward specific political goals—goals that took on topical urgency in 1431, the year Lydgate received his commission.

As well as their similarities of content, the libraries of Duke Humfrey and Bury St. Edmunds are joined by a common historical context, the threat of popular revolt, to which both responded.[93] If, as I have argued above, the popular attacks directed at Bury St. Edmunds in 1327 and 1381 led to the strengthening of its archives and library, Humfrey was motivated by similar concerns about popular uprisings, particularly those that advanced political ends through the means of literate culture. For Humfrey, these concerns coalesced around a figure who also plays a role in William Curteys's register: Jack Sharp, the leader of the 1431 rebellion. In the spring of 1431 William Perkins or Maundvyll, under the pseudonym "Jack Sharpe of Wygmoreland," was found distributing bills in the Midlands that pointed to a would-be rebellion unlike any that preceded it.[94] The bills themselves recycled many of the calls for religious disendowment advanced by earlier uprisings, such as the one engineered by Sir John Oldcastle in 1414.[95] But the conspiracy went much further. Not stopping at religious disendowment, the plan was to abolish private property itself, as Edward Hall would report in his *Chronicle*, with the aim "that priests should have no possessions; and that all thinges, by the order of charite amongst Christian people, should be in common."[96] And while earlier revolts had maintained loyalty to the ruler, Sharp's aimed "totally to destroy the estate and person of the king," to disendow lay lords, and to name Lollard successors, and thus, as one contemporary charged, "of ladds and lurdains [to] make lordes."[97] According to reports, Jack Sharp himself, a.k.a. William Perkins, planned to "take upon himself as a prince" and to replace the king's council with his own associates; Humfrey himself was to be replaced by one John Cook, a weaver from London.[98]

Once the plot was uncovered, Humfrey acted swiftly and harshly to suppress it. Perkins and his coconspirators were captured and spectacularly executed on 17 May, but fear that more plotters remained at large drove Humfrey to organize a large-scale campaign against Lollards that resulted in further executions. Humfrey himself traveled widely during the spring and summer of 1431 to suspected centers of instability; during this time the first letter of warning against Lollard uprisings that is preserved in Curteys's register was sent, alerting Bury to "heretiques in this oure Reaume, com[m]only called lollardis, the which now late by setting vp of cedicious billes, and o[ther]wise, treiturly exhorted, stired, and meued [th]e people of oure land, to assemble, gadre, and arise ayenst goddis pees and oures." Jack Sharp triangulates Curteys's register, Duke Humfrey, and *The Fall of Princes*: Humfrey finds a place in Curteys's register in the warning against Sharp (the king refers to Humfrey as "our saide lieutenant and consail") and Sharp figures in *The Fall of Princes*, since the anti-Lollard campaign of 1431 inspired Lydgate to observe in *The Fall of Princes* that "in this land no Lollard dar abide" and that Humfrey "sparith noon, but maketh himsiluen strong" against heretics (1.403, 405). William Curteys and Duke Humfrey are thus mediated not only by a common friend, John Lydgate, but also by a common enemy, Jack Sharp.

The Jack Sharp rebellion represented a new level of threat to English political and social order. While earlier Lollard rebellions counterbalanced religious critique with support for the monarch, that of 1431 plotted the overthrow of the monarch and his counselors—and did so, moreover, during a potentially vulnerable moment for the monarchy, with the ten-year-old Henry VI away in France and the nobility internally divided and sometimes at violent odds.[99] The king's response reflects the challenge that the rebellion posed to existing models of monarchical power and order. The king charges the rebels with seeking

> gou[ver]naile in no wise be langyng vnto hem [th]at owen to be go[ver]ned, and not so to gov[er]ne; [th]e which sturyng and vsurpacion of oure roial power, by [th]e lawe of this oure land is treson, ech resonable man may wel fele, [th]at in eschuyng of, chastisyng, and reddoure of oure lawes, [th]ei in so doing... dispose hem to be out of subjection, obeissance, or awe of vs, and of oure lawe; and as God knoweth, ne[th]ere wolde [th]ei be subgitt to His, ne to mannes, but wolde be louse and free.[100]

By putting men "who ought to be governed" in the place of those who govern, Jack Sharp and the rebels threatened to subvert not only the king but a social order grounded on "subjection," not just the king's law but God's law.

The rebellion itself coincides with the emergence of what I. M. W. Harvey identifies as a "popular politics" in the mid–fifteenth century that fed on a growing sense of political clout, coupled with increasing levels of literacy, within a group that identified itself as "the common people."[101] If the rebellion represented a "usurpation of . . . royal power," it was also a usurpation of literacy; in their sophisticated uses of bills, which included verse and other texts, Jack Sharp's rebels showed that they could use the tools of literacy for propaganda as effectively as the Lancastrians.[102] These were "acts of assertive literacy" in the mold of the broadsides of the 1381 rebels, of which Steven Justice observes: "they made their most important claim merely by being written documents that came (or claimed to come) from the hands of *rustici*."[103] Similarly, in nearly all contemporary and near-contemporary accounts, the literacy of the 1431 rebels became their hallmark. Thus, a letter from "Humfrey duke of Gloucestre, guardian of England," dated 13 May 1431, "To the Sheriffs of London" warns against Sharp and his allies, who "at the instigation of the devil have written and caused to be written diverse bills and writings false and seditious containing things contrary to the Christian faith and doctrine . . . and to publish the same to the people have wickedly posted them up and cast them forth in cities, boroughs and notable towns in places where people are wont most to congregate." The letter charges "all the king's lieges, his officers and others, to arrest them who write, communicate, cast forth or post up such bills and their abettors, them who tell tales and spread seditious rumours," so that the king and his agents can "zealously chastise them according to their desserts."[104] In similar terms contemporary Nicholas Bishop charges the rebels with "wryting fals bulles and fals scriptures and gilful."[105] The St. Albans chronicle (*Chronicon rerum gestarum in Monasterio Sancti Albani*) recounts how Sharp, "a certain rogue, tainted with Lollardy," "created a certain commotion among the people, by throwing about and dispersing written bills in London, Coventry, Oxford, and other towns," and was harshly suppressed, "together with the writers of his bills."[106] And the fifteenth-century *Chronicle of London* recounts how the rebels "casted billes aboughte in every good town in Engelond."[107]

Though the fear of future Lollard uprisings remained, Humfrey's suppression of the would-be rebellion was generally held to have been a success. With the king's return from France approaching, Humfrey was able to parlay his political victory into a more material reward, convincing the council on 20 November to approve a substantial raise in salary to reward his efforts in "the taking and execution of the most horrible heretic and impious traitor to God and the said Lord king, who called himself John Sharp, and of many other heretical malefactors his accomplices."[108] The raise funded a series of patronage projects that Humfrey pursued from 1431 to 1433, when he extended his sponsorship to Lydgate and initiated a major stage in the development of his library.[109] It is thus to Jack Sharp and his plot of 1431 that *The Fall of Princes* and Humfrey's library owe their common origin.

Humfrey's turn to literary patronage represented not a retirement from the public life but an attempt to extend his statesmanship from the level of practice to the level of doctrine. After the king's return from France, Humfrey resumed his earlier political role as First Counselor but positioned himself to be closer to Henry VI and the centers of power in the court.[110] In promoting his public status as a learned statesman, Humfrey confirmed his indispensability to the monarch by demonstrating the importance of books and reading to the maintenance of royal power. Where the rebels used ephemeral literacy, in the form of bill posting, to make their case, Humfrey turned to monumental textuality, in the form of his library and the enormous *Fall of Princes,* to demonstrate his political might.[111] Through these works of patronage, Humfrey reasserted literacy as a tool of the ruler over the ruled.

In his effort to build a spectacular library, Humfrey followed the practice of contemporary Italian statesmen like Cosimo de' Medici and Federico da Montrefeltro, Duke of Urbino, whose extensive libraries made the display of learning into an attribute of power.[112] Thanks to their examples, the library, marked by the extensiveness and richness of its holdings, became "a distinctive and characterizing element," as Armando Petrucci puts it, "of the new signorial state then taking shape."[113] This point is reflected in the Florentine bookseller Vespasiano da Bisticci's *Lives of Illustrious Men,* which eulogizes his famous contemporaries by recounting the magnificence of their libraries: the Duke of Urbino, Vespasiano reports, "had a mind to do what no one had done for a thousand years or more; that is, to create the finest library since ancient times. He spared neither cost nor labour, and when he knew of a fine book, whether in Italy or not, he would send for it."[114] Likewise, when Cosimo de' Medici built a splendid library, Vespasiano notes, "there was no lack of money."[115] Humfrey's ambition to emulate his Italian counterparts in building a seignorial library is reflected in his decision to employ as overseer of his collection the Milanese humanist Pier Candido Decembrio, whose brother Angelo authored a set of dialogues focusing on "the question of how a Renaissance prince and his courtiers and scholars should choose and use books."[116] As David Rundle wryly observes, "a well-stocked library was a sign, not of its owner's wisdom, but of his recognition of the importance of wisdom."[117]

But Humfrey was attentive to at least some of his books' contents as well as their appearance. Besides offering an outward manifestation of his learning, Humfrey's book collecting was inspired by a practical desire to locate models of rulership from the classical past. The linchpin of his collection— and the work most often cited as evidence of Humfrey's humanism—is

Decembrio's translation of Plato's *Republic*, which Decembrio purportedly carried out in the duke's honor. In the letters that passed between them, Decembrio promises Humfrey that the work "will impart to you the form of a good and true prince," while Humfrey in turn finds Plato's prince a model of "wise statesmanship": "Such is the dignity and grace of Plato," Humfrey writes in gratitude to Decembrio, "and so successful is your interpretation of him, that we cannot say to whom we owe most, to him for drawing a prince of such wise statesmanship, or to you for laboring to bring [this work] to light."[118] In the fifth book of the *Republic*, which Decembrio translated and sent first to the duke to advertise the *Republic*'s value, Plato famously formulates his model of the philosopher-king when he has Socrates insist:

> Unless philosophers become kings in our cities, or unless those who now are kings and rulers become true philosophers, so that political power and philosophic intelligence converge, and unless those lesser natures who run after one without the other are excluded from governing, I believe there can be no end to troubles, my dear Glaucon, in our cities or for all mankind. Only then will our theory of the state spring to life and see the light of day, at least to the degree possible.[119]

Plato's philosopher-king dovetailed with Humfrey's own self-cultivated persona as a learned statesman, which he attempted to project at home and abroad through his patronage. In Italy, where the mythology of the learned ruler was already familiar, humanists eagerly reflected back to the duke the terms of honor that he himself cultivated assiduously. The Venetian humanist Piero del Monte compared Humfrey to classical examples of learned statesmen like Caesar "who fought and judged by day, and wrote books by night." Similarly, Lapo da Castiglionchio dedicated his original treatise, "Comparatio studiorum et rei militaris," to Humfrey, citing his fame as both a soldier and a devotee of "learning, eloquence, and the humane studies."[120] The image of Humfrey as scholar-prince was anchored by his library, whose fame spread in England as well as Italy. The University of Oxford's official letter of thanks for his bequest of books echoes the Italian humanists in comparing Humfrey to Caesar as both a soldier-scholar and founder of a great library: just as "Julius Caesar founded a library at Rome to preserve by books the fame of his conquest of the world," it claims, so the library at Oxford "will be an everlasting monument of your fame."[121]

Lydgate's *Fall of Princes* needs to be read within the context of Humfrey's efforts to cultivate the persona of a learned statesman. Like the others, Lydgate compares Humfrey to Caesar, who "natwithstandyng his conquest

& renoun,/Vnto bookis he gaff gret attendaunce" (1.369–70). And further echoing his Italian counterparts, Lydgate praises his patron as a soldier-scholar who is "bothe manli and eek wis" (1.407), for whom "corage" and "studie" are congruent virtues:

> His corage neuer doth appalle
> To studie in bookis off antiquite,
> Therin he hath so gret felicite
> Vertuously hymsilff to ocupie,
> Off vicious slouthe to haue the maistrie. (1.393–99)

But Lydgate also adapts the classical and humanist figure of the soldier-scholar to the English contexts to which Humfrey's patronage responded. If Lydgate conceives Humfrey's literary activity in terms of the Benedictine injunction to "eschew idleness," he also identifies Humfrey's "maistrie" over "slouthe" in his study with his ability to "[make] hymsiluen strong" against Lollard challenges to the state (1.405).[122] Thus, where Humfrey's ruthlessness in quelling the Jack Sharp rebellion reveals his ability "to chastise alle that do therto tresoun" (1.413)—recalling Humfrey's 1431 letter to the sheriffs of London promising to "zealously chastise [the 1431 rebels] according to their desserts"—his work in his study also leads to the more abstract and literary chastisement of "errour":

> And to do plesaunce to our lord Iesu,
> He studieth euere to haue intelligence;
> Reedyng off bookis bryngith in vertu,
> Vices excluding, slouthe and necligence,
> Makith a prynce to haue experience,
> To knowe hymsilff, in many sundry wise,
> Wher he trespasith his errour to chastise. (1.413–20)

Chastising both treasonous Lollards and "errour" in himself, Lydgate's Humfrey offers the example of how statesmanship and reading are not only mutually supporting activities but two outcomes of the same activity: "chastisement," or *castigare*, an act of correction whose foundations in textual criticism Stephanie Jed has demonstrated.[123] What makes Humfrey a scourge of Lollards, in other words, also makes him a gifted scholar. By extension, Humfrey's ability to produce stability in the state begins with his ability to remain "stable in study" (1.389).

If Humfrey's library anchors his personal mythology as scholar-prince, *The Fall of Princes* deserves to be called "a phenomenon of the library" (in Foucault's words), since it makes libraries its recurrent setting and touchstone.[124] Libraries, Lydgate insists, are places to which writers are naturally drawn: "Poetis to sitte in ther librarie/Desire of nature, and to be solitarie" (3.3807–8). *The Fall of Princes* is a fiction of the library, a setting in which Lydgate goes out of his way to establish the scene of the work's composition. Where Boccaccio frequently refers to himself in the act of writing, Lydgate emphatically locates that act in a study or library, two terms he uses interchangeably. For instance, in a scene in which Boccaccio tells us only that "I was taking up my pen," Lydgate inserts details of location: "In his studi alone as Bochas stood" (6.1–2) and, a few lines further, "Bochas pensiff [was] in his librarie" (6.15).[125] Throughout *The Fall of Princes* Lydgate pictures Bochas not only in the act of writing but in a place where he is surrounded by books—a detail that figures importantly in Lydgate's vision of the work's composition and significance and is emphasized in the illuminations from a fifteenth-century manuscript of *The Fall of Princes*, Rosenbach Museum and Library, Philadelphia, MS 439/16.[126]

Though a place "to be solitarie," Lydgate's library is not set apart from the world—as reflected in the Rosenbach illuminations, which represent the poet continuously visited in his library by figures of worldly authority such as Emperor Mauritius (fig. 1). The library is not a retreat from worldly action but a privileged site for it. If Humfrey deserves praise because of his industrious literary activity ("Vertuously hymsilff to ocupie,/Off vicious slouthe to haue the maistrie"), Lydgate's Bochas shows how that industry is located in the library. In the prologue to book 8, when Bochas finds himself succumbing to idleness, Lydgate interpolates a scene in which he is visited by the shade of Petrarch, who admonishes him, "[Idleness] hath the drawe awey fro thi librarie" (8.101). Directing Bochas back to his library, Lydgate's figure of Petrarch advises him to take example from "the book I maad of lyff solitarye," which "techeth the weie of virtuous besyness" (8.108–10). Petrarch's *Of the Solitary Life* is not mentioned by Boccaccio or Laurent de Premierfait; however, it was one of the books in Humfrey's library, and its insertion in Lydgate's narrative was almost certainly directed by Humfrey himself.[127] The reference clarifies the meaning of Lydgate's observation about poets "in ther librarie" who desire "to be solitarie" by defining the kind of solitude that Petrarch describes as not a retreat from the world but an active engagement with it: "I mean a solitude," Petrarch writes, "that is not exclusive, leisure that is neither idle nor profitless but productive

Fig. 1. The emperor Mauritius visits Boccaccio in his library (Rosenbach
Museum and Library, Philadelphia, MS 439/16, fol. 198)

of advantage to many."[128] Solitude for Petrarch is a space of learning that
bears fruit in active application; thus, he approvingly cites "examples of
emperors and military leaders who liked solitude."[129] The "virtuous besyness" that Bochas learns to pursue in his library resonates with Lydgate's
description of Humfrey's own library as a factory of virtue, a place dedicated

to overcoming "slouthe and necligence," where "Reedyng off bookis bryngith in vertu." This business of virtuous reading recalls the wise rulers
whom Lydgate praises in his *Cartae versificatae*, who, aided by the literate
efforts of their monastic allies, essay "with lyght of verteu ther sogettys
tenlumyne/Both by example and vertuous doctryn" (223). Here, as in the
Cartae versificatae, the library produces virtuous doctrine that is necessary
to rulers.

The library setting of the *Fall of Princes* supports the book's larger aims
and methods. As Lydgate's prologue insists, Bochas intends his book "for
a memoriall," and he draws on the multiple sources that he "hath gadred
out . . . In dyuers bookes which that he hath rad," from which he undertakes
"to compile and writen as he fond/The fall of nobles in many dyuers lond"
(1.64, 72–73, 76–77)—an action of reading across multiple sources that is
enabled by the book's library setting. But again, this "memorial," like the
library from which it draws its sources, is composed not through accretion
but through selection. At the same time that Lydgate's Bochas "compiles"
and "gathers" his sources, Bochas pointedly omits "alle the stories which
that comoun be" (1.146), explaining:

> And lest that folk wolde haue had disdeyn,
> Thynges comoun to put in memorie,
> Therfore Bochas thoughte it was but veyn,
> To his name noon encres off glorie,
> To remembre no cronycle nor historie,
> But tho that wern for ther merit notable,
> Auctorised, famous and comendable. (1.148–54)

The "memorie" produced in this library filters out "thynges comoun" in
favor of the "auctorised, famous, and comendable," works granted their
status not through popular but through elite readers. Increase of glory, in
other words, comes through restriction of memory.

The reading program that Lydgate describes recalls Wycliffite charges
against religious libraries that exclude "comoun" readers and thus harm
"the comunte"—cognate terms that signify things or people of shared use
or identity and that emerged into political significance with the rise of "the
common people" as a self-conscious political force.[130] The Jack Sharp rebels
participate in this movement by issuing bills purporting to speak on behalf
of "alle comyns of the reme," while their calls for disendowment were taken
to signify "that all thinges, by the order of charite amongst Christian people,
should be in common."[131] In opposition, Lydgate's *Fall of Princes* advances a

literary model in which the "comoun" is grounds for exclusion. This project
of building a memorial edifice that excludes the "comoun" is consistent
with Lydgate's treatment of the terms "comoun" and "comounte" throughout *The Fall of Princes*: to signify unruly elements that require discipline
through literary chastisement. The prologue articulates the work's aim thus:

> to correct and a-mende
> The vicious folk off euery comounte
> And bi exaumplis which that notable be
> Off pryncis olde, that whilom dede fall,
> The lowere peeple from ther errour call. (1.206–10)

In a work that charts the rise and fall of Fortune, Fortune's vicissitudes are
frequently identified with just such "lowere people," called "comouns" or
"comounte": thus, Lydgate warns against "the stormy trust off eueri comounte" (3.2164) and "the chaunge and mutability / Founde in Fortune and
eueri comounte" (3.2162–63), warning princes "In trust off comouns is no
perseueraunce" (3.2203) and "Loo, what it is in comouns to assure! / Stormy
off herte, onseur off ther corage" (3.2921–22).

The Fall of Princes seeks to discipline the stormy "comouns" and bars
"thynges comoun" from the memorial library, and it praises Humfrey for
seeking his literary community in a more stable place: "With clerkis to
commune" (1.387).[132] Whereas "comouns" are associated with a literacy of
"thynges comoun," clerks produce a literate community of virtuous chastisement. Clerical literacy is both allied with and distinct from the literacy
of poets, as Lydgate describes the latter in a passage that is unique to his
version of Boccaccio's *De casibus virorum illustrium:*

> Ther cheeff labour is vicis to repreve
> With a maner couert symylitude,
> And non estat with ther langage greeve
> Bi no rebukyng of termys dul and rude;
> What-euer thei write, on vertu ay conclude. (3.3830–34)

In his insistence that poets' meanings ultimately produce "vertu," "what-
euer thei write," Lydgate deliberately echoes St. Paul from Romans 15.4:
"Whatever was written in former days was written for our instruction," a
passage that became one of the key texts for medieval *allegoresis*. Tradition-
ally used to justify the recuperation of classical texts for Christian meanings, this doctrine suggested that meanings that seemed to point away from

Christian truths could be interpreted allegorically in order to bring them into a Christian framework. In a similar vein, Lydgate insists that, even when poets appear to use "rebuking of termys dul and rude," their true intention is not to "greeve" any "estat" but to produce virtue. Lydgate thus adapts Paul's model in the service of upholding the truths, not of Christianity, but of social order and the traditional hierarchy of the estates; but it will take a concerted reworking of the monastic program of reading to do this.

As Lydgate asserts, clerks, trained as allegorical readers, are especially equipped to decode poets' "couert symylitude" and to derive moral lessons from recalcitrant texts. Embodying this assertion, *The Fall of Princes* is created through the compilation of poetic exempla followed by envois, which are Lydgate's most notable innovation to his sources; those envois gloss the exempla that precede them and uncover edifying moral lessons in line with Lydgate's charge to offer a work of instruction to princes. Thus, to cite an opening example that establishes the work's modus operandi, poets are responsible for producing fables such as that of Saturn:

> These olde poetis with ther sawes swete
> Ful couertli in ther vers do feyne,
> How olde Saturne was whilom kyng of Crete
> And off custum did his besy peyne,
> Off his godhed list for to ordeyne
> That he sholde, as off his nature,
> Echon deuoure as by his engendrure. (1.1401–7)

But having recounted this poetic fiction, Lydgate hastens to add that the story is a fable and thus should not be taken literally to refer to an actual king:

> To vndirstonde off poetis the processe,
> Thei meene pleynli that this word Saturne
> Doth in it-silff nothyng but tyme expresse;
> And philisophres bere also witnesse,
> That as in tyme, foorth euery thyng is brouht
> So tyme ageynward bryngith euery thing to nouht. (1.1409–14)

Through Lydgate's gloss, a story of an unnatural king becomes a lesson about the circularity of time, a lesson that, as Lydgate attests, "clerkis recorde eek in ther writyng" (1.1415).[133] Where poets write "couertli" and "with a maner couert symylitude," clerks "recorde" in clarifying language the virtuous lessons to be gleaned from those stories.

By aligning himself with clerks as a moralizing interpreter of poets, Lydgate establishes the project that will guide *The Fall of Princes*. Because Lydgate's training as a monastic reader prepares him to extract "covert" messages of Christian virtue from classical texts, he declares that he will emulate "these clerkis in writyng" who produce new lessons from

> Thyng that was maad of auctours hem beforn
> Thei may off newe fynde and fantasie,
> Out of old chaff trie out ful cleene corne. (1.22–24)

The lesson echoes the *Cartae versificatae*'s Augustinian injunction "To voyde the chaf and chesyn oute the corne" in the performance of allegorical reading. For Augustine, the metaphor of the corn and the chaff illustrates the possibility of recuperating Christian meanings from non-Christian texts. But, as he did with St. Paul, here Lydgate transforms Augustine's famous account of allegorical reading into a tool supporting the secular authority of princes.

In so doing, Lydgate further transforms the chaff and corn model by insisting on the corn's newness; thus, as Larry Scanlon points out, he makes the "corn," or moral lesson, less an anterior object to be uncovered than a product of "fantasie" or invention, a revision that allows clerks to approach their sources with "an almost unlimited latitude for innovation."[134] Lydgate claims precisely this latitude for himself in lines that open the prologue to *The Fall of Princes*, which assert that writers must be willing to "make and unmake" their sources

> In many sondry wyse,
> As potteres, which to that craft entende,
> Breke and renewe ther vesselis to a-mende. (1.12–14)

With this potter metaphor, Lydgate presents the creative process as a form of renewal that involves a certain amount of destruction; the transformation of "old chaaf" into "ful cleene corne," he suggests, requires the use of interpretive force.

In *The Fall of Princes* the main locus of that force is the envoi, a feature that Lydgate included at the special request of Humfrey, who charged him:

> That I sholde in eueri tragedie,
> Afftir the processe made mencioun,
> At the eende sette a remedie,

With a lenvoie conueied be resoun,
And afftir that, with humble affeccioun,
To noble pryncis lowli it directe. (2.148–53)

If breaking and renewing can be considered a practice of amending, it is also germane to the form of "remedie" that Lydgate's envois supply to his source texts. Humfrey's request for an envoi following every chapter significantly changes the tone of the work from that of its sources. Boccaccio conceived his own work less as a source of edification than as an example to the "vicious" and "debauched" rulers of his age illustrating the tenuous nature of power; where he extracts lessons, he offers them as occasional breaks meant to leaven the otherwise-relentless narrative of downfall: "In order that an unbroken succession of stories be not tiresome to the reader, I think it will be both more pleasant and useful from time to time to add inducements to virtue and dissuasions from vice."[135] But Humfrey's request forces Lydgate to turn each story into the basis of a moral lesson for princes.[136] Under that pressure, Lydgate constructs his envois as a secular commentary that extracts moral meanings from his sources. But those sources are not always amenable to Humfrey's wishes—especially given the ambivalence toward princes and monarchy that characterizes many of Lydgate's humanist sources, including Boccaccio himself.[137] Breaking and remaking his sources were necessary if Lydgate was to extract the kinds of moralized stories Humfrey sought from humanist texts that sometimes delivered a distinctly antimonarchical message.[138]

"Breke and Renewe": Lydgate Revises His Sources

When Humfrey lent Lydgate books from his library to incorporate into *The Fall of Princes*, he had a clear agenda: to advance his self-fashioning as a scholar-prince and to extract edifying lessons in the arts of statesmanship. Humfrey's lendings are concentrated in one chapter of book 2. While it represents only a short portion of the vast *Fall of Princes*, the section offers a telling illustration of how Lydgate and Humfrey collaborated through Humfrey's library—as well as of that library's role in the making of *The Fall of Princes*. Early in the second book appears "A Chapitle / descryuyng how prynces beyng hedis of ther comountees sholde haue noble cheualrie true Iuges &c ther commounte to gouerne &c" (2.806). This chapter represents a noteworthy departure from Lydgate's sources. Boccaccio's original presents a chapter of a different nature, entitled "In fastosam regum superbiam," which Lydgate's immediate source, Laurent de Premierfait, translates as

"Contre les roys & princes orgueilleux" (Against Proud Kings and Princes).
In both Boccaccio's and Laurent's versions, the chapter reminds kings that
their power derives from the people, who maintain the right to deprive them
of that power should they abuse it. Thus, Boccaccio asserts, "To conspire
against this kind of ruler, to take up arms, to deceive, to oppose this man is
an act of greatness and, even more, of necessity. Scarcely any offering is more
acceptable to God than the blood of a tyrant." In support of this assertion,
Boccaccio cites examples of "extraordinary men" who "have dared the greatest deeds" in overthrowing tyrants; thus, "Junius Brutus turned the Roman
people against Tarquin the Proud, Virginius against Appius Claudius."[139]

In his reading of Brutus and Virginius, Boccaccio follows a tradition that
took these stories to exemplify and justify popular revolts against tyranny;
they had an added resonance in Boccaccio's Florence, where they were held
to champion republican freedom.[140] Boccaccio's citation of them here becomes one of those moments in his ideologically complex text in which,
as David Wallace asserts, Boccaccio "shows a strong prorepublican, antity-
rannical bias in narrating histories of ancient Rome," reflecting his own allegiance to the Florentine republic.[141] Laurent translates the section faithfully while expanding it to catalogue the moral failures of princes who are
justly overthrown, before he concludes, following Boccaccio, "There is no
sacrifice that pleases God so much as that of the tyrant and evil prince, because he has corrupted both human and divine rights" (Il nest sacrifice a dieu
tant aggreable comme est le sang du tyrant et mauluais prince pource que il
corrompt les droitz diuins et humains).[142] And again, he cites, though also
amplifies, the stories of "Brutus a citizen of Rome and cousin of the chaste
Lucrece" (brutus vng cytoyen de romme et cousin de la treschaste Lucresse)
and "virgineus" who led "all the people of Rome against Claudius" (tout le
peuple de romme contre appius claudius) as examples of "those who dare to
achieve great things" (aucuns qui ont ose entreprendre & acomplir tresgrans
choses).[143]

In *The Fall of Princes*, the chapter is dramatically revised in ways that
reflect Lydgate's encounter with Humfrey's library. In place of Boccaccio and
Laurent's examples of the justified overthrow of tyrants and the "mauluais
prince," Lydgate offers an allegory of good government that is lifted from
John of Salisbury's *Policraticus*, a book that Humfrey himself owned and in
fact donated to Oxford; he almost certainly lent it to Lydgate for the purposes of this substitution.[144] In John's well-known allegory, a hierarchically
structured body politic is likened to the human body. "The place of the head
in the body of the commonwealth is filled by the prince." The various parts
of the body are represented by the prince's officers and governors, and so on,

down to the feet: "the husbandmen correspond to the feet, which always cleave to the soil, and need the more especially the care and foresight of the head...since it is they who raise, sustain, and move forward the weight of the entire body."[145] Borrowing from this allegory, Lydgate likewise compares the nation to a human body, at whose head is the ruler:

> Mihti pryncis for ther hih renoun,
> As most worthi shal ocupie the hed,
> With wit, memorie, and eyen off resoun,
> To keepe ther membris fro myscheeff & dreed. (2.841–44)

Also like John of Salisbury, Lydgate stations the commonwealth's laborers in the place of its feet: "Laboreris...Shal this bodi bern up and susteene / As feet and leggis" (2.891–92). From this model, Lydgate extrapolates a lesson about the interdependence of the parts:

> Hed, armys, bodi, and ther fressh visages
> Withoute feet or leggis may nat vaile
> To stonde upriht; for needis thei mut faile
> And semblabli subiectis in comountees
> Reise up the noblesse off pryncis in ther sees. (2.829–33)

As wielded in *The Fall of Princes*, the metaphor literally replaces an image of popular uprising with one that asserts princely rule as the natural order. Where in Boccaccio, and Laurent after him, the people rise up against princes, in Lydgate the people "reise up" princes, just as the legs raise up the body, an organic metaphor that not only stresses the interdependence of the body parts but calls on their mutual investment in the hierarchy of rule over ruled.[146] In Lydgate's "Chapitle / descryuyng how pryncis beyng hedis of ther comountees sholde haue noble cheualrie true Iuges &c ther commounte to gouerne &c" it is notable that "comountees" become subjects under rulers ("subiectis in comountees") rather than political agents in their own right, a hierarchical structure that is reinforced in Lydgate's appeal to the "thestatis that gouerne comou[n]tees,—/ As meires, prouostes & burgeis in citees" (2.865–66). This redefinition of "comounte" might be read alongside the narrowing of the term "common" that Maura Nolan and John Watts have identified at the beginning of the Lancastrian regime.[147] Where Jack Sharp and his followers claim to speak for "alle comyns of the reme," here such commons are incorporated into, and subjected within, "comountees" that are headed by rulers.

In keeping with his use of John of Salisbury to recast a critique of bad
rulers as an homage to political hierarchy, Lydgate similarly "amends" the
stories of Lucrece and Virginia that follow as examples.[148] Where Boccaccio
and Laurent cite these stories to support popular revolts against tyrannical
rule, Lydgate rounds out his "Chapter of Good Government" by retelling the
same stories through alternative sources that can also be traced to Humfrey.
As Lydgate recounts, Humfrey himself pressed him to incorporate the story
of Lucrece into *The Fall of Princes*, despite Lydgate's reluctance to retell a
story that had recently been treated by Chaucer:

> My lord bad I sholde abide,
> By good auys at leiser to translate
> The doolful processe off her pitous fate. (2.1006–8)

But the story that follows departs from Laurent's source text by instead
"Folowyng the tracis off Collucyus" (2.1009), again at the insistence of Humfrey, who apparently pressed his own copy of Coluccio Salutati's *Declamatio*
on Lydgate for the purpose.[149] Accordingly, Lydgate produces a lengthy and
faithful translation of Salutati's *Declamatio*, which tells the story of Lucrece's
rape by Tarquin by focusing on its aftermath: first, in an address to Lucrece
by her husband and father, urging her against the suicide that she threatens (2.1058–1211); next, in Lucrece's response, culminating in her suicide
(2.1212–1330); and finally, in a description of Lucrece's vindication in the
exile of the royal Tarquin and the establishment of the Roman republic.[150]

Humfrey's selection of the text for insertion into *The Fall of Princes*
seems incongruous, particularly as an example of "Good Government" in
the section that he so actively engineered. As written and received, the *Declamatio* is a story of supremely bad government; its author, Coluccio Salutati, the chancellor of republican Florence from 1375 to 1406, intended
the narrative to illustrate the origin of *libertas Romana* as an example for
Florentine republicanism by means of what Stephanie Jed reminds us is a
"humanist tradition which has celebrated Lucretia's rape as a prologue to
republican freedom."[151] As reflected in Boccaccio's version, this tradition
reads Tarquin's exile as a story of tyranny justly punished, a warning of the
evils of tyranny, and a reminder of the power of the people to overthrow
unjust rulers.

But as reread and glossed by Lydgate, the story of Lucrece is made to uphold a very different lesson. Following his faithful translation of Salutati's
text, Lydgate reinterprets the story as an example of the tragic aftereffects
of bad governance. Because of Tarquin's offense, moralizes Lydgate's envoi,

"Kynges [were] exiled for such mysgouvernaile" (2.1435). Thus, Lydgate offers Lucrece's story as an extension of his lesson, from *Policraticus*, that the
hierarchical ordering of the kingdom will produce harmonious coexistence,
while disorder and riot will ensue when that order is violated. Republicanism is not the glorious end that justifies tragic means, then, but a specter
that threatens a society out of order.

    Lydgate advances this reading of Lucrece's story by pairing it with a
retelling of the story of Virginia, echoing Boccaccio's and Laurent's linkage
of the two stories. But again, rather than following Boccaccio or Laurent,
he cross-references another source, "Titus Lyuyus" (2.1346). Although Livy
was a standard source of the Virginia story, I take Lydgate's reference to be
to a specific book. Humfrey owned a magnificently illuminated copy of Livy
that was translated by Pierre Bersuire; a gift from his brother John of Bed-
ford, it was in Humfrey's library at the time Lydgate wrote this chapter.[152]
Humfrey's desire for practical morality dovetails with Bersuire's stated goal
of transforming Livy's history into a store of exempla for royal readers; as
Bersuire writes in his prologue to King Jean le Bon, "Les Souverains doivent
s'inspirer des exemples du anciens."[153] Following Bersuire, Lydgate offers
the story of Virginia along with that of Lucrece as advice to "noble pryncis"
on how to maintain their rule. Thus, his envoi concludes:

> Noble Pryncis, your resoun doth applie,
> Which ouer the peeple ha[ue] dominacioun,
> So prudentli to gouerne hem and guie,
> That loue and dreed be trewe affeccioun
> Preserue ther hertis from fals rebellioun,
> Sithe to your hihnesse nothyng may mor preuaile
> Than trewe subieccioun expert in the poraile. (2.1457–62)

True to Humfrey's request, Lydgate's envoi "remedie[s]" his sources by rein-
terpreting their meanings for the benefit of "noble pryncis." Thus, Lydgate's
envoi inverts the meanings of the stories of Lucrece and Virginia by offering
them as lessons to princes in how to maintain their "dominacioun" and
"preserue" the people "from fals rebellioun."

    In his moralizing envois like this one, Lydgate applies the literate skills
he cultivated as a monk at Bury St. Edmunds to the library of Duke Humfrey.
In so doing, he shows why Humfrey valued him in the first place: because,
as a clerk, he was well trained in the exegetical arts, which prepared him to
extract apposite morals from otherwise-recalcitrant sources.[154] By replacing
the republican lessons that Boccaccio and Salutati drew from the story of

Lucrece with a commendation of princely rule, Lydgate could be following the model of his other source, Pierre Bersuire, who championed clerkly exegesis in his own *Ovidius moralizatus*.[155] There Bersuire justifies his practice of drawing Christian morals from pagan sources by asserting that "a man may, if he can, gather grapes from thorns, suck honey from a rock, take oil from the hardest stone, and build and construct the ark of the covenant from the treasures of the Egyptians. And Ovid says that it is allowable to learn from an enemy."[156] In a similar vein, Lydgate brings his monastic training into Duke Humfrey's Library, and from the "old chaff" of his sources he offers Humfrey the "ful cleene corn" of his envois' lessons in statesmanship.

Because of the rebellion of 1431, Humfrey's interest in marshaling literary lessons against the dangers of "fals rebellioun" is highly topical. The agents of the Jack Sharp rebellion threatened to "make lordes" out of "ladds and lurdains" and thus sought "gou[ver]naile in no wise be langyng vnto hem [th]at owen to be go[ver]ned, and not so to gov[er]ne" and thereby "dispose[d] hem to be out of subjection, obeissance, or awe" of royal rule.[157] In light of this threat, Lydgate's ability to produce lessons in "trewe subieccioun" is valuable to Humfrey, as is his ability to transform stories of popular uprisings into exemplary tales supporting the natural hierarchy of ruler over ruled. If Lydgate accomplishes this transformation on a local level in his chapter "descryuyng how prynces beyng hedis of ther comountees sholde haue noble cheualrie true Iuges &c ther commounte to gouerne &c" in book 2, that accomplishment is consistent with other alterations that Lydgate made to his sources in *The Fall of Princes* to condemn the political agency of "comouns" or "comouneres."[158] As Lydgate observes of the story of Spartacus:

> What thyng mor cruel in comparisoun
> Or mor vengable of will & nat off riht,
> Than whan a cherl hath domynacioun!
> Lak of discrecioun bleendith so the siht
> Of comouneres, for diffaute of liht,
> Whan thei haue poweer contrees to gouerne
> Fare lik a beeste [that] can nothing disserne. (6.778–84)

Moreover, if the rebels of 1431 put Humfrey and his agents on the lookout for "trublos langage or talys," Lydgate shows how language and tales can be disciplined through a program of reading that "remedies" their original meanings to bring them into line with the interests of rulers.

Resituating *The Fall of Princes* within Duke Humfrey's Library holds implications not just for Lydgate studies but for the history of libraries and literacy in the fifteenth century. My analysis of Duke Humfrey shows that he was sensitive to the contents of his books and that he developed his library in alliance with his literary patronage efforts, of which *The Fall of Princes* is perhaps the most monumental. As I have argued, both had topical political importance. Taken together, they show that Humfrey viewed his library not simply as an accumulation of books whose prestige emanated from their bulk and impressive appearance. Instead, Humfrey's library was a place of active literary production, which fostered not just the writing of new books such as *The Fall of Princes* but new ways of reading the old books that Humfrey collected. Humfrey's patronage of Lydgate, I am arguing, advanced a larger effort to respond to a recent history of popular unrest and monarchical instability by reclaiming literacy as a tool of rulers over the ruled. If the fifteenth century is "the age of libraries," Duke Humfrey imagined his own English library as a fortress of orthodoxy.

The University of Oxford Library: "Claustrium sine armario castrum sine armamentorio"

Duke Humfrey achieved lasting fame when he donated more than 280 books, in installments in 1439, 1441, and 1444, to the University of Oxford, thus establishing the university's library.[159] The gift is lauded in a translation of Palladius's *De re rustica* commissioned in the early 1440s by Humfrey himself, in which the translator, whom A. S. G. Edwards identifies as Thomas Norton, a clerk in Humfrey's service, describes Humfrey's "librair vniversal":[160]

> At Oxenford thys lord his bookis fele
> Hath euery clerk at werk. They of hem gete
> Metaphisic; physic these other feele;
> They natural, moral they rather trete.
> Theologie here bye is with to mete;
> Hem liketh loke in boke historial.
> In deskis xij hymselue, as half a strete,
> Hath boked thair librair vniuersal. (89–96)[161]

By "universal," Norton describes the scope of the collection, which extends, in his description, from natural and moral philosophy to theology and history—subjects that were indeed amply represented in Humfrey's donations. Included in the lists of the Oxford donations are medical texts by Averroës, Avicenna, Bartholomaeus Anglicus, and Hippocrates, philosophical texts by

Plato, Aristotle, Pliny, and Ptolemy, theological texts by Anselm of Canterbury, Augustine, Ambrose, and Nicholas Trevet, and historical texts by
Livy, Eusebius, Ranulf Higden (*Polychronicon*), Matthew of Westminster,
and Bede.[162] Although Humfrey's donations have been credited with in-
stigating an epochal shift in English literary and intellectual culture (as his
biographer announces, "in the book-chests of Oxford lay the seeds of the English Renaissance"), more recent scholars have pointed out that the texts,
while broad in scope, do not mark a departure from the conventional map
of medieval knowledge.[163] Indeed, despite the presence of works by humanists such as Petrarch, Boccaccio, and Coluccio Salutati, Lydgate's exegetical
treatment of these very sources in *The Fall of Princes* should caution us
against the temptation to use book lists alone to make assumptions about
how the books were read; likewise, the "librair vniuersal" that Norton describes is less a departure from, than an embodiment of, the idea of the
library as it came together in fifteenth-century England.[164]

In the prologue to his translation of *De re rustica*, what Norton finds
noteworthy is not the particular authors represented by Humfrey's donations but the novelty of encountering them in one room. Since the books are
fixed in place by chains—one of the earliest provisions of the library, which
Humfrey personally supervised—the "librair" must be navigated with the
reader's body, while the books remain stationary at their desks.[165] As modern excavations of the library have revealed, desks were built on the model
of lecterns, with reading surfaces positioned at a height of four feet, three
inches—indicating that readers were expected to conduct their reading while
standing rather than sitting.[166] This is not a space built for long periods of
stationary reading; instead, Norton describes the library experience as one
of mobility, as he compares the library to a city "strete." The reader in this
scene resembles a medieval flaneur, tempted to sample the library's various
offerings like a window-shopper or a consumer at a marketplace: "Theologie
here bye is with to mete;/Hem liketh loke in boke historial."[167]

Like the city street, the library is also heavily populated; Norton describes study there as a group experience, where the reader encounters not
just books but the plentiful, mobile bodies of other readers: "They of hem
gete/Metaphisic; physic these other feele;/They natural, moral they rather
trete." Yet this populous image of the "librair vniuersal" drops away when
Norton addresses his patron. Where the Oxford clerks divide themselves
among the various disciplines, which are physically divided among the library's desks, their command of the library's contents appears to be fragmented
by the layout of the room: some study "metaphysic," others "physic," and

so forth. Humfrey alone maintains ownership of the "librair vniuersal" in his prodigious memory:

> For clergie, or knyghthod, or husbondrie,
> That oratour, poete, or philosopher
> Hath tretid, told, or taught, in memorie
> Vche lef and lyn hath he, as shette in cofre. (97–100)

The stanza contrasts Oxford's populous library of desks and books with the inner library of Humfrey's own memory, which, with its books securely stored and "shette in cofre," recalls the traditional *armarium*. Contrasting with the openness and mobility of the streetlike library room, the "coffer" of Humfrey's memory also narrows and privatizes the image of learning with which the poem begins; what opens with an image of learning as a communal, public experience ends with one of learning as an enclosed object of private ownership. The description of Humfrey's learning as "shette in cofre" repeats the terms of Wycliffite critique against the Oxford Greyfriars, who enclosed books in libraries and "putte hem in tresorie," terms that were generalized to the libraries of clerks and monks, who were said to shut books in their libraries like "myche hid tresour biried in here houses fro Þe comune of cristen men," which "ben as castellis or paleicis of kyngis & emperouris, & suffre hem be closed Þer." Norton repeats these critical terms as praise, to suggest that the strongbox of Humfrey's memory encloses his library's content. But his image of Humfrey's cofferlike memory and learning also delimits the images of communal study invoked in the earlier stanzas. Humfrey's library, Norton thereby suggests, will have more in common with the libraries of the Oxford Greyfriars than those imagined to serve the "comune of cristen men."

Where later scholars have held that Humfrey's book donations to Oxford opened the door to English humanism, contemporary records indicate that the university welcomed them in different terms, as weapons with which to defend the church. Echoing St. Benedict's assertion that "a cloister without a book collection is a castle without an armory" (Claustrium sine armario castrum sine armamentorio), the university's letter "to a reputed executor of the Duke of Gloucester" asserted the value of Humfrey's donation in similar terms: "Books are as necessary to us as weapons are to soldiers; for by them we are enabled to defend the Church and overthrow heretics."[168] The formulation was repeated in acknowledgments of other book donations: a letter "To one of the executors of the late Bishop of Chichester" asserts, "As weapons to the soldier so are books to us, who fight for the church against heretics."[169] Likewise, a letter "To the Archbishop of Canterbury and Convocation" articulates what sounds like the university's mission statement when it asks, "What is more acceptable to God than to improve and maintain the true faith and worship, and expel heresy and idolatry, by the advancement of learning and promotion of learned clergy?"[170] Such statements are repeated often enough to count as commonplaces; yet in fifteenth-century Oxford, the threat of heresy was more than rhetorical. Although Lollards were the subjects of persecution and paranoia through the early to mid–fifteenth century and Wyclif's own bones were exhumed and burned in 1428, Wyclif continued to enjoy a high reputation among the Oxford arts faculty, where his works were still taught as late as 1410.[171] In response, Archbishop Arundel visited Oxford in 1411 and again in 1414 to investigate Wycliffite influences there, and he ordered an investigation of Wyclif's writings for heresies and errors shortly after his visit, possibly in an attempt to refute perceived Oxford Wycliffism.[172]

By soliciting and accepting book donations from Duke Humfrey, the renowned scourge of Lollards, and setting up a university library in his name, "to defend the Church and overthrow heretics," Oxford could publicize its commitment to intellectual orthodoxy and visibly repudiate its former association with Wyclif and Wycliffism.[173] The new library's location, situated on the floor above the new Divinity School, could be expected to serve these ends, positioning the new building, and the university that housed it, as a citadel of orthodoxy. In so doing, the university institutionalized a vision of Duke Humfrey's Library that is created in *The Fall of Princes*, which celebrates the library's origin, along with its own, in Humfrey's suppression of the Jack Sharp uprising. If Oxford welcomed Duke Humfrey's Library as a weapon against popular heresy, it took Lydgate's *Fall of Princes* to make it one.

CHAPTER TWO

The Lost Libraries of English Humanism: More, Starkey, Elyot

From Saint's Cell to Scholar's Study

The emergence of humanism as an international movement was bla-
zoned through an increasingly ubiquitous icon: the scholar in his study.
As Ruth Mortimer and Dora Thornton have shown, beginning in the fifteenth century in Italy and spreading out across Europe, author portraits feature their subjects in scholarly poses, sitting at desks in intimate spaces that
are circumscribed by borders or columns, and with their books, the accou-
trements of their literary authority, prominently displayed around them.[1]
Portraits of Erasmus and his associates by Quentin Massys and Albrecht
Dürer adopted such visual conventions, making the scholar in his study a
humanist trademark.[2] The idealized library spaces of such portraits became
the models for real ones, inspiring scores of lesser-known scholars, courtiers,
and ambitious bureaucrats to assemble their own private libraries.[3] While
ostensibly meant for secluded study, such libraries became objects of display, advertising their owners' humanist credentials in a world where books
and learning served as important social currency.[4] The private library, thus
made iconographic in study-portraiture, became coextensive with the humanist virtues of bookish learning and cultivated taste. It also announced
a paradigm shift in the social and cultural place of literacy, relocating literacy's sites, practices, and objects from the religious setting of the monastic
libraria to the domestic interior of the learned layman.[5]

Few were as well positioned to understand the cultural significance of
the private library as Thomas More. As the first layman to become chancellor in England, More epitomized the laicization of literacy and its privileges
that was an important precondition of English humanism.[6] Like many educated laymen in the early sixteenth century, he amassed a library of his

own, which, though now lost, has been speculatively called "perhaps the
first great working collection owned by a lay scholar."[7] More's writings reflect his awareness of libraries' centrality to humanist culture. In a letter to
Erasmus in 1516, More describes the humanist library of Jerome Busleiden,
the provost of Aire and counselor of Charles, Prince of Castille, whose generous letter of commendation graces the 1516 Latin edition of *Utopia*. During
More's ambassadorial trip to the Netherlands, Busleiden was his host; as
More informs Erasmus: "He gave me a tour of his home, which is very ar-
tistically decorated and fitted with exquisite appointments; he also showed
me his large collection of antiquities, in which, as you know, I am very interested. Finally, he displayed to me his remarkable well stocked library and
a mind even more so than any library, so that he completely filled me with
amazement."[8] Here the library is a sign of secular learning and acculturation, sharing space with Busleiden's well-decorated home and "collection
of antiquities," which signaled their owner's participation in a Renaissance
culture of collection.[9] Busleiden aptly saves his library for the climax of
More's house tour. Capturing the capaciousness of humanist learning, the
library's chief virtue lies in being "well stocked," externalizing the mind of
Busleiden himself. In More's account of it, Busleiden's library is no place of
solitary retirement. Rather, it forms both setting and pretext for the sort of social intercourse that was germane to humanism, generating not only the convivial exchange between More and his host but also the epistolary exchange
through which More extends this humanist fellowship to his absent friend,
Erasmus.[10]

More's description of Busleiden's library demonstrates his appreciation
for its symbolic richness; however, a very different model of the private library emerges from More's own biography. As described by More's son-in-
law, William Roper, More's library became a setting not of engagement with
the world but of escape from it: "Because he [More] was desirous for godly
purposes sometime to be solitary, and sequester himself from worldly company, a good distance from his mansion house builded he a place called the
New Building, wherein there was a chapel, a library, and a gallery. In which
[w]as his use . . . to occupy himself in prayer and study together."[11] Whereas
Busleiden's library shares space with his house and worldly goods, More's
"New Building" is set physically apart from his house, designed to produce
not convivial exchange but solitary contemplation. Libraries defined the
place of reading, and in the case of More's library, that place is contiguous
not with the household but with the chapel and the meditative space of the
gallery, which approximates the cloister. In bringing these spaces together,

More's New Building recalls no architectural and theoretical model so clearly as that of the monastery.

Humanist study-portraiture often implicitly or explicitly invokes the space of religious enclosure as a cultural antecedent: as Ruth Mortimer observes, "in the early sixteenth century, the prototype for the scholar writing was the scholar-saint," a model that appropriated the religious authority of the latter as a model to bolster the cultural authority of the former.[12] Erasmus himself cultivated identification with St. Jerome in part by invoking Jerome's study as a model for his own. In his *Life of Jerome (Hieronymi vita)* Erasmus approvingly describes Jerome's years of ascetic seclusion, when, "far removed from the assembly of men, he communed only with Christ and with his books" and "reread his entire library."[13] Jerome's library becomes a model for Erasmus's, a parallel that two engravings by Albrecht Dürer make explicit by inviting comparison between the solitary study of the saint and that of the humanist scholar (figs. 2 and 3).[14] But the comparison elides considerable differences. As Lisa Jardine has shown, in reality the worldly activity centered in Erasmus's study brought it closer to the printing house or the school than to the space of religious retreat.[15] Indeed, Erasmus's description of Jerome's secluded study quickly gives way to a social model approaching Erasmus's own: "Sometimes he was visited by friends, occasionally he went to see neighboring monks, and in the exchange of letters he enjoyed friends from whom he was separated."[16] And however austere Jerome's dedication to "Christ and [to] his books" in Erasmus's depiction, the books in his library range far beyond the expected scriptural and patristic canon to include touchstones of the humanist curriculum: "he gave an inordinate amount of attention to the imitation of the dialogues of Cicero and Plato," Erasmus notes, "overlooking no writer at all from whom he might glean something, whether pagan or heretic."[17] Erasmus's analogy between saint's cell and humanist study serves strategic purposes, allowing him to claim a line of continuity between sacred and secular spheres of knowledge that promotes his view of humanist learning, not as the antithesis of religious scholarship, but as its fulfillment. To further this claim, Erasmus continually abstracts the principles of monastic study and living to such a degree that they become indistinguishable from the world of the laity; "What else is a city," Erasmus asks, "but a great monastery?"[18]

More's New Building employs the monastic model very differently. Rather than positing continuity between the places and pursuits of secular and sacred study, More opens up a gap between them.[19] That gap marks a distance between hospitality and solitude, interaction and contemplation,

Fig. 2. Albrecht Dürer, *St. Jerome in His Study* (1514) (The Metropolitan Museum of Art, Fletcher Fund, 1919 [19.73.68]; image © The Metropolitan Museum of Art)

worldliness and *contemptus mundi*. As well as offering a stark contrast with Busleiden's library, that monument to a humanism of the active life, More's New Building challenges the Erasmian appropriation of the religious study, as made iconographical in humanist study-portraiture. Instead, More's library models itself on English forms of devotional literacy that had deep

Fig. 3. Albrecht Dürer, *Erasmus of Rotterdam* (engraving, 1526) (National Gallery of Art, Washington, 1943.3.3554, Rosenwald Collection; image © 2007 Board of Trustees, National Gallery of Art, Washington)

roots in the Middle Ages and that were still current and vigorously practiced in the early sixteenth century—as evidenced by the continued popularity of contemplative works like Walter Hilton's *Scala perfectionis* (*Ladder of Perfection*), editions of which were reissued in 1494, 1507, 1525, and 1533.[20] By mimicking such models of contemplative piety, More's library reveals that early Tudor English libraries were the sites of multiple and sometimes-competing forms of literacy. If the rise of private libraries signaled a shift in book ownership "from institutional collections into private hands," as Sears Jayne observes, such libraries did not necessarily indicate a diminution of institutional authority.[21] To the contrary, More's library offers one example of how, on the eve of the English Reformation, the private libraries of the laity could be conceived as outposts of monastic influence.

In its design and function, More's New Building replicates a model of monasticism that More himself encountered in his young adulthood when he lived without vow at a Carthusian monastery, the London Charterhouse, from 1500 to 1504.[22] Carthusians established a distinctive architecture of solitary cells arranged around a cloister. Those cells, in which the monks spent most of their time, were spaces for prayer, meditation, and, crucially, reading.[23] Through contemplative reading, Carthusian monks believed that they would be "enflamed with the desire for the celestial kingdom."[24] They promoted this model of literacy not just by practicing it themselves but by copying and disseminating religious books in the vernacular that were aimed at a reading public outside the cloister. Some of the most popular works of late medieval piety, especially those associated with contemplative devotion, were transmitted by Carthusians or held in Carthusian libraries, including the works of Walter Hilton, Nicholas Love's *Mirror of the Blessed Life of Jesus Christ*, and the best-selling *Imitatio Christi*.[25]

More's connection with the London Charterhouse played a major role in shaping the modes of literacy that he promoted throughout his life—not only the Carthusian practices of solitary and contemplative reading he pursued in his own library but also those he urged on the English laity more broadly when he had the power to do so as lord chancellor. In his *Confutation of Tyndale's Answer*, More recommends that lay readers immerse themselves in "englysshe bookes as most may norysshe and encrease deuocyon," as opposed to the vernacular learning that Tyndale promoted.[26] More identifies several such "englysshe bookes" by name: *Imitatio Christi*, Nicholas Love's *Mirror of the Blessed Life of Jesus Christ*, and Hilton's *Ladder of Perfection*, all works with strong Carthusian associations. More's promotion of these works recalls their official uses in the preceding century. As Nicholas Watson has shown, Archbishop Arundel affirmed their orthodoxy as part of his effort to defend vernacular, lay literacy from heretical influences.[27] Indeed, the *Mirror of the Blessed Life of Jesus Christ*, by Nicholas Love, the prior of the Carthusian Community of Mount Grace, won Arundel's personal endorsement as a work particularly suited "ad fidelium edificationem et hereticorum sive Lollardorum confutationem."[28] By singling out Love's *Mirror*, along with the equally sanctioned *Imitatio Christi* and *Ladder of Perfection*, for lay readers, More's *Confutation of Tyndale's Answer* extends the tactics and texts of Lancastrian anti-Lollard campaigns to the early-sixteenth-century campaigns against Luther and Tyndale that he himself spearheaded.

The model of Carthusian literacy that More promotes both officially as chancellor and personally in his associations with the London Charterhouse points in a fundamentally different direction from the pedagogical and intellectual projects espoused by his humanist associates. Despite the efforts of humanists like Erasmus to collapse the aims of secular and religious study, contemplative piety defined itself in avowedly anti-intellectual, and antihumanist, terms. Since contemplation implied the suspension of temporality and worldly engagement, many contemplative authors attack the aims and means of secular learning. In a chapter entitled "Ayenys the veyne and seculer science," the *Imitatio Christi* warns readers: "Rede never noÞinge to seme better taght or wiser; studie for mortificacion of synnes and vices, for Þat shal avayle the more Þen knowledge of many harde questions." Furthermore, it insists that readers will "[profit] more in forsakynge all Þinges Þenne in studyinge of soteltez."[29] In similar terms, Love insists that readers should abandon "kyndely reason" and submit to the teachings of Holy Church "with a buxom drede," even in instances where they appear to run counter to human reason.[30]

Taking the solitude of the Carthusian cell as a model, devotional works imagined the space of reading to be one of temporary enclosure and a respite from, rather than an extension of, worldly engagement. Hilton, for example, advises his readers in their devotions to "[leave] al manere bisynesse outward, and [g]eue he[m] vnto praieres and meditacions, redynge of hooli writ, and to oÞere goostli occupacions."[31] This practice was facilitated by the emergence of new domestic spaces that permitted lay readers to cultivate a quasi-monastic solitude within their own homes.[32] The *Imitatio Christi* counsels its reader to "entre into Þi pryue closet and exclude all worldely noyce," in common with contemporary devotional guides that presuppose the existence of a special room or "secret place" into which the reader can retreat for devout study and prayer.[33] Echoing such works, More himself continually depicts such private spaces as crucial to lay piety: in his *Dialogue of Comfort*, he writes of the need to "withdrawe our thought fro the respect and regard of all worldly fantasies, & so gather our fayth together into a little narrowe rowme." For this purpose, he recommends that his reader cultivate "some secret solitary place in his own house/as far fro noyse & companye as he conveniently can/And thyther lett hym some tyme secretly resort alone."[34] Where the humanist library symbolically appropriates literacy and its cultural privileges from the clergy to the laity, the "secret solitary place" of contemplative piety takes the cloister as its model. The result was a phenomenon that we might call the monasticization of the laity: by externalizing monastic models—and specifically Carthusian models—of reading as ideals for lay readers, vernacular books of devotion had the effect of strengthening, rather than eroding, the monastery's literate authority.[35]

Where humanist portraiture identified the private study as a setting for humanist acculturation, modern scholars of humanism have extrapolated a causal relationship between the vogue for private libraries and the spread of humanism. Thus, Denys Hay argues that private libraries in England created "a new mood of receptivity and an atmosphere propitious to the establishment of new ideas and practices" that encouraged "the importation of humanist ideas from Italy."[36] Yet as More's library illustrates, the quasi-monastic closets and spaces of contemplative piety represented opposing models of literacy that, far from heading toward cultural obsolescence, remained popular among the early Tudor English laity. It was with such contemplative literacy that humanism, as it moved from Italy and the Continent into England, competed for cultural primacy. The result of this encounter was less the organic "growth" or "rise" usually credited to humanism than an uneven process of local contestation and selective appropriation.[37]

In considering the expansion of humanism as a contested, rather than organic, process, I want to develop an argument that was first advanced by Anthony Grafton and Lisa Jardine in their well-known book of 1986, *From Humanism to the Humanities*, which suggests that humanism spread less by evolution than by revolution as it contended with and eventually replaced religious modes of learning. At the same time, they argue, humanists like Erasmus elided this conflict by claiming to synthesize religious and secular knowledge, a move that they call humanism's "intellectual sleight-of-hand."[38] Grafton and Jardine focus on the struggle between humanism and scholasticism in the universities and European intellectual coteries, whereas More illuminates a more local and material conflict that took place in England between two competing models of lay literacy: Erasmian humanism on the one hand and a Carthusian-tinged vernacular devotion on the other. For More, the private library is the battleground on which these literacies and their representatives enact a struggle for cultural influence.[39]

Where his humanist colleagues saw libraries as places of synthesis and intellectual continuity, in More's work libraries register deep institutional
divisions within early Tudor literacy itself. This is an argument I will develop further by turning to two texts in which More grapples with the spread
of humanism in England: his little-read translation of the life of Pico della
Mirandola and his best-known work, *Utopia*. Both works feature libraries as
key settings for cultural transmission in forms that recall humanism's governing trope, *translatio studii*.[40] But in More's libraries that transmission is
not an organic or seamless flow of cultural influence but rather a struggle
between competing models of literacy and knowledge.

I make this argument with two broader aims in mind. The first is to rethink More's place in literary history, as well as the literary-historical models of "medieval" and "Renaissance" that take More as their fulcrum. More's
many biographers have often seen their subject as a figure poised on the
threshold between the Middle Ages and the Renaissance, depicting his humanism as a sign of his forward-thinking liberality while accounting for his
more explicitly pious engagements, like his sojourn in the London Charterhouse, as marks of a backward-looking medieval mentality. This split has
been lodged deep within More's psyche and read as the sign of a subject
internally divided. The struggle between monasticism and humanism that
plays out in More's work has conventionally been interpreted as a sign of
what his biographers call More's "vocational crisis"—the tension between
the religious commitment represented in his life at the Charterhouse, his
antiheretical work, and his martyr's death on the one hand and the humanist commitment that is evident in his friendship with Erasmus and in works
such as "The Letter to Oxford" and *Utopia* on the other.[41] Thus, in an influential analysis, Stephen Greenblatt describes More's identity as wavering
between "humanist scholar or monk" as he personally struggled between active engagement in the world and an almost self-annihilating desire to escape
it, reflecting his dislocation on the cusp of two ages.[42] But I read More less
as a victim of historical dislocation or its psychological effects than as a particularly sharp observer of, as well as participant in, a conflict that emerged
within early Tudor literary culture around the place of books, reading, and
knowledge. More's experience of monasticism was not, I argue, a medieval
throwback; rather, situated within the specific milieu of Carthusian practice, it reflected a thriving form of literacy in the early sixteenth century that
posed a powerfully influential countermodel to humanism and its intellectual aims. Focusing on libraries as spaces where the conflict between humanism and vernacular devotion becomes visible, as I hope to show, relocates the
split between religious withdrawal and humanist engagement from More's

individual biography to the broader material and institutional conflicts surrounding the meanings and uses of lay literacy in early Tudor England.

My second and larger aim is to rethink the modes of cultural and intellectual commerce that take place in libraries and thus to reconsider libraries'
relation to historical change on a larger scale. Rather than viewing libraries
as ideologically unencumbered vehicles of humanist cultural transmission,
I find them to be centers of a far-reaching conflict that developed over the
meanings and uses of books, reading, and knowledge in the late fifteenth
and early sixteenth centuries, a time that witnessed both an upsurge in lay
literacy and considerable official concern about the forms that such literacy
would take. This conflict, registered in the symbolic afflictions that More
visits on libraries in his *Life of Pico* and *Utopia*, comes to a head in the early
Reformation, when struggles to define the nation's intellectual and religious
identity concentrate with particular intensity on the nation's libraries.
If More's libraries promote a laicized monasticism to counter humanist
influences, Henrician reformers and their humanist allies make libraries
the focus of reform. I find this point demonstrated in the works of two of
More's contemporaries, Thomas Starkey and Thomas Elyot, both of whom
found support in the humanist coterie of Henry VIII's chief minister and
the architect of the English Reformation, Thomas Cromwell. Starkey and
Elyot, like More, have been identified with a nascent English humanism of
the early sixteenth century; and, also like More, they took a keen interest
in the functions and forms of lay literacy, as manifested in libraries. Moreover,
they too saw libraries not as places of synthesis and unity—the hallmarks of
the humanist library as envisioned by figures like Erasmus and Pico—but,
like More, as places of cultural conflict. But they reflected on this conflict
from the countervailing perspective of Cromwellian humanism, which attempted to convert the libraries of contemplative piety, like More's "secret
solitary place," into institutions of literacy fit to serve the state. In so doing,
I argue, they confirm, albeit from a reverse angle, an insight that emerges
powerfully from More's own writings: the library is not a conduit but a cru-
cible.

The Missing Library in More's *Life of Pico*

Sometime between 1506 and 1511, More translated a biography of Pico della
Mirandola from a Latin original by Pico's nephew, Gianfrancesco Pico. Pico
has always been a humanist icon, and More's interest in him has long been
seen as an act of identification of one "humanist prodigy" with another.[43]
According to one of More's first biographers, Thomas Stapleton (writing in

1588), More's *Life of Pico* upholds humanism as the solution to the problem of how to live actively in the world as a pious layman. After leaving the Charterhouse, Stapleton writes, More sought the example of "some prominent layman, on which he might model his life. He called to mind all who... enjoyed the reputation of learning and piety, and finally fixed on John Pico, Earl of Mirandola, who was renowned in the highest degree throughout the whole of Europe for his encyclopedic knowledge, and no less esteemed for his sanctity of life."[44] By upholding Pico as a model for the reconciliation of knowledge and sanctity, learning and piety, Stapleton casts More as an English Erasmian who sought to reconcile humanism's active virtues with the aims of the Christian life. But More's *Life of Pico* also questions whether such a reconciliation is possible. Though the work represents More's first engagement with Italian humanism, he dedicates the work to Joyce Leigh, a member of the convent of Poor Clares—hardly a model of worldly living.[45] And if it offers Pico as an exemplum of piety, it does so in ways that radically downplay his secular learning; instead, the work represents Pico following textual models established by contemporary English devotional books, offering him up to readers as one "whos lyfe & warkys bene worthy & digne to be redd & oftyn to be had in memorye." To the extent that More's *Life of Pico* attempts to reconcile humanism and piety, it also suggests that such reconciliation cannot occur without a struggle that results in visible loss and fragmentation. The place where this struggle becomes most evident is a library.

In his own age and succeeding ones, Pico was famous for his library, which held nearly seventeen hundred volumes in a display of the "encyclopedic learning" that Stapleton praises. The capaciousness of Pico's library reflected his larger intellectual aim to reconcile diverse strands of learning—classical and Christian as well as Hebrew and Arabic—in order to establish the "obscure linkage" (occulta concatenatio) that, Pico believed, united the entirety of human knowledge.[46] This ideal is manifested in the library's surviving catalogue, which reveals Pico's efforts to collect a spectrum of sacred and secular learning—from theology to poetry and natural science—and to bring it together under one roof.[47] Pico treasured his library above all of his possessions; famously, he sold his patrimony to his nephew and later biographer, Gianfrancesco himself, in order to enlarge its holdings. Pico's library was no quasi-monastic cell of world-denying solitude. To the contrary, contemporary accounts confirm that Pico built it on the model of the Vatican library, aiming to create a place for debate and social exchange. Thus, as Anthony Grafton observes of Pico, "he treated his library as quasi-public, something to be shared with a larger community of those he regarded as learned and intelligent."[48] In ways that recall Erasmus's study—which was, in Jardine's words, "a classroom without walls"—Pico's library became the center of a broad intellectual community of lay scholars.[49] Pico's extensive correspondence reveals a network through which other scholars exchanged the inventories of their libraries as well as individual books, thus creating a kind of private interlibrary loan system.[50] The intellectual synthesis to which Pico's library aspired therefore produced "linkage" not only between fields of knowledge but also across a broad intellectual community of fellow readers.

This library assumes a central role in Gianfrancesco's biography of his uncle (and on one level, we could read Gianfrancesco's biography of his uncle as a tribute to the library to which his own fortune was so indebted). As Gianfrancesco represents it, the library secures Pico's own identity and place in the world: Pico insists that his library is his most valuable possession, exclaiming, in words that More would translate faithfully into English, "I set more bi my little house/my study/the pleasures of my bokes" than any other honor or glory in the world.[51] By extension, he can imagine no greater horror than his library's destruction: "if his chestis perished in which his bokes lay: that he had with grete trauaile & watch compiled" (65). These references make it possible to imagine the physical layout of Pico's library; he stored his books in "chestis" (in the Latin original, "scrinia," 322) that were permanently housed in a room set apart for the purpose. While More's Pico refers to his library as "my little house," Pico calls it "my little cell" (cellulam meam), echoing the collapse of secular and sacred study that Erasmus performs in his own library (350, 351).

Although More's translation of Pico's biography has been called an unusually faithful one, it reduces its original by nearly a third, making its most dramatic cuts in the passages that describe Pico's library. The following passage describes Pico's youthful decision to apply himself to serious study, represented by the "great libraries" (in the Latin original, "bibliothecas amplas") to which he turns:

> From thensforth he gave him selfe day & night most feruently to the studies of scripture in which he wrote many noble bokes: which welle testifie bothe his angelike wit/his ardent laboure/and his profounde erudition of which bokes some we haue & some as an inestymable tresure we haue lost. Gret lybraries hit is incredible to consider with how meruelous celerite he redd them ouer/and wrot out what him liked. Of [th]ᵉ olde fathirs of [th]ᵉ chirch: so gret knowledge he had as hit were harde for him to haue [th]ᵗ hath lyued longe & all his life hath don nothing ellis but

red them. Of these newer diuines so good iudgment he had [tha]ᵗ yt might
apere there were no thyng in any of them that were vnknowe to him. (60)

In More's translation, Pico consults libraries containing works by "the old
fathers of the church" as well as by "newer divines" that thus appear to constitute an entirely sacred body of knowledge. But in order to represent Pico's
learning as essentially religious, More drastically edits Gianfrancesco's Latin
text by excising a long passage that describes Pico's secular reading and writing. To cover the gap, More sutures two passages that fall on either side of
the missing text. The first passage corresponds to More's opening line in the
passage quoted above; it describes how Pico ardently embraced the study of
holy scripture (sacras deinde litteras ardentissimo studio complexus; 304,
305), which More translates faithfully as "From thenceforth he gave himself
day and night most fervently to the studies of scripture." The second describes how Pico "perused and excerpted whole libraries of Latin and Greek
books with incredible speed" (Bibliothecas amplas, tam Latinorum quam
Graecorum incredibili Celeritate & perlegit & excerpsit; 314, 315). More
translates: "Great libraries it is incredible to consider with how marvelous
celerity he read them over."

But in More's source, this second sentence appears many pages after the
first; between them comes Gianfrancesco's long discussion of the contents of
those libraries and Pico's own, which constitutes nearly a quarter of the original text. This discussion, which is missing from More's translation, details
Pico's philosophical writings and wide-ranging work in natural philosophy,
geometry, and mathematics, as well as his studies of classical, Hebrew, and
Arabic authors, all of which fueled Pico's larger project of establishing the
essential unity of all knowledge.[52]

In place of Gianfrancesco's account of his uncle's encyclopedic literacy,
More substitutes a short passage observing that Pico's books "welle testifie
bothe his angelike wit/his ardent laboure/and his profounde erudition of
which bokes some we haue and some as an inestimable treasure we have
lost." But, as comparison with the original makes clear, the "loss" of Pico's
secular works is of More's own making. Not only does More excise Gianfrancesco's description of Pico's reading in "great libraries" and the volumi-
nousness of his own, but he calls attention to that excision in the passage
that replaces it, which recounts, in their absence, a miniature narrative of
bibliographical loss.

By thus representing Pico's books as lost, More enacts Pico's worst night-
mare: as Pico himself imagines, no worse event could befall him than "if his

chestis perished in which his bokes lay: that he had with grete trauaile &
watch compiled" (65). But Pico's own words offer proleptic justification for
More's editorial destruction of his library. After imagining this horror, Pico
expresses faith that his library will find divine protection: "for as much as
he considered [tha]ᵗ he laboured only for [th]ᵉ loue of god & profit of his
chirch: & [tha]ᵗ he had dedicate unto him all his warkis/his studies & his
doinges & sith he saw [tha]ᵗ sith god is almighty they could not miscary but
if hit were either by his commaundement or by his sufferaunce" (65). God
would not allow a library to perish, in other words, unless he judged that it
ran contrary to the love of him and his church. As this testimony reveals,
Pico saw his intellectual effort to prove the unity of human and divine
knowledge as an essentially religious undertaking, and he saw his library as
the embodiment of that undertaking.[53] Yet the same passage also suggests
that libraries that do not uphold, in his words, "[th]ᵉ loue of god & profit of
his chirch" are justly vulnerable to destruction, thus inviting the judgment
that More passes on Pico's library. By reducing Pico's library to only the
most clearly doctrinal works and excising the rest, More manifests his serious disagreement with his subject over the nature of religious study and the
relationship between human knowledge and divine.

It is a quarrel that Gianfrancesco Pico himself had with his uncle. Despite benefiting from Pico's decision to enrich his library at the cost of
his patrimony, Gianfrancesco expressed skepticism about Pico's vision of
universal knowledge that would be embodied in Pico's library. In his own
Examen vanitatis doctrinae gentium (*An Examination of the Futility of
Pagan Learning*, 1520), Gianfrancesco reflects on Pico's project to unify the
different strands of knowledge represented by the pagan philosophers: "It
occurs to me, however, that it is more proper and more useful to render the
teachings of the philosophers uncertain than to reconcile them as my uncle
wished to. I prefer to follow in this matter those earlier theologians of our
faith, who held that some action must be taken against the pagan philosophers and that their teachings must be demolished."[54] For More, the great
defender of classical letters, the question is not whether to destroy the "pagan philosophers" but rather whether their study is compatible with the contemplative ideals that Pico upheld.

More's transformation of Pico's library from a center for humanist learning to an exclusively religious space responds to a larger debate about the
role of learning in which both More and Pico were engaged. In his famous
Oration on the Dignity of Man, Pico insists that "natural philosophy" will
"point out the way to theology and even accompany us along the path."[55]
More was clearly familiar with this argument: in his well-known "Letter

to the University of Oxford," written in defense of secular learning, he observes: "Some plot their course, as it were, to the contemplation of celestial realities through the study of nature, and progress to theology by way of philosophy and the liberal arts."[56] Yet if More acknowledges that "some" believe that the study of liberal arts can lead to "contemplation of celestial realities," he never fully endorses this project himself. Rather, in the same letter he insists that the liberal arts are most useful for teaching what he calls "prudence in human affairs"—in other words, the art of acting in the world. By distinguishing between worldly prudence and "contemplation of celestial realities," he opens a gap between secular knowledge and religious wisdom, which he plays out, I argue, in his treatment of Pico's library. Where Pico's encyclopedic library embodies aspirations of intellectual synthesis and unification, More's radical expurgation of that library suggests that contemplative knowledge can be achieved not through natural philosophy and the liberal arts but through religious study alone.

Pico's library, thus reworked by More, reflects a larger debate over the relative values of the active and the contemplative life that frames More's *Life of Pico*. Like Gianfrancesco's biography of his uncle, More's translation includes a short selection of Pico's letters treating the larger question of the place of study in the world. Responding to a letter from Andrew Corneus that counsels Pico "to surcease of study and put him self with sume of ye grete princes of Italy" (85), More's Pico retreats to his library, retorting, "I set more bi my little house/my study/the pleasures of my bokes/ye rest and peace of my mynde then by all your kingis palacis/all your commune besines/all your glory/all the aduauntage that ye hawke aftir/and all the fauoure of the court" (87). In this passage study becomes an architecturally secluded activity: the "little house" of study (which is translated from Pico's "cellulam meam," literally "my little cell" [350, 351]) recalls descriptions of contemplative spaces from contemporary English devotional guides such as *Instructions for a Devout and Literate Layman*, which refers to "that little house" (casa illa) or "cell" (cella) set aside for prayer, a space that is juxtaposed with the "kingis palacis," the site of worldly ambition.[57]

The alterations that More makes to his original further emphasize Pico's study as a place of religious retreat; following Pico's and Corneus's debate over the relative virtues of the *vita contemplativa* and the *vita activa*, More adds a line to his source to allow Corneus to advocate the possibility of a middle way, a *vita mixta:* "Love them & use them both as well study as worldly occupation" (86). But he does this only so that Pico can then reject even this possibility of compromise, when he retorts, "I loke not for this frute of my study y^t I may therby herafter be tossed in the flode and rombeling of

your worldly besynesse" (87). In More's translation these lines amount to an
absolute denial of any reconciliation between contemplative learning and
worldly action. To the same effect, More deletes from the original a line in
which Pico approvingly quotes St. Francis as saying, "A man knows only so
much as he puts into practice" (327).

In emphasizing Pico's total withdrawal from the world into a library
wholly devoted to religious works, More remakes Pico in the image of the
devout layman imagined in the contemplative works of Hilton or the *Imitatio Christi*. This identification is underscored by the textual layout of
More's translation; it is divided into short chapters that encourage the kind
of regular, devotional reading convenient for daily meditation. This intended
use is signaled by the work's title: as a book to be "redde" and "often . . . had
in memory," it becomes the object of the kind of rumination that Mary
Carruthers finds to be the hallmark of devotional reading in the monastery.
Moreover, by addressing the text to the cloistered Joyce Leigh, More follows
the lead of Hilton and other authors of devotional works that are addressed
to religious women; as these texts were circulated outside the cloister, the
figure of the religious female dedicatee became a stand-in for the vernacular reader of contemplative works.[58] In the 1525 edition of More's *Life of
Pico*, printer Wynkyn de Worde emphasized the book's contemplative purpose still further by giving it a frontispiece featuring a man kneeling before
the crucified Christ, surrounded by the instruments of the Passion (fig. 4).
Apparently specially commissioned for this volume, the woodcut quotes
the visual conventions that had become associated with printed works that
originated from the London Charterhouse and from the Bridgettine Syon
Abbey outside London, with which the Carthusians shared some connections.[59] In de Worde's edition, the woodcut serves a double function; it is
both a generic marker that directs lay readers to approach the work as a
contemplative handbook and an object of contemplation in itself.

Seen in the light of works like Love's *Mirror of the Blessed Life of Christ*
or Hilton's *Ladder of Perfection*, More's *Life of Pico* participates in a model
of English vernacular devotion that More would later advocate when he
advised lay readers "to occupye them selfe besyde theyr other busynesse in
prayour, good medytacyon, and redynge of such englysshe bookes as moste
may norysshe and encrease deuocyon. Of whyche kynde is Bonauenture of
the lyfe of Chryste, Gerson of the folowynge of Cryste, and the deuoute contemplatyue booke of scala perfectionis wyth such other lyke."[60] In aligning
Pico with these English models of lay piety, More crucially remakes Pico's
library in the image of the private space or closet of contemplative reading.
Thus, whereas Pico's humanist library produces social exchange and capacious

Fig. 4. Frontispiece, Thomas More, *Lyfe of Johan Picus* (London: Wynkyn de Worde, 1525) (Huntington Library, San Marino, CA, RB 62878)

knowledge, More replaces it with a space of enclosure and renunciation. And in place of the encyclopedic learning that was manifested in Pico's library, the devotional libraries that are More's models aim for reduction, rather than expansion, of books. Just as the *Imitatio Christi* advises readers that they will "[profit] more in forsakynge all þinges þenne in studyinge of soteltez [subtleties]," one of More's friends, the devotional author Richard Whitford of Syon, endorses a similarly radical reduction of the devotional library. In a work directed to pious laypeople, Whitford offers this prayer: "Be thou (good lorde) alone the hoole booke of all my study and lernynge.... And be thou (good lord) [th]ᵉ closet/arke/chest/coffer/and casket of all my juels/ treasure/and ryches."[61] Describing Christ as "closet/arke/chest/coffer/ and casket," Whitford invokes terms that were commonly applied to the care and preservation of books in monastic libraries, which were sometimes called "thesauri"—literally "treasure chests."[62] But Whitford invokes these images of books and libraries only to collapse them into the body of Christ, which is, according to the prayer, the only book and the only library that Whitford's lay reader will ever need. It is this exchange—library for body of Christ—that de Worde's frontispiece illustrates by picturing a devout man—a factotum for Pico, named above in the title—in contemplation of the Crucifixion. Like the book it prefaces and cannily reflects on, the woodcut produces a space of contemplative piety only by emptying that space of books.

More's *Life of Pico* similarly remakes Pico's library in the image of the library of the pious English layperson when it evacuates it of all books save those directly relating to scripture and devotion. More's editorial decision reflects his distance from Pico on the question of how books and study uphold "[th]ᵉ loue of god & profit of his chirch." For the Neoplatonic Pico, all human learning can be reconciled with Christian revelation; therefore, his encyclopedic library reflects faith in the unity—and essentially Christian identity—of all knowledge. By emptying out Pico's library and declaring most of its contents "lost," More reflects a different model of the lay library and, by extension, a contrasting understanding of the idea of knowledge that it represents. In place of a library of encyclopedic capaciousness, More substitutes a library that is incomplete—and in so doing, gives material form, not to the essential unity of human and divine knowledge, but rather to their irreconcilable division. If More's *Life of Pico* introduces Italian humanism to English readers, it illustrates the conflict between humanist modes of reading and the traditions of contemplative piety that shaped English lay literacy in the fifteenth and early sixteenth centuries. Significantly, this conflict becomes visible in a library, which for More represents, not the unity of human and divine knowledge, but rather a vision of human knowledge that is by nature finite, fragmented, and temporary, compared with the eternal durability of religious knowledge. In the empty space at the center of Pico's library falls classical philosophy, poetry, and science—the pillars, in other words, of the humanist curriculum. More's *Life of Pico* brings humanism into England, we could say, by losing it.

The Utopian Library

The debate over the contemplative and the active life that frames More's *Life of Pico* forms the backdrop for his better-known *Utopia*.[63] In the *Life of Pico*, Pico rebuffs Corneus's efforts to persuade him to apply his learning "to the ciuile and actiue life" (85), countering that "[I] set more bi my little house/my study/the pleasures of my bokes/[th]ᵉ rest and peace of my mynde then by all your kingis palacis/all your commune besines/all your glory/all the aduauntage that ye hawke aftir/and all the fauoure of the court" (87). Likewise, in *Utopia*'s opening scene, the figures of "Morus" and Raphael Hythloday engage in a similar debate when, like Corneus, Morus urges Hythloday to apply his learning "to the public interest" by becoming "councilor to some great monarch."[64] In upholding the *vita activa* as the worthiest outlet for learning, Morus articulates the utilitarian biases of English humanism, which flourished as the lingua franca of Henrician lay administrators and bureaucrats.[65] The Utopia that Hythloday describes in the work's second half offers an extended meditation on the question that underlies the "Dialogue of Counsel" in the first: is it possible to reconcile contemplative learning with civic engagement? In response, Utopia presents a social vision in which the spheres of contemplative study and worldly activity are perfectly integrated. The Utopian commonwealth is constructed so that its citizens need never forsake the active life for the contemplative, or vice versa: regular hours of work are offset by long periods specifically set aside for study. "There are not many in each city who are relieved from all other tasks and assigned to scholarship alone," we learn, because learning is integrated into the active life: "A large part of the people . . . men and women alike, throughout their lives, devote to learning the hours which, as we said, are free from manual labor" (159). *Utopia*'s balance of contemplation and action has struck many of its readers as a "paradoxical synthesis" of "court and cloister."[66] Its citizens' communal living, dedication to regular study, and "cloistral" household arrangements appear to universalize monastic living arrangements, as if to live out the implications of the civic experiment envisioned by Erasmus when he writes, "What else, I ask you, is a city than a great monastery?"[67] *Utopia* explores—and ultimately, I will argue, challenges—this Erasmian ideal by embodying an integration of contemplation and worldly action that is so complete as to erase any meaningful distinctions between them.[68]

The Utopians' integration of action and contemplation is enabled by their philosophy, which does not differentiate between knowledge of the natural world and that of the divine. Rather, recalling the historical Pico, Utopians adhere to a Neoplatonic belief that all knowledge culminates in apprehension of divine truth: "They think that the investigation of nature, with the praise arising from it, is an act of worship acceptable to God" (225).[69] Utopian scholarship makes contemplation its ultimate end—"to the soul they ascribe intelligence and the sweetness which is bred of contemplation of truth" (173)—but because learning is integrated into worldly matters, there is no need to encloister it in a separate space like a monastery or library. Instead, the world becomes the object of study, as the branches of Utopian knowledge reflect. Although Utopians are introduced from an early age to the study of "good literature" (159), the principal objects of their study are nature—through the study of astronomy and meteorology—and moral philosophy rather than books.

When the Utopians do encounter books, it is because Hythloday himself decides to bring to the island what Louis Marin calls a "humanist library."[70] As Hythloday recounts, "When about to go on the fourth voyage, I put on board, in place of wares to sell, a fairly large package of books," the contents of which represent the chief classical authors in the humanist canon: Plato, Aristotle, Theophrastus, Plutarch, Lucian, Aristophanes, Homer, Euripides, Sophocles, Thucydides, Herodotus, and Herodian (181).[71] Nearly all the books in Hythloday's "package" are represented in the surviving catalogue from Pico's library.[72] This is no accident, since Pico's library and Hythloday's derive from a common textual culture, as outlined by Erasmus in *De ratione studii* (On the Method of Study, 1511). Setting out the core curriculum of a humanist education, Erasmus insists that "almost all knowledge of things as well as of words is to be sought in the Greek authors," of whom he assigns "first place to Lucian, second to Demosthenes, and third to Herodotus"; among poets, he assigns "first place to Aristophanes, second to Homer, third to Euripides"; and of the philosophers he selects "Plato, Aristotle, and his pupil Theophrastus"—all works that Hythloday brings to the Utopians.[73]

Hythloday further establishes his library's humanist credentials by disclosing the detail that the books he brings are printed "in the small Aldine type." So fine is this type that it inspires the Utopians to emulate it themselves:

> When we showed them the Aldine printing in paper books, we talked about the material of which paper is made and the art of printing.... Though previously they wrote only on parchment, bark, and papyrus, from this time they tried to manufacture paper and print letters. Their first attempts were not very successful, but by frequent experiment they soon mastered both. So great was their success that if they had copies of Greek authors, they would have no lack of books. But at present they have no more than I have mentioned, but by printing books they have increased their stock by many thousands of copies. (183–85)

This story of humanist acculturation as told here is inextricably linked to that of printing, reflecting the historical intertwinement of humanism and print culture that has long been recognized by scholars of both movements.[74] English printers came belatedly to the international humanist book market; as David Carlson has noted, it was not until three years after the publication of More's *Utopia* that printers began to recognize the market's potential.[75] Until then, English humanism fed almost entirely on books imported from abroad, especially from Italy—a market condition that is reproduced in Utopia itself, which is also an importer of books from abroad.

Aldus Manutius, the Venetian printer who developed the Aldine type that is so admired by the Utopians, played a key role in the international spread of humanism by marketing classical books specifically to lay readers and creating the Greek, Roman, and italic fonts that gave humanist texts their distinctive appearance.[76] Aldine books were printed without the marginal commentary or textual apparatus that made scholastic texts so visually offensive to humanist readers. Rejecting the gothic appearance of the black letter font, Aldus's fonts attempted to recapture the look of classical lettering and thus claimed ancestry in the lost library of Alexandria rather than the medieval scriptorium.[77] As textual objects, Aldine books embodied some of humanism's strongest principles: the desire to recover classical texts in forms that made them legible to present readers, the belief that such texts could speak for themselves without the intervention of commentary, and the understanding that classical texts would attract a new kind of reader, whose literacy was not circumscribed by the monastery or university but who desired to build up personal libraries in new places. Aldus appealed directly to these readers with his collection of octavo classical texts that were designed to be carried and read in the midst of other daily activities and commerce. The effect was to create a "portable library," as Aldus himself called it, which promoted the idea that books belonged in the world rather than in enclosed spaces.[78] Here was the beginning of the notion of a "library without walls" that has been a powerful object of humanist fantasy ever since, promising to overcome libraries' material constraints to create a world in which knowledge could travel freely.[79]

By demonstrating the crucial importance of print to humanist ideals of lay education, Aldus became an icon for humanists, winning Erasmus's constant praise as a "defender of good literature" and "consummate scholar."[80] Pico himself owned many Aldine editions and developed a bibliographical alliance with Aldus in the mid-1480s that benefited them both; Pico provided Aldus with books that Aldus printed, thus extending the contents of Pico's library indefinitely outward to other scholars. The same "encyclopedic interests" underwrote both Pico's library and Aldus's book list, allowing "the one to serve as the vehicle of the other."[81]

When Hythloday brings this "humanist library" to Utopia, he enacts a drama of *translatio studii,* the movement of texts across historical periods and territories given prominence in humanist modes of cultural transmission.[82] Like Aldus himself, Hythloday extends the library beyond the physical constraints of the monastery or cell; and in ways that recall Pico, he offers his printed books as complements to the Utopians' intellectual aims. Having received the books, the Utopians attempt to assimilate them into their contemplative mode of inquiry, in the hope that books of men will advance their apprehension of the book of nature. Yet from the start, More indicates that this assimilation will not occur without impediment. Describing his introduction of books to the island, Hythloday offers this seemingly whimsical detail: "They received from me most of Plato's works, several of Aristotle's, as well as Theophrastus on plants, which I regret to say was mutilated in parts. During the voyage an ape found the book, left lying carelessly about, and in wanton sport tore out and destroyed several pages in various sections" (181).

The presence of "Theophrastus on plants" in his packet of books signals Hythloday's endorsement of humanist ideals of *sapientia* as "scientia omnium rerum divinarum et humanarum," which included the sciences of natural philosophy and botany alongside the philosophical realms of human knowledge represented by Plato and Aristotle.[83] Long revered as an important source for Pliny, *Theophrasti de historia plantarum* became part of the humanist canon when Aldus published it in an edition of 1497, a copy of which was owned and annotated by Erasmus himself.[84] But the fact that

Hythloday's copy of "On Plants" is "mutilated in parts" undermines the humanist enterprise that the Aldine Theophrastus, along with Hythloday's act of *translatio studii*, represents. Theophrastus is an apt object of textual mutilation for several reasons. Until his works *De historia plantarum* and *De causis plantarum* were recuperated and published in the fifteenth century, Theophrastus was known to the West only through fragments: thus, Theophrastus's corpus was "mutilated in parts" for much of its medieval existence.[85] A witness to the instability of textual transmission, Theophrastus was also associated with bibliographical loss.[86] According to a story well known from Strabo's *Geography*, the historical Theophrastus was entrusted with Aristotle's library, the greatest in the ancient world, and thereafter became a founding figure in the history of libraries:

> Aristotle bequeathed his own library to Theophrastus, to whom he also left his school; and he is the first man, so far as I know, to have collected books and to have taught the kings in Egypt how to arrange a library. Theophrastus bequeathed it to Neleus; and Neleus took it to Scepsis and bequeathed it to his heirs, ordinary people, who kept the books locked up and not even carefully stored. But when they heard how zealously the Attalic kings to whom the city was subject were searching for books to build up the library in Pergamum, they hid their books underground in a kind of trench.... The result was that the earlier school of Peripatetics who came after Theophrastus had no books at all.[87]

In its scope, Aristotle's library supplies the model for the library of Alexandria, but it also anticipates the fate of the Alexandrian library in its loss. Theophrastus may have been the classical world's first librarian, but in Strabo's account, he shares responsibility for that library's loss, unable to secure its future against mistransmission, careless storage, and human error. It is thus fitting that, of all the books in Hythloday's traveling library, Theophrastus's is the one singled out for destruction, because, through the bibliographical narratives with which he became associated, Theophrastus is a reminder of libraries' materiality, contingency, and temporal limitation. In this capacity, Theophrastus's mutilated book disrupts the library's *translatio studii* by representing instead a failure of transmission, or *translatio studii interrupta*.

The agent of the destruction of Theophrastus's book, the ape or monkey (as it is variously translated) who mutilates the book in "wanton sport," has generated numerous interpretations. In an ingenious reading, Louis Marin discusses the animal's intervention as a comment on the intransigent materiality of the book itself: "By mutilating an ancient work of botany the monkey obscurely symbolizes the passage from book—practical instrument to transform nature—to the scientific book-as-representation, representation of the mechanical spectacle of nature."[88] Thus reducing the book to an object, the ape/monkey succeeds in making it into a thing of nature, mistaking the work "on plants" for a plant itself; it thereby enacts a collapse of signifier and signified that Marin traces to medieval verbal play on *simia-similis*, becoming the playful symbol of symbolic activity itself.[89]

But the animal itself demands further comment—not least because, despite the near universality of English translations in using the category "ape" or "monkey," More's Latin original calls it a "cercopithecus" (180), which More's contemporary and onetime friend Thomas Elyot defines in his *Dictionary* as "a beast called a Marmoset."[90] A species of long-tailed monkey, the marmoset carries a set of literary references and associations beyond those of its simian relatives. In classical literature, the Kerkopes were deceptive dwarves whom Jupiter transformed into monkeys and banished to the island of Pithecusae; More would have been familiar with Ovid's reference to the "sly race" of "the Cercopes" in *The Metamorphoses*.[91] As men turned into monkeys, the Kerkopes reverse the civilizing mission that Hythloday believes he is carrying out; they also critique that mission, suggesting that reading natural philosophy does not elevate men's wisdom but reduces them to the level of animals; it is a "wanton sport."

Such a reading is consistent with broader medieval and early modern iconography surrounding monkeys, which regularly symbolize the limitations of human reason.[92] Leonardo da Vinci, writing in 1508, invokes monkeys in a criticism of "men" who confine their desires to the temporal and corporeal world; such men, Leonardo charges, "entirely lack any desire for true wisdom, which is the food and only secure wealth of the soul. Because they prize the soul no more than the body, they prize the riches of the soul no more than those of the body. And often when I see one of them take up a work of real wisdom, I expect him to stick it to his nose like a monkey or ask me if it is something to eat."[93] As Leonardo indicates, human readers who do not see that books of "real wisdom" point upward to celestial, rather than earthly, meanings are no better than monkeys. For such readers, books lead only outward to the world rather than to higher purposes. This is the point that More himself makes in his "Letter to the University of Oxford," in which he allows that the liberal arts have value in teaching "prudence in human affairs" but stops short of advocating their study as an avenue to "the contemplation of celestial realities." This is also the message conveyed by the marmoset on Hythloday's ship: the beautiful objects from the Aldine press belong to this world, not the next. We are primed for this reading by Hythloday's observation early in the *Utopia* that "the crow and the monkey like their own off-spring best" (57)—by extension, we are invited to conclude, the marmoset recognizes the Aldine Theophrastus as monkey business.

The message is driven home by Hythloday's companion, who contributes several more classical books to Hythloday's cargo: "some small treatises of Hippocrates and the *Ars medica* of Galen" (183). The Utopians "attribute great value" to these works as the means to "explore the secrets of nature," thereby believing themselves "to win the highest approbation of the Author and Maker of nature" (183); however, the companion's name, "Tricius Apinatus," implies that the works are "trifles and toys," echoing a meaning suggested by Hythloday's own name, "purveyor of nonsense."[94] Rather than representing "one of the finest and most useful branches of philosophy," the books are objects of "wanton sport" no less than "Theophrastus on plants" is to the playful marmoset.

At least one of *Utopia*'s early readers interpreted the marmoset as a figure for More himself. In Raphe Robynson's 1556 English translation, the animal becomes "a mormosett," a uniquely attested spelling variant that both puns on More's name and offers an anagram for "T[h]omas More."[95] More himself owned monkeys, which are memorialized in Erasmus's colloquy "Amicitia" and in the famous 1527 Holbein portrait of the More family, which contains a faint outline of a pet whose long tail and tufted ears reveal it to be a marmoset.[96] If the marmoset is More's playful signature in *Utopia*—as I suggest that it is—it also inserts More directly into a broader critique of the Utopian project of contemplative knowledge that Hythloday's traveling library represents. In my reading of it, the marmoset in Hythloday's library mocks the idea that secular books can be avenues to contemplative knowledge, and thus it subverts the principle on which libraries like Hythloday's—or Pico's or Erasmus's—were built: the notion that the accumulation of books will advance the apprehension of divine truth. In its place, as in his earlier *Life of Pico*, More produces as a counterimage a broken library, aptly figured in the mutilated work of Theophrastus. The broken library is the opposite of the syncretic library that is Pico's ideal; rather than unifying earthly and divine knowledge, humanist and monastic literacies, it insists on their irreconcilability.

By representing an alternative to humanism's narrative of its own advance, More's libraries counter what Jardine and Grafton call humanism's "intellectual sleight-of-hand," the illusion that humanism synthesized secular and religious knowledge, which papered over the real contentiousness surrounding humanism's conquest of lay literacy—its places, aims, and objects—in early Tudor England. Conceived as a vehicle of *translatio studii*, a secular monk's cell, and a natural ally of humanist learning, the library has played an important, if sometimes unexamined or mystified, role in this narrative. But against this vision of cultural and textual transmission, More's libraries stage the meeting of Erasmian humanist and Carthusian-tinged monastic literacies as a clash between irreconcilable entities, which are shown to stake competing claims on English lay literacy and its cultural spaces. By locating this conflict of literacies, humanist and monastic, in the library, More diagnoses a set of conditions that became volatile in the early stages of the Henrician Reformation. I have considered libraries in literary texts that embody theories of books and reading; and in the work of a passionate observer such as More, I have shown that libraries became powerful symbols of the divided place of lay literacy in the early modern period. But the library was not only a symbolic space; nor were the conflicts it witnessed and the losses it sustained in the Reformation era merely immaterial ones. Instead, and in ways that More can be said to have foreseen, the Reformation effort to reshape England's political and religious identity made libraries into its battlegrounds.

The Politics of the Library: Cromwell's Interlibrary Loans

For scholars of the early modern period in England, the relationship between humanism and religious reform has posed a constant but still-unanswered question: did humanism advance the cause of religious reform, or were reformers and humanists fundamentally different constituencies, with distinct ideological concerns?[97] Recent scholarship has cautioned against the tendency, always latent in the question, to consider "humanism" and "Reformation" as two monolithic and unified movements, a tendency that can obscure their multiple, and sometimes-conflicting, points of intersection on the level of individuals and institutions.[98] In England, as scholars such as Jonathan Woolfson and Alistair Fox have argued, humanism did not produce a coherent political or religious agenda so much as a set of postures and tools—chief among them, a commitment to classical learning, an interest in the *vita activa*, and a belief that the former could be applied, through the latter, to public-minded ends.[99] But if humanism itself was not a reformist movement, its postures and tools proved effective in the hands of that movement's English agents.

When More poses an opposition between humanist literacy and the orthodox vernacular literacy of the Carthusians, he anticipates the dismantling of Carthusian literacy that was carried out under the banner of humanist reform by Henry VIII's chief minister, Thomas Cromwell. An energetic patron of an Anglicized active humanism, Cromwell cultivated a coterie of educated laymen, most visible among them Thomas Starkey and Thomas Elyot, who applied their humanist training in the service of the state.[100] In so doing, Cromwell and his agents advanced the aim of rethinking and adapting medieval structures of learning and literacy to meet the changing political landscape of Henrician England. Thus, the members of New College, Oxford, wrote to Cromwell in 1534 to praise him as an educational reformer:

> While we consider the great wisdom and high judgment of your mastership... we know ourself much bound to God, which hath in our time sent such a favourable defender of the truth of God, that whereas of long time unlearned learning and rude barbarousness hath reigned, to the great hindrance of good learning and the true knowledge of God, yet now by your high wisdom is clean abolished and put to silence, and good learning brought in their place.[101]

Cromwell's program of educational reform was particularly suited to accommodate a generation of Henrician "new men" represented by Cromwell himself.[102] Cromwell's conjoined political and educational goals are reflected in numerous English translations of humanist works that were dedicated to him; the prefatory epistle of one such work, David Clapham's 1540 translation of Agrippa's *Commendation of Matrimony*, credits Cromwell with an educational reform movement that enabled "the noble mens children" to attain "lernyng of good letters sciences and craftes," through which "they shuld be earnestly taught, obedience to god, to the kynges hyghnesse, and to such rulers and lawes, as his maiesty shal ordeyn."[103] In terms calibrated to appeal to Cromwell, education produces ideal subjects, whose "learning" is measured by its result, "obedience" to God and Crown. As such an argument insinuates, Cromwell's humanism is a tool of state control.

Humanism offered Cromwell not only an educational program but also a textual method. Continental humanists like Poggio Bracciolini had come to value monastic libraries as treasuries of primary sources (Bracciolini's searches of monastic libraries in Germany and France yielded classical manuscripts of Cicero, Statius, and Vegetius and established a model for the humanist study of sources), and early in the Reformation Cromwell set his agents to work, like Bracciolini, searching England's monastic libraries for primary sources that could support the Supremacy.[104] Those agents, by their own report, "made search in all the libraries in our country," scouring their holdings for sympathetic sources and promising that "any opinions of doctors" that might support Henry's cause "they shall be had."[105] The reports that Cromwell received from his agents suggest that he sent them to search libraries with a shopping list of desiderata.[106] One commissioner, John Prior of Chistchurch, Twynham, indicates as much in a letter to Cromwell on 3 October 1535: "I send you Beda de Ecllesiastica Historica, and another chronicle, whose author I do not know, wherin is also another treatise de Gestis Pontificum Anglorum. The other book you desire, de Gestis Anglorum, cannot yet be found."[107] The results of these research expeditions were compiled into a massive manuscript collection, *Collectanea satis copiosa*, which would form the basis of the Act of Appeals (1533) and Edward Foxe's *De uera differentia regiae potestatis et ecclesiasticae* (1534), which provided the doctrinal support for the Supremacy.[108] As James P. Carley notes, the index of historical sources contained in the *Collectanea* resembles the list of monastic books appropriated by the royal library at the same time, including such medieval authors as Ivo of Chartres, Geoffrey of Monmouth, Henry of Huntingdon, and William of Malmesbury.[109] Thus, Cromwell's search for primary sources to support the Supremacy amounted to a large-scale acquisitions policy for Henry's library.

Monastic libraries proved invaluable to Henrician reform by yielding the primary historical sources that validated it; but they were also called on to supply the evidence that would support their own demise. To the king's agents who searched them, the libraries were sources of orthodoxy as well as heterodoxy, repositories of materials favoring both the Crown and his papal nemesis. If Cromwell's commissioners sought books that could be drafted into the *Collectanea*, they also eagerly confiscated others that could provide evidence of the monasteries' allegiance to Rome and its practices and thereby justify their disendowment. Thus, the commissioner John Placet wrote to Cromwell from Winchcombe, referring to his "commandment to bring in books touching his authority ["the bishop of Rome"], St. Patrick's Purgatory, miracles, &c, confounding simple souls."[110] Another commissioner, Richard Layton, appears to refer to the same directive when he promises Cromwell, "ye shalle receve a bowke of our lades miracles well able to mache the Canterberies Tailes. Such a bowke of dremes as ye never saw wich I fownde in the librarie."[111] Libraries could supply historical and doctrinal truth, but they could also generate religious "dreams"; the job of Cromwell's agents was to sift the former from the latter.

Cromwell's infamous persecution of the monks of London Charterhouse, in which More had formerly resided, turned particularly intense scrutiny onto their library, recognizing the Carthusian house's influential role as a literary center.[112] In October 1535 Jasper Fyllol reported to Cromwell on the "foreign printed books" that he "found in the prior's and proctor's cells," mentioning that the monks "have great pleasure in reading such, and little or none in the New Testament or other books."[113] In response, Cromwell ordered his commissioners "to take from them all manner of books, wherein any errors be contained, and to let them all have the Old Testament and the New Testament."[114] This attempt to replace Carthusian books with scripture may represent an effort to counter the Carthusians' historical efforts to promote extrascriptural devotional material like Love's *Mirror of the Blessed Life of Jesus Christ* to the laity in place of the English Bible proffered by Lollards.[115] In addition, Cromwell resupplied the Charterhouse with other books, according to his commissioner Bedyll, who at Cromwell's command brought the Carthusians "divers books and annotations...against the primacy of the bishop of Rome," "that they should see the Holy Scriptures and doctors thereupon concerning the said matters." But the attempt to convert the Charterhouse monks was not successful, as Bedyll reports: "yesterday they sent me the said books and annotations again to my house by a servant of theirs without any word or writing." When questioned, the monks retorted "that they saw nothing in them whereby they were moved to alter their opinion."[116] The public execution of the Charterhouse priors John Houghton, Robert Laurence, and Augustine Webster, together with Richard Reynolds of Syon, on 4 May 1535 was the culmination of Cromwell's attempt to discipline not only Carthusian disloyalty but also Carthusian literacy.

Following a similar pattern, More's persecution and imprisonment focused lethal attention on his library. While he was in the Tower, accompanied by the books he was allowed to bring with him, More insisted that he experienced his confinement less as a painful punishment than as the fulfillment of an ongoing desire for Carthusian-tinged ideals of contemplative solitude. As Roper recounts, More takes the occasion of his imprisonment to recall his youthful longing "to have closed myself in as strait a room—and straiter, too."[117] He expresses as much in his marginal annotations in his prayer book from the time of his confinement, which pray for "grace" "to set the world at nought" and "to be content to be solitary/Not to long for worldely company."[118] The prayer book annotations epitomize the kind of meditative literacy that More first encountered in the Charterhouse, suggesting that he attempted to re-create a Carthusian setting in his cell in the Tower.[119] Roper's biography underscores the connection between More's earlier practices of Carthusian literacy and his final days in the Tower when it describes More's Chelsea library as a place where More longed, as Roper puts it, "to be solitary, and sequester himself from worldly company." Roper's

description of More's Chelsea library repeats verbatim More's prayer book
annotations, with their prayer for the strength "to be content to be solitary /
Not to long for worldely company." Later published by More's nephew, William Rastell, as "A Godly Meditation" in Rastell's 1557 edition of More's
English Works, More's prayer book annotations were promoted by the More
circle as evidence of More's defiant fortitude at the time of his death. By
inscribing the lines within his description of More's "New Building," Roper
insists on a line of continuity between library and prison cell, suggesting
that in the private space of devotional reading More both anticipated his
eventual imprisonment and created a space of resistance.

More's Henrician persecutors appear to have recognized the symbolic
power of More's cell/library, and in Roper's account, they stage More's final
persecution over the seizure of his books. As Roper writes, several of the
king's agents "were sent to Sir Thomas More into the Tower to fetch away
his books from him. And while Sir Richard Southwell and Master Palmer
were busy in the trussing-up of his books, Master [Richard] Rich, pretend[ed]
friendly talk with him." In the course of this conversation, Rich entrapped
More into a self-incriminating statement against the king's supremacy that
would provide the pretext for his execution.[120] The "trussing-up" of More's
books offers a bibliographical parallel to More's entrapment in his conversation with Rich; it also suggests that the books will be not only bound and
carried away but also, like their owner, executed, another contemporary
meaning of the term "truss up."[121]

Although lost libraries feature in More's writings from the *Life of Pico*
to *Utopia*, the most famous lost library with which More would be associated was ultimately his own. The books More had with him in the Tower
are now for the most part lost, perhaps the victims of Cromwell's policy of
destroying "papistical" books after 1535.[122] More's lost library has featured
in his subsequent mythology and hagiography as a figure for the cruelty of
his persecution and execution, an association perhaps first made by More
himself. In a famous scene recounted by More's anonymous Elizabethan biographer, "Ro:Ba.," with the loss of his books, More saw that his cause, too,
was lost; once his books were removed, he is reported to have asked for his
windows to be covered, remarking, "Is it not meet to shut up my shop windows when all my ware is gone?"[123] Raymond Irwin speculates of More, "if
his spiritual anchorage was the orthodox faith, his material anchors were the
volumes on his library shelves."[124] But if More's quasi-Carthusian library at
Chelsea anticipated his library-like enclosure in the Tower, More is likewise
prophetic in seeing that library, like the contemplative, devotional literacy
it promoted, as incompatible with the pragmatic goals of English humanists.

Cromwell, the inheritor of this latter position, took humanism to be an effective tool for shaping subjects of the Henrician state, but he also took Carthusian literacy to be its opposite, a nursemaid of sedition. In the aim of separating the former from the latter, Cromwell initiated Henrician reform as a reformation of England's libraries.

From Monasteries to Schools:
Thomas Starkey's Modest Proposal

Thomas Starkey was one of the Reformation era humanists to enjoy Cromwell's support, and his career as king's chaplain and counselor and as author testifies to the success that humanists met in the later Henrician court.[125] Yet his early biography shares surprising details with that of his ill-fated predecessor Thomas More. As well as following More in his career path from lawyer to king's counselor, Starkey too experienced a period of Carthusian retreat early in his career. For a year, beginning in 1530, Starkey resided at the Charterhouse at Sheen, accompanying his patron, Cardinal Reginald Pole.[126] Starkey's stay at the Charterhouse was apparently a productive one; out of it came the work for which he is best known, his *Dialogue between Reginald Pole and Thomas Lupset*, whose debate about the ideal commonwealth is indebted, and often responds directly, to More's *Utopia*.[127] Like More's work, Starkey's also reflects on the extraclaustral applications of monastic learning and literacy, as befits the Carthusian setting in which the work was composed; but where More drew on his Charterhouse experience to promote the monasticization of the laity, Starkey's own experience seems to have fueled his interest in the reverse, the laicization of the monastery. Coming at a time when monasteries were poised to undergo their most dramatic redefinition in English history, Starkey's *Dialogue* develops a proposal for transforming the monasteries to meet the needs of the particularly English brand of pragmatic humanism that Cromwell cultivated and for which Starkey himself would become spokesman and representative.[128]

In June 1531 while lodged at the Sheen Charterhouse, Starkey received a letter from his friend Edmund Harvel—who was, like Starkey, a member of Pole's household who found favor and royal employment under Cromwell's patronage—that complained, "you have incloside yourself in the charter howse wher it semith that you have dedicate al you[r] worke to perpetual philosophye but wether tendith soche pertinacye?" Instead, Harvel urges Starkey to abandon his retreat in favor of a civic, and specifically Protestant, life: "Wil you not comme forthe & teche other qualiter sit humanum vivendum, and helpe to take out al barbarous custom [?] and bring the realme to an antike form of good living?"[129] By urging Starkey to leave the monastery for the active life ("qualiter sit humanum vivendum") and to redirect his intellectual focus from "perpetual philosophy" to the cause of reform, to "bring the realme to an antike form of good living," the letter makes Starkey the focus of a one-man Reformation. It thereby anticipates a number of themes—the contemplative versus the active life, the monastic retreat versus the pursuit of Protestant reform—that would occupy Starkey throughout his later career. But Harvel appears to have misinterpreted Starkey's experience at the Charterhouse; instead of seeing his time at Sheen as a retreat, Starkey himself would depict it as a unique preparation for his life as a Protestant humanist.

In 1534 Starkey wrote to Cromwell seeking preferment and used the letter as a chance to detail his educational background. The defining moment of his education, Starkey informs Cromwell, came when he "set apart" his study of "philosophy" following his travels in Italy and instead "applyd my selfe to the redyng of holy scrypture, judging al other secrete knolege not applied to some use & profit of other to be as a vanyte." From that point onward, he writes, he decided to pursue the study of "cyuyle Law," "by-cause my purpos then was to lyue in a polytyke lyfe."[130] The period between Starkey's Italian travels, from which he returned in 1529, and his legal studies, begun in 1532, coincides with his retreat at Sheen. The account of his background in his letter to Cromwell responds indirectly to Harvel's charge that Starkey was engaged in "perpetual philosophye" rather than the pursuit of "qualiter sit humanum vivendum." Instead, Starkey asserts that this monastic interlude in his life actually taught him to forswear philosophy for civic humanism, a point he makes by reducing Carthusian literacy to "the redyng of holy scrypture." In so doing, Starkey imaginarily reforms Sheen in the same way that Cromwell would attempt to reform the London Charterhouse in 1535, when he ordered his commissioners "to take from them all manner of books, wherein any errors be contained, and to let them all have the Old Testament and the New Testament." In fact, the Sheen Charterhouse promoted a contemplative literacy that was similar to that of the London Charterhouse, in alliance with the neighboring Bridgettines at Syon.[131] But, anticipating the dissolution of the monasteries, Starkey's account transforms the Sheen Charterhouse from a center of medieval devotion to a nursery of civic humanism.

On the evidence of his *Dialogue between Reginald Pole and Thomas Lupset*, Starkey's time at the Charterhouse apparently stimulated his developing critique of monastic literacy. Echoing the words of Harvel's letter to Starkey, the *Dialogue* opens by condemning those who allow themselves to be "drownyd in the plesure of letturys and pryuate studys," urging them to turn their talents to serve the commonwealth instead: "Who so euer he be wych, drawen by the swetenes of hys studyes, and by hys own quyetnes and plesure mouyd, leauyth the cure of the commyn wele and pollycy, he dowth manyfest wrong to hys cuntrey and frendys, and ys playn vnjust and full of iniquity; as he that regardyth not hys offyce and duty, to the wych, aboue all, he ys most bounden by nature."[132] The lines stage a debate between the contemplative and the active life in terms that could be lifted from the framing dialogue between Morus and Hythloday in *Utopia*; but here the admonition to public service is placed in the mouth of Lupset, the lecturer of rhetoric at Oxford, and addressed to Pole, Starkey's onetime mentor, who defends "the quyat and contemplatyue" life until Lupset's words convince him otherwise (4). Pole had in fact led Starkey to Sheen; some of his biographers suggest that it was during this time that Pole found that his resistance to the royal divorce made his position in England untenable.[133] This stance would drive Pole to Italy, while Starkey remained behind, charged by Henry VIII with the impossible task of correcting and changing his former mentor's thinking on the matter. As he composed the *Dialogue*, however, Starkey imaginarily converted Pole into an unlikely spokesman for reform who is brought to understand that private study should be a preparative for civic action rather than contemplation.

If service to the commonwealth is to be preferred over the secluded life of contemplation, Starkey's Pole extends this newfound ideal to the monasteries themselves, proposing that they be converted into schools for the sons of the nobility: "that, euen lyke as thes monkys and relygyouse men ther lyuyng togyddur, exercise a certain monastycal dyscyplyne and lyfe, so they nobyllys, being brought vp togyddur, schold lerne ther the dyscyplyne of the commyn wele" (188). The proposal transforms the missions of the monasteries, charging the new schools with instructing the noble youth "in the admynystratyon of justice both publyke and pryuate"—and thus making them into idealized law schools. In so doing, Starkey's Pole concludes, "They schold more profit to the commynyng of Chrystyn charyte and the veray Gospel of Chryst, then our monkys haue downe in great processe of tyme in they solitary lyfe, wych hath brought forth, syth lytyl profit to the publyke state, much superstycyon. Thys vthe [youth], as sterrys, schold light in al partys of the reame hereaftur, and they schold put in effect that thing wych thes solitary men dreme of in theyr cornarys" (189). Thus transformed, the new schools represent the fulfillment, Pole asserts, of what should be true monastic ideals: "Thys schold brung forth in few yerys, I trow, Plato's commyn wele, or els, rather, the true instytutyon of Chrystyan doctryne"

(189). The result sounds very much like the Erasmian vision of the monastic life extended to the world that More explores in *Utopia*, but here it anticipates and creates an intellectual justification for the dismantlement of the monasteries that would occur in the years immediately following.

While Starkey was composing the *Dialogue*, it was still possible to imagine a peaceful reformation of the monasteries; but the question took on greater urgency in the coming years, when the dissolution routed out the monks and left the former monastic properties open for new uses. In January 1537, when Starkey had been promoted to the lofty position of the king's chaplain, he wrote to Henry VIII, condemning the former monks who entered the monasteries because they were "more mouyd by the idul quyetnes & vayn plesure therin, then by any desire of perfayt vertue & true relygyon."[134] Instead, he develops his earlier proposal from the *Dialogue* concerning the transformation of the monasteries and urges Henry to "alter these fundatyonys & turne them to better use; provide they may be as commyn scolys to the education of youth in vertue & relygyon" (lvi). Starkey's proposal for converting the monasteries to schools recognizes the monasteries' former importance as centers of literacy while also redirecting them to benefit the "new men," humanist-educated counselors such as himself for whom literacy was an essential tool for employment and advancement. By encouraging "men of letturys & lernyng," he writes Henry, "I trust now to see many a nobul wytt incurragyd to learning by your gracys lyberalyte, & made apte to celebrate your fame & glory commendyng your princely virtues to eternal memory" (liv). Where the former monasteries had bred pockets of dissent and treason, the humanist academies that Starkey envisions would be propaganda factories, using all the educational and intellectual resources at their disposal to promote and celebrate royal authority.

Starkey shows that the advance of humanism in England depended on the conversion and displacement of monastic literacies and the architectural spaces that supported them. In so doing, he creates an ideological program for Cromwell's uneven and sometimes-contradictory approaches to the monasteries. Where Cromwell and Henry transformed the monastic libraries by appropriating documents useful to the intellectual foundations of the Supremacy while seizing and destroying those "books, wherein any errors be contained," Starkey's program reforms monastic literacy without violence. He does so by insisting, in a sleight-of-hand worthy of Erasmus, on the essential continuity between the goals of humanism and monasticism, so that his academies dedicated to the noble youth represent the fulfillment of monastic ideals rather than the destruction of them. Thus, while Starkey imported Italianate "civic humanism" to England, he also adapted it to the ideological and material goals of the dissolution, namely, the expropriation and secu-larization of monastic property and learning. Starkey's educational vision would not be brought to fruition until much later: in the sixteenth century the monastic spoils would be redistributed to benefit the Henrician "new men," who transformed them into manor houses, however, not schools. It was not until the seventeenth century that the monastic buildings—includ-ing the London Charterhouse itself—began to be converted into schools. But in its vision of a reformed monasticism, Starkey's program accomplishes what Cromwell could perform only through force: the transformation of monastic literacy and its institutions into tools of the state.

Thomas Elyot's Dangerous Enterprise: The Library of the State

If Starkey enjoyed success as a humanist supporter of the Cromwellian ref-ormation, Thomas Elyot has been harder to assess as to both his support for Cromwell and the level of success he may have achieved. In part this is because Elyot was a master of equivocation: those moments in which he appears to be expressing his most ardent support for his patron, as several of his biographers note, are also marked by an unsettling degree of evasive-ness.[135] In 1536, the year after the execution of Thomas More, Elyot wrote Cromwell a letter now preserved in the Cotton Library (Cotton MS Cleopa-tra E. iv). In it, Elyot appears to distance himself from the man who had formerly been his friend and protector, asking Cromwell "to lay a part the remembraunce of the amity betweene me and sir Thomas More which was but *Vsque ad aras*, as is the proverb"—a proverb that Elyot himself would define as meaning "to do all the pleasure that a man can for his friend, saving his conscience"—insisting, "I was never so moche addict unto hym as I was unto truthe and fidelity toward my soveraigne lorde."[136] In the same letter Elyot appears to pledge his allegiance to Cromwellian reform, asserting, "I have in as moche detestacion as any man lyving all vayne supersticions, superfluous Ceremonyes, sklaunderous jonglynges, Countrefaite Mirakles, arrogant usurpacions of men called Spirituall and masking Religions and all other abusions of Christes holy doctrine and lawes" (31). Yet as Greg Walker observes, Elyot's careful word choice in his letter also maintains the possibility of preserving "necessary ceremonies, legitimate miracles, and those aspects of belief and the liturgy that were not abused" and renders it nearly impossible to diagnose the state of its author's "conscience," whether conservative or radical.[137]

Walker issues an important corrective against earlier interpretations of El-yot as a hypocritical opportunist, calling attention instead to those examples

of Elyot's work that appear to critique the more brutal aspects of Cromwellian and Henrician reform.[138] One such example is Elyot's translation of
A Sweet and Devout Sermon of Holy Saint Ciprian (1534) from an original by
Pico.[139] The translation follows the model of More's own Pico translation,
particularly in its dedication to three sisters of the Bridgettine House of
Syon, echoing More's own dedication to Joyce Leigh of the Poor Clares. The
dedication, along with the text's message about Christian strength in the
face of persecution, seems especially pointed given Syon's uncertain future
in 1534.[140]

But Elyot's apparent sympathy for those whom the dissolution would
soon displace did not make him a critic of that policy. To the contrary, and
to a degree even greater than Starkey, Elyot was directly involved in that
policy's implementation. The letter in which Elyot distances himself from
More and "vayne supersticions" has a more pressing purpose: to ask for a
share of the expropriated monastic property, in the event that Cromwell
can convince "his highnesse to reward me with some convenient porcion of
his Suppressid landes, whereby I may be able to contynue my life according
to that honest degree whereunto his grace hath called me" (31). It was not
the first time that Elyot made such a request, but it was one for which he
had some reason to be hopeful because he had actually been employed as
a commissioner himself. As Elyot reminds Cromwell, "late I have traveled
about the surveying of certain monasteries by the King's commandment,
wherein my pains should appear not unthankful" (24).[141] Records from 1535
confirm that "Sir Thos. Elyot" was a member of Cromwell's commission in
charge of visiting monasteries and religious institutions in Oxfordshire and
the town of Oxford.[142] His reward came later, when Elyot was permitted to
purchase lands formerly belonging to Eynsham Abbey at a favorable rate.[143]

Elyot never forgot—nor would he allow Cromwell to forget—his service
to the dissolution. While documentation of his exact activities in that office
is sparse, the duties of the commissioners were clear-cut. Elyot would have
been expected to investigate the state of religious houses, the administration
of their properties, and the conduct of their inmates; to issue injunctions
that expelled young inhabitants and forbade the illicit use of relics; and
to report on abuses that would bolster the case for suppression.[144] This
work swiftly came to fruition in 1536, when the first Act of Suppression
dissolved the lesser houses because of the "manifest sin, vicious, carnal, and
abominable living" that the commissioners reported to Cromwell during
their visitations.[145]

The Oxford commissioners' charge to examine "loca alia ecclesiastica"
extended to the universities.[146] In a letter of 12 September 1535, Richard

Layton, writing on behalf of the Oxford commissioners, reports purging the university libraries of the works of the scholastic Duns Scotus:

> We have set Dunce in Bocardo [a pun, meaning a scholastic syllogism and an Oxford prison] have utterly banisshede hym Oxforde for ever, with all his blinde glosses, and is nowe made a common servant to evere man, faste nailede up upon postes in all common howses of easment: id quod oculis meis vidi. And the seconde tyme we came to New Colege, after we hade declarede your injunctions, we founde all the gret quadrant court full of the leiffes of Dunce, the wynde blowing them into evere corner.[147]

The letter shows that the two charges of the Oxford commissioners—inspecting and purging libraries and instituting humanist educational reform—were allied. Indeed, the lavatorial afterlife to which Duns Scotus's books are condemned links the purgation of the libraries with the purgation of the body in "howses of easment."[148] Scotus, the most reviled of medieval scholastic thinkers, was detested by Erasmus as one of the "men who conspire with such zeal against the humanities," and the commissioners' injunctions singled him out by name as an author "of inextricable labyrinths" who must be removed from the university curriculum.[149] Erasmus's comment, and its instantiation in Layton's report, are reminders that the official spread of humanism in England went hand in hand with the acts of destruction that marked the dissolution.

The scene of anti-Scotus biblioclasm that Layton reports to Cromwell prepared the way for a wide-scale curricular reform for which the commissioners also claim credit:

> Pleasit your goodnes to be advertisyde that in Magdelen Colege we fownde stablished one lecture of divinitie, two of philosophie, one morale another naturale, and one of Laten tonge, well kept and diligently frequentede. To thes we have adjoned a lecture in the Greke, that is, the grammer in Greke perpetually to be rede there, and all the yewthe thereunto to have confluence for ther principules. In New Colege we have stablisshed two lecturres publique, one of Greke, another in Laten, with a goode stipende and salarie thereunto assignede for ever. and made therefore for evermore an honest salary and stipend.[150]

In the model of More's Hythloday, the commissioners spread humanism by instituting the study of Greek at Magdalen, New College and elsewhere.[151] But they do so with the aim of sweeping away the vestiges of scholasticism in

the universities. Their most dramatic reform in this direction takes place in
the study of law; as they report, "we have also, in the place of the canon lecture, jonede a civel lecture, to be rede in evere college, hale, and in[n]."[152] The
abolishment of canon law in favor of civil law, couched "as a logical consequence of the royal supremacy over the church," was a reform with sweeping
implications, as F. D. Logan observes.[153] One of Cromwell's special projects,
this emphasis on legal reform is reflected in the backgrounds of Cromwell's
commissioners, who, like Starkey and Elyot, were trained in civil law.[154]

Elyot's humanist writings made him uniquely qualified for the Oxford
commission, with its double emphasis on humanist reform and antischolas-
tic biblioclasm. In his writings prior to his appointment, Elyot's humanism
is leavened with the anticlericalism of a Cromwellian iconoclast. In his satir-
ical dialogue *Pasquil the Playne* (1533), Elyot derides the priest Harpocrates
as a "Duns man" because of his linguistic hair-splitting and overreliance on
the traditions of "noble authors approved." Harpocrates is furthermore identified as having been a "student at Bonony." The University of Bologna—or
"Bonony," as it was called in medieval and early modern England—was
known to be a center for the study of canon law, as it was the birthplace of
Gratian's Decretum in 1140 and won the longtime favor of the popes. Identified with Duns Scotus and medieval canon law, Harpocrates embodies
the old learning that will be swept from the libraries at Oxford, a development that Pasquil presages when he rails against Harpocrates for upholding
a world in which "vertue [is tourned] into vice, vice into vertue, deuo-
cio[n] into hypocrisie, and in some places men saye, faythe is tourned to
herisye."[155] In *Pasquil the Playne*, Elyot performs a symbolic act of biblioclasm aligned with humanist reform that announces his readiness to serve
Cromwell's campaign.

But as a Cromwellian agent, Elyot was also forced to turn the focus of
persecution inward. On 25 October 1535, the king issued a proclamation
forbidding the ownership of "erroneous writings and books," defined as the
works of John Fisher and "any other writing or book wherein shall be contained any error or slander to the King's majesty, or to the derogation or
diminution of his imperial crown or of any authority knit to the same, or
repugnant to his statutes of this realm made for the surety of his grace's succession, or for the abolition of the usurped power of the Bishop of Rome."[156]
Elyot's own library came under official scrutiny, and in response, Elyot
wrote to Cromwell in March 1536 to assure him of "the similitude of our
studies" (26). He confesses that "as touching suche bookes as be now prohibited containing the busshop of Romes authorite, some in deede I have,"
but he insists that these are "joined with diverse other warkes in one grete

volume or twoo at the moste" (27), reflecting the accretive conventions of the medieval miscellany.[157] When Elyot found his library under scrutiny, he offered to lay open its contents to Cromwell: "if it be the kinges pleasure and yours that I shall bringe or sende theim I will doo it right gladly" (27), he insists, expressing the wish that he could likewise divulge the contents of his mind; if "he mowght see my thowghtes as godd doeth," Elyot assures Cromwell, he would thereby "finde a reformear of those thinges, and not a favorar" (28). Elyot's service with the commission trained him in the practices of biblioclastic reform responsible for searching and sacking the medieval libraries, and so Elyot expresses his readiness to turn these biblioclastic practices upon his own library, offering to "make diligent serche, and suche as I shall finde, savering any thinge against the kinges pleasure, I will putt theim in redyness either to be browght to you, or to be cutt oute of the volume wherin they be joined with other, as you shall advyse me" (27).

Around the same time that he was forced to disclose the contents of his own library, Elyot was granted access to the king's library, which he fulsomely acknowledges in the preface to his *Dictionary* (1538).[158] As that preface recounts, he was hard at work on the *Dictionary*—the first Latin-English work of its kind—when news of his project reached the king through Anthony Denny, William Tyldesley (the king's librarian), and Cromwell himself.[159] Taking an interest in the project, Henry extended the resources of his own library to Elyot, pledging (as Elyot recounts), "if I wolde trauayle therin," to supply him "with suche bokes as your grace had, and I lacked, wold therin ayde me" (*Dictionary*, preface). With Henry's support, and the material support of the king's library, Elyot is able to expand the scope of his work. From a Latin word list, the work grows into an encyclopedia of knowledge of all kinds that is Pico-like in its broad range and ambition, including not simply definitions of words but also "proper termes belongynge to lawe and phisike, the names of diuers herbes knowen among us: also a good number of fishes founden as wel in our ocean, as in our riuers: ... sondrie poysis, coyne, and measures. ... Nor I haue omitted prouerbes, callyd Adagia, or other quicke sentences, whiche I thought necessarie to be had in remembraunce" (preface).

Elyot's description of the king's library as a source of intellectual bounty seems calculated to support Henry's self-image as a patron of learning and a generous supporter of scholarship. Yet in Elyot's description, Henry's decision to admit Elyot into his library looks less like an act of benevolent patronage and more like an extension of the disciplinary practices that Elyot already knew too well. As his preface reports, Elyot's experience in the royal library fills him not with inspiration but with terror; after visiting it, Elyot

confesses, "I was attached with an horrible feare, remembryng my dangerous enterprise." That "dangerous enterprise" follows from his attempt to
bring together a wide range of sources and to reconcile them in a single book.
Aided by the king, Elyot undertakes "an augmentation of myn understan-
dynge" that will expand his *Dictionary* to include the additional sources
he discovers in the royal collections in a multipage appendix headed "The
Additions." Yet Elyot discovers to his dismay that his sources resist such
unifying efforts: surveying his authors, Elyot finds not a synthetic unity of
knowledge but an alarming diversity and discord: "dyuers other men haue
written sundry annotations and commentaries on olde latin authors, among
whom also is discorde in their expositions" (preface). Faced with the self-
imposed task of collating such diverse authorities into a single book, he is
driven nearly to despair: "desperation was euen at hand to rent al in pieces
that I had written." His experience in Henry's library recalls his response to
Cromwell's scrutiny into the contents of his own library: here, as there, the
necessity of imposing unity on a heterogeneous collection of sources drives
Elyot to the brink of mutilating his own books. But reducing his work to
"pieces" does not solve so much as it acknowledges and acts out the problem
of his sources' disunity.

The impossible challenge of imposing ideological unity on a diverse
and divided collection of sources applies not just to the dictionary but to
the library. Elyot's *Dictionary* resembles a library on a number of levels, a
resemblance driven home by its new title in the 1542 and later editions,
Bibliotheca Eliotae: Eliotis Librarie. The alphabetical order that structures
the *Dictionary* was also an organizing principle of the royal collections at
the time of Tyldesley's librarianship.[160] It contrasts with other modes of bibliographical ordering developed in the early sixteenth century, such as the
chronological order of John Bale's *Illustrium majoris Britanniae scriptorum*
(1548) or the subject headings of Conrad Gesner's *Bibliotheca universalis*
(1545), which group books under headings that differentiate "de Grammatica
et Philologia," "de Dialectica," "de Rhetorica," "de Poetica," "de Naturali
Philosophia," "de Morali Philosophia," "de Theologia Christiana," and "de
diversis artibus illiteratis, mechanicis, et aliis humanae vitae utilibus."[161]
It also contrasts with the traditional division of faculties ordering a library
like Oxford's, as Thomas Norton describes it in his 1440s translation of
Palladius's *De re rustica*, which separates theology, natural and moral Philosophy, medicine, and history.[162] Where these other organizational modes
group books according to similarities in period, faculty, or subject, in the
arbitrary classification scheme of alphabetical order all books stand alone.
Alphabetical organization produces both uniformity and incongruity; while

removing subject- and field-specific taxonomies and leveling its sources into a nonhierarchical field, it accentuates differences rather than similarities across the elements it organizes.[163]

This effect is especially pronounced in the royal collections beginning in 1530, when, as James P. Carley observes, "libraries in three of the royal palaces, Westminster, Hampton Court and Greenwich, were refitted as storehouses for monastic books."[164] These new contents produced jarring incongruities of subject matter and orthodoxy. In the Westminster library, for example, a listing of books classed under the letter *C* brings the following classical and religious works together: *Constitutiones Gregorii X* (now British Library, MS Royal 10 D. vii); *Ceremonia ecclesiae Romanae; Concilia generalia* (possibly *Tomus primus [secundus] quatuor conciliorum generalium*, ed. Jacques Merlin [Paris, 1524]); *Confessio Waldensium;*[165] *Commentariis Siluii in concilium Basiliense* (Pius II, *Comentarii de gestis concilii Basiliensis*); and Cicero's *De finibus bonorum ac malorum*.[166] At the same time that Elyot fell under suspicion for owning works "containing the busshop of Romes authorite," he would have seen numerous such works, such as the *Ceremonia ecclesiae Romanae*—perhaps one of the texts that had been expropriated from the monastic libraries and preserved to strengthen the case against the monasteries—among the king's own collections. The varied contents of the king's library reflect Cromwell's Janus-like response to the monastic libraries in directing his commissioners to search both for books that supported the Supremacy and for those that provided evidence against the monasteries, such as those supporting "the bishop of Rome's authority" sought by the commissioner John Placet.[167] Works of both kinds found their way into the royal library. There would eventually be a narrowing of the collections when, in 1551, by order of the Privy Council, "all superstitious bookes, as masse bookes, legendes and such like," were purged from the royal library at Westminster.[168] But at the time of Elyot's visit, the king's library (the repository for numerous "legendes" and "superstitious bookes" removed from other libraries as well as those remaining from earlier collectors) was paradoxically the most heterodox in the nation, containing books that would have made any other library, private or religious, the object of official scrutiny. And, as Elyot discovers to his distress, those books' arrangement by alphabetical order rather than topic or category offers no guide in discerning which were officially sanctioned and which were not.

Elyot's "Additions" to his *Dictionary* draw directly from the royal collections, reflecting their classical holdings as well as newly appropriated monastic books. In the process, they also reflect Elyot's experience in the library, as he encountered both licit and illicit sources side by side. Like the library, Elyot's *Dictionary* produces dissonance in its juxtapositions as well as unexpected connections across its otherwise apparently random listings. Take, for example, the entries that Elyot lists in "The Additions" close to the beginning, under "A ANTE N":

> Anabula, a beaste in Aethiope, hauynge a heed like a camell, a necke like a hors, legges like an oxe, and is of colour a bryght redde, full of white spottes.
>
> Anacephaleosis, a shorte recapytulation or repetition of thynges before rehersed.
>
> Anacharsis, a philosopher of a meruaylous wysedom, all be it that he was borne in the barbarous cou[n]trey of Scithia, whom Pliny supposeth to haue fyrst fou[n]den the potters whele: And beinge in the tyme that Solon made lawes to the Athenienses, he sayde, that lawes were lyke to copwebbes, which tyed fast lyttell flyes, & the great flyes brake them, and went clene through them. In like wyse the poore & meane men are fast wou[n]den in the penalties and dangers of lawes, but lordes and men in great auctoritie daily breake lawes, and are not corrected.
>
> Anachorita, an hermite: the interpretation therof is, he that lyueth a parte, and oute of companye.[169]

The definition of "Anabula" (giraffe) derives, as a marginal note indicates, from Pliny, *Historia naturalis*, of which Henry owned two copies.[170] Pliny is also the source for Elyot's discussion of Anacharsis, the pre-Socratic Scythian philosopher whom Pliny credited with the invention of the potter's wheel, a fact that also makes its way into Elyot's entry.[171] But Elyot goes on to embellish his entry on Anacharsis with a quotation from Plutarch's *Lives* that became a commonplace in works like Erasmus's *Education of a Christian Prince* (1516), a copy of which Erasmus himself sent to Henry VIII, and that attributes to Anacharsis the maxim "Laws are merely spider webs, which the birds, being larger, break through with ease, while the flies are caught fast."[172] By inserting this maxim into his *Dictionary*, Elyot reiterates a lesson from his *Boke Named the Governor* (1531) that rulers must obey the same laws to which the people are subject; thus, he approvingly cites Alexander Severus (emperor of Rome, 222–35): "God forbede that ever I shulde deuise any lawes wherby my people shulde be compelled to do any thynge whiche I my selfe can nat tollerate."[173] In the *Dictionary*'s entry "Anacharsis," Elyot underscores his lesson, just in case the reader misses the significance of the comparison between "lawes" and "copwebbes," by repeating it (a trope to which he calls attention in the definition that precedes it: "Anacephaleosis, a short recapytulation or repetition of thynges before rehersed"): "the poore & meane men are fast wou[n]den in the penalties and dangers of lawes, but lordes and men in great auctoritie daily breake lawes, and are not corrected."

Elyot's entry "Anacharsis" presents a miniature guide for princes, and one that derives lessons for rulership from the royal library itself.[174] In this mode of extracting lessons for rulership from the king's library, Elyot positions himself as Lydgate to Henry's Duke Humfrey, instructing the ruler in how to read his own books. The lesson on "lordes and men in great auctoritie" who "daily breake lawes" that govern their subjects also reflects the contradictory nature of the king's library itself, which, thanks to Cromwell, contains works that support both the king's authority and that of his nemesis, "the Bishop of Rome." Henry's library thus skirts the law that governs the libraries of Henry's subjects. While private libraries like Elyot's are forbidden books "containing the busshop of Romes authorite," no such restrictions applied to the king's library, whose postdissolution holdings embraced heterodox works that would have brought suspicion to nonroyal owners. Such is the case with many of the monastic materials that were seized by Cromwell's commissioners in their visitations of the monasteries, one example of which is indicated in the definition immediately following that of "Anacharsis": "Anachorita, an hermite: the interpretation therof is, he that lyueth a parte, and oute of companye." One of the works in the Westminster library at the time of Elyot's visit was *The Ancrene Wisse* (Guide for Anchoresses), listed in the catalogue as "vita anachoritarum utriusque sexus," a work that originated from Bardney Abbey, Lincolnshire.[175] The book was sought by later antiquarians like Sir Robert Cotton as a specimen of early English; Elyot's contemporaries, however, excoriated it as a "fabula vana" that exemplified the worst excesses of pre-Reformation superstition.[176] Elyot refers to this work in his entry "Anachorita," which he defines as "an hermite: the interpretation therof is, he that lyueth a parte, and oute of companye," thereby calling attention to the book's presence in Henry's library. But at a time when the presence of such a book in any other private library might be expected to attract official scrutiny, Elyot's citation recalls the charge in the previous entry, "Anacharsis," against "lordes and men in great auctoritie" who "daily breake lawes, and are not corrected." The ironic juxtaposition of "Anacharsis" and "Anachorita" in Elyot's *Dictionary* mirrors in print the incongruities and ironies that are produced in the alphabetical ordering of Henry's books on his library shelves. In it, Elyot exposes an anxious realization that plagues his "dangerous enterprise"—the laws impose an ideological unity on books and libraries that is impossible to maintain.

"The Additions" to Elyot's *Dictionary*, I am suggesting, not only reflects the contents of the king's library but allegorizes Elyot's "dangerous enterprise," his effort to impose ideological unity on a dangerously heterodox diversity of written material. This effort concerns more than the arrangement of books in libraries or words in dictionaries; it captures the larger Reformation challenge of imposing religious and political unity on the nation. In his *Dictionary*, Elyot insists that such unity from diversity inheres in the office and title of the monarch: "Unto that office of governance is (as it were by the general consent of all people) one name appropred, in the which, although by the diversity of languages, the letters and syllables are oftentimes changed, yet the word spoken hath one signification, which implieth as much as a KING in English" (Aii). The very title "king" carries a single meaning ("one name"/"one signification") despite the "diversity of languages" in which it is expressed, just as the king's authority enforces ideological unity on his subjects. As an example of the king's enforcement of this unity, Elyot cites the trial and execution of the sectarian John Lambert in November 1538, over which Henry himself personally presided.[177] Lambert's crime is in promoting heterodoxy that is not only religious but also hermeneutic, as Elyot describes: "The perverse opinions and interpretations of the arrogant masters of the said Lambert, in whose writings and his own proper wit he more trusted (as your highness truly alleged against him) than in the playne context of holy scripture, and the determinate sentence of holy and great learned doctors." Elevating individual wit over the "playne" message of scripture, Lambert rejects the ideological unity represented by "the determinate sentence of holy and great learned doctors" in favor of the "pernicious errours" multiplied by heterodox readers (prologue). By personally overseeing Lambert's trial and execution, Henry enforces orthodoxy's "determinate sentence" and the "one signification" of royal authority. Yet the very ideological unity that is demanded by the king is contradicted by the diversity of opinion that Elyot discovers in even the most weighty authorities, who are not unified in their judgments: those "dyuers other men [who] haue written sundry annotations and commentaries on olde latine authors" are divided among themselves (there is "discorde in their expositions"), and their "sentence" is anything but "determinate" or "playne." In the end, the reader who does not rely on "his owne proper wytte" to differentiate his sources is forced to reproduce that discord.

Elyot comes to terms with this paradox in the 1542 reissue of his *Dictionary* as *Bibliotheca Eliotae: Eliotis Librarie*, which cuts the mention of Lambert from the prologue while adding a warning to the reader that his *Librarie* contains heretical matter interlaced with its orthodox contents. Echoing his letter to Cromwell in 1535, Elyot confronts the problem of such interlacing by "divulging" his contents, but this time he rejects the impossible aim of reconciling his sources into an orthodox unity: "I . . . thought it necessary to enterlace the detestable heretykes, with theyr sundry heresyes, concernynge the substance of our catholyke faythe iustly condemned by the hold consent of all true chrysten men," he explains, "to the intente that those heresyes beinge in this wyse divulgate, may be the sooner espied and abhorred in suche bookes, where they be craftily enterlaced with holsom doctrine."[178] Elyot's practice of "enterlacing" heretical definitions within his *Librarie* imitates how such heresies are "craftily enterlaced with holsom doctrine"—just as in Elyot's own library prohibited books were "joined with diverse other warkes" in compiled volumes.

The new edition incorporates the definitions from "The Additions" while adding new ones: thus, Elyot's *Librarie* proffers a definition not only of the "anachorita" of the old religion but also of the radical "Anabaptistae": "A sect of heretikes, which began about the yere of our lorde. 1524. In Germany: wherof the first author was one Balthazar, which taught that baptisme dyd nothynge profit unto children, but that they ought eftsones to be baptized wha[n] they come to yeres of discretion. Wherefore they which were of that sect of heretikes be called Anabaptistae, whiche do signify re-baptisours."[179] Elyot's effort to "divulgate" the heretical meanings that are "enterlaced" in his *Dictionary* echoes his proem to *Boke Named the Governor* (1531), which informs his dedicatee, Henry VIII, that "I am (as God iuge me) violently stered to *devulgate* or sette fourth some part of my studie" (my emphasis) by offering the book as "the first fruits of my study" to the searching eyes of the monarch.[180] So too, we recall, his letter to Cromwell offered to divulge the contents of his own library—"if it be the kinges pleasure and yours that I shall bringe or sende theim I will doo it right gladly" (27)—no less than he would, if he could, divulge the contents of his mind; if "he mowght see my thowghtes as godd doeth," Elyot informs Cromwell, he would thereby "finde a reformear of those thinges, and not a favorar" (28). But just as alphabetical order enforces a neutral ordering on its contents, the catalogues of libraries cannot tell us how readers interpreted their contents. Nor can Elyot be certain that his *Librarie* will reveal him to be a "reformear" and "not a favorar" of the heretical matter it contains, any more than his own library did when it was under Cromwell's scrutiny. This is the problem of libraries as much as dictionaries: they invariably multiply meanings rather than reduce them, and disperse authority across a field of sources rather than unify it.

At around the same time that he resissued his *Dictionary* as his *Librarie*, Elyot published *The Image of Governance* (1541), which describes an idealized royal library.[181] The Roman emperor who is the book's subject, Alexander Severus (who also appears in *Boke Named the Governor*), enacts reform by beginning a campaign against "idelnesse, that is to say, ceasynge from necessarye occupation or study," which he identifies as "the synke, which receyued all the stynkyng canalles of vyce." The campaign is ruthless: "yet ere that shall be brought well to passe, a great parte of the people shall peryshe" (285). Targeting the same "idleness" that featured in Starkey's criticisms of the monasteries, Elyot's version of Roman reform recalls the bloody campaign of Henry and Cromwell in the years between 1535 and 1540.[182]

Also like Cromwell and Henry, Alexander Severus, we learn, focuses his reform on the library; "first he visited all the libraries that were in the citie" and ordered them to be "clensed" and their books reorganized: "as making for euery boke an huche locked, to the intent that wha[n] any man came to study there, he shulde haue no moo bokes to loke on, than one of the keepers of the lybrarye (wherof there were a good number retained to give their attendance, hauing therefore competent salaries) shulde delyuer unto them" (294–95). These well-salaried librarians are primarily guardians; they retain the books in "an huche locked," in order to ensure that readers have access to no more books than they are authorized to see. As well as reforming existing libraries, Alexander "made also a newe lybrarye, garnyshyng it as well with most principall warkes in euery science . . . whyche lybrarye was deuyded into sundry galeryes, accordynge to dyvers sciences, all byulded rounde in the fourme of a cerkle, and being separate with walles one frome an other" (295). The library's round reading room recalls the all-encompassing universality of knowledge to which some humanists, like Pico, aspired.[183] But Elyot presents the opposite of a library without walls: rather than being unified by the "obscure connections" championed by Pico, these books are "deuyded into sundry galeryes," ordered by the disciplines ("accordynge to dyvers sciences"), which are in turn "separate[d] with walles one from an other." If this is a reflection of the library reformed by royal authority, its driving aim is circumscription; the borders that separate books from one another are as carefully policed as its contents are restricted from readers.

It is the antidote to the problem of the composite medieval book in Elyot's library, in which forbidden writings are "joined with diverse other warkes," or that of heresie in Elyot's *Librarie*, in which the works of "detestable heretykes" are "craftily enterlaced with holsom doctrine." In *The Image of Governance* Elyot insists that the most important feature of the library is its walls.

Elyot's image of Alexander Severus's reformed library, with its physical and disciplinary divisions, returns us unexpectedly to the divided libraries of Thomas More. As I have argued, More's literary depictions of lost or broken libraries refuse the synthetic visions of learning promoted by humanist libraries like those of Erasmus and Pico, manifesting instead a field of literacy that is deeply divided in its objects and aims. The walls and locked cabinets of Elyot's library reflect a literacy that is no less divided, despite the Henrician Reformation's official imposition of ideological and religious unity. Although they upheld opposing loyalties, More and Elyot both project the Reformation's conflicts over the nation's intellectual and religious practices onto libraries. In so doing, they challenge a humanist vision of libraries as sites of intellectual transmission and social progress, which has been repeated in subsequent accounts linking "the rise of humanism" to the rise in book production, literacy, and libraries during the early sixteenth century. But in the works of More, Starkey, and Elyot that I have examined here, the rise of humanism looks more like the consequence of conquest, and the library, less like a nursery than a battleground. If, as Grafton and Jardine suggest, humanism spread through revolution, not evolution, More's libraries foreground the devotional literacies that dominated English literate culture in the early sixteenth century and came to represent pockets of resistance in the early Reformation.

As I have argued, More promoted a Carthusian-tinged devotional literacy that aimed to combat Lollard and Protestant heterodoxies starting with Arundel's Constitutions of 1409. But those who advanced the spread of English humanism were no less politically motivated; Cromwell, as we have seen, adapts the rhetoric of Erasmian humanism to the cause of Henrician reform by directing the "lernyng of good letters, sciences and craftes" toward "obedience to god, to the kynges hyghnesse, and to such rulers and lawes, as his maiesty shal ordeyn." This project took shape through the work of humanists who enjoyed Cromwell's patronage, such as Thomas Starkey, who redirected the monasteries toward "the dyscyplyne of the commyn wele." Cromwell's commissioners instituted humanist reform at the same time that they confiscated and, if Richard Layton's accounts of "Dunce in

Bocardo" are to be believed, destroyed books that were scholastic, super-stitious, or supportive of "the bishop of Rome's authority." Indeed, such examples make it possible to see how in Reformation England the rise of humanism came about not through the spread of books and literacy but through their restriction. If the icon of the scholar in his study promoted humanism as a natural and even inevitable outgrowth of the laicization of literacy, the libraries of More, Starkey, and Elyot reveal the institutional violence that it both produced and elided.

CHAPTER THREE

Reading Reformation:
The Libraries of Matthew Parker
and Edmund Spenser

Library Books

In the preface to the newly translated *Holie Bible* of 1568, the so-called Bishops' Bible, Matthew Parker, archbishop of Canterbury under Elizabeth I, describes the destruction of libraries throughout history:

> It is recorded, that Ptolomeus Philadelphus, King of Egypt, had gathered together in one Library at Alexandria, by his great Cost and Diligence, seven Hundred Thousand Books, whereof the Principal were the Books of Moses; which, reserved not much more than by the space of Two Hundred Years, were al brent and consumed in that Battail, when Caesar restored Cleopatra again after her Expulsion. At Constantinople under Zenon, by one common Fire, a Hundred and Twenty Thousand Books. At Rome, when Lucius Aurel. Antonius did raign, his notable Library, by a Lightning from Heaven was quite consumed. Yea it is recorded, that Gregory the first did cause a Library of Rome, containing only certain Painims Works to be burned, to thintent the Scriptures of God should be more read and studied.[1]

Among these infamous examples of lost classical libraries Parker includes the destruction of libraries in his own age: "What other great Libraries have there been consumed, but of late Dayes? And what Libraries have of old throughout this Realme, almost in every Abby of the same, been destroyed at sundry Ages, besides the Loss of other Mens private Studies, it were too long to reherse."[2] The archbishop is right to classify the loss of English libraries among the most devastating in the history of libraries. Given that England's religious institutions housed its greatest libraries in the Middle Ages, the dissolution of the monasteries meant the widespread loss of medieval books.[3] Some were deliberately destroyed, such as those of Duns Scotus, as reported by Cromwell's commissioner Richard Layton. Others were victims of passive neglect or active misuse, such as those that were dismembered and reportedly used for wrapping groceries or scouring dirty boots.[4] Innumerable books that escaped destruction in the initial waves of Reformation fell victim to the 1550 Act against Superstitious Books and Images under Edward VI, which required all medieval service books, including missals, prayer manuals, and saints' legends, among others, to be surrendered to church officials and "openly burnt or otherways defaced and destroyed."[5] Whatever the direct causes, the loss of medieval books in the years between 1536 and 1550 was immense. N. R. Ker estimates the scale of loss by comparing monastic library records with the rates of post-Reformation survival, finding, for example, that of the more than six hundred volumes in the medieval catalogue of the Austin friars of York, only five books have survived, while of the three hundred volumes that Duke Humfrey gave to the University of Oxford, only two survived the Reformation.[6] Some libraries that contained only a hundred or fewer volumes had no survivors at all. As the work of Ker and other library historians reminds us, what currently remains of England's medieval textual heritage represents a small fraction of the medieval books that existed before 1536.

Yet Parker's description of the loss of England's libraries "of late Dayes" is notably silent about the causes of loss, and his generalization about libraries "in every Abby" that have "been destroyed at sundry Ages" leaves unclear whether the religious institutions were the victims or the perpetrators of such destruction. Moreover, it is unclear from Parker's account whether the loss of libraries is a positive or a negative development in the history of Christianity: while he imagines the "Books of Moses" perishing with the fabled destruction of the Alexandrian library by Caesar, he also suggests that the destruction of libraries could promote Christianity, as when "Gregory the first did cause a Library of Rome, containing only certain Painims Works to be burned, to thintent the Scriptures of God should be more read and studied." Parker's ambivalence regarding the destruction of libraries reflects the complexity of his own position in relation to the monastic libraries during the Reformation and its aftermath. Parker was affiliated with Reformation bibliophiles John Bale, John Leland, and the lesser-known Sir John Prise and Stephen Batman, who searched the monastic libraries and gathered large collections of medieval books following the dissolution.[7] In 1568 Parker won a royal commission to catalogue surviving books from the former monastic libraries, from which he amassed the important library that he donated largely to Corpus Christi College, Cambridge, in 1575.[8] For Parker and his fellow post-Reformation book collectors, library building served the ends of nation building. Leland considered it his patriotic duty, as he reported to Henry VIII, "to peruse and dylygently to searche all the lybraryes of Monasteries and collegies of thys your noble realme" (Bviii r). On a similar note, Bale wrote to Parker that "only conscyence, with a fervent love to my Contrye moved me to save that myghte be saved," a motivation and goal shared by Parker himself; his secretary John Joscelyn notes Parker's great care to preserve medieval books as tangible links to the nation's past: "to the end that these antiquities [i.e., books] might last long and be carefullye kept he caused them [to be] broughte into one place."[9]

The work undertaken by these collectors is responsible for preserving much of medieval English textual culture that survives today: the Royal Library, which became the core collection of the British Library, "gathered together fragments of the wreckage of many monastic collections," as its cataloguers observe.[10] Likewise, as the ongoing scholarship of James P. Carley shows, the medieval English books currently housed in the major collegiate and cathedral libraries survived the Reformation largely through the active intervention of Henrician bibliophiles like Leland.[11] Yet the process of collecting—aligned as it was with the project of nation building—was motivated by strong political and religious interests.[12] Where library historians like Ronald Harold Fritze find that work like Leland's "stands as a great triumph of our respect for our past and the need to preserve the heritage of human knowledge," I see in that work less an expression of (what we now call) "respect for the past" than an invention of "preservation" and "heritage" as terms directed at supporting and upholding the interests of the state.[13] The library-building project initiated by Bale, Leland, and the book collectors in Matthew Parker's circle did not advocate "the collection, preservation, and protection of the monastic libraries" in any modern sense of the terms.[14] Indeed, far from opposing the official destruction of monastic libraries, these collectors supported it: likewise, the collections they built self-consciously advanced, rather than subverted, many of the same aims of the Reformation that resulted in the dissolution.[15]

This was certainly the case with Parker, who, as Elizabeth's archbishop of Canterbury, championed the causes and effects of England's Reformation. Hence it is that Parker minimizes the dissolution as a uniquely destructive event by aligning the loss of English libraries "of late Dayes" with that of "every Abby . . . destroyed at sundry Ages," while imagining the destruction of libraries as both threatening and protecting the study of the scriptures. It is no mistake that the archbishop's meditation on lost libraries prefaces the Bible whose translation and publication he oversaw. As Parker notes, through divine Providence God "hath preserved these bookes of the scriptures safe and sounde, and that in their natiue languages they were first written..., and contrary to all other casualties, chaunced upon all other bookes in mauger of all worldly wittes, who would so fayne haue had them destroyed, and yet he by his mightie hande, would haue them witnesses and interpreters of his will toward mankind."[16] Not only do the holy scriptures miraculously survive the destruction of the monasteries, but they are thereby liberated for the benefit of the people.

In place of the monastic libraries, Parker and his associates sought to establish new libraries that could be institutions of the state rather than of a church whose head resided in Rome, and repositories of historical knowledge rather than of so-called superstition and idolatry. Long after the flurries of Henrician and Edwardian iconoclasm were quelled by mollifying edicts, the English library remained both an object and a vehicle of reform. Reforming the English library meant reshaping the memorial functions formerly performed by monastic libraries. The Privy Council letter of 1568 authorizing Parker's bibliographical survey describes the destruction of the monastic libraries as a crisis of memory: whatever their offenses, it observes, the "divers Abbeys" that had been destroyed in the dissolution formerly served "as treasure-houses, to keep and leave in memory such occurents as fell in their time."[17] The use of the term "treasure-house" recalls the terminology that medieval thinkers such as Hugh of St. Victor and John of Salisbury employed to describe the workings of memory, and the monastic library itself was often taken to be a model memory chamber.[18] Yet the term also recalls earlier Wycliffite attacks that charged Franciscan libraries with hoarding bibliographical "treasures," as when *Jack Upland* accuses friars of imprisoning books: "[they] putte he[m] in tresorie, & do prisone hem from secular preestis and curatis."[19] Here the library as "treasury" is also a prison house of books: if it guards in memory, it also withholds that memory from lay readers. By calling the monastic libraries "treasure-houses," the Privy Council letter of 1568 invites Parker and his associates to take over the memorial function of the former monastic libraries and to liberate their contents for the public good. Under Parker's sponsorship, the post-Reformation library became a place of memory in content as well as form: those books deemed most worthy of preservation dealt with matters of national and ecclesiastical history, supplying the need for historical precedents to support the reformed state.[20]

The post-Reformation English library was dedicated not simply to the preservation of cultural memory but to the active remaking of it—and that remaking is still visible in the medieval books that this salvage effort recuperated.

Following the dissolution, the 1542 inventory of the Royal Library reveals an influx of formerly monastic books into the king's collection—the result, as James P. Carley has shown, of the systematic appropriation of medieval books by the state.[21] The contents of these books, moreover, reflect concerns with which Henry was preoccupied in and around 1535: the legality of the divorce, Britain's imperial status, and the history of England's relation to Rome.[22] In the Royal Library as much as in the private collections of Prise and Bale and the royally authorized library of Parker, individual books owed their very survival to active choices that were made on the basis of the collector's sense of what was worth preserving and, more broadly, of what national or historical roles the library should fulfill. As a result, a significant body of what now survives as the textual heritage of the English Middle Ages reflects the shaping interests of these post-Reformation collectors.[23]

Those shaping interests are manifested not only in the selection of individual books but within the books themselves: the marginal glosses and other readers' marks that post-Reformation collectors left in their pages bear witness to the fact that books were materially remade to meet the new requirements of the post-Reformation library.[24] If the work of these collectors represents an inaugural effort to recover rare books on behalf of national interests, it also shows how one effect of that "recovery" was the reinvention of the places, acts, and objects of reading.

As well as transforming the meanings of libraries and their contents, the work of collectors such as Parker, Bale, and Leland had wide-scale cultural reverberations that remain evident in post-Reformation literary works; one such work is Edmund Spenser's *Faerie Queene* (1590, 1596).[25] As I will argue in this chapter, Spenser's allegory of Protestant nationhood meditates on the post-Reformation transformation of the library and its broader implications for literary history and practice. Spenser, who received his baccalaureate in 1573 and his master of arts degree in 1576, was still a student at Cambridge when Parker began to transfer his books to the university. In 1574 Parker bequeathed seventy-five printed books and twenty-five manuscripts to Cambridge University Library at the request of Andrew Perne, master of Peterhouse; that bequest was followed by Parker's monumental gift of nearly six hundred books to Corpus Christi College in 1575, the collection that established the Parker Library there.[26] Together, these bequests constituted a bibliographical watershed, and they could not have escaped Spenser's notice as a noteworthy Cambridge event. Moreover, Spenser maintained literary connections with collectors and associates in Parker's circle, which I will discuss further below, that linked him to the literary and textual culture that the Parker Library fostered.

In *The Faerie Queene*, Spenser reflects on the cultural significance of the post-Reformation library, as exemplified by Parker's library as it was installed at Cambridge, while extrapolating from its example a larger practice and ethos of reading. The second book of Spenser's Protestant epic reveals its debt to the post-Reformation book collectors in a scene that allegorizes the human brain as an architectural space while representing the portion of the brain dedicated to memory as a vast library filled with history books.[27] This "Memory's Library" manifests the importance of memory and the textual past to Protestant self-definition in the period following the Reformation. Spenser's library is presided over by a librarian, Eumnestes (Good Memory), who, like Matthew Parker, preserves the past in written records, which he stores "in his immortall scrine,/Where they for euer incorrupted dweld" (2.9.56).[28] Extending the aims of the post-Reformation book collectors who sought to recover England's own origins from bibliographical ruin, Spenser makes the library into a center of Protestant memory. In so doing, he offers a dramatic illustration of this chapter's central argument: that in the politically contentious post-Reformation period, the library was conceived, and attained new cultural significance, not as a passive vessel for the preservation of the past but as a place where the past was actively remade. As Spenser's book 2 reveals, the post-Reformation library was dedicated to reshaping cultural memory from remnants salvaged from the ruined monastic past. If, to recall the Royal Library's modern cataloguers, the post-Reformation library "gathered together fragments of the wreckage of many monastic collections" to create an institution of national memory, in *Faerie Queene*, book 2, Spenser creates what we might call a poetics of wreckage, an extended meditation on the project of cultural recovery that accompanied England's long Reformation.[29]

Monuments of Antiquity, Monuments of Superstition

Spenser's affinity with the post-Reformation book collectors is signaled in the titles of two books in Eumnestes' library that are identified by name: *Briton moniments* and *Antiquitie of Faerie lond*.[30] In the wake of the dissolution, the terms "monument" and "antiquity" inspired and justified the project of rescuing and preserving medieval books. The Protestant bibliographer John Bale uses them liberally and pointedly, as when he laments the fact that, through the dissolution, monastic libraries were "wretchedly spoyled of so many noble monuments of Antiquite" (Eii r). Classifying books as "monuments of antiquity" sanitized them for Protestant readers by removing them from the formerly idolatrous setting of the monastic library to a new site of historical value. In so doing, the term also reimagined the library—the center for preserving "monuments of antiquity"—as a site of national memory. The "monument of antiquity" is crucial to developing notions of book preservation in the post-Reformation years. The term resurfaces in the Privy Council letter of 7 July 1568 that authorized Parker to undertake a survey of surviving medieval books: in the letter (probably drafted by Parker himself), the archbishop is charged with seeking out "such historical matters and *monuments of antiquity*" deemed important "both for the state ecclesiastical and civil government" (my emphasis).[31] As "monuments of antiquity," books became worthy of preservation, in other words, to the extent that they could be shown to bear a palpable link to the past. By extension, that link made the library a defining institution for the Tudor state.

Understood as a site of national identity, the library became an object of antiquarian desire in the generations after the dissolution. Bale was an early champion for a library system that could centralize the former holdings of the monasteries in the service of the state, advocating that "one sole[m]pne lybrary" be established in "euery shire of Englande [dedicated] to the preseruacyon of those noble workes, and preferrement of good lernynges in oure posteryte" (Bi r). Similarly, in the reign of Mary Tudor, John Dee carried on Bale's theme by lamenting the "destruction of so many and so notable Libraries, wherin laye the seat of all Antiquities," and he petitioned for the foundation of a "Library Royall" to preserve such "Antiquities," citing the example of "all the famose & worthy Monuments that are in the notablyest libraryes, beyonde the sea as in Vaticana of Rome S. Marc of Venise [etc.]."[32] In this, Dee aligns himself with the Italian humanists, for whom the Vatican library formed a center of intellectual activity, as well as suggesting to the Catholic Mary that a state library could revive and continue the religious traditions extirpated by the dissolution.[33] Mary ignored the proposal for a state library, but the idea was taken up again by the group of antiquarians who petitioned Elizabeth I to "preserve divers old books concernynge matter of hystorye of this Realm [such as] originall charters and monuments in a library" and who thus explicitly understood the library's significance as historical and political rather than religious: "This library to be intituled, the Library of Queene Elizabeth. and the same will be well furnished with divers Auncient books and monuments of Antiquity."[34] As employed throughout the post-Reformation discourse of library building, the term "monument" intertwines two etymologically distinct words: "monument," a memorial object, and "muniment," a written document used to defend legal rights and privileges.[35] The resulting "monument of antiquity" thus defines the library as a guardian of both heritage and inheritance while creating the English past as a primarily archival entity.

But making a case for the library that they desired required Protestant bibliophiles like Bale and Parker to define the preservation of books as a highly selective practice. Parker admits that not all books in the monastic libraries deserve preservation:

> If the Bishop of Rome's Laws, Decrees, Decretals, Extravagants, Clemen-
> tines, and other such Dregs of the Devil; yea, of Heytesburie's Sophismes,
> Porphyrie's Universals, Aristotle's old Logicks, and Dunse's Divinity,
> with such other lowsie Legerdemains, and Fruits of the bottomless Pit,
> had leaped out of our Libraries, and so become coverings for Books, com-
> ing from the foreign Nations, we might well have been therewith con-
> tented. But to put our antient Chronicles, our noble Histories, our learned
> Commentaries, and Homilies upon the Scriptures, to so homely an Of-
> fice of Subjection and utter contempt, we have both greatly dishonoured
> our Nation, and also shewed our selves very wicked to Posterity.[36]

The phenomenon of manuscripts that "leaped out of our Libraries, and so become coverings for Books" describes the practice of post-Reformation sta-tioners who unbound and recycled the leaves of medieval books into bind-ings for printed books or pastedowns—which Neil R. Ker calls "the un-wanted legacy of the Middle Ages."[37] What Parker objects to here is not the destruction of manuscripts per se but the destruction of those that serve present needs: histories, chronicles, commentaries, and homilies, all of which are well represented in the Parker Library. By differentiating these from books that deserve their fate, such as the writings of the scholastics and the pope, Parker shows that the "monument of antiquity" is an exclusive, rather than inclusive, category.

In 1567, the year before the Privy Council letter charged him with "the con-servation of . . . ancient records and monuments," Matthew Parker wrote to the warden and fellows of All Souls College, Oxford, ordering them to relin-quish the contraband books that remained in their library, which he deemed "monuments of superstition": "whereas [understanding] is given that you do retain yet in your college divers monuments of superstition, which by public orders and laws of this realme ought to be abolished as derogatory to the state of religion publicly received." According to Parker, these works in-cluded three portable breviaries ("portuisses"), several psalters, mass books, "an old manual of prayer," and "a legend."[38] In distinguishing "monuments of antiquity" from "monuments of superstition," Parker's office undertook both the preservation and the suppression of books.[39]

Parker was not alone in this equivocal task of simultaneously suppressing books and preserving them. As James Simpson has observed of John Leland, the famous bibliophile was also an agent of Henry VIII: thus, at the same time that he worked to preserve monastic books, he also actively supported the forces that led to their destruction.[40] Even more directly illustrative of this paradox is the case of Sir John Prise, one of Cromwell's relations (he was married to Cromwell's niece) who was personally sent with the commissioners to suppress the monasteries, a task that his letters show he completed zestfully.[41] From Bury St. Edmunds, for example, Prise reports to Cromwell on the "vanitie and superstition" he uncovered among the monks, with whom, he reports laconically, if not euphemistically, "we did use moche diligence in our examinacion."[42] Yet while Prise's letters reveal a violent antipathy to the monasteries, Prise himself was also an avid book collector; from the very monasteries whose dissolution he oversaw, he selected books not only for his own library but also, it appears, for the royal collections.[43] Like Parker's library, Prise's library, which was later bequeathed to Hereford Cathedral Library and Jesus College, Oxford, reflects a patriotic interest in matters of church and national history.

The conservation of books both counteracted Reformation biblioclasm and occasioned further destruction in turn. According to the Protestant writer Stephen Batman, a member of Parker's household, the archbishop personally chose to preserve only a small fraction of the monastic books that were made known to him.[44] Soon after the Privy Council's charge, Batman worked as one of Parker's agents, collecting books formerly housed in monastic libraries; as Batman recounts in his own work, *The Doome Warning all Men to the Iudgemente* (1583), "Thys reuerende father by vertue of commission from oure soueraigne Queene hyr Maiestie, didde cause to be diligently gathered many bookes of Antiquitie, whiche throughe default of heede takeing, when the religious houses of the Popish were suppressed, their Libraries we almost utterly spoyled, to the great hurt and hindraunce of learning. Among whose Bookes remayned, (althoughe the moste parte according to the tyme, Superstitious and Fabulous,) yet some worthy the view and safe keeping."[45] Batman's account distinguishes the former monastic books that are "worthy the view and safe keeping" from "the moste parte" of them, which, having been written "according to the tyme, Superstitious and Fabulous," share the worst characteristics of the discredited past to which they belong. Batman's view of selective "keeping" is aligned with Parker's collecting practices. In his capacity as Parker's book-collecting agent, Batman claims to have brought the archbishop, by his own estimation, "six thousand seauen hundred Bookes, by my onely trauale, *wherof choyse being taken*, he most gratiouslye bestowed many on Corpus Christi College in Cambridge" (my emphasis).[46] Of the four hundred and thirty-three manuscripts in Parker's library, only two are traceable to Batman: even if his claim to have provided Parker with six thousand seven hundred books is exaggerated, it nonetheless sheds light on how very restrictive Parker's collecting activities—and how narrow the "choyse" of books—were.[47] Concerning John Leland's collecting activities, Ker observes, "Some great national store-house of ancient manuscripts may have been dreamt of by Leland, but the reality was a rather small collection of selected books, not truly of the first interest and drawn from a restricted area."[48] Yet Batman's comments make it possible to see how such a restricted collection could represent, not the failed result of a more comprehensive aim, a "small collection" where a "great national store-house" was intended, but rather the successful outcome of a collecting effort in which restrictedness and selectivity were precisely the point. In such a model, what gave value to the books that were preserved was the very restrictiveness of the "choyse" applied to them. Some books were determined to be library-worthy, in other words, only through distinction from the many other books that were not.[49]

Reformation library making is thus aligned with, and even contingent upon, the act of library breaking. In Bale's account, Leland's "serche of lybraries" is an act of purification—one that is simultaneously conservative, in recovering the textual origins of the nation's history, and destructive, in purifying those origins of accretions of false doctrine. Thus, as Bale explains, Leland was motivated by the wish "that the scriptures of God myght therby be more purely taught then afore in the Romish popes time. Moreover, that al kyndes of wicked superstycyons, and of the sophystical doctrynes, myghte be removed hens" (Ci r). The description of Leland's purificatory act echoes Bale's own attempts to differentiate the books he calls "the profytable corne" from those he calls "the unprofytable chaffe," the "wholesome herbes" from "the unholesome wedes" (Avii v). Expressing the wish that the one would not be lost along with the other, the corn thrown out with the chaff, Bale's model of book preservation assumes that for every book to be saved, others will be destroyed: in order to separate the one from the other, it calls for a threshing.

In practice, it appears that the catalogues that Leland drew up from the monastic libraries created a template from which books were either selected or rejected for the royal collections. Leland's list of books belonging to Lincolnshire monasteries has been annotated with crosses (perhaps, it has been suggested, by the king himself) in order to distinguish books to be transferred to the royal collections: out of eighty-six books, only thirty-five were selected, leaving those that remained unmarked to an uncertain fate.[50] Those that were preserved reflect a distinct interest in historical matters: thus, authors such as William of Malmesbury and Geoffrey of Monmouth are overrepresented, as are texts relating to the pressing matters of Supremacy and royal divorce.[51] Similar inventories of other monastic libraries, such as Reading Abbey, appear to have been drawn up, also for purpose of selection.[52] As Carley notes, medieval manuscripts from at least four religious houses that found their way to the Royal Library seem to have been likewise chosen for a focus on theological and historical topics.[53]

The selection of library-worthy materials produced its own vocabulary of differentiation. Like Leland, Parker himself followed similar practices of distinction in his search for "ancient records and monuments" formerly housed in the monastic libraries, as reflected in a letter that Parker received in response to his request for information: his correspondent, Bishop Robinson, reports from Wales, "There is not in this country any monuments of antiquity left, but certain fabulous histories and that lately written."[54] Here the category of the "fabulous" distinguishes the matter of Catholic doctrine and belief from the "monuments of antiquity" recuperable for Protestant national identity; thus, Bale notes in his letter to Parker cataloguing surviving monastic books, "Joannes Rufus, a black fryer in England, wrote a lyttle boke, *de vitis Romanorum pontificum*. I haue seane an olde coppye therof at Norwich, full of newly deuysed lyes and fables."[55] But if the task of the post-Reformation library is to differentiate the "fabulous history" from the "true history," the "monument of superstition" from the "monument of antiquity," medieval book production made the separation of works of "antiquity" from those "fabulous" works of "superstition" decidedly difficult. Given the porous boundaries between historiographical and religious genres in medieval writing, the saint's legend, a genre Parker designates among the "monuments of superstition" to be purged, could be easily copied within or alongside the work of chronicle history, which post-Reformation readers like Parker deemed eminently worthy of preservation.[56]

This interpenetration of historical and "superstitious" genres and texts forced the post-Reformation reader and collector to be ever vigilant against the intrusion of erroneous matter between the covers of an otherwise-licit book (a challenge that Thomas Elyot faced when his own library fell under suspicion). Again describing Leland, Bale observes that the conservation of books facilitated his aim of purifying books from within: "He ded wele to commyt certen of those worthy workes to the kinges noble libraries to their conseruacyon, and also in reseruyng a certen of them to hym selfe, at that tyme myndynge to haue polyshed our Chronycles, by fabulouse wryters sore blemyshed" (Ciiii v). This work of "polishing" as Bale defines it—as an act of restoration that removes Catholic "blemish" and thus recovers chronicle history for Protestant use—shows that processes of selection and purification take place in Reformation libraries not only from book to book, as some are selected for preservation while others are rejected, but also within books. The troubling amalgamation of the categories "fable" and "history" causes Bale to lament, "we fynde for true hystoryes, most fryvolous fables and lyes, that we myghte the sonner by the deuyls suggestion, fall into most depe errours, and so be lost, for not beleuynge the truth" (Diiii r). The task of distinction that was germane to post-Reformation library making and aimed to separate, in Bale's words, "the profytable corne" from "the unprofytable chaffe" did not end, then, with the distinction of books from one another; rather, because of the pollution of "true hystoryes" with "most fryvolous fables and lyes," the work of distinction extended to the act of reading itself.

Bale's corn/chaff terminology not only authorizes the destruction of the monastic libraries but appropriates and refigures the central terms of medieval reading as defined by *allegoresis*. According to Augustine's well-known elaboration in *On Christian Doctrine*, "the letter covers the spirit as the chaff covers the grain. But to eat the chaff is to be a beast of burden, to eat the grain is to be human. He who uses human reason, therefore, will cast aside the chaff and hasten to eat the grain of the spirit. For this reason it is useful that the mystery be covered in the wrapping of the letter."[57] For Augustine the metaphor implies the need to move from literal level to spiritual meaning. Following such a model, *allegoresis* designated *fabula*, the "poetic fiction," as the *integumentum* or husk to be penetrated through attentive reading, to arrive at the truth.[58] In this scheme, the "fabulous" represents an outer covering for a hidden truth, as the author of the *Ovid moralisé* asserts, "sous la fable gist couverte/la sentence plus profitable" (beneath the fable, the most profitable meaning lies hidden).[59] By reading *fabula* as integument, *allegoresis* preserves the category of the fabulous; as Rita Copeland points out, its effect is to allow texts that do not outwardly conform to orthodoxy to be read: "such exegesis does not discard the given text once its truths have been delivered up. Instead, it invests the given text with a new tropological significance (as integument)."[60]

By contrast, Bale's suspicion of "the fabulous"—shared by his fellow library makers Leland and Parker—materializes the Reformation critique of *allegoresis*, which is articulated by William Tyndale in his *Obedience of a Christian Man* as an attack against what he calls "chopological sophisters."[61] For Tyndale *allegoresis* reduces all writing—from poetry to

scripture—to the status of fable, as he retorts in what appears to be a reference to the *Ovid moralisé*, "Yea, thou shalt find enough that will preach
Christ, and prove whatsoever point of the faith that thou wilt, as well out
of a fable of Ovid or any other poet, as out of St. John's gospel or Paul's epis-
tles."[62] Against *allegoresis* and its insistence on multiple layers of meaning,
Tyndale asserts "that the scripture hath but one sense, which is the literal
sense."[63] The need to preserve the primacy of scripture over other kinds of
writing led to the degradation of "the fabulous" as a catchall for describing
all medieval religious genres. Thus, George Puttenham was able to observe
of the Middle Ages that "[in] registring of lyes was the clergy of that fabulous
age wholly occupied."[64] Similarly, Francis Bacon describes the Reformation
as a process of enlightenment through which "error in ecclesiastical history"
such as "reports and narrations of miracles wrought by martyrs, hermits, or
monks of the desert, and other holy men, and their relics, shrines, chapels,
and images" came to be recognized and discredited as "old wives' fables."[65]

When "the fabulous" was seen not as the *integumentum* of truth but
as a dangerous perversion of it, it became possible to argue, as Bale does,
for the necessity of stripping libraries of their fabulous accretions in order
to preserve the "profytable corn" alone. This Reformation compulsion to
separate the "true hystorye" from the "most fryvolous fables and lies"—
and to preserve the former by extirpating the latter—generated in turn new
material reading practices. Where medieval *allegoresis* produced distinctive
technologies of reading in the form of marginal commentary, Reformation
reading produced new glossing practices of its own that were dedicated
to rooting out the "fryvolous fables and lies" that Bale insists pervert the
"truth" of Protestant universal history. Bale's theory becomes method in a
book that he appears to have owned, later acquired by Parker for his own
library. Corpus Christi College, Cambridge, MS 43 is a fourteenth-century
manuscript miscellany of mostly chronicles and historical materials that begins with William of Malmesbury's *De gestis pontificum Anglorum*.[66] Like
another copy of Malmesbury's *De gestis* in the Royal Library, the Corpus
Christi College book is filled with sixteenth-century annotations—many
of which belong to Parker and his secretary, John Joscelyn—that reflect an
interest in issues concerning papal authority of relevance to contemporary
events in Henrician reform. But one note appears in a different hand, which
appears to be Bale's own.[67] Following Malmesbury's text is a shorter document entitled "Tractatus de visione monachi Eveshamie anno do[mini] 1196."
This "Vision of the Monk of Eynsham" describes a vision of St. Nicholas experienced by Edmund, a monk of Evesham, in which Purgatory and Paradise
were revealed and explained to him. As proof of the vision's veracity, its

copyist, one Adam of Evesham, cites the fact that the sickly Edmund was miraculously cured of a long-standing illness. The work was widely circulated and was not uncommonly inserted into chronicles under the year 1196, thus demonstrating the medieval classification of visions and miracles as potential species of historical writing.[68] In Corpus Christi College, Cambridge, MS 43 it has been incorporated into a chronicle to represent an apparently historical event. However, the copy that reached the Parker Library is annotated in what appears to be Bale's characteristically spindly hand, labeling it a "false and fabulous vision" ("visio fallax et fabulosa"; fol. 120r). While the text itself calls on revelation and miracle as evidence of its veracity, by the Reformation such categories were consigned to the category of the "false and fabulous."

Bale's annotation "purifies" the chronicle by setting the false and fabulous apart from the "true history" in which it is embedded. Similarly, a manuscript owned by Prise now housed in the British Library contains both chronicle histories and a shorter text "on the life, miracles, and translation of St. Thomas of Canterbury." While the histories are largely unadorned with marginal notes, the shorter legend of St. Thomas is copiously annotated in notes from Prise's own hand that contest its version of the history and dismiss its subject as "a stynkyng martyr."[69] Prise's annotation practice, like Bale's, is meant to distinguish the false from the true and thus reveals books to be the sources simultaneously of history and of history's corruption.

The marginal glosses with which Bale and Prise amend their manuscripts exemplify, I am arguing, a distinctly post-Reformation approach to the uneasy textual legacy that was salvaged from the monasteries. The same is true of the marginal glosses that Stephen Batman, Parker's indefatigable agent, left in his own manuscripts.[70] As well as selecting manuscripts to be presented to Parker—and possibly from those the archbishop rejected—Batman selected medieval books for his own collection, many of them devotional texts in Middle English of the Carthusian variety favored by More.[71] Batman's annotations reveal that he read them closely and, in so doing, grappled with the same problem that troubled his fellow book collectors: amid the textual remains of monastic literary culture, what was worth preserving, and how was it to be preserved? In a manuscript of *The Pricking of Love*, an English translation of the popular medieval devotional text *Stimulus amoris*, Batman reflects at length on the problem (fig. 5):

In mani placis of this stimulus amoris this pricke of Love are veraye good & sounde documents of scripture, and what the rest are consider the tyme. He is no wyse man [tha]t for the haveng of spiders. scorpions.

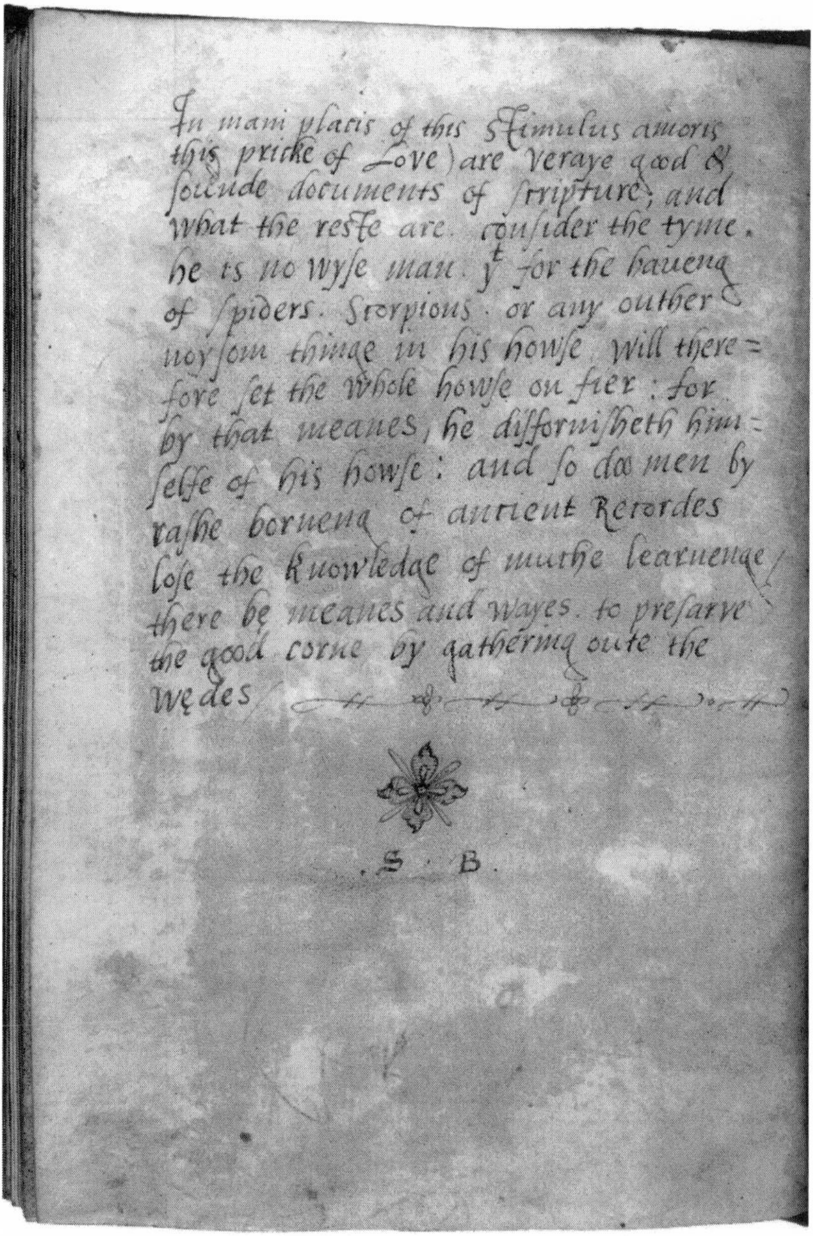

In mani placis of this Stimulus amoris
this pricke of Love) are veraye good &
sollude documents of scripture; and
what the reste are. consider the tyme.
he is no wyse man. y^t for the hauenq
of spiders. Scorpions. or any outher
noysom thinge in his howse. will there=
fore set the whole howse on fier: for
by that meanes, he disformisheth him=
selfe of his howse: and so do men by
rashe borneng of antient Recordes
lose the knowledge of muthe learnenge/
there be meanes and wayes. to presarve
the good corne by gatherinq oute the
wedes

S . B .

Fig. 5. Stephen Batman's annotation on *Stimulus amoris* (reprinted by permission of
the Masters and Fellows, Trinity College, Cambridge, MS B.14.19, fol. 67v)

or outher noysom thinge in his howse will therefore set the whole howse
on fier: for by that meanes, he disfornisheth himselfe of his howse: and
so doo men by rashe borneng of ancient Recordes lose the knowledge of
muche lernenge / there be meanes and wayes to presarve the good corne
by gathering oute the wedes.[72]

Insisting that there remain things of value in even so objectionable a text
as *Stimulus amoris*, one of the texts More singled out for praise in his re-
futation of Tyndale, Batman refers to the parable of the wheat and the tares
in Matthew 13.29–30: "lest while ye gather up the tares, ye root up also the
wheat with them. Let both grow together until the harvest: and in the time
of harvest I will say to the reapers, Gather ye together first the tares, and
bind them in bundles to burn them: but gather the wheat into my barn."
Batman's meaning—that good matter can be gleaned from otherwise-bad
books—echoes Bale's on the need to distinguish the "profytable corn" of
historical truth from the "unprofytable chaffe" of superstition. Insisting that
"there be meanes and wayes to presarve the good corne by gathering oute the
wedes," Batman imagines a harvest undertaken through the act of reading.

Like Bale, Batman uses his annotations to develop a theory and practice
of reading that reverse the devotional literacies that are elaborated in and
around the very same medieval books that he annotates. The same *Stimulus amoris* on which Batman exercises his pen is a guide to a contemplative
practice that is grounded in reading, addressing itself to "ho-so hath grace
for to ransake hooli writte. and grave aftir wisdom with bysynesse of studie"
and promising that "he shal mow fynde in hit swetnesse of deuotioun and
fedyng of his soule."[73] The devotional practice of "ransacking Holy Writ" retains the original meaning of "ransaken," to search for something hidden or
stolen, by seeking the lesson of the Passion even in texts in which it appears
hidden, such as when it is "hidde in figure & in shadow of Þe olde testament."[74] This process of ransacking the text, through meditation, to reach
its hidden meaning is justified through the tenet of *meditari aut legere* that
defined the monastic *lectio divina*.[75] *Scala claustralium* (1150; translated in
the late fourteenth century into Middle English as *The Laddyr of Cloystreris*
or *A Ladder of Foure Ronges by the Which Men Mowe Clyme to Heven*),
by the Carthusian Guigo II, articulates the founding principles of monastic *lectio*.[76] Reading, or "lesson," formed the first rung of a ladder of four
rungs (reading, meditation, prayer, and contemplation) reaching toward contemplative knowledge: "Lesson sekyth, Meditacion fyndith, Orison askith,
Contemplacion felith . . . Lesson puttyth as it were hole mete to Þe mouth;
Meditacion chewith & brekith it; prayere fyndith savoure. Contemplacion

is the liking swettnes that so myche comfortith./Lesson is wiÞoutforth in the barke. Meditacion is wiÞynforth in the pythe."[77] Guigo's hermeneutic model owes its layering of inside and outside, shell and nut ("barke" and "pythe"), to Augustinian *allegoresis*, which moves through the word's shell to arrive at the nut of meaning. It rests on the idea that, through meditative reading, all texts can be reconciled to an ultimate meaning, *caritas*. In common with his *Stimulus amoris*, Batman also undertakes a hermeneutic ransacking; but instead of reconciling texts through meditation, his relies on selective appropriation, the extraction of "good & sounde documents of scripture" from "the rest."

Batman elaborates his reading method in annotations to another copy of *Stimulus amoris* that he owned, which note, "Many thinges following/ar supersticius: yet some/thinges worthie kepenge." And he follows the text with this admonitory verse:

> Thowgh some thing in thys booke
>   Be rude and of smaule price
> Some other thinges are goode
>   And pleasure maye the wyce [i.e., "wise"]

> The best with [th]e Bee
>   So gather the sweete
> The euel thow shalte see
>   From thenc ye maiste fleete.[78]

If these annotations allow that some medieval texts yield worthy matter to discerning readers, they also follow Bale and Prise by insisting that other texts, or parts of texts, are fit only to be discarded: thus, Batman notes at the beginning of a popular medieval penitential work, *Psalterium sancti hieronymi*, "Here is to be senne the ignorance of tyme past/Praie that soche tyme be neuer a gayne," while in his copy of the *Ancrene wisse*, Batman labels one section of the text a "fabula vana."[79]

Batman advocates a process of reading that distills truthful from superstitious matter through the application of "reason," as Batman counsels when he inscribes his *Ancrene wisse* with this gloss:

> *Let reason Rule the,* [that] this booke shall reede:
> Muche good matter shalt thow finde in deede/
> Thowghe some bee ill, doo not the rest dispize
> Consider of the tyme, else thow art not wize. (My emphasis)[80]

Batman's "reasonable" reading advocates a level of historical detachment toward medieval books. Unlike other Protestant readers—"Frantik braines" who would destroy any apparently "papisticall" book, as Batman notes in a manuscript of *Piers Plowman*—Batman reads selectively for "thinges worthie kepenge."[81] But harvesting these also involves "gathering oute the wedes," a process that his annotations both describe and perform.

Although the marginal annotations of Bale, Prise, and Batman visually recall the glosses that monastic readers left in the margins of their books, they were employed toward antimonastic ends. Bale, Prise, and Batman were not alone in this: as Anthony Grafton has shown, Italian humanists explicitly rejected the textual practices of scholastic readers, claiming that their glosses represented "a visual as well as an intellectual distortion of [the books'] content"; yet humanists developed their own glossing practices that were no less motivated by contemporary concerns.[82] When Florentine republicans hoped to trace a direct line of inheritance to republican Rome, the study of old texts became a means of establishing this connection. But the genealogy could be established only by "purifying" the ancient texts of what was seen to be the corruption introduced by scribes in those texts' later circulation: thus, as Stephanie Jed argues, "in order to verify the uninterrupted descent of Florence from Republican Rome, it became a moral imperative to purify the texts dealing with this issue of accumulated errors. To liberate the ancient texts of corruption was to restore integrity to the Florentine republican identity."[83] As Jed shows, the word with which the textual scholars described their work was "castigare," to chasten, both punishing and purifying, to make chaste. Thus, genealogical purity was created through textual purity. Similarly for Bale and Prise, who also sought to establish national origins from the evidence of old books, the annotating pen becomes a chastening scourge.[84]

But if marginal annotation like Bale's or Batman's is meant to "purify" the recovered monastic library books by separating the fabulous from the true, it also testifies to the persistence of the one alongside, and indeed within, the other. The post-Reformation library reveals "monuments of antiquity" to be inseparable from "monuments of superstition," as is the "true hystorye" from the "fabulous"—a point witnessed by Bale's own manuscript, Corpus Christi College, Cambridge, MS 43, which, despite the presence of the "visio fallax et fabulosa," found its way into the Parker Library. Indeed, Parker himself admits in the preface to Thomas of Walsingham's *Historia brevis*, which he edited from a manuscript in his library, that in the process of preserving "antique histories," he could not help but preserve in their midst "some monastic fragments or rather old wives' fables" introduced by their monkish writers.[85]

The task of distinguishing "true hystorye" from "fabulous" was never-ending, not just because of the intrusion of Catholic "fable" into the sources of "antique history" but because of the notorious instability of British antiquity itself, starting with its founding figure: King Arthur. Despite Arthur's importance to national identity, even his stalwart champions were forced to admit that they could not easily distinguish fact from fiction when it came to determining his historicity.[86] As William Caxton admitted of Arthur in the prologue to his 1485 edition of the *Morte dArthur*, "dyuers men holde oppynyon that there was no such Arthur, and that alle suche bookes as been maad of hym ben but fayned and fables."[87] For Caxton, however, the story of Arthur does not need to be true to be valuable, and he instructs his readers to follow his lead in suspending their judgment: "For to gyue fayth and byleve that al is trewe that is conteyned herin, ye be at your lyberte. But al is wryten for our doctryne."[88] He here invokes St. Paul from Romans 15.4: "Whatever was written in former days was written for our instruction." This was one of the key texts for medieval theories of *allegoresis*—the same that Chaucer invokes at the end of *The Nun's Priest's Tale* to defend his use of fable: "For Seint Paul seith that al that writen is,/To oure doctrine it is ywrite, ywis;/Taketh the fruyt, and lat the chaf be still."[89] In contrast to these Pauline justifications of the fable, following the Reformation's rejection of *allegoresis* and the reading practices it supported, the story of Arthur, in order to be preserved, needed to be proven true. Arthur became a crucial figure for post-Reformation library makers, whose search for evidence of Arthur's historicity is reflected in the numerous annotations in Parker Library manuscripts to passages relevant to Arthurian matter, such as occur in Parker manuscripts of William of Malmesbury and Matthew Paris.[90] The same desire accompanied Leland in his search of monastic libraries; but if, as Bale writes, that search was motivated by the hope "to have polyshed our chronycles, by fabulous wryters sore blemyshed," telling fable from chronicle in the case of Arthur was no easy task.

Arthurian history received its most devastating blow from Polydore Vergil, whose *Historia Anglicana* (1534) dismissed histories of Arthur as mere "feining" and "things to be laughed at."[91] Leland sought to defend the Arthurian history against Vergil in his *Assertio inclytissimi Arturii regis Britanniae* (1544) and was joined in this enterprise by John Prise, who wrote a defense of the British matter, *Historiae Brytannicae defensio*, published posthumously by his son in 1573.[92] But in the process of defending Arthur as a historical figure, both Prise and Leland were forced to acknowledge that not all sources of Arthurian history were credible. Prise conceded that some accounts of Arthur were as mythical as those of Hercules, but he insisted that these did not make British history itself "groundless, fictious, or false."[93] The point is similar to one made by Leland, when he insists that, in order to arrive at the truth of British history, fictitious elements must be distinguished from truthful ones and eliminated:

> It appeareth most evidently, that both obscure and absurde reportes have crept into the historie of Arthure.... But this in deede is not a cause sufficient iust, why any man should neglect, abiect, or deface the Historie otherwise of it selfe, lightsome and true. How much better is it (casting awaye trifles, cutting off olde wiues tales, and superfluous fables, in deede of stately porte in outwarden shew, but nothing auayleable vnto credite, beeing taken away) to reade, scanne vpon, and preserve in memorie those things which are consonant by Authorytie.[94]

Recalling Bale on the need to separate "profytable corne" from "unprofytable chaffe," Leland advocates the production of historical truth through a process of selection and distinction whose result is "memorie."

The model of reading and memory production that Leland develops here pointedly rewrites the monastic *lectio divina*, which aimed at the refinement of memory through what Mary Carruthers calls *meditatio*'s "process of memory-training, storage, and retrieval."[95] For, as Jean Leclerq observes, "to meditate is to read a text and to learn it 'by heart' in the fullest sense of this expression, that is, with one's whole being: with the body, since the mouth pronounces it, with the memory which fixes it, with the intelligence which understands its meaning, and with the will which desires to put it into practice."[96] If memory was the product of monastic *lectio divina*, the monastic library became its factory, supplying the books that *lectio divina* made into the necessary fuel for contemplative practice.[97]

In contrast, where the *memoria* of *lectio divina* internalizes its textual objects, for Leland the actions that compose the reading process—"to reade, scanne upon, and preserve in memorie"—work by "casting awaye trifles, cutting off olde wiues tales, and superfluous fables." Leland's memory *preserves* by *casting away* and *cutting off*; its integrity is determined as much by what it excludes as by what it takes in. In place of Caxton's allegorical reading of Arthur, Leland's defense of the Arthurian matter produces a *modus legendi* for the post-Reformation library. If the library is built through "choyse being taken" (to recall Batman's description of Matthew Parker's collecting practices) that distinguishes the "monument of antiquity" from the "monument of superstition," the act of reading internalizes this selective process to the faculty of memory. But the ongoing need for such selectivity on the part of the individual reader registers the failure of post-Reformation collectors ever fully to separate truth from fable, antiquity from superstition; as long as these materials remain intertwined in the post-Reformation library, the act of reading itself must continually repeat the acts of selection and distinction that the book collector initiated but could not finish and thereby ensure the complete elimination of the "fabulous."

Like Leland, Parker's associates Prise and Batman also reform memory and the reading processes that produce it by reshaping the libraries on which they depend. In place of monastic reading that reconciles diverse texts to a unifying truth, they subject medieval books to a process of distinction aimed at separating truth from falsehood, and history from fable. Thus, the same books that were the objects of monastic meditation become the objects of post-Reformation castigation. *Lectio divina* gives way to what we might call a *lectio* of suspicion.[98] If *lectio divina* produces, and ultimately takes shape in, the memory of the individual monastic reader, the memory produced through the reformed *lectio* of the Parker circle represents not so much a positive recovery and preservation as the perpetual apprehension and castigation of error.

Spenser's Library of Memory

Edmund Spenser's time at Cambridge coincided with the formation of Parker's library there, and his writings reveal literary affiliations with Parker's circle that inform, I will argue, the ethos of reading he develops in *Faerie Queene*, book 2. Richard Robinson, who translated Leland's *Assertio inclytissimi Arturii regis Britanniae* (1544) as *A Learned and True Assertion of the Original Life, Actes, and Death of the most Noble, Valiant, and Renoumed Prince Arthur* (London, 1582), dedicated the work to Spenser's patron, Arthur Lord Grey de Wilton, thereby associating him with the Elizabethan Arthurians in Parker's circle.[99] Spenser shared Lord Grey's interest in Arthur, whom he brings to life in *The Faerie Queene*, as well as Robinson's specifically antiquarian perspective on Arthur, a perspective that Robinson's *Assertion* links to the Parker circle; not only was the *Assertion* written by "the learned English Antiquarie of worthy memory Iohn Leyland," as Robinson's translation declares, it is prefaced by a note that Robinson claims to have arrived at "by conference with Master Steuen Batman, a learned Preacher and friendlie fauourer of vertue and learning (touching the praise worthie progenie of this K. Arthur)."[100] Citing evidence "taken out of [Batman's] Auncient records written at Aualonia" and "Verses found in certaine Cronicles," Robinson identifies Batman as his authority for tracing Arthur's genealogy back to Joseph of Arimathea; moreover, he claims, Batman "shewed me out of his auncient records the interchaunges of king Arthures armes" from a "booke... in an English mans handes" who "willingly shewed it & lent it me."[101] As the source of Arthurian genealogical knowledge deriving from "Auncient records" and books, Robinson's Batman is a true denizen of Memory's Library, with its "old records from auncient times deriv'd" and textual trove of Arthurian history (Faerie Queene, 2.9.57).

Batman's connection with Spenser's library may be closer still: Batman's own long poem The Travayled Pylgrime (1569)—according to Ann Lake Prescott, "England's only significant nondramatic Protestant quest allegory before Spenser"—appears to be a source for The Faerie Queene.[102] The thematic parallels between the works are compelling: like Spenser's protagonist in book 2, Batman's takes guidance from an allegorical figure of Memory, who is, like Spenser's, a guardian of British history. Batman's Memory presents that history in a distinctly post-Reformation mode, celebrating Henry VIII's victory over the pope, when he "puld the Abbeys downe / And spoyled the Romishe lubbers all, which lurckte in every towne," and praising Edward VI, who "purged the Englisshe church" and "the bookes of God he made be read... / The which Antichrist the Pope had hid long time and rent."[103] And while Batman's Memory is the guardian not of a library but of a cemetery, Batman's protagonist prefigures Spenser's Guyon and Arthur when he is conducted into the House of Reason's Room of Knowledge "with characters straunge & pictures wrought" (Diiv) in which he is shown "things of worthie Memorie, which long agoe hath beene" (Ei).

If Spenser owes his bookish, Protestant Arthur to Batman and Leland, Spenser's broader intellectual associations with the Parker circle are reflected in the ethos of reading that he develops in The Faerie Queene. The emergence of a post-Reformation reading practice that aimed to separate (Protestant) "plain truth" from (Catholic) "feigned fable" underlies the defensiveness with which Spenser explains his decision to make allegory the mode of The Faerie Queene. In his introductory "Letter to Raleigh," Spenser admits, "to some I know the Methode will seem displeasant, which had rather haue good discipline delivered plainly in way of precepts, or sermoned at large, as they use, then thus clowdily enwrapped in Allegorical deuises" (737). In the English Renaissance allegory shifted venue from monastery to court—a move enabled in no small part by George Puttenham—but the problems of knowledge and interpretation that allegory raised were still theorized in theological terms, hence allegory's opposition, for Spenser, to the "sermon" as the place of "plain" speaking and "discipline."[104] For the Protestant writer after Tyndale, employing allegory meant courting the charge of willful falsification or obscurity, a charge that Spenser takes up directly in his proem to book 2. At the outset, the proem expresses the concern

> That all this famous antique history,
> Of some th'aboundance of an idle braine
> Will iudged be, and painted forgery,
> Rather then matter of iust memory. (2.proem.1)

Recalling the Reformation critique of allegorical reading along with Bale's earlier distinction between "true hystoryes" worthy of preservation and "most fryvolous fables and lyes" that need to be cast aside (Diiii r), Spenser anticipates that his own poem will be subjected to a similar judgment that uplifts "matter of iust memory" while casting down "painted forgery." Likewise, the proem's anxious meditation on how the poem "will iudged be" reflects an awareness of the reading process as directed at separating the true from the false. In so doing, book 2 offers itself as both diagnosis of and solution to what I will argue is a distinctly post-Reformation problem of knowledge production.

With this focus, I reconsider what the Reformation meant to those like Spenser who lived in the generation after Henry VIII. While Spenser's readers have long seen book 2 as a work deeply concerned with the Reformation, they have focused on the climactic destruction of the Bower of Bliss, frequently taking it as an allegory of dissolution era iconoclasm.[105] By shifting the locus of book 2's Reformation concerns to the library of Eumnestes, my reading shifts the defining act of the Reformation from iconoclasm to biblioclasm, an act that both inspired the work of post-Reformation book collectors and continually haunted their efforts.[106] As book 2 shows, the dissolution's longest-lasting creation was a dialectic of remembering and forgetting that began in the library.

The judicial reading process that is described in book 2's proem is anatomized in cantos 9 and 10, which depict the culminating stage of Guyon's and Arthur's visit to the Castle of Alma. Alma's castle renders the human body as an architectural space of which the brain is the uppermost turret, which Spenser divides into the three chambers of Imagination, Reason, and Memory. Following Aristotle, a similar division of the brain was widely adopted in medieval and Renaissance theories of the mind.[107] But for Spenser, this three-chambered brain gives bodily form to the material practices of reading and distinction that I have identified with library building in the wake of the dissolution, while locating them, literally, "deepe within the mynd" (6.proem .5) of the anatomized subject.[108] Most resonantly for our purposes, the third chamber, Memory, takes the shape of a library, in which Guyon and Arthur lose themselves reading the above-mentioned books of national memory, *Briton moniments* and *Antiquitie of Faerie lond*. If, as I have argued above, the post-Reformation reshaping of the library extended to the acts of reading that took place within it, here the library, displaced to the interior of the brain, displays its power to reshape the reader at the level of cognition itself.

Memory, as the library presents it, is infinite: Eumnestes (Good Memory), the librarian-scribe, is a "man of infinite remembrance," who preserves the written records of the past in his "immortal scrine," which is at once archive, shrine, and skull (9.56).[109] The infinitude of memory in this library, as becomes clear, is not to be confused with the kind of comprehensiveness dreamed of by Petrarch when he describes his own library as a "thesaurus," a great storehouse reflecting in its encyclopedia-like ambition of scope, as Armando Petrucci observes, a "universal conception of written culture."[110] To the contrary, Eumnestes' "remembrance," like that of his library, is "infinite" to the extent that it lacks limits. It cannot be bounded, because it will never achieve—and does not aim for—comprehensiveness. Instead, it manifests the very incoherence that is the hallmark of Spenserian allegory, of which Jonathan Goldberg observes that "its very endless quality denies hermeneutic closure."[111] This resistance to closure is embodied in *Briton moniments* and *Antiquitie of Faerie lond* themselves, whose very endlessness makes them exemplars for *The Faerie Queene*.

Briton moniments, the book in Eumnestes' library that appears to choose its reader Arthur rather than the reverse, is incomplete because it is unfinished. Like many of the "monuments of antiquity" collected by post-Reformation library makers such as Sir John Prise and Matthew Parker, it compiles historical matter from chronicle histories such as Geoffrey of Monmouth's in order to trace an elaborate prehistory of the British monarchy. But when it comes to the story of Arthur himself, it stops abruptly. Following an account of Arthur's father, Uther Pendragon,

> There abruptly it did end,
> Without full point, or other Cesure right,
> As if the rest some wicked hand did rend,
> Or th'Authour selfe could not at least attend
> To finish it. (2.10.68)

The gap in the record at precisely the moment of Arthur's expected appearance reflects the instability of the written record around the question of Arthur. That the book stops without "Cesure"—caesura—highlights one of the objections raised against Geoffrey of Monmouth, whose version of the British matter was damagingly perceived to differ from the one advanced in Julius Caesar's authoritative historical writings.[112] If the lack of "Cesure" here points to the incoherence of the historical record, the record's "abrupt" end—a new word Spenser employs to mean brokenness or rupture—indicates its material instability: "as if the rest some wicked hand did rend."

Hands rending texts fill the literary subconscious of the post-Reformation era. Yet such rending was not confined to either friends or enemies of British history: while Leland decries those who would "neglect, abiect, or deface the [British] History," he defends the importance of "casting awaye trifles, cutting off olde wives tales, and superfluous fables" in search of truth and thus advocates a reading that produces rupture as much as it repairs it. To which rending hand has Arthur's own story been lost? While Prise and Leland advocate a selective approach to Arthurian history in order to preserve authentic records of Arthur's historicity, a marginal note in Bale's *Scriptorum illustrium maioris Brytanniae catalogus* accuses Polydore Vergil of destroying records that did not accord with his own conviction of Arthur's fictitiousness: "Polydore Vergilius . . . had the randsackings of all the Englishe lybraryes, and when he had extracted what he pleased he burnt those famouse velome manuscripts, and made himself father to other mens workes."[113] This description of Vergil "randsacking" "all the Englishe lybraryes" both recalls and rewrites the hermeneutic "ransacking" advocated in the *Stimulus amoris*: "ho-so hath grace for *to ransake* hooli writte. and grave aftir wisdom with bysynesse of studie . . . shal mow fynde in hit swetnesse of deuotioun and fedyng of his soule" (my emphasis).[114] If "ransacking" is the foundation of *lectio divina*, Vergil transforms it, via Bale's annotator, into the basis of a *lectio* of selective and destructive appropriation—which, to be sure, could just as easily describe the methods of Reformation era book collectors like Bale, Prise, Leland, and Parker, whose preservation of "monuments of antiquity" called for eradicating "fables and lies." Spenser's silence about the identity of the hand that rent Arthur's history suggests that it might have belonged to either camp.

Whether it is the textual victim of an unjust act of censorship or the purified object of an act of correction, the ruptured record is, unexpectedly, a source not of trauma but of "secret pleasure," as Arthur finds:[115]

that so vntimely breach
The Prince him selfe halfe seemd to offend,
Yet secret pleasure did offence empeach,
And wonder of antiquitie long stopt his speach. (2.10.68)

By its end (or, more precisely, lack thereof), *Briton moniments* reduces
Arthur to wonder-filled silence. Arthur's response recalls Spenser's earlier
discussions of "antiquitie." After book 2's proem anxiously wonders how
The Faerie Queene "will iudged be"—whether "painted forgery" or "iust
memory"—it articulates the poem's principal challenge, to discover how
to "vouch antiquities, which no body can know" (2.proem.1). While for
Bale and Parker the "monument of antiquity" was grounded in the antiquity's unquestioned authenticity, Spenser embraces the uncertainty of post-
Reformation knowledge production, which produces an endless process of
differentiation without a positive object. In his effort to "vouch antiquities,
which no body can know," Spenser implies that the "antiquity" represents
the limits of knowledge rather than its basis.

Similarly, in Eumnestes' library "antiquity" is marked by gaps and rup-
tures.[116] However, the absence of positive knowledge produces "wonder,"
a term that had accumulated an array of meanings in the sixteenth century. Where medieval wonder, as Carolyn Bynum points out, marks the
encounter with phenomena that are not understood, early modern wonder
was transplanted to the wonder-cabinet (cabinet of curiosities) or the encyclopedia, where it was an instigation to knowledge.[117] Arthur's experience
in the library supports Lorraine Daston's and Katharine Park's contention
that wonders captivated medieval and early modern subjects because they
were "markers of the outermost limits of what they knew, who they were,
or what they might become."[118] But rather than a "seed of knowledge" (as
Bacon called wonder), Arthur's wonder resides in the unknowable.[119] His
"wonder of antiquitie" defies discursive or rational explanation—it "long
stopt his speach"—because, unlike the knowledge-producing objects of the
wonder-cabinet, the textual objects of the library, the "antiquities, which
no body can know," cannot be known fully. They defy knowledge because,
like Arthur's ruptured book, they are fragments of a lost whole; yet Arthur's
response, his "secret pleasure," suggests that he experiences the unknowable not as an absence to be filled but as a source of pleasure in itself. By
extension, the pleasure of the library—its production of wonder—comes not
from its comprehensiveness but from its incompletion.

If the Spenserian library calls attention to the perennially fragmentary,
incomplete nature of the post-Reformation archive, that very incompleteness

forms the basis of a new literary aesthetic, one that favors silences and gaps over comprehensiveness and totality. Arthur's "secret pleasure" over the gap in the record reinscribes an aesthetic of incompleteness that runs throughout *The Faerie Queene*. As Jonathan Goldberg has pointed out, in other textual moments in the poem incompleteness generates narrative: "leaving an ending 'to be perfected' in 'another place'; the fundamental quality, as the narrator calls it, is 'endlesse worke.'"[120] The book that picks up where Arthur's leaves off, Guyon's *Antiquitie of Faerie lond*, is literally such an endless work, since, as we learn, it has no end:

> But Guyon all this while his booke did read,
> Ne yet has ended: for it was a great
> And ample volume, that doth far excead
> My leasure, so long leaves here to repeat. (2.10.70)

Antiquitie of Faerie lond recounts a legendary British history that begins with Prometheus and proceeds, through the mythical lineage of Elves and "Faeryes" (2.10.71), to the exotic lands of India, America, and finally "Cleopolis," the seat of Gloriana, the Faerie Queene herself.[121] India and America are earlier linked to Faeryland in the opening of book 2, when the proem defends its project to "vouch antiquities, which no body can know" by comparing the unknown antiquity to the undiscovered country in order to ask, "Why then should witlesse man so much misweene / That nothing is, but that which he hath seene?" (2.proem.3). In the scene in Eumnestes' library, the *Antiquitie of Faerie lond* grounds the legitimacy of its allegorical landscape on its unknowability, thereby drawing a connection between the unknowable antiquity (the antiquity "which no body can know"; 2.proem.1) and the colonial category of the marvelous, which both provokes and resists the desire to know it.[122]

Rather than taking *Briton moniments* and *Antiquitie of Faerie lond* to represent opposing camps of "history" and "fiction"—as a number of previous readings have—my reading sees them as complementary halves of a Spenserian category of "memory," which is neither, strictly speaking, fictional nor historical.[123] Spenserian memory, as it is produced in Eumnestes' library, bears comparison with Pierre Nora's discussion of the differences between history, which aspires to a totalizing account of the past—"the reconstruction, always problematic and incomplete, of what is no longer"—and memory, the ever-shifting forms of human understanding through which the past is experienced and given shape: "Memory is always a phenomenon of the present, a bond tying us to the eternal present; history is a representation

of the past. Memory, being a phenomenon of emotion and magic, accom-
modates only those facts that suit it.... It is vulnerable to transferences,
screen memories, censorings, and projections of all kinds."[124] In a similar
vein, Michel de Certeau observes, "Memory is a sort of anti-museum: it is
not localizable. Fragments of it come out in legends."[125] Memory, presented
in comparable terms in book 2's proem, is neither "famous antique history"
nor "painted forgery"; it is neither an objective representation of the past
nor an attempted misrepresentation of it. Rather, by upholding the legitimacy of "antiquities, which no body can know," the proem produces "iust
memory" as a kind of "matter" that resists positive knowledge (2.proem.1).
Guyon's *Antiquitie of Faerie lond* is a work of memory to the extent that
it operates in the realm of the marvelous (in its stories of Elves and Fairies)
and the symbolic (such as the setting of Cleopolis) and is thus, in Nora's
words, "a phenomenon of emotion and magic." Its effect is not to produce
an interpretive grid through which "real" history can be decoded, as many
of its more recent readers have discovered to their frustration, but to evoke a
degree of wonder that extends into narrative form the "secret pleasure" that
Arthur experiences at the end of *Briton moniments:* in both cases, what is
being exposed and admired represents the limits of knowledge and knowa-
bility. Together, *Briton moniments* and *Antiquitie of Faerie lond* produce
a species of memory that, like wonder, springs up in the gaps of knowledge. Where Arthur's monumental work produces "wonder" at the point of
the historical record's rupture, Guyon's book of antiquity takes up where it
leaves off by producing a seemingly inexhaustible, wonder-filled legendary
narrative, which, like the "antiquities" of the proem, "no body can know."

If Spenserian memory resembles Nora's in its opposition to a historiography "of what is no longer," it also reveals the historicity of "memory" as a
category for understanding the past.[126] Spenserian memory belongs to a historical moment after the dissolution had scattered the contents of monastic
libraries but before the construction of what Thomas Richards calls "the
imperial archive," which represented the "merger of the Victorian project
of positive knowledge with the Romantic project of comprehensive knowledge."[127] Following the Reformation, knowledge, like its textual sources,
was fragmentary rather than comprehensive; likewise, post-Reformation
memory was an unstable object to be constructed rather than a positive
vision of the past to be recovered whole—less a return of the repressed, that
is, than an act whose own repressions were only too conscious and visible.
Spenserian memory reflects this historical moment. Like the texts it com-
prises, it exists in fragments and in a perennial state of incompletion—which
is why, for Spenser, memory is a library.

At the Limits of Memory: Imagination and the Bower of Bliss

Like the post-Reformation library that I argue it echoes, Eumnestes' library is the product of a distinction or culling process that remains visible in its incomplete holdings. Just as Leland advocates a process of "casting awaye trifles, cutting off olde wiues tales, and superfluous fables" from those matters that one should "reade, scanne vpon, and preserve in memorie," so Spenser upholds the library-worthiness of *Briton moniments* and *Antiquitie of Faerie lond*—and, by extension, the category of memorial writing that they exemplify—by implicitly contrasting them with "th'aboundance of an idle braine" and "painted forgery" that book 2's proem distinguishes from "iust memory." The material that is excluded from Eumnestes' library exists on the other side of its threshold: in the forecourt of the headlike tower of the Castle of Alma, the chamber of Phantastes, the imaginative faculty, is filled with

> idle thoughts and fantasies
> Deuises, dreames, opinions unsound,
> Shewes, visions, sooth-sayes, and prophesies,
> And all that fained is, as leasings, tales, and lies. (2.9.51)

With their emphasis on imaginative feigning and deception, these "idle thoughts" directly recall the proem's anxious invocation of "th'aboundance of an idle braine" and "painted forgery" while at the same time explicitly translating that anxiety into the discursive realm of Reformation anti-Catholicism. "Opinions unsound / Shewes, visions, sooth-sayes, and prophesies" name precisely the dangerous fabrications that Protestant readers chastised in the medieval books they salvaged from the monastic libraries: thus, Bale castigates the "Vision of the Monk of Eynsham" by naming it a "visio fallax et fabulosa," just as Robert Burton's later *Anatomy of Melancholy* would debunk Catholic visions or "extasies" such as appear "in Bede and Gregory, Saint Bridgets revelations," and so forth by classifying them as "common apparitions" belonging to "the force of the imagination."[128]

For Protestant library makers, no less than for Protestant theological writers such as William Tyndale, the imagination was the realm of idolatry: thus, in *The Obedience of a Christian Man*, Tyndale insists that nothing "bringeth the wrath of God so soon and sore on a man, as the idolatry of his own imagination."[129] Excoriations of "fantasy" and "imagination" run through Protestant polemic: a work reprinted by Foxe called "The Phantasy of Idolatry" accuses papists of misleading believers with false shows;

Archbishop Cranmer attacks idolatrous "images and phantasyes"; and the iconoclastic Royal Visitor's Injunctions of Edward VI in 1547 targeted for destruction images "devysed by mennes phantasies."[130] In this Reformation discourse, the antidote to the idolatrous imagination and fantasy was memory: thus, the very injunctions that forbid the works "devysed by mennes phantasies" permit the uses of images as objects of "remembraunce, whereby, men may be admonished, of the holy lifes and conversacion of theim, that the sayd images do represent."[131] Likewise, while Cranmer dismissed idolatrous fantasy, he helped retain Holy Communion in the Protestant service by defining it as an act of "remembraunce."[132] The terms "imagination" and "memory" as Spenser anatomizes them in the Castle of Alma cannot help but recall the Reformation contexts that charged them with political, as well as religious, meaning in the sixteenth century.

What separates imagination from memory in Spenser's anatomy of mind is the middle chamber of reason or judgment, which performs a culling function, determining which thoughts are to pass from the imagination into the memory. This function is consistent with the medieval and Renaissance theories of mind that distinguish the three faculties of imagination, reason, and memory: as Stephen Batman writes in *Batman uppon Bartholome*, his 1582 translation of Bartholomaeus Anglicus's *De proprietatibus rerum*, reason performs the role of a judge: "For what the vertue imaginatiue shapeth & imagineth, she sendeth it to the iudgement of reason. And what that reason taketh of the imagination, as a Judge, iudgeth & defineth it sending to the memory."[133] Here Batman articulates a common early modern conception of memory as the product of judgment: in 1631 John Doddridge similarly calls memory "the receptacle wherein is reposed and laid up what-soever thing the Understanding hath apprehended and judged worthy of receipt or entertainment."[134] The process of judgment has an extractive function: in the Renaissance, the action that Batman assigns to reason, which "defineth," signified the power to reduce to or extract an essential nature, looking forward to a later signification, "to distinguish."[135] In describing the judging and defining actions of reason, Batman repeats the lessons from his own marginal annotations to his copy of the *Ancrene wisse*, in which he counsels:

> *Let reason Rule the*, yt this booke shall reede:
> Muche good matter shalt thow finde in deede/
> Thowghe some bee ill, doo not the rest dispise
> Consider of the tyme, else thow art not wize. (My emphasis)[136]

In the very same manuscript, Batman enacts this practice of reasonable reading by marking off a section as a "fabula vana."[137] Batman's reason-driven reading process recalls Leland's comments on his own practices as a reader, when he declares that his aim is "to reade, scanne upon, and preserve in memorie those things which are consonant with Authoritie" by "casting awaye trifles, cutting off olde wiues tales, and superfluous fables." Not only is the faculty of reason as theorized in *De proprietatibus rerum* exemplified in the selective reading practices that post-Reformation readers performed on pre-Reformation texts, but it guides the creation of the post-Reformation library. It is worth bearing in mind that the translator of *De proprietatibus rerum* was the same man who collected books for Matthew Parker, whom Batman describes in terms similar to the terms he applies to reason when he notes the archbishop's selective construction of his own library through a process of "choyse being taken."[138] Like the construction of memory, the post-Reformation library is built through a process of elimination.

In Spenser's tripartite model of the brain, the middle chamber of Judgment or Reason, which intervenes between Imagination and Memory, is represented by a room whose walls are painted with murals "of laws, or iudgments, and of decretals" (9.53) that are consistent with Batman's description of "the iudgment of reason." There its guardian exercises his sole function: to "meditate all his life long," an action that, as David Lee Miller points out, involves "the reduction of images to ideal essences."[139] As a center for extraction and purification, the chamber of Reason thus performs a digestive function similar to the stomach described in stanzas 29–31, in which nourishment is refined from waste.[140] This function both recalls and recasts "the activities of digestive meditation" that Carruthers ascribes to monastic readers who took written texts into their memories through such meditative practices.[141] Spenser's turret of the brain in the Castle of Alma takes over the activities of monastic reading by appropriating them on behalf of a decidedly antimonastic aim: the library of Memory may recall the monastic library and scriptorium, but it Protestantizes their memorial function by banishing "shewes, visions, sooth-sayes, and prophesies," as did Bale and Prise, to the realm of imagination, classifying them under the rubric of "all that fained is, as leasings, tales, and lies." This principle of refinement and purification is responsible for what I have noted above is the library's incompleteness, as exemplified in the rupture of Arthur's *Briton Moniments*. In the chamber of Reason or Judgment, in which memory is produced through the extraction and exclusion of imagination, rupture is the condition of reading. It is this process that Guyon learns in Eumnestes'

library and enacts, I want to further suggest, in the Bower of Bliss. Guyon
journeys to the bower immediately after leaving Eumnestes' library, and in
it, he puts into practice the acts of extracting, reducing, and thus distinguishing imagination from memory that are modeled in the library.[142]

The bower's presiding figure is Genius, a personification, like the Middle
English poet John Gower's Genius, of imagination.[143] But here imagination
is inflected with dangers: he "secretly doth vs procure to fall,/Through
guilefull semblaunts, which he makes vs see" (2.12.48). In its emphasis on
deceitful imaginings, Spenser's description of the bower recalls Bale's earlier fulmination against the "fryvolous fables and lyes" that mislead readers
into "depe errours": "we fynde for true hystoryes, most fryvolous fables and
lyes, that we myghte the sonner by the deuyls suggestion, fall into most depe
errours, and so be lost, for not beleuynge the truthe" (Diiii r). The Bower of
Bliss embodies the very qualities that are excluded from the library of Memory, the "idle thoughts and fantasies . . . leasings, tales, and lies" (2.9.51)—
and, by extension, the "painted forgery" and "aboundance of an idle brain"
that the proem juxtaposes with "iust memory." Where these were Catholi-
cized in the chamber of Phantastes, in the Bower of Bliss they are secularized and abstracted. As Ernest Gilman observes, the veneration of the idol
is absorbed into the Bower's "idle" pleasures.[144]

If the library of Eumnestes is a seat of memory, the Bower of Bliss is a
seat of forgetting. Its centerpiece is the postcoital pietà formed by Acrasia
and Verdant; through them, sensual surfeit, whatever its other dangers, is
shown to be specifically a threat to memory.[145] Thus, Verdant is overcome
with forgetfulness of his own origins:

> His warlike armes, the idle instruments
> Of sleeping praise, were hong vpon a tree,
> And his braue shield, full of old moniments,
> Was fowly ra'st, that none the signes might see. (2.12.80)

The "erased" monuments on Verdant's shield embody historical amnesia
and forgetting of origins. It was precisely such a forgetting that prompted
the book collectors after the Reformation to attempt to restore such "old
moniments" to legibility. For Parker's secretary Joscelyn, textual criticism
offered a way to undo this corruption: as he writes in the preface to *A
Testimonie of Antiquitie*, the texts that were recovered after the dissolution bore the marks of corruption by ignorant readers and writers. In one,
"a very auncie[n]t boke of Cannons of Worceter librarye," a key passage has
been "rased out by some reader," an action that demonstrated the negligence

of pre-Reformation religious libraries, which allowed the corruption of writ-ten "moniments" either by neglect—such as Bale charged when he accused monks of storing manuscripts "among wormes and dust" (Evii r)—or by design, as Joscelyn charges here. Yet such corruption could be corrected through textual criticism, Joscelyn holds: by comparing texts, he announces, "consider how the corruption of hym, whosoeuer he was, is bewrayed" in allowing the "rased" passage to be restored.[146] Upholding this principle, Joscelyn "corrected" numerous texts in the Parker Library, leaving copious marginal annotations and inserted passages that "bewrayed" the "corrup-tion" of his sources. The "moniments...fowly ra'st" on Verdant's shield instigate a similarly corrective effort, which I argue Guyon carries out in his destruction of the Bower of Bliss.

Guyon's response to his discovery of Verdant and Acrasia is to bind them in what Maurice Evans calls (in a term that recalls Batman) "fetters of reason."[147] He releases Verdant after delivering "counsell sage" (2.12.12), the substance of which is undisclosed, but it is perhaps embodied in the stanza that immediately follows, when Guyon applies himself to the bower. Guyon's destruction of the bower has been read as a scene of iconoclastic fury which replays the dissolution's most destructive excesses.[148] Yet the climactic moment reveals few direct religious references: rather than seeing it as a literal description of dissolution iconoclasm, I read the passage's Ref-ormation resonance in its effort to correct and purify a source of corruption and thereby to restore the forgotten knowledge of origins first glimpsed in the "moniments...fowly ra'st" on Verdant's shield:

> all those pleasant bowres and Pallace brave,
> Guyon broke down, with rigour pittilesse;
> Ne ought their goodly workmanship might saue
> Them from the tempest of his wrathfulnesse,
> But that their blisse he turn'd to balefulnesse.
> Their groues he feld, their gardins did deface,
> Their arbers spoyle, their cabinets suppresse,
> Their banket houses burne, their buildings race,
> And of the fairest late, now made the fowlest place. (2.12.83)

Although the objects of Guyon's violence—bowers, groves, arbors, and so forth—are emphatically secular, the verbs owe their historical and moral force to the Reformation: "broke," "feld," "deface," "spoyle," "suppresse," "burne," and especially the final act, "race."[149] The repetition of the word "race" in this crucial passage suggests to A. C. Hamilton that Guyon's destruction of the bower is "fitting revenge" for the "'moniments... fowly ra'st' on Verdant's shield."[150] Similarly, Guyon's "defacement" of the bower's gardens recalls and responds to Verdant's self-defacement: "certes it great pittie was to see/Him his nobilitie so foule *deface*" (2.12.79; my emphasis). But in chastising defacement through defacement, razing through razing, Guyon's destruction appears to be less an act of revenge than an attempted correction, which is akin to the acts of correction performed in the post-Reformation library. Where Verdant's "ra'st" monuments and defaced nobility represent a historical amnesia, Guyon's razing of the Bower of Bliss aims to recall its denizens to their forgotten origins. Thus, after this orgy of destruction, Guyon is moved to observe,

> See the mind of beastly man,
> That hath so soone forgot the excellence
> Of his creation, when he life began. (2.12.87)

If the bower is a seat of forgetting, in other words, Guyon's destruction of it is an act of violent remembering. In this, Guyon recalls the chastening scourge of post-Reformation readers and library makers like Leland and Bale, who sought to recuperate England's lost origins in its "monuments of antiquity" by purifying those monuments of the corrosive accretions of monastic influence. Thus, Bale (whose name it is difficult not to read as punningly encrypted in the "balefulness" of the bower's destruction) castigates the "fallax et fabulosa" "Vision of the Monk of Eynsham," just as he will also condemn the *De vitiis Romanorum pontificum* as "full of newly devis'd lies and tales," thereby advancing his project to preserve "true history" from "fryvolous fables and lyes." Similarly, Leland advocates "casting awaye trifles, cutting off old wiues tales, and superfluous fables," in order "to reade, scanne upon, and preserve in memory." Like Leland's and Bale's acts of "polishing" or "purifying" the written records of the past, Guyon's destruction of the Bower of Bliss is an act of unmaking, whereby "painted forgery" is castigated in order to produce "iust memorie." But the "memory" that Guyon instigates does not produce a positive knowledge of origins; indeed, despite Guyon's command, "Let them returned be vnto their former state" (2.12.85), the bower's former denizens never quite recover their original human identities: "being men they did vnmanly looke" (2.12.86). Instead, Guyon produces ruins—a broken landscape that offers neither knowledge nor enchantment—as the locus of post-Reformation memory.[151]

In the Bower of Bliss, Guyon performs the very action of which book 2's proem expresses fear when it worries how it will be "iudged" and whether or not it will be dismissed as "th'aboundance of an idle braine" and "painted forgery / Rather then matter of iust memory" (2.proem.1). By tracing Guyon's training, through his progress from Eumnestes' library to the Bower of Bliss, in the castigation of "forgery" and the production of "memory," book 2 inoculates itself against the very judgment it fears by offering itself up as a lesson in such judgment, rather than judgment's object. In so doing, it reveals how the preoccupations with distinction, chastisement, and correction established by post-Reformation book collectors and library makers shaped the conditions of reading in *The Faerie Queene*. If, as I have argued, the new English library institutes a *lectio* of suspicion whose object is less the recovery of positive knowledge than the endless castigation of error, *The Faerie Queene* is the first work after the Reformation to be written for its shelves.

A Library of Evidence:
Robert Cotton's Medieval Manuscripts and
the Generation of Seventeenth-Century Prose

The Cottonian Middle Ages

The *Anglo-Saxon Chronicle* (Cotton MS Tiberius B. i; Cotton MS Tiberius B. iv), *Sir Gawain and the Green Knight* (Cotton MS Nero A. x), *Ancrene wisse* (Cotton MS Nero A. xiv; Cotton MS Titus D. xvii; Cotton MS Cleopatra C. vi), *Beowulf* (Cotton MS Vitellius A. xv), *Piers Plowman* (Cotton MS Vespasian B. xvi)—without Robert Cotton, the corpus of medieval written works would be very different, and considerably smaller.[1] The most accomplished collector of the early seventeenth century, Cotton dominates the history of the Renaissance English library.[2] He likewise dominates the history of the English Middle Ages, since much of what we know about the period's history and literary culture is thanks to the original sources that he amassed. The Cotton Library shows that the history of the English Middle Ages is a history of the Renaissance, since post-Reformation collectors like Cotton selected, organized, preserved—and, in so doing, I argue, remade—medieval books and documents in line with their own contemporary concerns and fantasies about the past. But the story of collectors like Cotton equally shows that the English Renaissance, as represented by the Cotton Library and its users, was a medieval creation, since those later readers and researchers could not handle and archive medieval materials without also being touched and shaped in turn by them.

Cotton belonged to a second generation of late Elizabethan and early Jacobean antiquarians, who followed the groundbreaking efforts of early-sixteenth-century collectors like John Bale and Matthew Parker.[3] In the preceding chapter I argue that Reformation era figures like Parker built up libraries through an art of selection. Since they obtained their books from, or at one remove from, the monasteries that held them until their dissolution, sixteenth-century collectors developed and promoted strategies to distinguish manuscripts worthy of preservation from those that were not. By the seventeenth century, collectors like Cotton acquired books not from dissolved monastic libraries but from other collectors; their overriding concern was less selection—picking and choosing the individual texts that went into their collections—than the challenge of organization, as they consolidated the large numbers of texts that they acquired, many of them en masse.[4] Their signature achievements are their catalogues and cataloguing techniques, which reflect seventeenth-century preoccupations with the taxonomy and right ordering of knowledge, as well as with the idea that the individual book or text is made meaningful by the classifications and taxonomies through which it is ordered and navigated.[5] Projecting the needs and interests of active library users, they recognized that an uncatalogued book is as useless to readers as an absent one.

The seventeenth-century regard for the right ordering of knowledge fueled a parallel literary development, the rise of nonfiction prose. Departing from the sixteenth-century aims of Ciceronian eloquence, seventeenth-century writers of prose were concerned with reflecting the world as it was, and they developed methods of documentation and textual evidence that supported this concern by representing the truth in a plain style.[6] I contend that the rise of nonfiction prose was an outgrowth of the rise of the library—and, furthermore, that such a development would have been unthinkable without Robert Cotton, whose support of numerous scholars and antiquarians of his generation is widely documented in grateful dedications and acknowledgments.

As well as lending manuscripts and other materials that became direct sources for writers of nonfiction prose—whose best-known practitioners include William Camden, John Speed, John Selden, and James Ussher—Cotton established the very idea of the documentary source by defining the meanings and uses of manuscripts for a generation of scholars and writers.[7] Indeed, for an extended community of writers associated with the Cotton Library, it was the manuscript as source that guaranteed the nonfictionality of nonfiction prose, by grounding its contents in a realm of recoverable truth. The idea of the documentary source as Cotton shaped it persists in the archival doxa undergirding scholarship today—which makes manuscripts into privileged vessels of historical knowledge and primary evidence more authoritative than the secondary source.[8] For the early users of the library, no less than for those today, being able to cite a Cotton manuscript became a marker of scholarly legitimacy; and thus, the many seventeenth-century writers of nonfiction prose who identified their sources with the marginal notation

"Ex MS Cot. Bibl." embedded their work in a powerful cultural narrative of archival research, underpinned by compelling dramas of bibliographical discovery and recovery.

At the same time, by inventing the idea of the archival source and its uses for the early seventeenth century, Cotton reinvented the medieval manuscripts that were its primary objects. Most of these, like the manuscripts that composed the Parker collection, came originally from monastic libraries that were sacked and dispersed in the Reformation. And like Parker, Cotton collected books not out of a desire to create a universal or comprehensive collection but in the interests of Protestant nation building, an ideological project manifested in his library's holdings on British subjects. Despite Cotton's personal interest in antiquities and histories of the classical past—reflected in his late practice of organizing his materials under busts of the Caesars, from Julius to Domitian—the actual contents of Cotton's library reflect a concern less with classicism than with British history, for which his collection became, and remains, an essential archive.[9]

Cotton's interests were informed by Reformation historiography—and, as we shall see, figures like Foxe, Bale, and Parker provided recurrent touchstones for Cotton—but further, much of Cotton's collecting focused on historicizing the Reformation itself.[10] Thus, Cotton sought and collected primary documents like the memoranda and original correspondence of Thomas Cromwell (Titus B. i, fol. 441; Cleopatra E. iv), a draft of the Act of Six Articles with corrections in the hand of Henry VIII (Cleopatra E. v, fol. 327), records of the anti-Henrician prophecies of Elizabeth Barton and Mrs. Amadas (Cleopatra E. iv, fols. 75r-85r), and numerous charters and records from the dissolved monasteries as well as from those who carried out the visitations.[11] In the Cotton Library the Reformation became a documented event. At the same time that he collected the materials of pre-Reformation British history, Cotton also enacted a kind of bibliographical Reformation of his own, by redirecting manuscript materials from monks to antiquarians. With this, we can identify a defining goal of the Cotton Library: to convert medieval manuscripts into sources of British history, and thus to transform artifacts of superstition, as shaped by their monastic makers, into vehicles of truth, as the term was understood by a seventeenth century newly fixated on questions of evidence and the fact.[12] The Cotton Library became a laboratory for a particular form of scholarly alchemy, in which the straw of medieval belief could be spun into the gold of early modern knowledge.

The religious conflicts of England's long Reformation not only formed the context of Cotton's collecting but also permeated the library's interior—where they were continuously replayed by the library's visitors in the reading and research they undertook there. This point is suggested by two anecdotes recounted in the "Memorials" of Father Augustine Baker, which are among the most vivid contemporary descriptions of Cotton's library as a place of historical research and discourse.[13] Despite his own Protestantism, Cotton maintained a number of English Catholic friends and close associates, among them Baker, who led the English Benedictines in Cambrai.[14] Baker knew Cotton to be a collector of medieval English books and even asked him to send him some for the Cambrai nuns, since "Thair lives being contemplative the comon bookes of the worlde are not for their purpose, and litle or nothing is in thes daies printed in English that is proper for them," whereas, he continues, "there were manie good English bookes in olde time."[15] Baker also consulted Cotton's library himself when seeking material for "a collection of all manner of ecclesiastical antiquities." On one such research visit, sometime between 1622 and 1624, he recalls overhearing a conversation between Cotton and Camden:

> Being once upon a time in the library of Sr Robert Cotton, there chanced to come in Mr William Camden, the auther of the *Description of Britanne*, and of *The Life of Queen Elizabeth*, and of other workes. And as he set down at the fire, with Sir Robert Cotton, in a room adjoyning to the library, Sir Robert told him how he had latly for a small price got a chest of writings, which belonged to Sir Francis Walsingham, Secretary of Estate to Queen Elizabeth; which writings did contain the principall passages of state under that queen, and by the which (as Sr Robert Cotton said) Mr Camdens History of the Queen might well be amended in many points, for that certainly his informers had misled and deceived him. To the which Mr Camden replyed that he knew well enough since the putting out of [*The Life of Queen Elizabeth*] that he had bin egregiously abused by his informers, and had thereby abused others against his will, whereof he was now sorry, and wished he had never undertaken the worke, or having undertaken it, had followed his own and other better friends information. This passed in the hearing of Fa. Baker, whereby you may gather, what opinion Mr William Camden himself had of his own issue, *Elizabetha*; which yet others (against the judgment of the auther himselfe) do vainly canonize.[16]

This account reframes the religious turmoil of Tudor and Stuart England as a drama of primary sources. Whether or not it is seen as evidence of Cotton's and Camden's ability to rise above "the conventional prejudices of the age," as Graham Parry suggests, Baker deploys the anecdote in the context of his own archival labors, "searching and collecting antiquities" in defense of the English Benedictines, and thus reclaims what had become one of the chief weapons in the arsenal of English anti-Catholicism: the manuscript as a primary source of historical knowledge.[17] As I have been arguing, the religious conflicts of England's long Reformation made libraries into arsenals and manuscripts into weapons: Baker's anecdote reveals that these could be wielded by both sides. If historians like Camden "abuse" Catholics on the word of their (human) "informers," the same "informers" can also "abuse" them with false words; but manuscripts, the artifacts of historical truth, have the power to set the record straight, this time by exonerating English Catholics.

Religious conflict in the Cotton Library was not confined to the historical records but drove the research of, and exchanges between, the scholars visiting the library, if a colorful second anecdote that Baker presents immediately following is to be believed:

> Another thing which happened in the same library of Sir Robert Cotton was this. There happened a dispute there about the worship of images (as I remember) between James Usher, the Protestant Bishop of Armach, in Ireland, and another who was a Catholike preist, and reputed a very great scholar. But the said preist happened (as it seemed) to be worsted in that disputation. Whereupon [Baker], seeing a necessity to speake in defence of Catholick religion, entered into disputation, and gave the Bishop such good satisfaction, as he got not so much credit by foiling the preist as he lost by disputing with Fa. Baker.[18]

The Cotton Library, which housed exemplary medieval illuminated manuscripts like the *Lindisfarne Gospels* and the Cotton Genesis (Cotton Otho B. vi), was an apt setting for a disputation on the religious use of images. As Baker's account reveals, the library was dedicated not only to preserving books like this but to facilitating their uses—and, as this anecdote shows, their contestation—in the present.

These two anecdotes establish the Cotton Library as a space open to the "Catholike preist" as well as the "Protestant Bishop," a source for Baker's collection of "ecclesiastical antiquities" for "a Monasticall History of our Order in England" no less than Usher's polemical *Britannicarum ecclesiarum antiquitates* (1639), and a forum for disputes both for and against such volatile religious topics as "the worship of images." But, as Baker reveals, this openness did not make the library a neutral setting for disinterested research. To the contrary, the Cotton Library was a major political battleground, as witnessed by its forced closure by royal order in 1629, after supplying precedents for sensitive issues from tithing practices and the debasement of currency to, most damagingly, the king's use of his council.[19] Cotton's practice of applying his library materials to such contemporary matters reflects the pragmatic objectives that drove Cotton's collection: his concerns were not "antiquarian" in the modern sense of being divorced from present realities, but rather, they aimed to establish the documentary basis of a past that was directly relevant to the present and its most urgent conflicts.

Historians have long recognized that Cotton's collections of documents were driven by, and used in ways that made them instrumental to, the legal and political concerns of Cotton's Stuart contemporaries; yet Cotton's collections of medieval religious and literary manuscripts, however important they remain as primary sources for medievalists, have largely been read outside the Tudor and Stuart contexts in which Cotton collected them and his contemporaries consulted them. I contend that Cotton's religious and literary collections were no less motivated and touched by contemporary concerns than his archives. Just as the modern distinction between "archive" and "library" breaks down in relation to the Cotton collections, the Cotton Library observed and enforced no real distinctions between documents and literary or religious texts. Instead, it appears that Cotton collected medieval literary and religious texts for the same reason he collected cartularies— because he saw their potential utility in addressing the most contentious matters of his day.

As Baker's accounts of his researches in the Cotton Library indicate, religious conflicts lingering from England's long Reformation shaped the motives of Cotton's contemporaries who sought and used his "antiquities," as well as the modes in which they did so. The patriotic antiquarians who first consulted the Cotton Library struggled to sift historical matter from the manuscript sources of England's pre-Reformation past. At the same time, they also engaged in hermeneutic struggles with contemporary Catholic users of the Cotton Library, who wrested their own meanings from the same manuscripts—sometimes, as in the case of Baker and Ussher, in the very same room. Both struggles shaped the antiquarians' approaches to medieval manuscripts and the concepts of "truth," "evidence," and "source" that they brought to them. In this chapter, I will argue that the first users of the Cotton Library generated protocols concerning the uses of medieval manuscripts that became foundational for modern scholarship—chief among them, a conviction in the truth-wielding capacities of the original source. But they did so, I will further argue, by effacing the original contexts and drastically

altering the protocols of reading from which those manuscripts first drew
their meaning.

The Archive of Saints

Cotton never aimed for his library to be a universal or comprehensive collection, in the model of some of his Italian contemporaries. Instead, like other
post-Reformation collectors in the Parkerian tradition, he concentrated on
sources of English history, with an emphasis on several basic categories:
Anglo-Saxon manuscripts; monastic cartularies and chronicles; genealogies
and state records; and saints' lives. This concentration explains why some
of the major works of English hagiography are now Cotton manuscripts, like
the *South English Legendary* (Julius D. ix), John of Tynemouth's *Legenda
Anglia* (Tiberius E. i), and countless other collections of vitae (such as Julius
F. x; Tiberius D. iii; Tiberius D. iv; Tiberius B. iii; Caligula A. viii; Nero
E. i; Otho D. viii; Cleopatra B. ii). Indeed, when Thomas Bodley began to
collect books, Cotton sent him an early-fourteenth-century *Legenda sanctorum* by Jacobus de Voragine, originally from Christ Church, Canterbury;
the library, the gift suggests, begins with saints.[20] Yet for some of Cotton's
readers, the presence of such manifestly "superstitious" texts required explanation and defense. Writing in 1696, the Cotton librarian Thomas Smith
justifies Cotton's inclusion of saints' lives in the collection because "among
the confused mass of rubbish and dross, veins of purer metal lie hidden for
good sense and hard work to sort out, many of which throw light on the civil
and ecclesiastical state and history of those times."[21] And in fact, borrowing
records show that many of Cotton's contemporaries who used the library,
such as William Camden, drew actively from its collection of saints' lives
as historical sources.[22] Yet for Smith, hagiography makes problematic history because "the monks corrupted the truth with a mixture of stories...,
feeding the credulity of the superstitious in a vicious and ignorant age with
inventions tacked on by dull minds and designed less to teach than to mislead" (54).[23] As Smith suggests, the medieval writers were at fault not just
because they told stories but because they mixed stories ("fabulis diversi
generis") with the truth, and refused to say which was which.

    Smith's comment suggests both a savvy reading of medieval hagiogra-
phers' writing practices and an effort to distance himself and the Cotton
Library from such practices. Writers of saints' lives frequently call themselves "collectors" or "compilers" of texts, stressing the variety of their
sources and their own role as gatherers, rather than as original writers.[24]

Thus, the *Kalendre of the Newe Legende of Englande* (1516), which derives from John of Tynemouth's fourteenth-century *Nova Legenda Anglie*, draws attention to the fact that it is "gatheryd togyther," and not an original composition, while the *South English Legendary* gathers hagiographical texts together in ways that encouraged successive readers to select and redistribute them across other sources.[25] Such texts follow the medieval practice of *compilatio*, which created single works from diverse sources.[26] The practice is exemplified by one medieval book that played a key role in Cotton's collection, Ranulf Higden's *Polychronicon*, whose author, as Andrew Galloway notes, "elaborated with unprecedented vigour the posture of the compiler."[27] This immensely popular fourteenth-century work, which was translated into Middle English by John Trevisa in 1387, undertakes a massive amalgamation of fact, miracle, and legend under the umbrella of universal history.[28] In a well-known preface, Higden (as translated in Trevisa's Middle English) describes *compilatio* as "a medling to gidre of profits and sweetness... mervalles and wonders, greet deeds of our forefathers, and diverse maner men that were in olde time."[29] Higden practices compilation with a high degree of self-consciousness, listing "Þe auctours names of Þe whiche Þis cronycle is nameliche i-gadered and i-drawe," and claims to "take for schelde and defens, me for to saue and schilde a[y]enst enemys Þat me wolde despise stongly and blame," by differentiating the words of his sources from his own, which he sets off under the authorial initial "R" (1.21). His careful attributions to his sources are a "schelde," he insists, that allow him to escape blame for sources that are disputed or inaccurate. As is commonly the case with medieval compilers, Higden shies away from differentiating the truth claims of "marvels and wonders" from "deeds," arguing that even those things that are not factually true are still valuable: "Wherfore in the writynge of this storie I take nought vppon me to aferme for sooth all that I write, but such as I have seie and i-rad in dyverse bookes, I gadere and write withoute envie, and comoun to othere men. For the apostel seith nought, 'All that is write to oure lore is *sooth*,' but he seith 'Al that is I-write to oure lore it is I-write'" (1.19).[30] As Higden puts it, the compilation's "lore" (its pedagogical use) overrides the factual truth (here, "sooth") of its constituent parts.[31] What makes particular stories useful to history, in other words, is not their factuality but their edificatory value, their adherence to a higher truth.[32]

In these meditations on his practice of *compilatio*, Higden acknowledges the diversity of his sources but stresses the essential unity of all writings: he explains the presence of classical and other non-Christian sources in the

Polychronicon ("They feynynge and sawes of mysbileued and lawless men, and wonders and merueillis of dyuerse contrees and londes" [1.17]) by appealing to an overarching Christian meaning that unites them. Such was the purpose of universal history in Higden's hands: beginning with the belief that human history revealed the unity of the divine purpose on earth, it sought to reconcile and thus unify history's diverse strands and narratives into a single chronology of salvation.[33] The model for such Christian historiography was Eusebius, whose *Chronicon* replaced the cyclical models of classical history with a linear chronology beginning at the Creation and continuing to the Last Judgment.[34] Higden similarly orders human history into a Christian chronology of six ages, which he promises will impose "rule and ordre" on a diversity of sources by revealing the "soothnesse" that unites them: "That is in other bookes i-write welwyde and parcel mele i-pluanted, here it is i-putte togidre in rule and in ordre; so merthe to sadnesse and hethen to Cristen, euerich among other, that straunge stories beeth so abregged, schorted and i-lengthed that the storie is hool, in soothnesse nought i-chaunged" (1.17). Higden's conviction in history's single truth, the "soothnesse" of the Incarnation, underwrites the diversity of his sources, despite the fact that many of them defy credibility: "Meny wonders thow schalt fynde that thou woldest nought bileue, and yit they beeth ful sooth" (1.17). "Also of many thinges that seemeth ful sooth, notheless skilfulliche me douteth" (1.19). Yet he concludes with Jerome that Christian truth redeems even these dubious texts: "It is semeliche to trowe her sawes that withseith nought oure byleue nother soothnesse that is knowe" (1.19).

Higden's reflections on the possibility of reconciling the various truths of written histories with the central truth of Christian history fuel his production of the "accretive bricolage" that is the *Polychronicon*. The term belongs to James Simpson, who notes that the medieval "accretive reception of texts implies historical continuity" of the sort that I find embodied in the *Polychronicon*.[35] In contrast, the late-seventeenth-century Cotton librarian Thomas Smith signals a break from this model when he articulates the belief that history must separate truth from story—"among the confused mass of rubbish and dross, veins of purer metal lie hidden for good sense and hard work to sort out"—as contrasted with the accretive practices of "the monks," who "corrupted the truth with a mixture of stories." In so doing, Smith also articulates a shift in the history of truth, away from Higden's model, in which human truths are necessarily fragmented reflections of the universal truth, to that of the later seventeenth century, in which historical truth was grounded in fact, which was itself underwritten by the documentary source.[36]

Cotton's *Polychronicon*

Higden's *Polychronicon* was the second book that Robert Cotton owned (a copy now preserved in Cotton Nero D. viii), making it one of the founding works of the Cotton Library.[37] It was apparently a book that Cotton himself valued and read carefully; the Nero text is annotated throughout by Cotton himself, who went on to acquire several more manuscripts of the work for his collection (Cotton Julius E. viii, Tiberius D. vii, and Otho C. xvi).[38] How—and, more to the point, why?—did Robert Cotton read his *Polychronicon*? A. S. G. Edwards has shown that the *Polychronicon* attracted English readers throughout the sixteenth century, including Matthew Parker.[39] Part of its post-Reformation appeal came from its association, through its English translator, Trevisa, with the cause of English Bible translation: when William Caxton printed an edition in 1482, he notes that it was "englisshed by one Trevisa," who had "translated this sayd book/the byble & bartylmew de propretatibus reru[m] out of latyn in to englysshe."[40] Caxton's belief that Trevisa was responsible for the Wycliffite Bible may reflect the fact that Trevisa and Wyclif were historically connected: Wyclif, who cites the *Polychronicon* as a favored historical source, probably knew Trevisa at Queen's College, Oxford.[41] Trevisa also advances arguments for vernacular Bible translation and disendowment in the *Dialogue Between a Lord and a Clerk*, a short translated text that prefaces five of the extant manuscripts of Trevisa's *Polychronicon* translation, including Cotton's own Tiberius D. vii.[42] We could imagine that Cotton, like other Protestant readers, similarly valued the work because of these Wycliffite associations.

Yet, as D. R. Woolf points out, by the seventeenth century the *Polychronicon* was outdated as a work of history, its place supplanted by other forms of history writing organized by topic or topography rather than by the broad temporal sweep of the chronicle, as exemplified by Higden's *Polychronicon*.[43] Indeed, given the *Polychronicon*'s availability in numerous printed editions issued as late as 1528, it is worth asking why Cotton bothered to collect the work in manuscript, let alone in multiple copies.[44] For Cotton, I will argue, the *Polychronicon* was valuable not only as an artifact of manuscript culture itself but as a bibliographical model of how to organize manuscript artifacts.[45] The *Polychronicon*'s self-conscious discussion and exemplification of *compilatio* under the chronological arc of universal history offer a solution to the problem of how to bring together texts of varied natures and origins, a challenge that Cotton himself confronted as he organized his own books. In this respect, it is worth noting that Higden appears to have been a librarian himself: one of Higden's few surviving life-records refers to "all your chronicles, and those which are in your charge," suggesting that Higden was at one point responsible for the book collection at the Benedictine Abbey of St. Werburgh's in Chester, where he became a monk in 1299.[46] While few books survive today from St. Werburgh's, it appears to have maintained a large and varied collection, containing classical works by Ovid, Seneca, and Virgil and chronicles and annals, as well as conventional theological works.[47] In Higden's efforts to present primary sources in their own words, his interest in ordering, rather than composing, knowledge, and his capacious embrace of diverse authors, classical as well as Christian, Higden's meditation on compilation in the *Polychronicon* might be seen to derive from, and apply to, the challenge of how to order books in collections.

By all accounts, Cotton expended extraordinary efforts organizing his own library; yet his practices were controversial by modern standards. Cotton has long been criticized for unbinding and redistributing the medieval texts he received into his library. In Cotton's hands or under his orders, manuscripts were routinely split apart; a twelfth-century passional was divided in two, a document from Christ Church, Canterbury, into three, four leaves from a Worcester cartulary were detached and rebound with different materials, and so forth, in countless outrages to contemporary bibliographical sensibilities.[48] As Colin G. C. Tite dryly observes, "the dissolution of the monasteries hugely disrupted the libraries of medieval England but so did Sir Robert Cotton."[49] Unlike later collectors, however, who commonly unbound medieval books and sometimes sold off the contents individually, Cotton unbound his own manuscripts in order to reorganize and rebind them into volumes of his own making.[50] The individual manuscripts in the Cotton collection, as anyone who has used it will know, are mostly preserved in large volumes that bring diverse materials together between two covers. Within the volumes, materials are roughly grouped according to subject and ordered chronologically, although the organizing principles are sometimes obscure.[51] Nevertheless, the volumes were apparently compiled with care: they frequently bear tables of contents, paginations, and notes to the binders in Cotton's own hand or in the hands of his librarian and close associates, indicating that Cotton himself took an active, careful role in putting the volumes together and that their organization was anything but haphazard.[52] Researchers today commonly consult the Cotton volumes in search of individual sources and thus encounter them as repositories of discrete manuscripts; but contemporary evidence suggests that Cotton intended them rather as compilations whose contents were closely interconnected, and even sequentially arranged, rather than standing alone.

If Cotton's practice of unbinding and rebinding manuscript materials is bibliographically incorrect by modern standards, it was less so by earlier standards. Medieval librarians commonly bound together texts with related subjects, as Malcolm Parkes reports of "a fifteenth-century librarian of Gunville Hall" who "bound a booklet containing Kilwardby's Intencions along with copies of the texts of Augustine to which they relate."[53] Cotton often seems to follow a similar practice; for example, the Nero D. viii manuscript, which preserves Cotton's first copy of the *Polychronicon*, binds it along with Gildas, Bede, and Gerald of Wales. These were Higden's own sources, all of whom Higden names in his second chapter; in the Nero manuscript, Cotton has annotated the relevant section in his *Polychronicon*, "Autores" (fol. 188r), suggesting that he not only noted Higden's sources but attempted to supply them. Like the medieval librarian, Cotton compiles texts in a way that facilitates cross-referencing, providing source texts in the form of extended footnotes on one another. This practice made Cotton into Higden's early modern inheritor, as he extended the practice of compilation from the level of the book to the level of the library.

Cotton's associates, the writers of nonfiction prose who mined his library for sources, sometimes compared their methods to those of medieval compilers: for example, John Weever, who incorporated numerous Cotton sources into his *Ancient Funerall Monuments* (1631), immodestly compares himself to "Venerable Bede, when hee compiled the Chronicles of the English Saxons," because he has brought together, in Weever's words, "Letters, Scrowles, and writings" to make up his history ("Epistle to the Reader"). However self-serving, the comparison tellingly illuminates a continuity in method between medieval monks and early modern antiquarians that belies more recent attempts to differentiate between medieval and antiquarian historiography.[54] Cotton too may have seen his work in the tradition of the medieval compilers, whose example he follows in the ways in which his compilations arrange and sometimes transform their sources in order to tell new stories about the past.[55] Like medieval chronicles that present themselves, in Thomas Betteridge's words, as "unadorned repositories of the truth of the past," Cotton's volumes of manuscripts present themselves as authorless compilations; they exemplify the compiler's drive to allow sources to speak for themselves and to produce historical narratives through organization rather than original composition. Yet just as the Reformation era compiler "deploy[ed] the genre conventions of chronicles, in particular their claim to be a simple mimetic record of the passing of time, to represent as truthful his own partial view of the past," Cotton's compilations produce or suggest narratives that reflect the political and religio-historical concerns of their maker.[56]

As a compiler, Cotton is no less careful a crafter of narrative than Higden, with his practice of bringing together primary sources of diverse generic backgrounds to produce a story about the past. The ordering tool of Cotton's compilations is chronology, an organizational model that had been adopted for post-Reformation bibliography by John Bale's *Scriptorum illustrium maioris Brytanniae...Catalogus* (Basel, 1557–59), complementing the historical model that John Foxe was developing for his *Acts and Monuments of These Latter and Perilous Days* (1563), or "Book of Martyrs."[57] Although chronological order was pioneered by Eusebius and related Christian traditions on which Higden draws, it became an object of increasing concern and critical interest in the sixteenth and seventeenth centuries.[58] As Anthony Grafton has shown, the Huguenot scholar Joseph Scaliger, author of *De emendatione temporum* (1583) and *Thesaurus temporum* (1606), monumentalized the mode of critical chronology by painstakingly comparing histories and other historical data in an attempt to reconcile the major events of biblical and world history into a unified timeline.[59] Scaliger's English counterparts were William Harrison, whose manuscript *Great English Chronology*, written in the 1570s, attempted to fit English Reformation history into the greater temporal schemes implied by the Bible and prophesies, and James Ussher, whose *Annales Veteris Testamenti a prima mundi origine deducti* (The Annals of the Old Testament Deduced from the First Origin of the World; 1650) assembled evidence from primary sources to create a universal chronology beginning with the creation of the world.[60]

Yet as early modern chronologers knew as well as did their monastic predecessors, chronology was a far from neutral system of ordering historical events; rather, chronological order not only crafted history as the arrangement of events in time but implied arguments about imminence, causality, and precedent, topics that became critical to Reformation historiography.[61] It was no coincidence that the major early modern practitioners of critical chronology were Protestants, since chronology played a central role in Protestants' justification of the Reformation as a return to ancient precedent, rather than a "novelty," as Catholics contended. Establishing such a chronology would be a driving antiquarian project; that project found its fullest expression in Ussher's *Britannicarum ecclesiarum antiquitates* (1639), which rigorously applies this use of chronology to the sources of ecclesiastical history in order to establish the antiquity of the British church.[62]

Cotton engaged seventeenth-century practices of critical chronology at close range. He actively encouraged the authors of chronological works by opening his library's sources to them, as Ussher himself reveals when he acknowledges his debt to "the rare treasury" of Cotton's library.[63] Cotton's personal interest in chronological modes is also inscribed in his library itself, whose most notable characteristic is a distinctive shelf-marking system organized by a chronological succession of Roman emperors' busts; as opposed to the alphabetical arrangement or subject matter divisions that organized other seventeenth-century libraries such as the Bodleian, Cotton's library takes its organizing principle from a temporal order.[64] But even before the emperor pressmark system was in place—a development that was not undertaken until the end of the 1620s and was still incomplete at the time of Cotton's death in 1631—chronology formed the main ordering system for Cotton's individual volumes of primary materials, which, even when they leap across generic boundaries, are commonly arranged with close attention to dates.[65] Cotton's practice of organizing primary materials chronologically recalls the practices of medieval chronicles, with their sequential ordering of historical events. But in keeping with contemporary critical chronology such as Ussher's, Cotton's chronological arrangement of manuscript materials in his volumes follows the outlines of a distinctly Protestant argument about history.

Cotton's Compilations: Reading as Reformation

A series of volumes in the Cotton Library, Cleopatra E. i-iv, bring together a treasure trove of late medieval and Reformation era manuscripts, including papal bulls and records, sources on late medieval religious controversy, and letters, official documents, and proclamations relating to the dissolution of the monasteries. These volumes have long been mined for primary sources on the individual topics they comprise: the archive of letters contained in Cleopatra E. iv, for example, has supplied many of the documents that have come to define the chronology and key events in the history of the visitation and dissolution of the monasteries for modern scholars.[66] Indeed, many of them have been cited in preceding chapters of this book, including letters to Cromwell by Thomas Elyot and others, reports on the visitations by Sir John Prise, and Prise's own copy of "The Legend of St. Thomas a Becket" from the South English Legendary, along with his annotations. But the Cleopatra volumes are more than repositories of autonomous materials or raw data; rather, it is clear from their organization and framing that the volumes, which Cotton referred to as "My own Collections of Ecclesiasticall causes," are intended as a multipart chronicle of English Reformation history, told through original sources.[67] This intention is reflected in the sequential titles

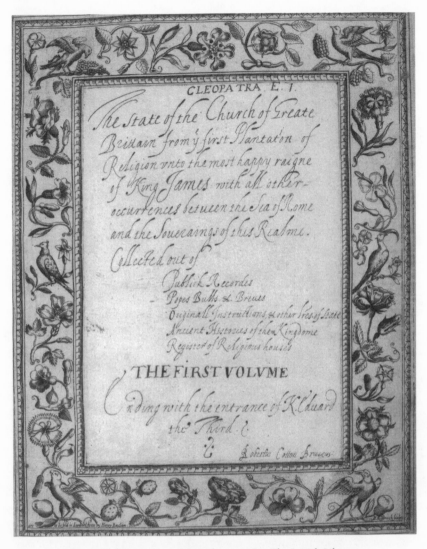

Fig. 6. Title page, Cotton MS Cleopatra E. i, The British Library.

that the volumes bear. The first volume in the sequence, Cleopatra E. i,
opens with a title page (fig. 6) on which is written:

> The state of the church of Great Britain, from the first plantation of reli-
> gion, unto the most happy reign of king James; with all other occurrences
> between the see of Rome, and the sovereigns of this realm: collected out
> of public records.

Popes bulls and breves.
Original instructions, and other letters of state.
Ancient histories of the kingdom.
Registers of religious houses.
THE FIRST VOLUME.

Ending with the entrance of king Edward the third.

This volume is followed by Cleopatra E. ii, whose title clearly indicates that it is meant as a continuation of the first: "The state of the Church of Great Britain, &c. THE SECOND VOLUME." This volume is followed in turn by Cleopatra E. iii, whose title "The state of the Church of Great Britain, &c. THE THIRD VOLUME," confirms its place in the sequence.

These first three volumes chart the prehistory of the Reformation through documents that record longstanding conflicts between the popes and the English kings, as well as domestic struggles over heresy, exemplified by "De conclusionibus Wicliffi, et earum condemnatione" (Cleopatra E. ii). Cleopatra E. iv and v bring together documents that are identified in Smith's catalogue as "multa de reformatione Ecclesiae" (Cleopatra E. iv) and that in many cases come from the pens of the very agents who were the English Reformation's key players—Thomas More, Thomas Cromwell, and Henry VIII himself. And, concluding the series, Cleopatra E. iv compiles the primary sources supporting Henry's divorce and the royal supremacy, including the *Collectanea satis copiosa*, the work compiled by a team of scholars on the king's behalf and annotated by Henry himself.[68] If medieval chronicles like Higden's presented themselves as repositories of primary materials that they painstakingly transcribed, Cotton goes one step further by compiling the primary sources themselves in the hands of those who wrote them. The volumes contain organizational notes throughout that were written by Cotton himself, reflecting the active role that he played in assembling them.[69]

The Reformation narrative that is charted in the Cleopatra E. volumes extends to successive volumes; Cleopatra F. i and ii, immediately following (which likewise contain Cotton's organizational notes)[70], bring together later sources in Tudor ecclesiastical history, classified as "Collectanea de potestate Ecclesiastica," and carry the narrative of Reformation into the Elizabethan period. At the other end of the sequence, the volumes preceding Cleopatra E. i can be read as a prehistory of the English Reformation: Cleopatra D. i through ix bring together numerous chronicles and other historical sources of particular interest to post-Reformation readers, including the works of Higden (Cleopatra D. iv) and Giraldus Cambrensis (Gerald of Wales)

(Cleopatra D. v), which Protestant historians and book collectors made into standard sources as they sought evidence concerning the early English church, while also including religious material such as saints' lives extracted from the *South English Legendary* and a short work entitled in Smith's catalogue, "narrationes quaedam fabulosae de visionibus & miraculis."

Taken together, the Cleopatra volumes reflect not only a chronology of events but a version of Protestant history that took its general outlines from the stories that the Reformation promoted about its own origins and outcomes. For example, the presence of "De conclusionibus Wicliffi, et earum condemnatione" in Cleopatra E. ii reflects a Protestant historiography from John Foxe onward that drafted Wyclif into the long history of the English Reformation as a formative figure.[71] Similarly, a concentration of Anglo-Saxon sources at the beginning of the sequence reflects a belief—prevalent in the seventeenth century but traceable to the Anglo-Saxon studies fostered in the Parker Library—that the period represented a font of English national identity.[72]

Cotton's historiographical context is reflected not only in the volumes' lists of contents but in indications, both in the titles and in other framing devices, of the modes in which they were intended to be read. The title page of Cleopatra E. i, the first of the sequence on ecclesiastical history, stresses the volume's contents as original sources that are authenticated by their age ("Ancient histories of the kingdom") or provenance ("Original instructions . . . "). It thus reflects the antiquarian context that shaped the volume's compilation and use, which elevated the primary source as a privileged piece of textual evidence. That context is extended in a collection of original papers that opens the volume by way of a preface; written for a meeting of the Society of Antiquaries on 29 November 1604, it includes contributions by society members like William Camden and Cotton himself, along with lesser-known antiquarians such as Arthur Agarde, the keeper of state archives, and the herald Sir William Dethick.[73] Like the volume's title page, the papers reflect a culture of manuscript research that was fostered within the society. For instance, Agarde opens his remarks by foregrounding his use "of auncyent manuscript Englishe aucthours, they being the bookes wherin I have for many late yeares together trayvelled for many speciall matters" (Cleopatra E. i, fol. 8r), wielding an antiquarian rhetoric of manuscript research that demonstrates how the Cleopatra documents, like those showcased in Agarde's own paper, are meant to be used: as primary sources for a Protestant history of England.

The common topic of the antiquarians' papers is the history of the English church, which was apparently the focus of the particular meeting for which the papers were composed. In their position at the opening of the

Cleopatra volumes, the essays produce a historical narrative and argument that will organize the collected primary materials that follow. Cotton's own paper is entitled "Antiquity of Christian Religion on this Island." It articulates a conventional Reformation belief that the English church preceded Augustine's mission in 597—"that we had a profession of Christ at and before the landing of our last restorer Austyn" (fol. 3r)—thus establishing its independence from Rome, which Cotton claims is supported by "consent of all authors." As evidence for this argument, Cotton's fellow antiquarians Agarde and Camden cite the second-century British king Lucius, who was for English Protestants a key figure of pre-Augustinian British Christianity. Following an apocryphal account by Bede, Lucius was believed to have become the first Christian king in Britain after he wrote to Pope Eleutherius sometime between AD 160 and 180 announcing his intention to convert.[74] Lucius's historical identity was always tenuous, supported by scant evidence of dubious authority. But he maintained a place in British history nonetheless because of his importance as a precedent for the early church. The Cotton Library played a central role in supporting Lucius, since it was the repository of the main piece of "evidence" for his historical existence, a letter purporting to be from Eleutherius himself in response to Lucius's request for conversion that was preserved in the Cotton Library as Claudius D. ii, fol. 33.[75] Though long suspected to be a forgery (and indeed it would later be shown to have been written in a fourteenth-century hand), the letter was reproduced verbatim by nearly every Protestant writer who treated the early history of the British church, beginning with Foxe. Camden himself cites the letter as evidence for his own assertion of the British church's antiquity, defending its authenticity against Catholic critics by asserting that its dating system was "unknowne to the counterfetting and unlearned Monkes of latter times" who might have forged it (fol. 13v).

The antiquarians' claims about—and use of documentary evidence for—the antiquity and independence of the English church establish a polemical context and *modus legendi* for the documents collected in Cleopatra E. i. Following the antiquarians' papers "on the Antiquity of the Christian Religion on this Island" come a set of "Professionum antiquorum Angliae episcoporum," professions of obedience from Eadulf, bishop of York (796), Denebert, bishop of Worcester (798), and Herewin, bishop of Lichfield (816) to the archbishops of Canterbury, transcribed (and selectively forged) in the twelfth century.[76] Representing an important chapter in the pre-Conquest English church in relation to the pope and Crown, the English bishops' practice of professing obedience to the archbishop of Canterbury was curtailed in the second half of the ninth century (possibly through papal intervention), only to be reestablished in the eleventh century and subsequently contested by succeeding popes and, later, English kings who sought to oversee episcopal professions.[77] This triangulated history of struggle between the pope, the English church hierarchy, and the English monarchs continues in documents that follow, which trace the conflict between Thomas, archbishop of York, and Lanfranc, the archbishop of Canterbury who reestablished the professions of obedience: "Narratio de Thoma Eboracensi Archiep. qui noluit professionem facere Lanfranco Cantuariensi" (Account of Thomas, Archbishop of York, who refused to profess obedience to Lanfranc of Canterbury) and "Epistolae Lanfranci, et Alexandri Papae" (Lanfranc's letters to Pope Alexander II) (Cleopatra E. i, fols. 45v, 48v).[78] John Foxe treats this conflict in detail as initiating "the lamentable decay of true Christianity amongst the christian bishops"; where Foxe bolsters his claim by citing historical evidence, including "the letter of Lanfranc sent to Pope Alexander," Cotton's volume incorporates the very primary texts that featured in Reformation historiography.[79]

Successive documents in the Cleopatra E. volumes bear out their title pages' promise to deliver a history of "occurrences between the sea of Rome and the soueraings of this Realme" by recording the Crown's negotiations with, and occasional victories over, papal authority through original documents or copies arranged in chronological order and keyed to Reformation historiography. In "Responsio Abbatis Bangor ad Augustinum Monachum petentem subjectionem Romanae Ecclesiae" (Cleopatra E. i, fol. 58r), which purports to be a copy "ex antiquissimo libro manuscripto," the abbot of Bangor writes to Augustine, archbishop of Canterbury, refusing subjection to the pope's authority;[80] in "[Bulla Alexandri IV.] ad R. Angliae de eodem argumento" of 1261, Pope Alexander IV releases Henry III from an oath to the barons (Cleopatra E. i, fol. 213r);[81] in a bull of 1278 Pope Nicholas III acquits Edward I of eight years of census payments (Cleopatra E. i, fols. 224v–225r);[82] and in a 1281 letter to John Pecham, archbishop of Canterbury, and the council at Lambeth, Edward I forbids the bishops and prelates from discussing issues of royal authority (Cleopatra E. i, fol. 226v).[83] Many of the documents in the Cleopatra E. volumes touch on events that are also discussed by Foxe.[84] The bulls and original (or copied) documents brought together in these volumes are carefully selected and arranged to form a chronology of the British church from Augustine's mission to the Elizabethan settlement, following the historical narrative established in the antiquarian papers that preface them.[85] Cotton brought his materials together, then, not just as a collector but as an active compiler who seeks to reconcile the methods of Higden with the teleology of Reformation historiography.

Saints and the Subjects of History

I have argued that in compiling the volumes that make up his library, Cotton followed the model of medieval compilers like Higden who presented their chronicles as repositories of primary sources. A crucial difference between them, which points to the transformation of compilation techniques in the seventeenth century, is the status of saints, who inhabit a shifting border between historical knowledge and religious belief. In Higden's *Polychronicon*, saints' stories are absorbed into British history, a characteristic that will drive the Cotton librarian Smith to complain that "the monks corrupted the truth with a mixture of stories..., feeding the credulity of the superstitious in a vicious and ignorant age with inventions tacked on by dull minds and designed less to teach than to mislead" (54). Higden himself admits that many saints' lives appear to stretch the boundaries of credibility; still, he insists, they testify to a higher truth that transcends rational knowledge. While he allows that "more certeyn som is I-holde than other," he asserts nonetheless, citing Augustine, "We schul [believe] and worschippe the miracles of God and nought hem despreue by despitusoun" (1.17).

The *Polychronicon*'s fifth book draws especially heavily on hagiographical sources to stress saints' formative role in English history, a story replete with miracles: Saint Birinus, sent by sea on a mission to England, leaves some of his belongings behind and walks over the water to retrieve them (5.3). The eighth-century Saint Guthlac establishes himself in the haunted Croyland and performs "meny myracles" that establish his "power over unclene spirites" (5.169). Saint Kenelm, a child king murdered in the ninth century, is miraculously found "by a scrowe that was i-wrete in Englisshe with golden letters, that a colvere [dove] broghte and leyde and lefte tofore the pope upon Seynt Peter his auter" (5.307). Higden's fascination with miracles follows the practice of his sources, such as Bede, in whose ecclesiastical history miracle stories constitute the main focus of "about forty out of a hundred and forty chapters."[86] For Higden, as for Bede, miracles authenticate history by proving not just that an event occurred but that human events fulfilled God's will on earth; in Chris Given-Wilson's words, miracles provide "the most direct form of evidence of God's purpose—not just eyewitness testimony, but Godwitness testimony."[87] Where Thomas Smith faults writers like Higden and his sources for "corrupt[ing] the truth with a mixture of stories," Higden defends the practice of mixing "deed" and "marvel." For Higden and his contemporaries, miracles do not corrupt historical truth; they make history true.

As Smith explains, users of the Cotton Library attempted to recover medieval hagiography for the uses of post-Reformation historiography, driven
by the belief that "among the confused mass of rubbish and dross veins of
purer metal lie hidden for good sense and hard work to sort out, many of
which throw light on the civil and ecclesiastical state and history of those
times" (54). Among those, he cites:

> Many distinguished men—Ussher of Armagh in his famous work on the
> antiquities of the British churches, Ware the diligent researcher of an-
> tiquities (especially of Ireland), Dugdale and Wharton, all of whom were
> equally industrious in reading and copying out these Cotton manuscripts.
> If indeed these had not been saved from the general holocaust the mem-
> ory of many illustrious saints produced by the British Isles would have
> been lost. (54)

Applying antiquarian methods to Protestant ends, Archbishop Ussher, James
Ware, Sir William Dugdale, and Henry Wharton labored in the tradition of
Matthew Parker and his circle. Their interest in recuperating the "many
illustrious saints produced by the British Isles" served a national "memory"
project embodied by the Cotton Library itself.[88]

Thus, antiquarians removed saints from the church to the archive. But
there they encountered Catholic researchers whose interest in saints and
their records took a similarly archival turn. At the same time that Cotton
and the users of his library were attempting to rewrite the meanings and uses
of medieval hagiography for Reformation history, contemporary Catholic
writers and scholars were attempting to recuperate and mobilize saints'
lives as a major salvo in the Counter-Reformation. This effort also involved
a return to the archival sources of hagiography. In 1586 Pope Gregory XIII
commissioned Caesar Baronius to revise the *Martyrologium Romanum*, in
an effort to standardize the calendar of saints while purging it of some of
the more egregiously apocryphal entries.[89] It was a calculated response to
the Reformation's challenges to the cult of the saints and established a
model for later Counter-Reformation hagiographical scholarship like that
of the Bollandists in the early seventeenth century, initiated by Héribert
Rosweyde in 1603.

Baronius and Rosweyde shared a commitment to the archive as a source
of hagiographical truth; returning to original sources that they gathered
from libraries with the help of legions of research assistants, they aimed to
strip the accretions of legend and fable from the authentic saints' lives and
thus to reinvigorate the cult of the saints for the faithful through heroic

acts of scholarship.[90] In England, Baronius and Rosweyde found counter-parts in John Wilson's *English Martyrologe* (1608) and Nicholas Roscar-rock's *A Breife Regester or Alphabeticall Catologue of such sainctes (& sainct like persons) as the Collector hathe taken notice of, to haue graced our Island of great Brittaine, Ireland and other British Islands bordering about it*, a manuscript concordance of saints' lives composed between 1616 and 1621.[91] Directed at recusant reading communities, these works reveal the persistence of hagiography as a devotional genre for Catholics in early-seventeenth-century England. They also show that the drive to uncover the historical and archival identities of the saints was charged with con-temporary political significance, producing a struggle not just between the Renaissance and its medieval precursors but between seventeenth-century Protestants and Catholics as they debated the meanings and uses of the past in a divided present.

Wilson's *English Martyrologe* self-consciously follows Baronius's model of archival hagiography by listing "in the margents . . . the bookes and places of the Authors, out of whome I haue gathered al that is here alleaged . . . re-jecting all Apocryphall Legends or other fabulous Historyes, that may be any way suspected or the least note of falsity or errour whatsoeuer" ("An Ad-vertisement of the Authour to the Catholicke Reader"). Those sources that met with his approval include Capgrave, Bede, and Matthew Paris—sources that are all represented in the Cotton Library and were used by Protestant antiquarians and historians in their own work. Yet for Wilson, the archive of the saints is a battleground; in his preface Wilson offers his saints to the "Catholicks of England, Scotland, and Ireland" as "a certaine inheritance, as it were, of your forfathers, descended still, by good right and title, vnto yow, and shall hereafter vnto your, and all posterity," and he presents "this, that I haue here gathered together, and restored vnto yow againe, that which the iniury of tymes had violently taken from yow, and sought to abolish all memory therof . . . as a duty of my loue towards yow, & my dearest Coun-trey" ("Epistle," n.p.). If the battle over the saints takes place in libraries, it is a battle over not just recuperation but interpretation. In the seventeenth century, the saints were not only "violently taken from" Catholics by the Reformation but were co-opted by Protestants like Cotton and Camden.

Nicholas Roscarrock acknowledges the seventeenth-century struggle over hagiography in his own manuscript. Like Wilson, Roscarrock took his archival materials from the same sources that Protestant antiquarians wielded for their British histories; indeed, Roscarrock maintained personal ties to both Cotton and Camden, and he frequently cites Camden as a source of manuscript material.[92] When researching his British saints, Roscarrock notes the existence of "a written booke in the librarie of Martin Colledge in Oxford" that "I learne by Mr Camden, my learned frind" (Cambridge University Library, MS Add. 3041, fol. 102r), and he acknowledges elsewhere his consultation of "ane auntiant maniscript which I had of my learned & laborious friend Master Camden" (fol. 393v), as if they were involved in a collaborative enterprise. In their approaches to, not to mention sharing of, primary materials, Camden and Roscarrock meet and overlap in many unexpected ways, though there remain telling and significant differences between their methods and aims. In his verse preface Roscarrock condemns with vehemence those who "nothing will beleiue/but self conceipt and self wills false pretence," insisting

> What God can doe to make his power appeare
> When it is done no wise man will denye,
> If it be truly prou'de as it is here,
> Except the wise be fooles and true men lye. (fol. 24v)

Here he appears to target the Protestant antiquarians, who part ways with their recusant counterparts not in the books they read—which in many cases turn out to be one and the same—but in their methods of interpretation and differing standards of truth, proof, and belief. In hagiography, Roscarrock insists, God's power on earth is "truly prou'de" and thus compels belief. In contrast, Cotton and his Protestant associates turn to the material "proof" supplied by documentary and historical evidence as an antidote to the false belief they impute to their Catholic counterparts.

Cotton recognized the contemporary volatility of martyrs and the hagiographical narratives that supported them. A tract that Cotton composed between 1617 and 1618, "Twenty-four Arguments," later published under the title *Serious Considerations for Repressing of the Increase of Iesuites, Priests and Papists without Shedding Blood*, argues against capital punishment of recusants, which, he insists, succeeds only in creating martyrs; so much is attested, Cotton writes, "if we read the volumes written in praise of their Priests constancy [such as] their Martyrologie or Kalender of Martyrs."[93] Instead, Cotton insists that judicious handling of such papist offenders makes visible their errors and strips them of their sainthood: "I need not envy the name of a Martyr to the Jesuit; for his cause if it be rightly weighed, will blanch that title."[94] Cotton approaches the hagiographical volumes in his library in a similarly forensic mode of analysis. Cotton's case against executing Catholics, extended to his library, presents a case for preserving, rather than destroying, Catholic texts: once preserved, they can be judiciously examined and thereby stripped of their seditious and superstitious power.

In the antiquarian essays that open Cleopatra E. i, both Cotton and Camden reveal their awareness of the archival hagiographical enterprise that Baronius and Rosweyde were spearheading on the Continent. Cotton writes approvingly of "Baronius in his laborious work of the church story," while Camden similarly cites "an old manuscript which Baronius saw in the Vatican Librarie." Following Baronius's example, both identify documentary sources on saints and martyrs as evidence for their arguments about the antiquity of the British church; Cotton cites "the old original martrilog, a monument of a thousand yeares" (fol. 4r), while Camden cites "the Romane martyrologe which no doubt is of auncient and good credite" (fol. 13v). Yet even while they approve of—and draw inspiration from—Baronius's archival hagiography, both Cotton and Camden attempt to remake the archive of saints, in a self-conscious effort to transform the sources of superstition into new sources of British historiography.

Cotton demonstrates the critical approach to hagiography advocated in *Serious Considerations* when he assesses the legends of individual saints in his essay on the history of the British church prefacing the Cleopatra volumes. While promoting the use of martyrology as historical source, Cotton insists that its evidence must be "rightly weighed"—and, in so doing, rejects the recorded lives of certain saints as inauthentic, such as "the doubtfull relation of our Saint Ursula [and] her 1100 [sic] virgins, and Saint Emerita sister to our Lucius" (fol. 3v). His statements on these particular saints represent a concerted attempt to wrestle hagiography away from medieval writers and their contemporary Catholic readers by redefining the forms of evidence that could establish their authenticity. They also represent a shift away from the archival tactics of earlier Protestants, for whom Saints Emerita and Ursula were admissible evidence for British history.

As an early Christian Briton, Ursula had been cited by Foxe, whom Cotton follows in his error in identifying Ursula's companions and fellow martyrs as 1100 virgins, as opposed to the usual 11,000, indicating that Foxe may have been Cotton's source.[95] Similarly, John Bale eagerly claimed "Emerita kynge Lucyes syster" as a proto-Protestant martyr in his *Lattre Examination of Anne Askew*, which lists her among the early Christian female martyrs whom Bale identifies as Askew's saintly precedents, such as Blandina.[96] While Foxe and Bale happily claim Catholic saints such as Ursula and Emerita as evidence in their Protestant histories, Cotton rejects them, showing how Protestant antiquarians of the seventeenth century applied

critical chronology and other research techniques that differentiated them
from the first generation of post-Reformation history writers.

Of the two female saints, Emerita is the lesser known; in some chronicles, she makes an appearance as the sister of the legendary British king
Lucius. While Protestants from Foxe to Ussher eagerly claimed Lucius as
an important precedent for the independent British church, Catholics coun-
tered by arguing that Lucius's conversion only strengthened the pope's historic authority in Britain, since it occurred, as Thomas Fitzherbert contends
in *A Defence of the Catholyke Cause* (1598), "when there was no other
but our Catholyke religio[n] vniuersally professed, & this of the protestants
not so much as dreamt of."[97] As Fitzherbert shows, the stories about Lucius in Catholic sources threatened his iconic status in Protestant history.
Troubling to Protestant historians were accounts of Lucius's postconversion
career, in which Lucius was said to have renounced his crown in order to
embark on a missionary trip, finally stopping in the Swiss city of Chur,
where he became the city's first bishop until he was martyred.[98] This aspect of Lucius's story earned him a brief entry in Baronius's revised *Roman
Matryrology*, which records his martyrdom at Chur: "Curiae in Germania
S. Lucii Britannorum Regis," an account that is characteristically inflated
in Wilson's *English Martyrologe*: "At *Chure* in *Helvetia* the Passion of S.
Lucius the first Christian King of *Britany* and Martyr, who being conuerted
to the faith of Christ . . . afterward became himselfe a preacher of the same
Doctrine, and went over into *France* and thence into *Germany* [and] . . . was
there finally put to death by the incredulous people of that Nation."[99] Foxe
attempted to discredit this segment of the Lucius story as a "fable of some
writers falsely feigning," insisting that it "disagreeth from all of our English
stories," which instead record that King Lucius was "deceased with great
tranquility in his own land, and was buried at Gloucester."[100]

Emerita belongs to this second stage of Lucius's career, which made her
a political liability as Protestants researched the history of England's first
Christian king. Emerita was held to have accompanied her brother both in
his conversion and travels as well as in his martyrdom; according to the
English Martyrologe, "S *Emerita* Virgin & Matyr, sister to King *Lucius* of
Britany, who going into Germany with her said brother, was by the paga[n]
people of that Cou[n]trey, for the confession of Christian faith, put to death,
ending her glorious martyrdome by fire, about the yeare of Christ, one hundred fourscore and thirteene."[101] Long after her death, Emerita continued
to be celebrated as a Catholic saint, thanks to the persistence of her relics
in Chur (still preserved in a magnificent fifteenth-century reliquary in the

cathedral's treasury) and the presence of her legend in the Breviary of Chur, where her feast day was celebrated on 4 December.[102]

Emerita's historical identity was questioned by later Protestant historians, who sought to dismiss accounts of Lucius's martyrdom in Chur, even as they insisted, often in reference to the Cotton forgery, on the authenticity of Lucius as Britain's first Christian king. To account for the two different versions of the Lucius story, Raphael Holinshed distances King Lucius from the story of Saint Emerita, insisting that Emerita was the niece of King Lucius rather than his sister; he makes the point, he writes, in order to confute those who would "affirme our *Lucius* to renounce his kingdome, and afterward to become first a bishop, then a preacher of the gospell, and afterward a pope: but to the end such as hold this opinion may once vnderstand the botome of their errors, I will set downe the mat|ter at large, whereby they shall sée (if they list to looke) how far they haue béene deceiued."[103] John Speed, who wrote his *British History* in close association with Cotton, similarly questions Emerita's authenticity in an effort to preserve the historical identity of Lucius as Britain's first Christian king: "As for those who would haue this *Lutius* after his *Baptisme* to saile into *Gallia* and other forrein parts, where subduing many Pagans, he became the Apostle to the *Bauarians,* and that his sister *Emerita* fifteene yeeres after was martyred in the City *Augusta:* I find thereof no warrant in any sufficient writer; but in this all others agree, that he raigned twelue yeeres, and lieth buried in *Gloucester.*"[104] In the battle over British history, then, Lucius and Emerita are at odds. For Protestants like Speed, Lucius could become an exemplary Christian ruler only if he was uncoupled from Emerita; yet Emerita's continued cult and sanctified presence in the Breviary of Chur allowed sources like Wilson's *English Martyrologe* and Roscarrock's *Breife Regester* to claim Lucius as a precedent for Catholic, rather than Protestant, religious identity.[105]

When Cotton demotes Emerita in his essay prefacing Cleopatra E. i, he does so in order to retain Lucius as a precedent for the British church; and in so doing, he promotes a rationale and method for the use of manuscript sources like those contained in the Cleopatra volumes themselves. The Cotton Library developed a reputation among Cotton's contemporaries as a source of precedents: as John Chamberlain wrote on 13 July 1615, Cotton "has ever some old precedent in store."[106] Likewise, when Cotton cites historical records in works of his own like *A Relation of Proceedings against Ambassadors who have Miscarried* or *A Short View of the Long Life and Raigne of Henry the Third, King of England,* he offers them as "precedent examples" that hold meanings relevant to matters of contemporary concern.[107]

Cotton's emphasis on precedent reflects the textual milieu of early-seven-teenth-century English jurisprudence, in which cases of common law increasingly stressed the authority of precedent-centered arguments.[108] As the citation of precedents grew more common in legal arguments, so did recourse to the textual records that preserved them. As John Selden asserts in a speech to the Commons in 1629, "the law speaks by record"—a belief that gave Cotton's library, as a source of historical legal records, an impor-tant role in seventeenth-century jurisprudence.[109] Cotton himself "mined his library of antiquities for precedents to revive lapsed privileges and dues on his manors," observes legal historian Richard J. Ross, who traces "the memorial culture of early modern lawyers" as it came to place increased weight on historical and textual evidence.[110] When Cotton sifts through the textual evidence concerning Lucius and Emerita, he imports the forensic skills of legal antiquarians to the realm of church history. Lucius continued to be cited in seventeenth-century histories in large part because of the piece of primary evidence for his existence housed in the Cotton Library, the let-ter to Lucius in Claudius D. ii, fol. 33. By demoting Emerita, Cotton defends not only Lucius's integrity as a precedent for the British church but also the integrity of the Cotton archive—along with one of its prized holdings—as a source of authentic evidence for British ecclesiastical history.

Ursula, the other saint whom Cotton dismisses as "doubtfull," likewise challenged key precepts of British history as practiced by users of the Cotton Library. The early British Saint Ursula occasioned discussion in the Middle Ages because evidence for dating her story was wildly variant. *The Golden Legend* acknowledges this variance after recounting the legend of Ursula and the eleven thousand virgins with whom she was martyred:

> Their passion took place in the year A.D. 238. There are some, however, who maintain that the events above related could not have occurred at that date. Sicily, they reason, was not a kingdom, nor was Constantino-ple, at the time when the queens of these kingdoms are alleged to have been with the virgins. It is therefore thought to be more likely that this wholesale martyrdom took place when Huns and Goths were warring upon each other, long after the reign of the emperor Constantine.[111]

Historical accounts likewise acknowledged the controversies over Ur-sula's story, as does *Fabyan's Chronicle* (1533), which refers the reader to church doctrine as a final authority: "Of the martyrdome of these maydens dyuers authours wryte dyuersly. wherfore I remytte them that wyll haue far-ther vndersta[n]dyng in this mater, vnto ye legende of saynts redde yerely in the chyrche, where they maye be suffycyenly taught and enformed."[112] The writer of *The Kalendre of the Newe Legende of Englande,* which was drawn from John of Tynemouth's *Nova Legenda Anglie,* similarly acknowledges the problems of dating but reports that he was induced to believe the legend himself by a vision that appeared to him, in which "the sayde blessyd Seynt Vrsula & dyuerse other of the sayde virgins apperyd vnto hym as he was wrytynge therof affermynge it to be true," an experience that causes him to decry skeptics who are "slowe to beleue thyngys which they see not nor cannot comprehende by theyr blynde reason."[113] In contrast, for Camden, Ursula challenges not just the Protestant version of British history but history itself, whose truth is founded in chronology. In the *Britannia's* chapter on Cornwall, Camden writes:

> The place requireth here, that I should say somewhat of the holy and devout virgin Ursula descended from hence, as also of the eleven thousand British virgins. But such is the variety of writers, whiles some report they suffered martyrdome under Gratian the Emperour about the yeere of our Lord CCCLXXXIII, upon the coast of Germanie, as they sailed to Amorica; others by Attila the Hun, that scourge of God, in the yeare CCCL. At Coleine upon Rhene, as they returned from Rome; *that with some it hath brought the truth of History into suspition of a vaine fable.* (My emphasis)[114]

Camden's treatment of Ursula reflects his effort, shared with Cotton, to read the saint's life forensically in order to yield the "truth of History." This truth, read as a unified chronology produced through the collation of sources—"consent of all authors," in Cotton's words—cannot admit "the variety of writers" whom Camden finds at odds over Ursula's story. Like Emerita, Ursula is sacrificed in the name of history: as Camden would have it, either history is to be considered "a vaine fable," or she is. Likewise, in Cotton's essay, if Emerita falls victim to a Protestant historiography grounded in the precedent, Ursula falls victim to the demands of critical chronology. Cotton's treatment of both saints reflects his approach to medieval hagiography, and medieval manuscript sources more broadly, which he promotes as a model for other users of his library through documents like the essay prefacing Cleopatra E. i. Rather than dismissing the medieval sources outright as superstitious fables, Cotton submits them to the truth-yielding protocols of reading that underwrote Protestant historiography. If Cotton's methods share the archival orientation of the Bollandist hagiographers, his aim is the opposite: not to allow saints, "truly prov'de" in the archive, to compel the "belief" of a resurgent, post-Reformation Catholicism (in the words of Roscarrock), but to wield archival "proof" against the allurements of Catholic "belief." Thus scrutinized and desanctified, Ursula and Emerita recall the counterfeit "martyrs" whom Cotton proposes to desanctify through judicious weighing in his *Serious Considerations for Repressing of the Increase of Iesuites, Priests and Papists without Shedding Blood*, of whom he avows, "I need not envy the name of a Martyr...for his cause if it be rightly weighed, will blanch that title; but I desire to have all those Lineaments defaced, vvhich may compound that counterfeit Image" (51).

Not all saints in Cotton's library shared the fate of Ursula and Emerita. In the same essay prefacing Cleopatra E. i in which Cotton dismisses the two female saints, he readily asserts the historicity of Saint Alban, as does Camden in his own essay in the same collection. An exemplary early Christian, Cotton writes, "Albon the martyr [was] executed for the testimony of Christ," and further, "the next step of our testimony followeth on the last persecution by Dioclesian, when Albon was made our protomartyr." Cotton's reference to his history as "testimony" is shared by Camden, who deploys his sources as "testimonies" to the truth of the past: "the Romane Martyrologe, which no doubt is of auncient and good credite, testifieth that...some [came] hither to teach the Christian Religion at the request of king Lucius" (fol. 13v).[115] The language of historiography as testimony further reflects how the antiquarians' uses of documentary sources were shaped by contemporary jurisprudence, reflecting the legal background and training that many society members shared.[116] Cotton's and Camden's transformation of hagiography into a source of documentary evidence for British history, for example, parallels the contemporary presentation of evidence in court; when Camden's martyrology "testifieth" to historical fact, it becomes an eyewitness to the past. This use of the term rewrites the significance of martyrs: in the original Greek, after all, the word "martyr" means *witness*, because martyrs testify to God's truth with their lives, as when, in Cotton's words, "Albon the martyr [was] executed for the testimony of Christ." But Camden and Cotton use hagiographical documents as witnesses not to religious but to historical truth. Such a use of manuscripts as historical witnesses reflects the confluence of early modern historiography and jurisprudence, as both came to stress the value of written records, material evidence, and historical precedents.[117] In the mid-sixteenth century, the influential historian and jurist François Baudouin called history (particularly in the form of original archival records, whose use he favored and promoted) "the witness of time."[118] The same meaning is implied in the title of Matthew Parker's edition of Aelfric, *A Testimonie of Antiquitie* (1566), which makes the ancient author, retrieved from the archive, into an eyewitness of his time.[119] Following in the Parkerian mode, in the Cotton Library, "auncient" manuscript martyrologies are similarly privileged not only as firsthand accounts of events from the long-distant past but as material emissaries from the past to the present.[120] Thus, the manuscript martyr becomes a witness of history.

Martyrs to History

In the Cotton Library saints' lives become historical sources following a process that could be compared to one that Lorraine Daston observes at work in seventeenth-century natural philosophy, which, in its concern with preternatural phenomena, "stripped [medieval marvels] of their religious significance" and made them into "the first scientific facts."[121] Similarly, in the hands of post-Reformation collectors like Cotton, saints' lives became the first histories. But they do so only when they can be reclassified as artifacts of historical knowledge rather than religious belief.

This appears to have been Cotton's intention for the *Legenda sanctorum* that he gave to Thomas Bodley in 1603, now Bodley 336 (fig. 7). The opening page bears a small sketch of a reading monk, a reminder of its origin, Christ Church, Canterbury; but next to the monk, Cotton has written one of his characteristic *"ex dono"* inscriptions within a drawing of a Roman *votiva ara* (votive altar).[122] Cotton first encountered such an altar during his archeological expeditions around Hadrian's Wall with Camden, who includes a sketch of a similar altar in *Britannia*, "taken out by the hand of Sir Robert Cotton of Connington, Knight, a singular lover of antiquity."[123] Such altars were originally intended for votive offerings to the *genius loci*, the presiding spirit of the place.[124] But in the *votiva ara* inscribed in Bodley 336, Cotton has furnished the altar with the inscription "GENIO LOCI BODLEO RESTI: BONO PUBLICO ROB: COTTON Conningto: HAC LL.M.D.D.," or (as Colin Tite paraphrases it): "For the public good, Robert Cotton of Conington, happily, freely, and justly made this thank-offering to the spirit of the library restored by Bodley."[125] This inscription enables Cotton to redirect a book originally meant as a religious work, the *Legenda sanctorum*, to "the spirit of the library," by means of the "antiquity" represented by the *votiva ara*, the altar that Camden and Cotton encountered as an archeological artifact. That transformation of religious book into antique artifact is commemorated in the two illustrations on the opening page of Bodley 336, which represent two modes of literacy, the monastic and the antiquarian. If Cotton's gift to Bodley suggests that the library starts with saints, his inscription also

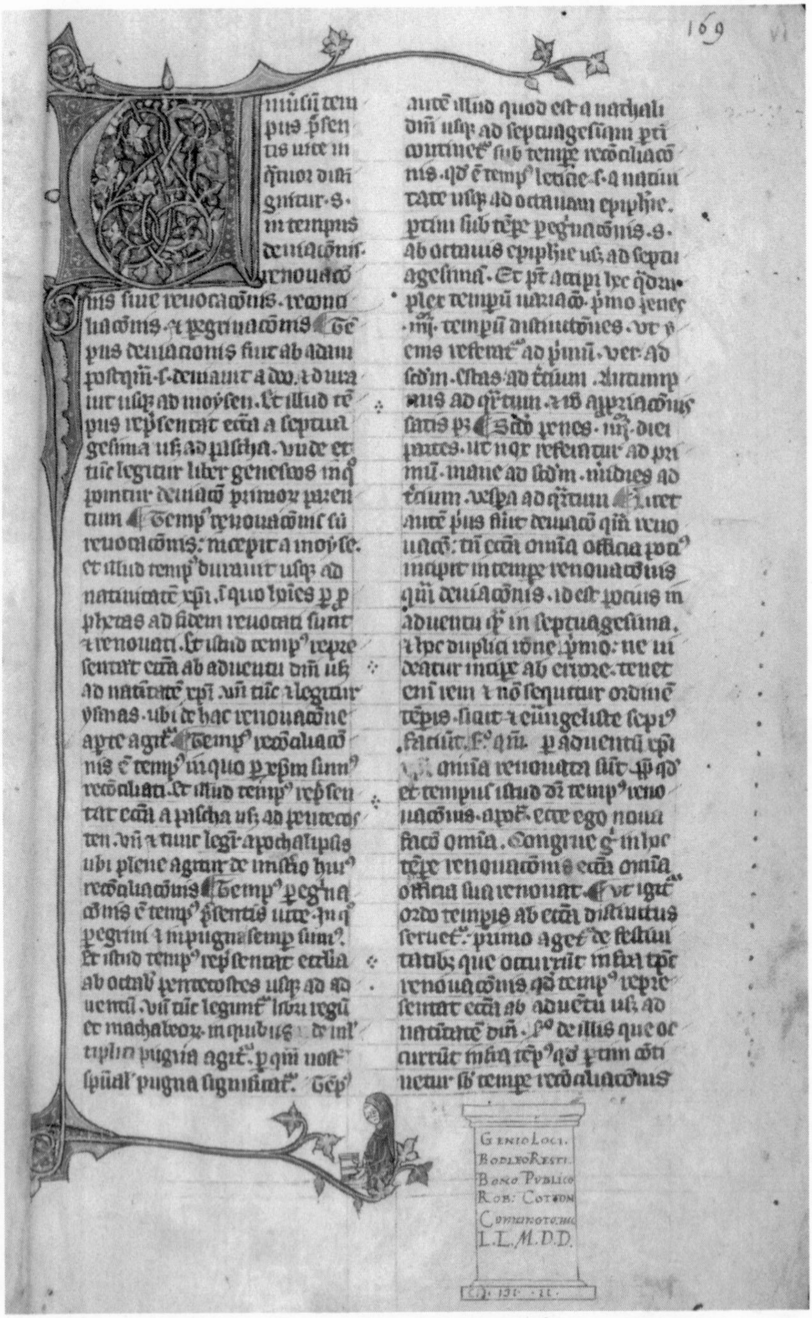

GENIO LOCI.
BODLIO RESTI.
BONO PVBLICO
ROB. COTTON
CVMHONOTEMO
L.L. M.D.D.

Fig. 7. Robert Cotton's drawing of a votive altar in *Legenda sanctorum*
(Bodleian Library, University of Oxford, MS Bodl. 336, fol. vi r)

indicates the method by which saints become library books: through the transformation of monastic into antiquarian literacy.

This, I argue, is how Cotton envisioned his library. An example of such transformation in action appears not in Cotton's library but in his cabinet of curiosities, which adjoined his library and in many important ways complemented its holdings.[126] In place of the natural oddities and quasi-scientific specimens fashionable with other seventeenth-century collectors, Cotton's cabinet focused on what John Speed called "old monuments," material artifacts of British history.[127] These included Roman coins in abundance, royal seals, old maps, pottery shards, and broken statues.[128] Along with these valuable but not atypical archeological finds, Cotton's cabinet also housed a highly unusual specimen: a fragment of the skull of St. Thomas Becket.[129] Becket, of course, was notorious among early modern Protestants; by memorializing his struggle with Henry II, his cult upheld the preeminence of church over Crown that the Reformation sought to overturn, and the Reformation's agents in England targeted Becket's relics and shrine with focused determination. Becket's relics and their fate also attracted the attention of post-Reformation antiquarians.[130] John Stow's *Chronicles of England from Brute vnto this Present yeare of Christ* (1580) describes the destruction of Becket's shrine and relics in Christ Church, Canterbury:

> Saint Austin[es] Abbey at Canterbury was suppressed, and the Shrine and goodes taken to the Kings treasurie as also the Shrine of Thomas Becket in the Priory of Christ Church, was likewise taken to the Kings vse, *and his bones scull and all, which was there found, with a péece broken out by the wound of his death, were all brent in the same Church by the Lord Cromwell.* The Monkes there were commanded to change their habites &c. (My emphasis)[131]

For Stow, the story of the disposal of Becket's skull fits into a larger story of appropriation and desanctification; the abbey's "goods" are "taken to the king's treasury" and Becket's shrine is "taken to the king's use," just as the monks are forced to "change their habits" and thus to become men among men. Amid these examples of holy objects and people secularized, the treatment of Becket's skull stands out as an act of destruction: at Cromwell's command, the bones, including the skull—which bore the mark of Becket's martyrdom—"were all burned in the same church."

But not all accounts agree with Stow's. A contemporary manuscript record of 1539, *Vindication of the Changes Recently Effected in England,* insists that Becket's "shrine and bones [were] therefore taken away and bestowed where they will cause no superstition afterwards."[132] This account places Becket's bones in the larger story of transformation and desanctification that frames Stow's account of the Reformation as enacted at Canterbury: holy goods are appropriated into the king's treasury and monks change their clothing, and likewise, the bones, transported to a new (though unnamed) place and context, are cleansed of the taint of superstition.

Cotton's cabinet of curiosities is such a place, where medieval objects can be "taken away and bestowed where they will cause no superstition afterwards." Just as Cotton's library desanctifies the formerly holy books in its holdings, so too his cabinet desanctifies the holiest of medieval relics—the skull fragment from St. Thomas Becket, which bore witness to his martyrdom and secured his sainthood, along with the sanctity of his shrine in Canterbury. Cotton's treatment of the skull fragment represents a late stage in the story of desanctification recounted by Stow, enacted not through destruction but through preservation. By preserving the skull fragment alongside the Roman coin or the pottery shard, Cotton reclassifies relic as artifact.[133] Becket's skull fragment in Cotton's cabinet is no longer an object of belief but a specimen in the history of belief.

The same process of reclassification extends to the Cotton Library and its use of religious texts as historical sources. Cleopatra D. ix, a volume that immediately precedes Cotton's volumes of collected materials on the Reformation, Cleopatra E. i, contains as its final entry the "narratio de vita, miraculis, et translatione Thomae Cantuariensis, rhythmis Anglicus." The text is extracted from the *South English Legendary*, which Julia Boffey calls "one of the most varied and extensive Middle English collections of lives," as well as one of the most "widely transmitted."[134] But Cleopatra D. ix situates the legend of St. Thomas within a markedly political context, binding it with Simon Islip's "Speculum Edwardi III," a complaint against royal exaction that parallels Becket's struggles with Henry II. This treatment of Becket as a political figure extends to the Cleopatra E. sequence, with its sources documenting the political and legal conflicts between popes and kings beginning in the ninth century. Among these, the volume includes a "Collectanea de litibus inter Henricum II et Thomam Beckettum, aliisque historici argumenti."[135] In this section appear transcriptions of letters and other accounts relating to the Becket affair, which originally appeared in the *Ymagines historiarum* of the twelfth-century chronicler Ralph of Diss (Diceto).[136] Ralph was a favored source for post-Reformation antiquarians: Bale lists him among the forgotten medieval authors whose work deserved to be recuperated "to the bewtie of our nacyon," while Holinshed approvingly describes "Radulfus de Diceto, whose noble historie is yet extant in ther librarie."[137] Ralph may have owed his popularity among post-Reformation antiquarians to his royal sympathies; as Charles Duggan and Anne Duggan observe of Ralph, "his loyalty was manifestly secured to the English crown."[138] This impression is borne out by the letters on Becket that are reproduced in Cotton E. i.[139]

Early modern historians read Becket's letters to Henry II as evidence supporting the Crown: Holinshed, for example, cites them to illustrate Becket's arrogance and insubordination: "the said Thomas Becket was so proud, that he wrote to king Henrie the second, as to his lord, to his king, and to his sonne, offering him his counsell, his reuerence, and due correction, &c."[140] This evidence leads Holinshed to conclude, "Thus we sée, that kings were to rule no further than it pleased the pope to like of; neither to chalenge more obedience of their subiects than stood also with their good will and pleasure."[141] Where Holinshed cites Becket's letters to justify his downfall, Cotton, by inserting them into the Cleopatra volumes, places that downfall within a long narrative of English Reformation that begins in the ninth century and ends with the collected letters and original edicts of Henry VIII himself.

As presented in the Cleopatra D. and E. volumes, the story of Thomas Becket reflects a larger Reformation history as written by its winners. The inclusion of the *South English Legendary* extract in Cleopatra D. ix is also a case of hagiography being made to tell the story of its own desanctification. This story reaches its climax in the Cleopatra E. iv volume, which includes a letter to Thomas Cromwell by his agent and son-in-law, Sir John Prise (whom we met in the preceding chapter); the letter reports on the excesses of relic and saint veneration, which were cited in order to justify the dissolution of the monasteries. From Bury St. Edmunds Prise mockingly writes, "Amongest the reliques we founde moche vanitie and superstition, as the coles that Saint Laurence was tosted withal, the paring of S. Edmundes naylles, S. Thomas of Canterbury penneknyff and his bootes, and divers skulles" (Cleopatra E. iv, fol. 120v).

What happened to the boots and penknife of St. Thomas, skulls, and other relics that Prise describes to Cromwell is impossible to say—unlike the books that Prise found in his monastic surveys, many of which he appropriated for his own library. Prise was, in fact, the source of Cotton's copy of the *South English Legendary*'s legend of Thomas Becket, which is preserved in Cleopatra D. ix. Prise obtained the work from Cirencester, in his capacity as commissioner, and he left marginalia throughout the legend that are aimed, like his work for Cromwell, at discrediting Becket's cult. As annotator, Prise plays the role of Becket's judge, charging the saint with

"arrogance" and "obstinacie" for refusing to recognize King Henry's authority (Cleopatra D. ix, fol. 138v) (fig. 8). When Becket predicts that he will
"deie . . . in martyrdom," Prise responds with the marginal condemnation
"yea, a stynkyng martyr" (Cleopatra D. ix, fol. 137v).

The comment recalls a marginal note in Foxe's *Book of Martrys*, also concerning Becket. In his 1562 edition of *Acts and Monuments* Foxe reprints "A
Compendious Olde Treatise, Shewing how that we Ought to Have the Scripture in Englishe," which cites and translates from Richard Rolle's psalter on
the "foetentes martires" who offend God: "and thoughe such as be slaine
doo miracles, neuertheless they be stinking martirs." To this, Foxe affixes
a marginal note that comments, "He meneth by like Thomas Becket."[142]
Becket is a "stinking martyr" because his sacrifice is not sanctified by God;
thus, the term, as wielded by Foxe, performs an act of desanctification.
By annotating his manuscript of the *South English Legendary* to condemn
Becket as a "stynkyng martyr," Prise extends Foxe's desanctifying critique
to the medieval legend itself. In so doing, he transforms the Foxian compulsion to distinguish true martyrs from false ones—and thus to differentiate
his own saint-making project from medieval hagiography—into a model of
textual criticism, directed at detecting and desanctifying the false martyr
through the critical medium of marginalia.[143]

The legend of St. Thomas as preserved in Cotton's volume illustrates the
contrast between sixteenth- and seventeenth-century collectors and their
approaches to the medieval manuscripts they handled. Sir John Prise and Sir
Robert Cotton were both Protestant collectors of Catholic books of saints;
and in the case of the legend of St. Thomas, both Prise and Cotton engaged
in the practice of desanctifying the saint's life. But they handle the book
in dramatically, and tellingly, different ways. Prise aggressively interrogates
his text of Becket, as he did the monks of Bury, of whom, as he reported to
Cromwell, "we did use moche diligence in our examinacion" (Cleopatra E.
iv, fol. 120v). Similarly, as a reader, Prise conducts a diligent examination by
marginally responding to, rebuking, and correcting the legend, as if dressing
down an adversary in public.

In contrast, Cotton compiles the text within the Cleopatra D. ix volume,
and in the process, he trims Prise's marginalia—an example of his notorious
instruction to his binder, "I car not for the new notts," that has made Cotton
the bane of modern scholars.[144] All the same, Cotton's compilation method
represents a shift in post-Reformation approaches to pre-Reformation texts.
If Prise adapts a Foxian reading model in his compulsion to distinguish
truth from falsehood, Cotton adapts another facet of Foxian historiography:
its artful compilation of primary sources to rewrite the medieval past as a

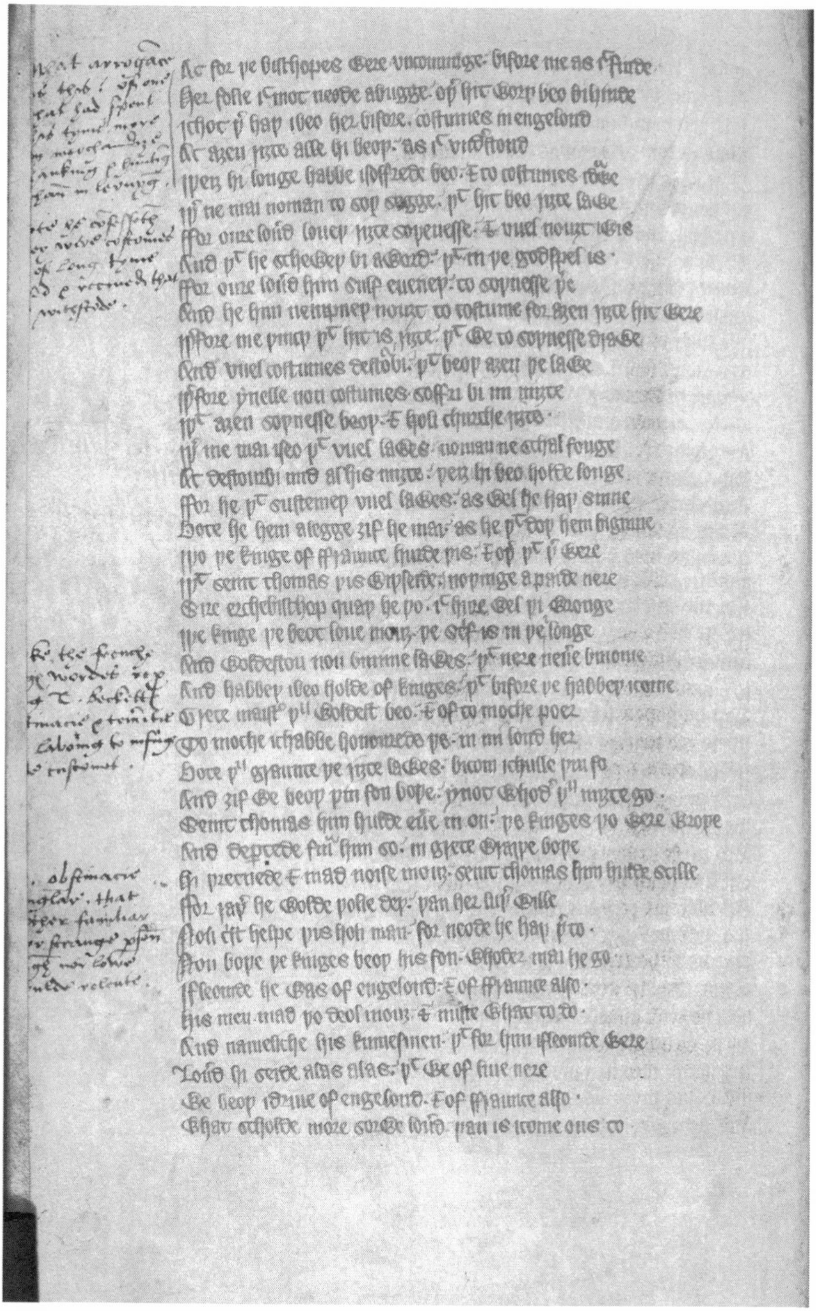

Fig. 8. John Prise's annotation on *The South English Legendary* (Cotton
MS Cleopatra D. ix, fol. 138v, The British Library). Photograph: ©
The British Library Board. All Rights Reserved.

prelude to religious reform.[145] Rather than attempting to correct his book from
the margins, he preserves it—in his own way—by cutting out the "newer
notes" and collating the text with historical materials that place the text
within an ongoing story of royal exaction and conflict between church and
Crown. As with the skull fragment of Thomas Becket in Cotton's cabinet, here
the legend of St. Thomas is desanctified by context; once interpolated into the
Cleopatra volumes, it becomes a historical artifact, valuable not for the truth
that it conveys but for the light it sheds on the false beliefs of the past.

The Reformation project of desanctifying hagiography, I am arguing,
is continued and advanced through Cotton's archivization of medieval
manuscripts.[146] Cotton's practice of binding saints' lives with sources of
Protestant historical interest, following the example of the Cleopatra volumes, incorporates them into the long history of the Reformation. In Otho
C. xvi, a work that was partially destroyed in the fire of 1731 but whose contents are recorded by the seventeenth-century librarian Thomas Smith, the
lives of St. Kenelm and St. Guthlac are bound with extracts from Higden's
Polychronicon, making these hagiographies into footnotes of the chronicle
that recounts their stories. The *Polychronicon*'s historical arc is extended
through the dissolution of the monasteries through the interpolation of a
series of notes on "events from 1536 to 1542."[147] It is followed by Roger
Dymmok's "Liber contra duodecim errores et heresies Lollardorum," a text
both containing and refuting the "twelve Conclusions of the Lollards,"
which is followed in turn by a "Sermon in Defense of the Scripture, in
English." This work has been identified with the same Middle English tract
that circulated among the Parker circle, reprinted by Foxe as "A Compendious Olde Treatise, Shewing how that we Ought to Haue the Scripture
in English."[148] In support of vernacular Bible translation, this work cites
"Sistrence" and "Cistrence" (i.e., Higden) several times: "Sistrence in his
fifte booke the 24. c°. seith the euangelie of Jon was drawen into Englice be
the for seide Bede" and "Cistrence in his sext boke the i. seith that Al[f]-
rede the kynge ordined opone scolis of diuerse artes in Oxenforde; and he
turnede the best lawes in to his modir tunge, and the sawter also."[149] Bound
with Higden's *Polychronicon* and other materials relating to late medieval
and Reformation era religious controversy, this text confirms the historical interests that drove the compilation of Otho C. xvi. If the lives of the
saints become footnotes to the *Polychronicon*, the *Polychronicon* itself becomes a footnote to the "Sermon in Defense of the Scripture." Finally, they
all become footnotes to the Reformation, which is presaged in the Lollard
controversies and completed in the "events" of 1536–42.

A text like Otho C. xvi shows how Cotton read his Higden.[150] From Higden, Cotton inherits a mode of imposing order on a wide array of textual sources through compilation, while his uses of chronological order likewise imply narrative continuities and relationships of cause and effect. Like Higden's *Polychronicon*, Cotton's compilations include both "marvels" and "deeds," the "narratio de vita, miraculis, et translatione Thomae Cantuariensis, rhythmis Anglicis," as well as "Collectanea de litibus inter Henricum II et Thomam Beckettum, aliisque historici argumenti." A telling difference is that while Higden includes the lives and stories of saints in order to authenticate history, Cotton includes them in order to submit them to a rigorous historical authentication, in which the losers will be discredited, like Ursula and Emerita, and others, like Thomas Becket, will become villains in the larger history of the Reformation, which transforms medieval articles of belief into "narrationes quaedam fabulosae de visionibus & miraculis." Where Higden's order of history is founded on a chronology of six ages, the chronology that orders Cotton's materials in his Cleopatra volumes is based on a post-Reformation periodization that separates the medieval age of belief from the modern age of knowledge.[151] The Reformation becomes a master narrative not only of historical change but also of a process of transformation that is carried out in the Cotton Library itself.

At least, this is how Cotton's Protestant contemporaries viewed and used the Cleopatra volumes. John Speed's *History of Great Britaine* (1611) was indebted to the Cotton Library for numerous sources, but especially those relating to the Reformation.[152] Speed reveals Cotton's influence most clearly in his chapters treating Henry VIII, the margins of which bear references to Cottonian sources: "Ex MS," "Ex Original MS," and "Ex MS R. Cot." Presenting original sources on the visitation of the monasteries, the references draw almost exclusively from Cotton's compilation Cleopatra E. iv, with its "Divers originall Letters, copyes of Articles inquirable, Injunctions and directions, tending to the Suppression of the Monasteryes in H.8. time. As also the substance of what was certified touching very many Monasteryes by the visitors; together with the values of them," as the volume's table of contents, signed "Robertus Cotton. 1612," reports (fol. 4r).

The same volume of materials also supplies the source for a table of monasteries and priories that Speed appends to his history, with this heading:

> The tempestuous stormes in the Raigne of this king Henrie the eight, and the violent deluge rased against the church . . . bare downe so many religious strong foundations, and were the destruction of so many beautiful

Monasteries, as the only relation of their numbers and names, would have much interrupted the narration of this history. *Wherefore to reteine their memorials (though their walles are laid waste) as well for the reuerence we owe unto venerable Antiquity,* as for the example of their Founders holy zeale, we have inserted a cataloge of their names, orders, and true valuations, as in the originall Booke thereof taken by commission, and given unto the king. (786; my emphasis)

To compile this table, Speed drew directly on Cotton's records of monastic holdings that were preserved in Cleopatra E. iv and that were originally compiled by Cromwell's commissioners as they carried out the dissolution. Where the commissioners intended these documents to record the spoils yielded by the newly closed monasteries, for Speed they provide a "memorial" to what is lost.[153] The dissolution is responsible for the effacement of the monasteries as well as for the production of original documents recording the history of the effaced monasteries; it destroys religious institutions and produces memorials, becoming the means by which the medieval is both lost as an object of belief and recovered as an object of memory.

The Cotton School of Prose, I: Camden's *Britannia*

Cotton's influence can be read in the numerous works of prose nonfiction that were written in connection with his library. Their writers—Speed, Camden, Ussher, and many others—shared with Cotton a commitment to the authority of documentary evidence, and much of the documentary evidence they used was supplied directly from the Cotton Library. Like Cotton, these writers struggled to adapt medieval texts to the central concerns and methods of seventeenth-century scholarship, even as they revealed themselves to be the sometimes-uneasy heirs of medieval textual methods and models. In this and the following section, I turn to two texts that were written in close association with Cotton and his library: William Camden's *Britannia* (1586; trans. Philemon Holland, 1607) and the lesser-known *Ancient Funerall Monuments*, by John Weever (1631). Both were extraordinarily influential examples of prose nonfiction in their own day—*Britannia* went through numerous reprintings, and Weever's text was one of the best-known antiquarian works of its time. Both, moreover, incorporate substantial selections from their primary sources, medieval texts that they borrowed from the Cotton Library, to such an extent that they have been called anthologies or even one-volume "libraries" of medieval verse. In so doing, I argue, they show how seventeenth-century prose nonfiction produced literary forms that approximated and adapted to the needs of print readership the models of compilation that Cotton used to organize medieval books and documents in his library.

Camden's *Britannia* has long been celebrated as a landmark in the history of scholarship for its pioneering use of primary research.[154] First published in a quarto Latin edition in 1586, it accrued ever-increasing amounts of archival material in its successive reissues, for which Camden turned to his friend Cotton, formerly his student at Westminster School.[155] As well as sharing an interest in antiquarian matters, Cotton and Camden were close collaborators in research ventures: in 1599 Cotton and Camden undertook a tour of Roman sites in the north of England, the resulting findings of which Camden recorded in illustrations of archeological remains that were printed in the 1607 edition of *Britannia*.[156] These were augmented by illustrations of coins and other materials that Camden borrowed from Cotton's cabinet of curiosity, showing how Camden's experience of Cotton's collections extended from books to other physical objects; indeed, in Camden's accounts of his research, books become a form of archeological artifact, the physical remains of the past that speak in a language that is no longer that of the researcher.[157] *Britannia* itself could be called a romance of the archive, in which the library is a central imaginary setting.[158] But in Camden's description, the library is not a simple repository of written records so much as the embodiment of strenuous firsthand research of a kind that recalls his tours with Cotton. As Camden asserts in his preface, "I have looked into most Libraries, Registers, and memorials; I have poored upon many an old Rowle, and Evidence: and produced their testimonie (as beyond all exception) when the cause required, in their very owne words (although barbarous they be) that the honor of veritie might in no wise be impeached" ("The Author to the Reader"). The library as a trove of primary evidence uncovered through heroic effort guarantees the authority of primary evidence on which Camden grounds his work. By presenting the *Britannia* itself as a compilation of original sources carefully selected and quoted "in their very owne words," Camden reproduces in a work of prose nonfiction what Cotton achieved in his library, with its volumes of primary sources similarly recounting their writers' stories "in their owne words."

Camden has been called the first modern historian because of his use of primary sources to establish, in Hugh Trevor-Roper's words, "a new base of scientific documentation."[159] Camden's passion for documentation and his incorporation of sources, as I argue above, reflect his alliance with the Cotton Library; yet Camden's long-held reputation as an early archival positivist has been challenged by Patrick Collinson, who argues against the tendency "to credit him with writing a history close to its sources, equivalent to the truth as he saw it, and even as it very probably was," pointing out that such expectations "may prove to be an inappropriate and anachronistic way to judge Camden, or any other historian of his age."[160] Following Collinson, I argue that Camden took a more skeptical and adversarial approach to the documentary source than his own preface, not to mention his later readers, would acknowledge. For Camden, manuscript research involves more than "neopositive performances of archival discovery and description" (in the words of Karen Newman, critiquing the archival turn of more recent scholarship).[161] If Camden lets his sources speak "in their own words," it is not because he sees documentary evidence as a transparent bearer of a self-evident truth. Rather, research as represented in Camden's model requires an active struggle to extract the truth of the past from sources that are sometimes written from the perspective of opposing models of truth: such is the dilemma of the Protestant historian at work on medieval texts.

In his preface to the *Britannia* Camden famously pronounces, "I would restore antiquity to Britaine, and Britaine to his antiquity," a statement commonly taken to identify Camden's historical interests with classical antiquity.[162] But Camden's project takes on a decidedly post-Reformation cast in the lines that immediately follow: "I would... cleare doubts, and recall home veritie by way of recovery, which the negligence of writers and credulitie of the common sort had in a manner proscribed and utterly banished from amongst us. A painefull matter I assure you." This project of recovering "veritie" from "credulitie" is one that Camden shared with Protestant library makers like Cotton who sought, as I have argued, to transform objects of belief into documentary sources or evidence for historical truth. As Camden insists, his aim is to write a British history that, unlike medieval sources such as Geoffrey of Monmouth, extracts truth from fables and thus produces history: "not out of feined fables, which were vanitie to recite, and meere folly to beleeve, but out of the incorrupt and ancient monuments."[163] But what makes the project "painful," as Camden puts it, is that manuscripts will not speak the truth themselves; instead, they must be made to do so through active intervention. Perhaps nowhere is this clearer than in the case of the saint's life.

In preparing and expanding the *Britannia*, Camden borrowed numerous saints' lives from Cotton, as shown in Cotton Library lending records, which reveal that Camden read hagiography attentively, including William of Malmesbury's life of St. Dunstan, Felix's life of St. Guthlac, a life of

St. Birinus, and several vitae by Henry of Avranches.[164] The voluminous manuscript notes that Camden took from these sources indicate that he used hagiography as a source of local history; many of the details about place-names and chronologies that he gleaned from his researches in hagiography are invisibly incorporated into the text.[165]

Other examples of Camden's use of hagiography are more explicit. In his discussion of St. Alban, whom Camden praises as "a citizen of singular holiness and faith in Christ," Camden cites Venantius Fortunatus, the late-sixth-century Italian priest and bishop of Poitiers who was a prolific poet and hagiographer. Camden credits Fortunatus with a Latin line that he then translates into verse:

> *Albanum egregium foecunda Britannia profert.*
> Fruitfull Britan bringeth foorth
> Alban a Martyr of high worth. (2.410)

But Camden's source for this line is not Fortunatus but Bede, who changes Fortunatus's original wording to produce the line that Camden quotes.[166] For Bede, the quotation from Fortunatus prefaces a conventional hagiography: chapter 7 of his *Ecclesiastical History* recounts Alban's devout life and martyrdom, culminating in a set of miracles that in Bede's account continue to the present: "To this day sick people are healed in this place and the working of frequent miracles continues to bring it renown."[167] Where Bede presents Alban as a figure of belief, Camden makes him into a historical artifact. As Camden reports from "A Legend of his Passion and Martyrdome," "the citizens engraved his Martyrdom in a Marble Stone, and inserted the same in their walles" (2.410). Here the writing of the saint's life becomes an archeological event: where the hagiographical lines of Fortunatus are cited as tributes to Alban's historical fame, the production of his legend is identified with the creation of material artifacts. Camden implicitly contrasts his own archeological exhumation of Alban's record with the medieval reverence for his burial site when he notes that St. German "commended the sepulcher of Saint *Albane* to be opened: and *therin bestowed, certain reliques of Saints, that when one in heaven had received, should also in one sepulcher be together lodged.* Thus much I note by the way, that yee may observe and consider the fashions of that age" (2.410).[168] In Camden's retelling, this account of relic veneration becomes itself a kind of archeological artifact: a reflection of the ancient religious practices and cultural alterity of their Catholic practitioners, safely removed to the medieval past.

As further support he cites the twelfth-century poet and scholar Alexander Neckham, who wrote about the Roman town of Verulamium (present-day Saint Albans):

In the commemoration of Verulam an Hexastich of Alexander Necham, who 400. yeares since was there borne.

> *Vrbs insignis erat Verolamia, plus operosæ*
> *Arti, naturæ debuit illa minus.*
> *Pendragon Arthuri patris haec obsessa laborem*
> *Septennem spreuit ciue superba suo.*
> *Hic est martyrii roseo decoratus honore*
> *Albanus, ciuis, inclita Roma, tuus.*
> The famous towne whilom cald Verolame,
> To Nature ought lesse than to painfull art;
> When *Arthurs* Syre *Pendragon* gainst it came,
> With force of Armes to worke her peoples smart;
> His seven yeeres siege did never daunt their heart.
> Heere *Alban* gain'd the Crowne of Martyrdome,
> Thy Citizen sometime ô noble Rome. (2.412)

Camden closes his discussion by noting, "*Verolamium* at this day being turned into fields: The towne of Saint *Albans* raised out of the ruins thereof flourisheth" (2.412). Camden approaches the history of the town of Saint Albans as an archeologist would: he excavates historical evidence from hagiographical sources, making the story of the saints part of the story of the town's sedimented past.[169] Camden's literary archaeology performed on medieval hagiography runs in a direction counter to the archeological impulse that Leonard Barkan explores, for example, in *Unearthing the Past*; Camden is not uncovering "initiations of a historical—and transhistorical—dialogue," but by unearthing the medieval past, he is remaking it as artifact and thereby establishing its historical alterity.[170] Where later "scientific" practices of archeology would contrast the authority of "things" with that of written sources, Camden's use of medieval manuscripts turns the written source into a thing: its authority comes not from what it says, and far less from the truth claims it presents, but from its status as a found object, whose physical age makes it into a material emissary from and a firsthand witness to the past it represents.[171] Camden's textual archeology might be compared to Cotton's cabinet, with its curious holding of the fragment of Becket's skull. By rejecting their miraculous claims, Camden, like Cotton, reclassified the objects of medieval hagiography as sources of historical knowledge.

A similar archeological performance occurs in Camden's use of other hagiographical sources borrowed from Cotton's library; one book that Cotton lent to Camden, Vitellius D. xiv (destroyed in the fire of 1731), contained the lives of English saints by Henry of Avranches and became Camden's source for discussions of St. Guthlac and St. Fremund.[172] In his discussion of Croyland Camden mentions "Guthlake a right holy and devout man [who] led there an Eremit's life. In whose memorial Aethelbald king of the Mercians founded to the honor of God at his great charges, in the yeere of our salvation 716 an Abbay very famous both for opinion of the religious life of the Monkes, & also for their Wealth" (2.529). Camden quotes from Henry of Avranches's life of Guthlac (which he misattributes, calling them "verses of Faelix a Monke of good antiquity") to describe the abbey founded in Guthlac's memory.

> Nunc exercet ibi se munificentia regis,
> Et magnum templum magno molimine condit.
> At cum tam mollis, tam lubrica, tam male constans
> Fundamenta palus non ferret saxea, palos
> Præcipit infigi quercino robore cæsos,
> Leucarumque nouem spatio rate fertur arena;
> Inque solum mutatur humus, suffultaque tali
> Cella basi, multo stat consummata labore.[173]
> His bounty now the King doth there bestow,
> An Abbay faire with much expense to reare.
> But seeing that the waterish fenne below,
> Those ground-workes laid with stone uneath could beare,
> (So quaving soft and moist the Bases were)
> He caused piles made of good heart of oke,
> Pitch't downe to be with maine commanders stroke.
> Then nine leagues off, men sand in barges brought,
> Which once fast ramm'd by painfull workmans hand,
> Of rotten earth good solide ground was wrought;
> On which for ay such workes might firmly stand:
> And thus by this devise of new plantation,
> The Church stands firme and hath sure foundation. (2.530)

This story of firm foundations pitched on unstable ground makes a compelling allegory for the Reformation in England, which continually proclaimed

the solidity of its ancient foundation. But in order to unearth the solid
ground of historical knowledge, Protestants complained that they had to cut
through the watery topsoil of medieval belief.[174] A similar act of excavation
is reenacted in Camden's reading of Henry of Avranches; while he accepts his
story of the abbey's foundation as historical fact, he rejects Henry's accounts
of Guthlac's miracles, the basis of his sainthood, which he presents to his
readers as comic relief:

> If I should exemplifie unto you out of that Monke, the divels of *Crowland*,
> with their blabber lips, fire-spitting mouths, rough and skaly visages,
> beetle heads, terrible teeth, . . . which heeretofore walked and wandered
> up and downe in these places, and very much troubled holy *Guthlake*
> and the Monkes, you would laugh full merily; and I might be thought a
> simple sily-one full worthily. (2.530)

For Camden, the fabulous accretions of miracle stories must be stripped
away to reveal the solid ground of historical fact.

The same Cotton manuscript, Vitellius D. xiv, contained a life of St.
Fremund, which Camden cites in his account of Off-Church.[175] After sum-
marizing the saint's life and death, Camden observes:

> which death of his notwithstanding turned to his greater glorie. For,
> beeing buried at his fathers Palace, now called *Off-Church*, hee liveth
> yet unto posterity, as who being raunged in the Catalogue of our Saints
> hath among the multitude received divine honours: and whose life is by
> an ancient writer set out in a good Poeme, out of which let it bee no
> offense to put downe these few verses following:
>
>   . . .   .
>   Past hope, whiles *Fremund* liv'd, to speed of wished regalty,
>   All secret and unworthy meanes he plots to make him die.
>   With naked sword, prophane slaue he, assaileth cowardly
>   His Lord unwares, and as he lay beheads him cruelly.
>   At *Widford* thus Prince *Fremund* did this glorious crowne attaine,
>   Whiles slaying guilty folke, at once, himselfe is guiltlesse slaine.
>   (2.561–62)

Again, Camden retools a hagiographical manuscript into a historical source
that reinforces the lasting value of the written record. Fremund's death is
"turned to his greater glorie" not because he becomes a saint but because his

life is written "in the Catalogue of our Saints." This "Catalogue" is probably a Cotton manuscript, John of Tynemouth's *Nova Legenda Anglie* (Tiberius E. i), which records the Fremund legend alongside those of many other English saints.[176] Camden asserts that in this "Catalogue" Fremund "liveth yet unto posterity," replacing sainthood with the archive as the safeguard of immortality. Rather than through religious veneration, then, Fremund's glory is secured when he becomes the subject of "a good Poem."

Camden transforms hagiography into epitaph, which commemorates rather than sanctifies. This use of verse as memorial is consistent with Camden's interest in epitaphs elsewhere; in *Remains concerning Britain*, Camden collects numerous epitaphs as examples of how "memory was continued to posterity" through written forms.[177] The Society of Antiquaries made epitaphs the focus of several meetings. At one, a member notes that epitaphs should "taste of nothing of the moderne, but be all al'antiche," a formulation that resonates with Camden's citation of medieval verse to emphasize its alterity and participation in "the fashions of that age."[178] Similarly, the antiquarian-lawyer James Ley's essay "Of Epitaphs" speculates on the earliest history of the poetic form, wondering whether

> I may be licensed to call that an Epitaph, which was found, notifying the place of the burial of Kenelm called the Martyr:
>
> > In clene kan hath kenelin kynebeane
> > Lith under thorne heave byreaued.[179]

The "epitaph" is actually a miraculous scroll written in golden letters (as we might recall from the retelling of St. Kenelm's legend in the *Polychronicon*). Like Camden, Ley transforms hagiography into epitaph.

In Camden's collection of epitaphs in the *Remains*, as his editor notes, he "restores scholarly interest in medieval Latin verse [by producing something] like an anthology."[180] The same is true of Camden's *Britannia*; in its compilation of hagiographical material, it contains within it a virtual library of medieval verse. It is noteworthy that Camden chooses to cite hagiography in verse, even when his source, such as Bede or Felix, actually writes in prose. While Camden mines his prose sources for facts that he invisibly incorporates into his text, he cites his verse sources directly. Camden's tendency to incorporate medieval verse into his text has been a noted feature of the *Britannia*.[181] I argue that his aim in so doing was to create a distinction between his medieval sources and his own prose.

The distinction between prose and verse in the Middle Ages is closely related to changing ideas about narrative truth, as Gabrielle Spiegel has shown in her account of "the rise of vernacular prose historiography in thirteenth-century France."[182] In France, Spiegel shows, as prose became increasingly associated with truthfulness, it replaced verse as the preferred medium of historiography. In England, however, the shift from verse to prose was belated, and the relatively later acceptance of prose historiography is witnessed by the existence of verse chronicles like that of Robert of Gloucester in the late thirteenth or early fourteenth century, the fourteenth-century *Short Metrical Chronicle*, and fifteenth-century historical works by Lydgate such as *Verses on the Kings of England* and John Hardyng's midcentury *Chronicle*.[183] Indeed, a work like Michael Drayton's *Poly-Olbion* (1612) attests to the long English afterlife of historiographical forms in verse.[184] But where Drayton frames history in verse, Camden, for all the verse he incorporates into the *Britannia*, is careful to differentiate it from his own prose historiography.[185] Thus, he sets off the verses he cites by noting their antiquity: "Touching that King an antient Poet wrote thus" (1.224); "Of which, a Poet of good antiquity writeth thus" (1.225); "whereupon these verses were made ... by one living in those daies" (1.247); "whereof the said old Poet hath these pretty verses" (1.248); "and hence hath been taken up this od barbarous verse" (2.547). His verse citations fulfill Camden's prefatory promise to quote his sources "in their very owne words (although barbarous they be) that the honor of veritie might in no wise be impeached." The "barbarous" verses of his medieval sources do not produce "veritie" because they are transparent receptacles of the truth—far from it. Rather, they represent archeological fragments, the broken remains of a long- and safely distant past.[186]

By putting his medieval sources into verse, Camden distinguishes their "simple" claims and "barbarous words" from his own prose, producing fragments of medieval verse as specimens of temporal otherness, not continuity. Although Camden creates an anthology of medieval verse in the *Britannia*, he does so in order to bolster the authority of Renaissance prose. The authority of Camden's historiography comes not from the primary source but from the distance he erects between that source and the historian who frames it. As a compilation of primary sources, Camden's *Britannia* establishes its own periodization based on a historical break between a culture of prose, grounded in fact-based knowledge, and a verse-based culture of infantile belief.

Camden's prose, which becomes a massive receptacle of medieval verse fragments, reproduces in literary form the experience of working in the Cotton Library. Following Cotton, Camden aims to recuperate the objects of medieval religion as evidence toward a Protestant historiography. Toward this end, *Britannia's* primary sources become archeological fragments of a safely distant past, like the religious experiences they document. If the Reformation is an occulted story in Camden's history, it nonetheless everywhere informs Camden's representation of the medieval past, as a cataclysmic event that has turned the past's monuments into ruins. But those ruins make up the foundation of Camden's writing, recalling the ancient town of *"Verolamium* at this day being turned into fields: The towne of Saint Albans raised out of the ruins thereof flourisheth" (2.412). The description could offer an allegory of the Cotton Library itself, which, like Saint Albans "raised out of the ruins" of the former medieval pilgrimage site, drew from the raw materials of the medieval past to make a modern library. Similarly, Camden claims to give the manuscript remains of medieval verse new life by redeeming them as historical evidence in his capacious prose.

The Cotton School of Prose, II:
John Weever's *Ancient Funerall Monuments*

John Weever's *Ancient Funerall Monuments* (London, 1631) ranked with Camden's *Britannia* as one of the best-known works to emerge in connection with the Cotton Library.[187] Weever came belatedly to antiquarian studies, after essaying the genre of Protestant hagiography in his earlier work, *The mirror of martyrs, or The life and death of that thrice valiant capitaine, and most godly martyre Sir Iohn Old-castle knight Lord Cobham* (London, 1601). In it, Weever proposes to replace Becket with Oldcastle, condemning the tomb of the former ("this mocke-ape toy, this vaine alurement") while calling for some "immortal verse" to memorialize the latter's "entombless worth."[188] *Ancient Funerall Monuments* extends the earlier work's fixation on tombs and memorials to the level of material history, surveying and carefully describing all of the English tombs and memorial artifacts that its industrious author could locate within the dioceses of Canterbury, London, and Norwich.

Like other contemporary antiquarian projects, Weever's aims to repair damages that Reformation era iconoclasm inflicted on English material history.[189] As Weever explains in his preface, he conceived his work out of distress at the loss of funerary inscriptions that had been "erased, torne away, and pilfered" from "Ancient" (meaning medieval) tombs. In the wake of the dissolution, funerary monuments—particularly those in churches—were specifically targeted for destruction, reflecting their association with a range of "superstitious" medieval practices, from intercessory prayers to pilgrimage.[190] So widespread was their destruction that Queen Elizabeth issued a "Proclamation against breaking or defacing Monuments of Antiquitie, being set up in Churches, or other publike places, for memory, and not for superstition." Weever reprints this proclamation in full as justification for the recuperative efforts that underlie *Ancient Funerall Monuments* itself (52). Yet in 1631 it was possible to imagine a return of such iconoclastic practices, Weever writes, as Puritans threatened to "deface or quite demolish all Funerall Monuments, swearing and protesting that all these are remaines of Antichrist, papisticall and damnable" (38).[191] Thus, Weever determined, as he records, "to collect such memorials of the deceased, as were remaining as yet undefaced; as also to reuiue the memories of eminent worthy persons entombed or interred, either in Parish, or in Abbey Churches" ("Epistle to the Reader"). Many of those monuments were indeed destroyed in the seventeenth century, making Weever's their only surviving record.

Weever's search for funeral monuments in the face of Protestant iconoclasm places him in a parallel position to that of his more-famous Reformation era predecessors John Leland and John Bale, who searched and catalogued England's libraries at the very moment that the dissolution threatened their destruction. It is a parallel that Weever actively cultivates: after describing Leland's own gravesite in Saint Michael's Querne, London, Weever reprints "The Laboryous Iourney and Serche of Johan Leylande, for Englandes Antiqutiees," which describes its author's project "to serche all the Libraries of Monasteries and Collegies" so that "the Monuments of auncyent Wryters . . . myghte be brought out of deadly darkenesse, to ly[ve]ly light" (688). For Weever, Leland's project is continued into the seventeenth century by "such men in these dayes, who like Sir Robert Cotton with labour and charges, collect, and safely preserve these ancient Monuments of learning for the publique good and commodity of the whole kingdome" (692). This description of Cotton's collection and preservation of "ancient Monuments" clearly echoes Weever's own project to collect ancient funeral monuments, making Weever himself, along with Cotton, Leland's seventeenth-century inheritor. Like Leland, Weever also attempts to recover forsaken monuments from "deadly darkenesse to ly[ve]ly light." But where Leland seeks to repair bibliographical loss, Weever addresses human loss, by attempting to recover the forgotten dead from oblivion. Where for Leland the grave is a metaphor for historical amnesia, for Weever it becomes the literal object of recovery and rescue.

Ancient Funerall Monuments is a book obsessed with mortality: as a verse beneath the author's portrait declares, "His studies are of Death." Not only does the work describe the sites and catalogue the inscriptions of every funeral monument with which Weever's extensive travels brought him into contact, but it places funerary practices and artifacts into a broadly historical perspective, opening with chapters on such topics as "funeral monuments, graves, tombes, or sepulchers: of the ancient custome of burials; of Epitaphs and other Funerall Honours" (chap. 2); "Of the care and cost anciently used in the preserving whole and entire, the bodies of the dead" (chap. 6); and ultimately, "Of the rooting up, taking away, erasing and defacing of Funerall Monuments in the severall raignes of K. Henry the eight, and Edward the sixt. Of the care Queen Elizabeth, of famous memory, had for the preservation of the same" (chap. 10), which contains a full-length historical account of the Henrician Reformation, replete with primary sources.

Weever's retelling of Reformation history as a prelude to the destruction of funeral monuments owes its outlines and sources to Robert Cotton, who proved to be a generous supporter of Weever's project. As Weever records in his preface, Cotton lent him "out of his inestimable Librarie, such Bookes and Manuscripts as were most fitting for my use" ("Epistle"), allowing Weever to supplement his original records of tombs and their inscriptions, as he puts it, "with variety of historicall observations, annotations, and brief notes, extracted out of approved authors" ("Epistle"). The result is a massive compilation of historical and textual sources, whose derivation from Cotton is reflected in the plentiful marginal reference "Ex MS Cot," familiar from the work of Speed and Camden.

But Weever departs from his contemporaries in his reliance on literary manuscripts, which Cotton's readers, and Cotton himself, mostly ignored or grafted onto historical sources. Given the Cotton Library's important holdings in medieval literary manuscripts, it is ironic that Cotton himself showed little interest in literature. Records of the Cotton Library reveal that its early users shared Cotton's preference for historical documents over literary manuscripts; while a book of ecclesiastical laws like Nero A. i was frequently loaned to and excerpted by Cotton readers, who included Henry Howard, James Ussher, and John Selden, for example, there are no records of contemporary loans of a neighboring volume, Nero A. x, the now-famous manuscript of *Sir Gawain and the Green Knight*, *Patience*, *Pearl*, and *Cleaness*, despite its historically minded seventeenth-century classification as "Gesta Arthurii Regis et aliorum versu anglico."[192] In contrast, Weever made use of medieval literary manuscripts that were overlooked by his contemporaries, including those of John Gower (Tiberius A. iv), William Langland (possibly from Cotton Caligula A. xi), and Richard Rolle (from a manuscript "in the Earle of Exceters Libraire," 151).[193] Weever's text also abounds with citations of medieval literary authors from unidentified or printed sources, such as Chaucer, Hoccleve, and Lydgate, which are so plentiful that one of the few modern critics to comment on *Ancient Funerall Monuments* calls it "a florilegium of English medieval verse," identifying the recuperation of undervalued medieval literature as one of Weever's chief purposes in the book.[194]

Yet Weever's interest in medieval literary texts moves beyond recuperation toward a larger goal: to secure the post-Reformation library as the guardian of a collective memory that had formerly resided in the church. In his introduction, Weever classes books and manuscripts as privileged funerary monuments themselves; in a lengthy prefatory discussion covering the varieties of "Tombs and Sepulchres," Weever asserts, "Aboue all remembrances . . . for worthinesse and continuance, bookes, or writings, haue euer had the preheminence" (1). Of these, literary texts are privileged: "Bookes then and the Muses workes are of all monuments the most permanent" (3), because "it is only the Muses works which giue unto man immortality" (5). Such a treatment of literary texts is consistent with what I am arguing is Weever's larger project, the transformation of medieval cultural artifacts for post-Reformation purposes. Just as Elizabeth's edict defends "Monuments of Antiquitie" as vehicles "for memory, and not for superstition," for Weever, literary texts become privileged tools for the construction of memory.

In keeping with his memorial theme, the verse extracts that appear in Weever's work largely take the form of epitaph. Some of those epitaphs are transcribed from the actual tombs that Weever surveyed in his travels, as in Sittingborne, Kent, where Weever recorded this epitaph of one Elizabeth Poodde:

> I was as yee be, now in dust and clay,
> Haue mercy on my sowl that bought hit with thi blood,
> For *Elisabeth* of Cherite a *Pater-noster* say
> Sumtymes I was the wyff of *Edmuonde Poodde*. (279)

The erasure or loss of many inscriptions on other tombs forces Weever to seek the missing epitaphs in other archival sources. So in Faversham, Kent, he describes the tomb of Maud, the wife of King Stephen, "Whose Epitaph I found in a namelesse Manuscript." A marginal note reveals its source: "in bib. Cot." (278).

Weever approaches the Cotton Library as a trove of memorial writing. For example, Weever describes the monument of Robert Waldby, once archbishop of York, in Westminster Abbey, whose "Epitaph is quite worne or torne away from his monument": "yet I found it in a Manuscript, in Sir Robert Cottons Librarie" (481). Likewise, Weever concludes an account of the life and death of Thomas Becket with an epitaph in "Hexamiters" he claims to have "found in an old Manuscript in Sir Robert Cottons Library." The "old" Cottonian manuscripts that Weever consults in search of missing epitaphs establish the model for his use of literary sources. For example, in Canterbury Cathedral, Weever comes across the tomb of Henry IV, which, though "richly adorned and garnished," lacks an "Inscription" (206). Weever supplies this want by turning, characteristically, to the archives, writing, "Let this memorial of him, in such rimes as I haue it, stand for his Epitaph" (207). There follows an extract from Gower's *Cronica Tripertita* (*Tripartite Chronicle*), marginally cited "MSS. In bib. Cot.," which can be traced to Cotton Tiberius A. iv.[195] Weever reprints an extract that praises Henry by contrasting him with his predecessor, Richard II:

O quam pensando mores variosque notando,
Si bene scrutetur R. ab H. distare videtur.
Clarus sermone tenebrosus et intus agone.
R. pacem fingit, dum mortis federa stringit,
Duplex cautelis fuit R. pius H. que fidelis
R. pestem mittit, mortem pius H. que remittit.
R. plebem taxat, taxas pius H. que relaxat.
R. proceres odit et eorum predia rodit.
H. fauet heredes que suas restaurat in edes.
R. regnum vastat vindex & in omnibus astat,
Mulcet terrorem pius H. que reducit amorem. (207–8)

(If he be closely scrutinized through weighing and taking note of various character traits, O how different R. seems from H.! Brilliant of speech yet inwardly dark with suffering, R. made a pretense of peace even as he drew tight the bonds of death. R. let loose destruction and the merciful H. forsook bloodshed.... R. laid taxes upon the people and the merciful H. alleviated their taxes. R. hated the nobles and plundered their estates; H. cherished them and restored their heirs to their homes. The vindictive R. laid waste his kingdom and stood over everyone; H. mitigated fear and brought back brotherly love.)[196]

Weever turns to the same source in a later section of *Ancient Funerall Monuments*, when he seeks a memorial for Richard II, whom Weever encounters buried in Westminster Abbey.[197] After describing the "glorious Tombe" built for him by the guilty Henry V, Weever extracts a moralizing epitaph, again from Gower's *Cronica*, in lines that follow those above:

> Hoc concernentes caueant qui sunt sapientes;
> Nam male viuentes Deus odit in orbe regentes:
> Est qui peccator non esse potest dominator,
> Ricardo teste finis probat hoc manifeste. (473)

(Let those who are wise beware as they look upon this, for God abominates rulers on earth who live evilly. He who is a sinner cannot be a ruler; as Richard is my witness, his end proves this clearly.)[198]

Weever selectively reads Gower's *Cronica Tripertita* as a mirror for princes while casting himself in the mode of John Lydgate, whose archival research extracted similarly edifying lessons from Duke Humfrey's Library for *The Fall of Princes*.[199] Yet where Lydgate gleans his lessons to Humfrey from the duke's own books, Weever gleans his from Cotton's library, which was forcibly closed in 1629 on the order of Charles I—in part, as Kevin Sharpe reveals, because Cotton attempted to advise the king with lessons extracted from archival sources, thus promoting his library as a source of extramonarchal authority.[200] By identifying Cotton's library as his source for lessons on rulership and warnings to tyrants, Weever uses it in exactly the mode that threatened Charles. Moreover, lessons like Gower's, that Richard "hated the nobles and plundered their estates," directly recall Charles's forcible closure of the Cotton library itself. *Ancient Funerall Monuments* was published in 1631, and Weever's readers could be expected to know that the very library that supplied his sources had been closed for two years. Yet the legacy of monarchs, Weever insists, endures in libraries long after their earthly end. It is a lesson that Cotton understood no less than Parker himself: those who make libraries make history.

Gower, one of the most frequently cited medieval poets in *Ancient Funerall Monuments*, earns his place there as a master of the epitaphic mode. Gower makes his first appearance in *Ancient Funerall Monuments* when Weever cites in full the Latin verse "Dicunt Scripture," which closes Tiberius A. iv:

> Dicunt scripture memorare novissima vite;
> Pauper ab hoc mundo transiet omnis homo.
> Dat fortuna status varios, natura sed omnes

Fine suo claudit, cunctaque morte rapit.
Post mortem pauci qui nunc reputantur amici,
Sunt memores: anime sis memor ipse tue:
Da dum tempus habes, tibi propria sit manus heres;
Auferet hoc nemo quod dabis ipse Deo. (19)

(They say in Scripture to remember the end of life./Everyone will pass from this world as a poor man./Fortune gives various conditions, but Nature brings to an end/All with her own conclusion, seizing everything at death./ After your death few who are now considered friends/Will be mindful of your soul; therefore, you should be mindful of it yourself./Give, while you have time, let your heir be your own hand;/No one will take away what you yourself give to God.)[201]

This verse appears in the opening section of *Ancient Funerall Monuments*, as an example of epitaph. Identified as Gower's "additions to his booke called *Vox clamantis*" and cited from "Mss in bib. Cott." (19), it exemplifies "the reasons wherefore so many have made their owne Monuments in their life-time," namely, "because thereby they thought to preserue their memories from obliuion" (18). If Weever—whose "studies are of Death," and who, in 1631, was only a year away from his own death—meant his own work to serve as his monument, he calls on Gower to articulate the guiding mission of *Ancient Funerall Monuments* itself.

In selecting Gower as a model for epitaphic writing, Weever performs a canny reading of the medieval poet, both acknowledging the importance of Gower's frequent meditations on death while also transforming their meaning. Gower's signature mode as a poet is the memento mori, as epitomized by the lengthy conclusion to *Vox Clamantis*, the work with which Weever identifies the poem above. But for Gower, the memento mori is a spur to repentance, just as the "novissima vite" (end of life) in the "Dicunt Scripture" refers to the "four last things" (death, judgment, hell, and heaven), which gain their meaning through Catholic eschatology.[202] Within such a framework, the injunction to remember one's soul because friends and family will not ("Post mortem pauci qui nunc reputantur amici,/Sunt memores: anime sis memor ipse tue") must be taken to refer to the need to secure prayers for one's soul after death.[203]

Gower himself was mindful of this need to the point of obsession. As Siân Echard has established, several manuscripts of Gower's works fixate on the author's own death; where other literary manuscripts typically end by gesturing toward a more abstract posterity, the Gower manuscripts conclude with a short Latin text offering 1,500 days' indulgence to those who pray for Gower's soul, reproducing the wording of an actual indulgence that was written (and remains) on a plaque hanging next to Gower's tomb at Southwark Cathedral.[204] Weever's Cottonian source text, Cotton Tiberius A. iv, is among the manuscripts that ask readers to remember the author in their prayers—"orate pro anima Johannis Gowr"—and offer a generous indulgence in return (fol. 174v). Like the poem "Dicunt Scripture," these indulgenced texts locate Gower and his writing in a medieval culture of the intercessory graveside prayer—and in the process, they conflate the poet's manuscript with his tomb.[205]

By selecting Gower to exemplify those who "have made their owne Monuments in their life-time," Weever accurately reflects on Gower's provisions for his own death. But Weever also rewrites the intercessory and eschatological contexts from which Gower's writings on death drew their original meaning. Insisting that self-monumentalization arises from the desire to "preserue their memories from obliuion," Weever remakes Gower into a memorial writer, one who secures the afterlives of his subjects and himself not through intercessory prayer or other superstitious practices but through the durable writing of the monumental epitaph.

Weever's treatment of Gower as a memorial writer resonates with the medieval author's seventeenth-century reputation. As Helen Cooper points out, that reputation emphasized his antiquity—as in Shakespeare's *Pericles*, when "from ashes, ancient Gower is come" "to sing a song of old."[206] Weever similarly stresses Gower's age, calling him "that old Poet Sir John Gower" (626) and "An Author contemporary" with the medieval subjects he chronicles (226). Where Shakespeare's Gower comes from ashes, Weever's comes from manuscripts—which Weever sometimes calls "vet. MS," or old manuscript—whose very age underscores both their authority and their distance from the present.

As Weever insists in his prefatory "Epistle to the Reader," the use of manuscript sources is consistent with—and even necessary to—the memorial project to which *Ancient Funerall Monuments* is dedicated, by facilitating material encounters between the present and the past. Weever claims to extend those material encounters to the readers of his printed text by reproducing, rather than modernizing, "the orthographie of the old English as it comes to my hands," as he explains, "for I hold originals the best" ("Epistle"). He even reprints some of his quotations from manuscript in black letter, to replicate the visual appearance of gothic hands. By thus locating epitaphs in sources like Cotton Tiberius A. iv, Weever makes the manuscript not just a memorial to the past but an emissary from it.

Cotton Tiberius A. iv features Gower's *Vox Clamantis* and *Cronica Tripertita* alongside a collection of Gower's occasional and political verse; its seventeenth-century cataloguer classifies the whole work as a "Chronica," suggesting that Cotton himself may have seen Gower as an author worth collecting on the strength of his reputation less as a poet than as a writer of history.[207] Like Cotton, Weever also reads Gower as a historical writer, but his epitaphic quotations suggest a historicism focused less on the truth of the past (the concern of fellow antiquarians like Camden) than on its meanings in the present—less, that is, on fact than on memory. Memory, as Weever puts it in a lengthy introduction on the history of funerary practices, is the defining function of epitaph: through epitaphs, "memorie was continued to posteritie, ... and the Reader put in minde of humane frailtie," and he commends "the frequent visiting ... of the Tombes and monuments of the dead (but without all touch of superstition)," along with "the often reading, serious perusal, and diligent meditation of wise and religious Epitaphs or inscriptions, found vpon the tombes or monuments" as "a great motiue to bring us to repentance" (9). Weever continues that epitaphs "are sometimes called memories, *a memoria vel a monendo*, in that by them we are put in minde, and warned to consider our fragile condition" (9). For Weever, the perusal of and meditation on epitaphs "without all touch of superstition" constitute a memorial act that replaces the medieval practices of tomb-side prayers, whether the paternoster requested by Elizabeth Poodde, the prayers offered at the tomb of the saint, or, indeed, the indulgence hanging by Gower's tomb.

In substituting memory for superstition, reading for prayer, Weever's discussion of epitaphic writing directly recalls the terms of Queen Elizabeth's "Proclamation against breaking or defacing of Monuments of Antiquitie, being set up in Churches, or other publike places, for memory, and not for superstition." Where the medieval tomb-side prayer reaches across time to redeem a soul from purgatory, the epitaph establishes the place that the dead will hold in the world of the living. But the epitaph also occupies a paradoxical position; by redeeming its subject into cultural memory, it also pronounces, and establishes as a permanent fact, its subject's death.[208]

The paradoxical position of the epitaph—mediating past and present, death and immortality—informs Weever's survey of the famous tombs at Canterbury. In his treatment of Thomas Becket, Weever describes at length the medieval shrine that was destroyed in the Reformation and notes that "Diuers Epitaphs were composed to the memory of this much honoured Martyr" (203). Along with these, Weever elects to reproduce one very well known passage of English verse:

Fro euery shires end
Of Englond, to Canterbury they wend:
The holy blisfull Martir for to seeke,
That hem hath holpen wher they were seke. (202)

Weever cites the opening of Chaucer's *Canterbury Tales* not from manuscript, as he had with Gower, but from Thomas Speght's printed edition of
1598, revised in 1602. Yet as Stephanie Trigg has recently noted, Speght's
Chaucer is conspicuously grounded in early modern manuscript-based antiquarianism, which would find its apotheosis in the Cotton Library.[209] Identifying Speght by name as his Chaucerian source, Weever praises the editor
for having "by old copies"—that is, through manuscripts—"reformed [Chau-
cer's] workes" (489). He thereby underscores Speght's own claim to have "restored [Chaucer] to his own Antiquity," a claim that echoes Camden's in
the *Britannia*, to "restore antiquity to Britaine, and Britaine to his antiquity." Speght antiquates Chaucer by presenting him in black letter, as
Weever will do with his own medieval sources in *Ancient Funerall Monuments*.[210] Following Speght's example (and that of Speght's occulted source,
John Stow),[211] Weever contributes to Chaucer's "medievalization" by citing
a conspicuously archival Chaucer, whose orthographically correct presentation "reforms" its subject by "restoring" him "to his antiquity" and thereby
distances him from the present.[212] Invoking Chaucer's lines from the *Canterbury Tales* to serve as Becket's epitaph, Weever mitigates any charge of
superstition against his own visit to the defunct shrine by allowing himself to assume the detached posture of a reader in the archives. Rather than
endorsing the claim that Becket miraculously healed those who visited his
shrine, Weever cites Chaucer's account of the Canterbury pilgrims' belief
that the saint "hem hath holpen wher they were seke," thereby memorializing the alien practices of a former time. Thus, Weever turns Chaucer's
oeuvre, like Gower's, into the epitaph for an age; at the same time that they
represent the past, Chaucer and Gower also establish its alterity, just as the
epitaph memorializes its subject by pronouncing his or her death.

Weever's description of the salutary value of "reading, serious perusal,
and diligent meditation" of epitaphs forms the model for a new form of
manuscript study, which, like the perusal of epitaphs, transforms the dead
past into the present's living memory. By drawing his epitaphs from manuscript sources, with his omnipresent references to the "Bibl. Cot.," Weever
displaces such memorial perusal from the church to the library. For Weever,
manuscripts preserve the memorials to the dead that church monuments
too often lose. In his praise of Cotton's collection and preservation of "these

ancient Monuments," Weever calls on libraries to do what churches can no longer be trusted to do: to preserve the memories of the dead. In a library like Cotton's, reading replaces prayer as the chief contact between the living and the dead, just as the memorializing works of the Muses replace indulgences and other works of purgatorial redemption as the means of securing immortality.

Weever was not the first to suggest a similarity between the Cotton Library and the funerary monument. In a letter of 1612, Edmund Bolton compares the Cotton Library as safeguard of cultural memory to the mausoleum: "For your Studie, if we respect the glories of saincts there carefullie preserved in authentick Registers, it is a Pantheon and all-hallowes of the memorials of the honorable deceased; it is a Mausolae[m]," suggesting that the Cotton Library's chief function, preserving the memories of the dead, both follows from and redeems the memorial practices contained in the "authentic registers" and hagiographical manuscripts it safeguards.[213] If Bolton's letter to Cotton envisions the library as a repository of epitaphs, Weever follows Bolton in reassigning to the Cotton Library the function of the mausoleum which imparts immortality to its inhabitants.

Its ultimate inhabitant is Cotton himself. The date of Weever's publication, 1631, was also the year of Cotton's death, and Weever commemorates him by inserting a lengthy verse, "Viro clarissimo Roberto Cottono, ab antiqua Regum prosapia oriundo, Epicedium," which lauds Cotton's achievements by stressing their specifically literary contributions:

Qualis Homerus erat, cuius de fonte furores
Sacros hauserunt veteresque nouique Poetae:
Talis eras nostros inter, Cottone, Britannos,
Rerum explorator veterum.

(Just as Homer was, from whose source both ancient and new poets have drawn their inspiration, just so were you, Cotton, among our fellow Britons, as an investigator of ancient matters.) Weever continues his eulogy in English: "this worthy repairer of eating-times ruines, this Philadelphus, in preserving old Monuments, and ancient Records: this Magazin, this Treasurie, this store-house of Antiquities, Sir Robert Cotton, is now lately deceased" ("The Author to the Reader"). In memorializing Cotton as "Magazin," "Treasurie," and "store-house of Antiquities," Weever applies terms to Cotton himself that were commonly used to describe libraries; indeed, Bolton's letter of 1612 calls the Cotton Library a "Magazin" and praises Cotton for having "engross[ed] into your hands all the rarities which concern

the policie, or Antiquitie of Britain."[214] In Weever's account, Cotton appears
not only to have engrossed national antiquities into his library but also to
have engrossed them into his person. In commemorating his illustrious
subject as "magazin," "treasurie," and "store-house of Antiquities," Weever collapses Cotton into the Cotton Library itself, making the library both
Cotton's monument and his mausoleum. Cotton thereby confirms what to
Weever is the key attribute of the Cotton Library—to have assumed the
memorial function of the church.

As well as being one of the Cotton Library's most dedicated and prolific
users, Weever also contributed to Cotton's collection. In the course of his
fieldwork researches for *Ancient Funerall Monuments*, Weever reports discovering

> Many letters of important affaires, which I found in certaine Chandlers
> shops of our Parish, allotted to light Tobacco pipes, and wrap up peni-
> worths of their commodities (all which I gaue to Sir Robert Cotton,
> Knight and Baronet, the onely repairer of ruined antiquitie whom I knew
> (the contents therof showing some passages of former times) would pre-
> serve them for better uses. (81)

The letters in question, which Weever reprints verbatim, were incorporated
into Cotton's Cleopatra E. vi volume, where they are still preserved and catalogued among what the seventeenth-century catalogue calls "Collectanea de
potestate regia in Ecclesiastica concilia, & Episcopos."[215] Written by Henry
VIII himself to several members of the nobility, the letters warn them not
"to extol, set foorth, maintaine, or defend the authoritie, iurisdiction, or
power of the Bishop of Rome, or of his See" (83), recalling the fates of "the
late Bisshop of Rochester and Sir Thomas More knight" (85) as examples
of disobedience justly punished. They include a letter in which Henry condemns those who continue to revere "Bisshop Beckett of Canterbury, which
they have tofore called Saynt Thomas," detailing Becket's offenses against
the Crown: "These and soche other detestable and vnlawfull liberties of the
Church, nothing concerning the common weale, but only the partie of the
Clergie, the said Thomas Becket most arrogantly desired, and trayterously
sweyd to haue, contrary to the law of this our Realme" (87).

Weever incorporates these documents into the introductory chapters
of his *Ancient Funerall Monuments* to tell the story "of the abrogation,

abolition, and extinguishment of the Popes supreme and exorbitant authoritie, within the King of Englands Dominions," the title of his chapter 13
(78), in the words of its chief agents—in this case, Henry VIII himself. Such
a use of primary sources to retell English history marks Weever's work as a
representative of what I have been calling the Cotton School of Prose Nonfiction, with its reliance on the authenticating primary evidence found in
manuscripts "Ex Bibl. Cot." Weever's affiliation with this school, moreover,
is reflected in the particular historical episode that he selects to narrate as
the culmination of English ecclesiastical history with sources drawn from
the Cotton Library: the Reformation. In his use of materials gathered in
Cotton's Cleopatra E. volumes, as well as his contribution to those very volumes, Weever joins his contemporary antiquarians like Camden and Speed
in identifying the Cotton Library primarily as an archive of the Reformation.

Cotton's Cleopatra series, I have argued, arrange their medieval and early
modern materials to construct a multivolume chronicle of the Reformation
told through original sources. That narrative is repeated in contemporary
works of prose nonfiction by writers and library users such as Camden,
Speed, and Weever, for whom the Cotton Library becomes not only a repository of documentary sources but also an example of how to compile those
sources to tell particular stories about the past. Such works reveal the Cotton
Library's influence in making the Reformation an archived event through
its collections of primary materials in ecclesiastical history. But the Reformation also provided a narrative framework—a chronology of two ages, "before" and "after"—through which Cotton ordered and classified medieval
materials, making the events of the 1530s only the culmination of long-
standing conflicts and cultural practices in evidence through texts from the
early edicts of British rulers to the works of Wyclif and his associates. Cotton's interests in and uses of medieval hagiography, as I have argued, reveal
how a medieval religious genre could be drafted as evidence in support of
Protestant historiography.

By adducing the centrality of the Reformation both in the Cotton Library
and in the works of prose nonfiction that it fostered, I have aimed to revise long-held assumptions about the "Renaissance" interests that drove its
founder and his associates. The Reformation provides a master narrative and
chronological order that arranges the primary materials in volumes like the
Cleopatra D. and E. sequences, but it also establishes a master narrative of
the Cotton Library. Cotton owed his collections to the dissolution, which
dispersed the textual holdings of the monasteries and other religious institutions into private hands, enabling them to be consolidated in Cotton's and
other post-Reformation collections. As well as a transformation of religious

practices and objects, then, the Reformation as it is represented in the Cotton Library stands for a massive redistribution of texts. If Cotton and his associates often saw themselves as inheritors of monastic textual culture—as does Weever, when he compares his compiling practices to Bede's, or Cotton, when he follows those of Higden in preparing his own compilations—it was because they were literally the inheritors of monastic texts, which they transformed into sources and models for Protestant historiography. Cotton's compilations of Reformation documents would continue to resonate in the works of those who used his library: Ussher, Speed, Camden, and Weever among them. They reflect, as I have argued, his effort to impose a new chronology and horizon of interpretation on the materials of British history as gathered in the Cotton Library. But further, they also represent Cotton's self-conscious attempt to explore, document, and reconstruct the history of the library itself.

CHAPTER FIVE

"Cogitation against Libraries": Bacon, the Bodleian, and the Weight of the Medieval Past

In an address to King James I opening the second book of *The Advancement of Learning* (1605), Francis Bacon writes: "Libraries are as the shrines, where all the Reliques of the ancient saints, full of true vertue, and that without delusion or imposture, are preserved, and reposed."[1] The comment presents a miniaturized history of the post-Reformation English library. While its language of shrines, relics, and saints acknowledges the library's medieval past, it converts those medieval forms to serve the new intellectual aims of a Protestant nation: in libraries the "relics of the ancient saints" are transvalued, stripped of the "delusion" and "imposture" of their past, and recast in the service of "true vertue," not false.[2] Bacon's terms echo the founding narratives of the major post-Reformation libraries, whose makers were Bacon's illustrious contemporaries and personal affiliates. A parliamentary colleague of Sir Robert Cotton, Bacon actively consulted materials from Cotton's library, to which he himself donated a life of St. Alban (Nero D. vii) in 1623.[3] Bacon also maintained a close connection with Sir Thomas Bodley, to whom he sent a copy of his *Advancement of Learning* in 1605 to mark the opening of the Bodleian Library. Bacon's letter accompanying the book echoes—and thus appears to underscore for Bodley's benefit—*The Advancement of Learning*'s pronouncement on libraries: "Books," he writes to Bodley, "are the shrines where the saint is, or is believed to be: and you having built an Ark to save learning from deluge, deserve propriety in any new instrument or engine wherby learning should be improved or advanced."[4] Bacon's description of the Bodleian as "an Ark to save learning from deluge" echoes John Speed's description of the Reformation as a "generall deluge of Time, whose stream bore down the walles of all those foundations, carrying away the shrines of the dead, and defacing the Libraries of their ancient records."[5] So too his description of libraries and books as the "shrines" of "ancient saints" uses the same language in which Edmund Bolton praises the Cotton Library and "the glories of saincts there carefullie preserved in authentick Registers."[6] Bacon is well versed, these moments reveal, in the language of destruction and preservation, redemption and transformation, that had come to define the post-Reformation library.

Yet this language is at odds with the intellectual mission that Bacon declares in *The Advancement of Learning*. For a work so invested in the forward-thinking experimental sciences, the "repose" that Bacon identifies with libraries contrasts with the "advancement of learning" promised in the book's title.[7] Thus, while Bacon associates libraries with receptacles of received knowledge—which, he writes, "would soone perishe and vanishe to oblyuion, if it were not preserued in Bookes, Traditions, Conferences, and Places appoynted"—he goes on to appeal for royal help in advancing learning beyond the boundaries of tradition, asking "why should a fewe receiued Authors stand vp like Hercules Columnes, beyond which, there should be no sayling, or discouering, since wee haue so bright and benigne a starre, as your [Majesty] to conduct and prosper vs?" The ship sailing beyond the columns of Hercules—and hence past the boundaries of the known world into an open sea—emblematizes the spirit of "discovering" in which Bacon conceived his enterprise, an image that would famously appear on the frontispiece to his *Great Instauration* (1620).[8] Bacon's venturing ship contrasts with Bodley's "Ark" in the letter that accompanies Bacon's gift of *The Advancement of Learning*, which, even in its words of praise, implies a similar hierarchy of discovery and advancement over preservation: while Bodley's "Ark"—the Bodleian Library itself—will "*save* learning," Bacon offers a "new instrument or engine wherby learning should be *improved* or *advanced*" (my emphases).[9] In place of the library's repose, Bacon offers active engagement, instrumentality, and progress.

Bacon's brief but telling comments about books and libraries in *The Advancement of Learning* and in his letter to Bodley reflect a broader effort throughout his work to define and differentiate the branches of learning by mapping them onto the spaces of early modern knowledge production.[10] Throughout Bacon's oeuvre the library is continually set against real and imagined spaces of experimental knowledge production, such as the laboratory-like "still-house" (*Gesta Grayorum*), "Inginary" (*Commentarius solutus*), "workshop" (*Novum organum*), or "engine-house" (*New Atlantis*).[11] In Bacon's seventeenth-century milieu, such literary and scientific spaces were more contiguous than distinct, their interrelations often more visible than their differences: as Anthony Grafton observes of Bacon's German contemporary Johannes Kepler, "the laboratory could not exist without the library."[12] Indeed, Bacon himself never uses the word "laboratory" to designate the space of scientific experimentation and discovery but continually imagines laboratory-like settings under familiar names—such as "workshop," "house," or "cabinet"—that produce analogies to existing spaces of mechanical and intellectual production in early modern England.[13] Bacon similarly compares libraries to these places of experimental science, though he does so, crucially, by defining their relationship as one of *difference*, not similitude. Bacon's articulation of that difference begins with the subtle terminological comparisons embedded in the passages from *The Advancement of Learning* and the letter to Bodley, but by the *Novum organum* (1620) and other later works it forms the basis of an epistemological distinction, one with broad implications for the taxonomy of research and knowledge.

Early Stuart "science," as Howard Marchitello observes, was "still embedded within a range of cultural practices" and thus not "an already autonomous feature of early modernity."[14] Yet by mapping the various branches of knowledge onto the places of their production, Bacon inaugurates a rudimentary disciplinarity based on spatialized divisions of intellectual labor and function.[15] The relationship that Bacon stages between library and laboratory-like space represents an effort to distinguish between the preservation of tradition and the discovery of new knowledge—intellectual functions that today are projected onto an opposition between the humanities and the sciences—just as his *Advancement of Learning* invites comparison between the sedentary "repose" of the library and the venturing ship of his own experimental enterprise.[16]

Yet if Bacon's descriptions of libraries self-consciously invoke the founding narratives of destruction and redemption habitually employed by post-Reformation library makers, they also misrepresent the intellectual work that was carried out in seventeenth-century libraries by framing those libraries as places of contemplative "repose" rather than active knowledge production. In this juxtaposition, Bacon also tactically expropriates for experimental science a set of key tools and functions that developed within the libraries themselves. As I argued in the preceding chapter, seventeenth-century libraries and their makers were preoccupied with problems of the right ordering of knowledge and the disposition of manuscript evidence, and similar problems of order and evidence likewise played a central role in Bacon's experimental method.[17] Indeed, the "new form of Induction" that Bacon sets out, in which data are "arranged in Tables" and elements of knowledge ordered "like an alphabet," owes its outlines and basic forms to the catalogues and indexing systems then being developed in libraries, which have led scholars to call the seventeenth century the golden age of

systematic bibliography.[18] The investigation of evidence and classification
of knowledge that define the Baconian project, I argue in this chapter, derive
from the very libraries from which Bacon attempts to distance them.

Bacon's understanding of libraries and their functions was shaped by
his practical experiences with the libraries of his day. Not only was Bacon an experienced library user, but he also had an opportunity to put his
experience to work in 1610, when James I called on him to oversee the organization of the new Lambeth Palace Library. Compiled by Richard Bancroft,
archbishop of Canterbury, the Lambeth Palace collection resembled other
post-Reformation libraries in content and provenance; it included many
manuscripts that, like those of other post-Reformation libraries studied in
this book's earlier chapters, derived from the former monasteries and were
acquired from Henry VIII and prominent post-Reformation collectors, such
as Baron Lumley and John Foxe.[19] Bacon personally issued the order "that
a catalogue of the bookes should be accurately and exquisitely made," a decision that reflects the intellectual and institutional concerns driving both
contemporary library science and Bacon himself.[20] If the seventeenth century is the age of the library catalogue, its librarians and cataloguers were
increasingly preoccupied with the challenge of ordering individual books under the *loci communes* of general subject headings that aspired to a systematic disposition of universal knowledge.[21] The movement from particulars to
universal categories that is the focus of the seventeenth-century library catalogue would become a central preoccupation for Bacon as well, as he formu-
lated his own inductive method.[22] Bacon's efforts to systematize knowledge,
its examination and classification, I will argue, appropriate both the form
and the function of the library catalogue, culminating in Bacon's "Catalogue
of Particular Histories," which plots a grand schematization of knowledge
at the end of the *Novum organum*.[23] In this, Bacon reveals the continuing influence of post-Reformation discourses and practices of libraries in
shaping intellectual projects that would otherwise appear to be—and that,
Bacon insisted, were—at odds with them.

In making this argument, I observe a continuity between the classification of books in libraries and that of natural phenomena, an observation
that belies a growing seventeenth-century distinction between "words" and
"things." Bacon's contemporary Abraham Cowley lauds Bacon for turning
"from Words, which are but Pictures of the Thought . . . / To Things, the
Minds right Object," and Bacon himself laments in *The Advancement of
Learning* that "men study words and not matter." Yet, by revealing the in-
terconnectedness of early modern "literary" and (proto-)"scientific" inquiry,
recent scholarship on Bacon and his intellectual contexts has cautioned

against too readily accepting this distinction.[24] My argument extends this insight to the level of the institution, showing that Bacon's experimental knowledge-making enterprise owes more to seventeenth-century library science than he allows when he sets the two in opposition; further, it finds that Bacon's very attempt to differentiate libraries from laboratory-like spaces followed from early modern efforts to spatialize knowledge and taxonomize the disciplines that began, not outside, but within libraries themselves.

In this chapter, I locate Bacon in the tradition of Reformation era and post-Reformation library makers that begins with Matthew Parker, John Bale, and Stephen Batman and extends to Bodley's first librarian, Thomas James. Reading Bacon as a practitioner of early modern library science as well as a writer engaging with the libraries of literary history, I also situate Bacon at the end of a line of writers beginning with John Lydgate and progressing to Thomas More, Thomas Elyot, Edmund Spenser, and William Camden, for whom writing about libraries was a way of theorizing and imagining the objects, shapes, and limitations of human knowledge. The very terms in which Bacon formulates his scientific project—as a reasoning process involving the active and critical creation of practical knowledge—draw on earlier literary imaginings of libraries like that of Spenser's Eumnestes as well as on more material discussions that were taking place in and around seventeenth-century libraries themselves—not only Lambeth Palace Library, in which he had a personal stake, but also the Bodleian, with which Bacon maintained a personal connection through its founder, Thomas Bodley. I make this argument by examining, first, the recurring and shifting but also unexpectedly central role that libraries play in Bacon's oeuvre, an examination I extend to Bacon's correspondence with Thomas Bodley and, finally, to Bodley's own correspondence with his brilliant librarian, Thomas James, as they produce a three-way debate over the roles of books, knowledge, and libraries in the seventeenth century.

Bacon's Libraries

Bacon begins to imagine the relationship between libraries and other places of knowledge in one of his earliest writings, an entertainment at Gray's Inn presented to Elizabeth I as part of the *Gesta Grayorum* (1594–95). The work features a counselor (transparently Bacon's spokesman) who advises his monarch to pursue the study of philosophy, defined as "the searching out, inventing, and discovering of all whatsoever is hid and secret in the world."[25] These goals are to be carried out in four distinct but interconnected locales, whose construction and function the counselor describes in detail.

The first entails "the collecting of a most important and general library, wherein whatsoever the wit of man hath heretofore committed to books of worth, be they ancient or modern, printed or manuscript, European or of the other parts, of one or other language, may be made contributory to your wisdom." The second is "a spacious, wonderful garden" showcasing plants, birds, beasts, and fish and thus providing "in small compass a model of universal nature made private." The third resembles an early modern museum: "a goodly huge cabinet" in which "shall be sorted and included" things made by "the hand of man by exquisite art or engine" and "chance," as well as "whatsoever Nature hath wrought in things that want life." The fourth and final knowledge zone comes closest to resembling a laboratory set aside for scientific experimentation: the counselor calls it "a still-house, so furnished with mills, instruments, furnaces, and vessels, as may be a palace fit for a philosopher's stone."[26]

The interconnection of library, garden, cabinet, and laboratory is not unusual for its time. Conrad Gesner, author of the *Bibliotheca universalis* (1545) as well as the five-volume *Historia animalium* (1552–57), moved freely between libraries and zoological "museums" both in his work and in his home, where he maintained collections of books alongside those of plants, animals, fossils, and minerals.[27] Working on a similarly contiguous model, Bacon's older contemporary John Dee maintained a voluminous collection of natural curiosities and a garden connected to his famous library, which was also adjoined by three rooms equipped for alchemical experimentation.[28] Dee's library, as William Sherman notes, "was part of a general intellectual and scientific space in which the books coexisted with laboratories, gardens, and cabinets of curiosities."[29] Although Bacon recalls the example of Dee—and, thus, the contiguity of early modern modes of knowledge—this moment in the *Gesta Grayorum* also attempts to impose a taxonomy on these spaces of knowledge that is absent from Dee's *Bibliotheca Mortlacensis*.[30] By locating "instruments" and curiosities in the "still-house" and "cabinet," and "books of worth" in the library, Bacon subdivides objects that were routinely classed together in early modern libraries, which commonly contained plentiful nonbook items, such as globes and coins, scientific instruments, and other objects alongside books.[31] Distributing these objects among distinct places with distinct functions, Bacon also arranges those places along a line of progression from library to "still-house" that culminates in the monarch's "discovering of all whatsoever is hid and secret in the world." Bacon's truth-seeking enterprise may begin in the library, but it progresses from there to the world outside.

The counselor's advice in the *Gesta Grayorum*, as Donna Coffy observes, "provides a blueprint for Salomon's House" in one of Bacon's last works, the utopian fiction *The New Atlantis* (written in 1624 and published in 1627).[32] Recalling the *Gesta Grayorum*'s counsel regarding "the searching out, inventing, and discovering of all whatsoever is hid and secret in the world," *The New Atlantis*'s Salomon's House, or "The College of the Six Days' Works," is dedicated to "the knowledge of Causes, and secret motions of things; and the enlarging of the bounds of Human Empire, to the effecting of all things possible."[33] At Salomon's command, select "Fellows or Brethren" are ordered "to bring unto us books, instruments, and patterns of every kind" that will be incorporated into the larger aims of knowledge production to which Salomon's house is dedicated.[34] Those responsible for collecting material from books are called "Depredators," a term meaning "plunderers" (from *de + praedari*, "plundering" or "pillaging"). These are followed by agents who are responsible for undertaking old experiments and examining their results, as well as those who direct new experiments and extrapolate new knowledge from them. Just as the library appears as the first locus of knowledge in the *Gesta Grayorum*, the work of the Depredators occupies the first order in Salomon's House, making it preparatory to the work that follows. Yet Salomon's House also imposes a distinct hierarchy of value onto these divisions of intellectual labor. The collectors are followed by the "Lamps," who "direct new experiments, of a higher light, more penetrating into nature than the former," and who are in turn followed by the "Interpreters of Nature," who "raise the former discoveries by experiments into greater observations, axioms, and aphorisms."[35] In the progression from the Depredators to the Interpreters of Nature, Bacon suggests that the accumulation of written knowledge is preparatory, but subordinate, to the "higher" and "greater" work of experimentation.

Bacon's *New Atlantis* continually acknowledges its precursor, More's *Utopia*, in explicit and implicit ways, and the book collectors of Salomon's House directly recall the act of *translatio studii* that Hythloday enacts by transporting the "package of books"—Aldine editions of Aristotle, Plato, and Theophrastus—to Utopia.[36] If that act of translation is interrupted en route by the playful plundering of the marmoset, in *The New Atlantis* the collectors themselves are the plunderers: for Bacon, plundering does not interrupt *translatio studii* but defines it. Rewriting book collection as plunder, Bacon also reads *Utopia* through the history of the post-Reformation library. Rooted in the history of *compilatio*, the term "depredator" recalls the compilation method that was so crucial to early modern library makers like

Robert Cotton; it also recalls the work of Reformation era collectors such as Stephen Batman and John Prise, for which "plunder" may not be an inaccurate description, as they extracted books from the wreckage of the monastic libraries.[37] Bacon's book collectors are plunderers because their acquisition of knowledge is restricted to others' treasures. In this, they are implicitly contrasted with the "Lamps," who "direct new experiments" in the many laboratory-like spaces in the "College of the Six Days' Works" (which include "chambers of health," "furnaces of great diversities," "perspective-houses," "sound-houses," and "engine-houses," but no library),[38] and finally the "Interpreters of Nature," whose "observations, axioms, and aphorisms" deriving from experimentation identify them with no one so much as Bacon himself. "The very art of Interpreting nature," as Bacon defines it in the *Novum organum*, is the philosopher's highest goal: "for Interpretation is the true and natural work of a mind freed from the fetters that restrain it" once it has "set aside received notions and opinions."[39] If the Depredators collect and compile received wisdom in the form of books, their work is preparatory to, but also distinctly secondary to, that of the Interpreters of Nature, who, in the model of the Baconian philosopher-scientist, do not merely gather and conserve prior knowledge but actively produce new knowledge.

Between the *Gesta Grayorum* of 1594–95 and the *New Atlantis* of 1624 Bacon's *Novum organum* of 1620 sharpens his representation of libraries into a pointed critique. In it, libraries explicitly impede the production of knowledge:

> If any one turns his attention from workshops to libraries, and is amazed at the huge variety of books which we see, he will surely be stupefied in quite a different way when he has examined and carefully looked into the manner and content of those same books. For then he will see that there is no end to their repetitions, and that men are forever working over and talking about the same things, and he will switch from amazement at their variety to wonderment at their poverty and at the scantiness of the matters which have taken over and tenanted the minds of men. (NO 137)

Where in the *Gesta Grayorum* the library prepares for experimental discovery, in the *Novum organum* libraries' storage of received knowledge stifles new knowledge by inducing stupefaction. The comment about "the matters which have taken over and tenanted the minds of men" in libraries illustrates Bacon's larger point that "human reason in its present condition is just a farrago and mass made up of a good deal of faith, a lot of accident, and a fair few infantile notions which we swallowed when young" (NO 155).

Among his contemporaries, Bacon was not alone in his critique of libraries. As they attained institutional prominence in the seventeenth century, libraries were identified with a newly perceived problem of information overload.[40] Thus, in the *Anatomy of Melancholy* Robert Burton lodges a complaint against libraries and their "vast chaos and confusion of Bookes," while in *Religio Medici* Thomas Browne celebrates the destruction of the Alexandrian library as a salutary purge of textual excess.[41] Bacon targets a similar textual excess when he criticizes libraries' stupefyingly "huge" holdings. But Burton's and Browne's critiques anticipate a library of the future, which faced a seemingly uncontrollable and ever-growing accumulation of printed works; for Bacon, on the other hand, libraries stupefy through their massive accumulation of the past. In charging that "there is no end to their repetitions," Bacon expresses a larger anxiety about the accumulation of past knowledge that threatens his own forward-looking philosophy of discovery and innovation; in Bacon's critique, the library is a place in which the past is forever doomed to repeat itself.

As spatialized models of knowledge, Bacon's libraries manifest the limitations of the thinking mind itself—a recurrent theme in Bacon's work—but they also reflect Bacon's engagement with post-Reformation English libraries: the particular historical conditions that shaped them, the rhetorics that accompanied their emergence, and the forms they took. Like Spenser, Bacon represents the library in terms that analogize it to the place of memory in the brain. In *The Advancement of Learning*, Bacon's division of learning into the three faculties of Memory, Imagination, and Reason makes Memory an information store that supplies the "raw material," as Lisa Jardine explains, "for all mental operations."[42] Memory thus contrasts with Reason, which "compares and combines" the past impressions stored in the memory in order to produce rational judgments.[43] Bacon inherits this tripartite structure of the mind from a long line of classical and medieval thinkers, beginning with Aristotle and Galen; but he innovates by making this structure the basis of a broad classification of knowledge, whereby Imagination becomes the seat of poetry, Reason, of philosophy, and Memory, of history.[44] Bacon proposes further subdivisions: "Of Histories, wee may finde three kindes, MEMORIALLS, PARFITE HISTORIES, and ANTIQUITIES: for MEMORIALLS are Historie unfinished, or the first, or rough draughts of Historie, and ANTIQUITIES are Historie defaced, or some remnants of History, which haue casually escaped the shipwrack of time" (AL 65). With its histories of defaced remnants, Bacon's faculty of memory resembles nothing so much as the post-Reformation libraries of Parker, Cotton, Spenser, and Weever. Like Bodley's "Ark to save learning from deluge," their libraries of "memorials" and "antiquities" preserve the "defaced remnants" of the medieval past from "the shipwrack of time." The English library becomes the internal structure of the human brain; and its contents, the substance of human memory itself.

But if libraries externalize the faculty of memory in their storage of written knowledge, they also manifest the limitations of that knowledge, revealing, as Bacon insists, "the scantiness of the matters which have taken over and tenanted the minds of men." As an example of such "degenerate learning," Bacon returns to the history of pre-Reformation thought, citing "the Schoole-men, who hauing sharpe and strong wits being shut vp in the Cels of a few Authors (chiefly Aristotle their Dictator) as their persons were shut vp in the Cells of Monasteries and Colledges... [did] spin out vnto vs those laborious webbes of Learning which are extant in ther Bookes" (AL 24). The attack on scholasticism shows how easily Bacon conflates the place of thinking with the mode of thought practiced therein: the Schoolmen shut up their wits, just as they shut up their bodies, in cells. So too in the *Novum organum* Bacon counsels his readers to seek knowledge "not arrogantly in the *narrow cells of human wit* but humbly in the wider world" (NO 25; my emphasis). The monastic cell contrasts with the voyaging ship, Bacon's emblem for the intellectual enterprise as a global voyage of discovery; as he asserts, "surely it would be disgraceful if, while the regions of the material globe—that is, of the earth, of the sea, and of the stars—have been in our times laid widely open and revealed, the intellectual globe should remain shut up within the narrow limits of old discoveries."[45] In contrast, like the monastic cells they resemble, the "narrow cells of human wit" are immured within the learning of the past.

The solution to a mind afflicted with "degenerate learning," Bacon argues in the same work, is to purify it—"to rid ourselves of excessive respect and admiration for things discovered already (and to do that briskly and without pretense)" (NO 11)—and thereby to undertake "the eradication of the *Idols* from the intellect" (NO 113; emphasis in original). As Michele le Doeuff observes of Bacon's analysis, "the Idols present the danger of shutting up the mind in an autarkic existence," producing the greatest threat to true learning: a mind fixated on false beliefs.[46] Devon L. Hodges points out that the idols underlie Bacon's thought, recurring, "in one form or another, in almost all his works, because to reach the tangible and certain facts that lie at the foundation of knowledge, he has first to tear away the superstitious notions that hide the truth from sight."[47] This iconoclastic project of intellectual reform propels Bacon toward a vocabulary and imagery of religious reform taken from the English Reformation's attack on the monasteries. Bacon inherited such a language from his mother, Anne Cooke, Lady Bacon, whose translation of Bishop John Jewel's *Defense of the English Church* (1564), a work that won the admiration and endorsement of Matthew Parker himself, stresses the need to extirpate Roman corruption in the form of "ignoraunce, errour, superstition, Idolatrie, [and] mennes Inventions."[48] Bacon adapts such reformist language and postures while internalizing them to the mind. Where the reformers targeted the idolatrous remains of Catholic material and textual culture, Bacon's famous attack on the "Idols which beset human minds" in the *Novum organum* (79) erects targets that are internal to the human intellect; and where the Reformation purged and purified the churches, Bacon applies himself no less energetically to purging and purifying the mind (NO 111). Thus, when describing the weakness of the human mind and its need for reformation in *The Advancement of Learning*, for example, Bacon observes that "the mind of Man ... is rather like an inchanted glasse, full of superstition and Imposture, if it bee not deliuered and reduced" (AL 116).

Bacon's adaptation of Reformation era rhetoric in his allegory of intellectual reform helps explain why, in the midst of an attack on "fantastical learning" and "vaine imaginations"—terms inescapably associated with attacks on papistry—Bacon cites as his hero none other than Martin Luther, by whose example "the ancient Authors, both in Diuinitie, and in Humanitie, which had long time slept in Libraries, began generally to be read and revolved" (AL 21). Luther's sudden appearance in this passage has struck many of Bacon's readers as anomalous; yet it makes sense within the larger context of Bacon's use of the Reformation.[49] Bacon's description of Luther directly recalls the language of Bale and Leland, who "peruse[d] the Libraries" during the dissolution of the monasteries, seeking "to saue the precyouse monume[n]tes of auncyent wryters ... and so to brynge them from darkenesse to a lyuely light."[50] But Bacon describes an interior reform. The "revolution" that his Luther effects "in Libraries" models the revolution Bacon himself hopes to effect in the intellect; where Luther liberates books from the libraries in which they slept, Bacon claims to liberate learning from its confinement in the weak human mind.[51]

Bacon's critique of libraries, I am arguing, plays a central role in his broader critique of the weakness of the human mind and the contemporary state of learning. But even while Bacon positions his intellectual project outside libraries in works like the *Novum organum*, Bacon's governing models of knowledge and the mind—from memory's antiquities to the need to purge idolatry and superstition—draw from the post-Reformation English libraries themselves, reflecting his direct experience with those libraries and their makers. Bacon's father, Sir Nicholas Bacon (Elizabeth's Lord Keeper of the

Great Seal), joined Archibishop Matthew Parker as one of a small group of donors supporting the restoration of the University Library in Cambridge, to which he personally contributed seventy books, including an Anglo-Saxon psalter (MS Ff.1.23).[52] If Matthew Parker invented the post-Reformation English library, he was also—through his close connections with Bacon's mother and father—an intimate of the Bacon household.

Bacon also experienced a brief career as a library maker himself. In 1610 Bacon himself was appointed to oversee the foundation of the first library at Lambeth Palace, established by the will of Archbishop of Canterbury Richard Bancroft.[53] In 1608 Bacon had sought to cultivate the aging archbishop of Canterbury as a possible patron for his "Great Instauration," on the understanding that (Bacon notes in a private memorandum) Bancroft was "single and glorious, and beleeving the sense" of the project, an intellectual sympathy Bacon hoped would pay off.[54] Instead, Bacon inherited Bancroft's library, or stewardship of it. George Abbot, the archbishop of Canterbury who succeeded Bancroft, recounts how James I "with his royall affection embracing this good purpose of the forsaid Archbishop" took up the project and, determining that "these bookes should be preserved," turned to Bacon for advice on how best to undertake such preservation:

> [Thus, James] did . . . commend the care and consideration hereof unto Sr. Frauncis Bacon knight his Ma[ties] Sollicitor, that he should think upon some course, how the custody of this Library might be established, and by the negligence of those that came after, so excellent a worke might not be frustrated, to the hurt of the Church and Commonwealth. Sr. Frauncis Bacon therefore, as a man learned and a true lover of learning, (for by both those titles the King was pleased to stile him) after good consideration did hold it fitt, that a Catalogue of the Bookes should be accurately and exquisitely made, that it might be knowne in the ages to come what were those Bookes, which the aforesaid Archbishop Bancrofte did leave to his successors.[55]

Comprising nearly 5,600 printed books and 470 manuscripts, the collection presented Bacon with the practical challenge of managing large bodies of written materials.[56] It also posed the same challenge faced by other early modern English library makers: how to balance the demands of preservation and use. Bancroft was, as Abbot observed, "a great gatherer together of bookes," many of which derived from the monasteries via other collections; some five hundred of these came from the Royal Library of Henry VIII, while other books had been initially gathered but ultimately rejected by the commissioners in 1530 as irrelevant to the king's "Great Matter," which drove their bibliographical acquisitions.[57] But like the library of Bancroft's predecessor Matthew Parker, Bancroft's library was not simply a vessel for conserving written traditions but a resource for active theological engagement and production—which is why Bancroft collected religious works passed over by the commissioners—comprising books of theology, religious controversy, and biblical commentary by Protestants as well as Puritans and Catholics.[58] This part of the collection played a crucial role for Bancroft, who was beset by contemporary religious controversies, such as the Martin Marprelate affair and ongoing Puritan, Catholic, and Presbyterian skirmishes, which played out in the sphere of the popular press and generated a loop of refutations and defenses in print.[59] Bancroft himself was an avid user and supporter of libraries. A lifelong friend of William Camden, Robert Cotton, and Thomas Bodley, and a patron of the first Bodleian librarian, Thomas James, Bancroft shared these Protestant library makers' interest in scholarly and text-based ecclesiastical history, borrowing a number of medieval religious books from Cotton, including his sequence of materials on English ecclesiastical history, Cotton Cleopatra E. i–iii.[60] True to Cotton's intentions, Bancroft used these archival materials in the service of contemporary concerns, the same concerns that informed his own collection of religious materials in his library.

The religious materials form the core of Bancroft's collection, as reflected in their careful treatment and classification in the catalogue. The library also included large holdings in civil and canon law, history, and "libri Humanioris literaturae," in which Bacon could have found copies of his own works, including his Essays (1597) and Advancement of Learning (1605).[61] Bancroft's books were stored in presses that were grouped by subject and ranged along the four walls of a square gallery. The catalogue that resulted from Bacon's direction presents a basic shelflist, whose order reflects the physical ordering of the books on shelves, according to their placement in the room's west, south, east, and north sides.[62] Within those four categories, the books are also subdivided by subject.[63] The "books gathered on the West side of the Lambeth Library" (libri collocantur in parte Occidentali Bibliothecae Lambethanae) included Bibles "et eius partes," patristic commentaries, theological and controversial works of both Protestants and Catholics; the south side, sermons and homilies, scholastic writers, works of canon, civil, and common law and humane letters (libri Humanioris Literaturae); the north, manuscripts, liturgical works, both Catholic and Protestant, writings by Puritans, and dictionaries; and the east, historical works (libri in Bibliotheca Historica).[64] The last subcollection includes five copies of the *Polychronicon* and two of the *Brut*, along with copies of the *Legenda Aurea*, an English legendary, and other works that are also represented in the libraries of Parker or Cotton.[65]

As recorded in the 1612 Lambeth Palace Library catalogue, the four sides of the library impose a basic ordering of subjects roughly following traditional disciplines: theology, law and letters, and history. The main headings "libri in Bibliotheca Historica" and "libri Humanioris Literaturae" both comprise vast collections whose contents are differentiated by the alphabetically ordered authors' names. Anticipating a later development in libraries whereby manuscripts were distinguished from printed works, the Lambeth Palace Library sets apart "libri manuscripti" in a category of their own on the north side of the library ("in parte Boreali Bibliothecae Lambethanae"), thus instantiating a division between the bibliographical past and present.[66]

Yet in contrast to the more capacious secular headings of history, literature, and manuscript collections, the theological works are methodically subdivided by subject, genre, and denomination. Thus "libri Protestantium" are distinguished from "libri controversialu[m] Protestantiu[m]"; "libri Pontificii" from "libri Controversiarum Pontificii" (24v); "Commentatores Pontificii" from "Protestantes," as well as "Commentatores partim Protestantes partim Pontificii" (17v). This topical shelving system reflects the library's intended and actual status as a working collection.[67] If the lists of secular works suggest inventories of objects to be preserved, the theological lists are ordered to prepare them for active use in the religious controversies of the day, in which Bancroft himself was tirelessly involved.

Bacon may have been responsible for ordering "that a Catalogue of the Bookes should be accurately and exquisitely made," but he appears to have been concerned less with the organization of the catalogue than with its safekeeping, since he stipulates foremost "that this Catalogue should be sent unto the Deane and Chapter of the Cathedrall Church of Canterbury, that it may be there layd up in Archivis."[68] Bacon thereby establishes the catalogue primarily as a list of possessions rather than an instrument facilitating use.[69] This perspective runs counter to Bancroft's own active uses of his collection; but it supports a critique that Bacon later formulates in his *Novum organum* (1620), a copy of which he personally presented to Abbot himself (Lambeth Palace 1620.45). As Bacon charges, libraries present their materials in forms that resist, rather than encourage, intellectual engagement. Bacon illustrates this critique by projecting his reader into an imaginary library: "let him look at the libraries and, among other things, at the corpus of civil and canon law on one side, and the commentaries of the doctors and jurists on the other" (NO 471). The description of this imaginary library directly recalls the disposition of books in Lambeth Palace Library, which indeed ranged "commentaries" on one side of the library (the west) and "civil and canon law" on the other (the south).[70] In Bacon's description, however, books thus arranged overwhelm the reader with their aggregate bulk: "the numberless host of opinions, tenets, and speculations goes on forever" (NO 473).

If Bacon's critique of libraries misrepresents the intended and actual uses of libraries like Bancroft's, it establishes the library as a foil for Bacon's "instauration," while camouflaging Bacon's debt to the very libraries whose example he rejects. Just as Bacon "did hold it fitt, that a Catalogue of the Bookes should be accurately and exquisitely made" for Lambeth Palace Library, cataloguing plays a central role in Bacon's project from its earliest forms.[71] He insists, however, that his cataloguing project differs in kind and function from the merely preservative and accretive practices that he identifies with libraries. Instead, Bacon aspires to create new catalogue forms that do not simply record information but help to generate new knowledge through their dynamic arrangement of materials. *Cogitata et visa* announces this intention to create "Tables of Discovery" that will replace the traditional disciplines: "The branches of knowledge we possess are presented with too much pretension and show," Bacon asserts, "in such a way as to enslave belief instead of provoking criticism."[72] In their place, he asserts that "a great storehouse of facts should be accumulated," and "further, the material collected should be sorted into orderly Tables, so that the understanding may work upon it and thus accomplish its appropriate task."[73]

Building on this intention, Bacon's *Novum organum* differentiates libraries, with the "numberless" bulk of their contents, from his own project: to organize a comprehensive collection of natural history into "A Catalogue of Titles of Particular Histories" (NO 474-85). The distinction Bacon makes between intellectual approaches—passive "belief" versus active "criticism" and "understanding"—hinges, he insists, on the presentation and organization of "material." Bacon's underlying tenet, that thought is limited or enabled by the forms that organize it, reflects the taxonomic mania of Bacon's contemporaries, such as Conrad Gesner, whose *Pandectae* sought to order all knowledge by submitting it to a methodical system of categories and subdivisions.[74] Likewise, Bacon's "Catalogue" embraces all possible branches of knowledge in its "Particular Histories," from the "History of the Heavenly Bodies" (including the "History of Rainbows" and the "History of Clouds"), to the "History of Air" and other "Masses," "History of Plants," and animals, concluding with the "History of Man" (including the "History of the Faculties" and "History of Motions"), "Machines," and "the Natures and Powers" of "Numbers" and "Figures." For Bacon, a "History" is a repository of facts, meant in a synchronic sense that might be contrasted with the diachronic histories produced in Cotton's chronologically ordered volumes.[75] Rather than producing a unified teleology of the kind pursued by Archbishop Ussher and other seventeenth-century practitioners of critical chronology, the "Particular Histories" in Bacon's "Catalogue" organize individual facts under subdivisions that aspire to reflect the scope and order of nature itself.

Bacon differentiates his "Catalogue of Titles of Particular Histories" from the libraries he disparages by calling his "a granary and storehouse of things, not comfortable accommodation for staying or living in, but a place we go down to when we need to fetch out something useful" (NO 459). His history of knowledge will not be a monastery, a space of enclosure, or a library, a space of "repose" and "endless repetition," but a means to an end, a warehouse fitted out for use. In contrast to the library as he depicts it, Bacon's "Catalogue" is a data-processing center.[76] Bacon proposes to compile "the currently accepted opinions in all the variety of the different schools" in order to facilitate their comparison and critical collation. Because "there are things which are "downright unreliable but which are bandied about and celebrated all the same" (NO 467), Bacon suggests that his "Catalogue" will allow researchers "to make up their minds whether it is trustworthy or not" (NO 269) or to "note the origin of this or that piece of nonsense or gullibility" (NO 469). For this reason, Bacon stresses the value of including even false beliefs, because, by identifying their origin, researchers can pinpoint and eradicate them, given the proper bibliographical procedure: "If there is anything in any narration which is doubtful or worrying, I would not want it to be suppressed or kept quiet but to be put in writing plainly and clearly by way of a note or advice" (NO 469). To this end, the crucial corollary of the "Catalogue" is an indexing system that Bacon describes as a method of appending "a note or advice" to mark the origins of false beliefs and thus to allow their dismantlement—since, as Bacon observes, "what ruins and destroys a believer will perhaps help out an inquirer" (NO 471).[77]

Bacon's efforts to distinguish his project from the endlessly repetitious and enclosed library follows on the model of his larger distinction, first mapped out in *The Advancement of Learning*, between the retentive faculty of Memory and the critical faculty of Reason; where libraries (as represented by Bacon) merely collect and preserve the learning of the past, Bacon proposes to submit that learning to a critical process—what he calls "the tribunal of the intellect" (NO 221)—and thus to combine Memory with Reason in a single institution. In so doing, he offers a corrective to a problem he diagnoses in the universities: "that they make too great and mischievous a divorce between invention and memory" (AL 289). Bacon similarly projects the faculty of Memory, divorced from invention or Reason, onto libraries—a process that misrecognizes, I am arguing, the critical practices that were fostered in contemporary libraries like Bancroft's. Bacon's history of thought, as we have seen, abstracts and internalizes the history of libraries; but it derives from, and continually refers back to, the libraries of his day. However boldly Bacon's "Instauration" proclaimed its independence from libraries, it owed them an unacknowledged debt.

Bodley's Ark

As his correspondence reveals, Bacon maintained a close personal connection, through its founder, with one of the great libraries of his age, the Bodleian.[78] In 1607, Bacon sent Sir Thomas Bodley a manuscript copy of his *Cogitata et visa de interpretatione naturae, sive de scientia operativa* (Thoughts and Conclusions on the Interpretation of Nature, or A Science Productive of Works), which followed *The Advancement of Learning*—a copy of which Bacon had earlier sent Bodley—in calling for a revolution in philosophy. Apparently receiving no response, Bacon wrote a second time to Bodley, charging him, "You are, I bear you witness, slothful, and you help me nothing; so I am half in conceit that you affect not the argument; for myself I know well you love and effect. . . . or else I would add a Cogitation against Libraries, and be revenged on you that way."[79] Bacon's jesting threat to pen a "Cogitation against Libraries" deflects the fact that the *Cogitata et visa* already contains such an attack, which could suggest why Bodley might be imagined to "affect not the argument" of the work. Only a few pages into his book, Bacon launches into a by-now familiar critique: "a library," he charges, "exhibits a wonderful variety of books, but, if you look closer, you find only infinite repetition, new in the manner but not in the substance," which leads Bacon to conclude that "book learning look[s] great but on examination [is] found to be small."[80] Bacon's presentation of *Cogitata et visa*, with its critique of libraries, to a committed library maker like Bodley is as audacious as his presentation of *Novum organum*, with its comments on libraries' "numberless" bulk, to Archbishop Abbot, founder of Lambeth Palace Library. But it suggests that Bacon developed his critique of libraries in a dialectical exercise: as much as he seemed to renounce libraries and their makers, he continually elicited their responses.

Despite Bacon's threats, Bodley did, in fact, respond to the work. In a letter of 19 February 1607, Bodley acknowledges it and diplomatically concurs with Bacon's appeal to an experience-based knowledge; but he takes exception to Bacon's stated aim (as Bodley summarizes it) "to disclaim all our Aximes and Maximes, and generall assertions that are left by tradition from our Elders to us which (for so it is to be intended) have passed all probations of the sharpest wits that ever were."[81] Bodley responds to Bacon's attack on axioms ("Aximes and Maximes, and generall assertions"), particularly the Aristotelian model of knowledge that subordinated observed particulars to inherited generalizations.[82] For Baconian induction, generalizations must be proved through particulars; in opposition, Bodley insists that they have already been proved "by tradition" and thus "have passed all probations of the sharpest wits that ever were." Were thinkers "to renounce our common Notions, and cancel all our Actions, Rules, and Tenents, and so to come Babes, *ad regnum naturae*," Bodley objects, "there is nothing more certain in my understanding, then that it would instantly bring us to Barbarism, and after many thousand years, leave us more unprovided of theoreticall furniture, then we are at this present."[83]

In articulating the value of preserving traditional knowledge to defend against "Barbarism," Bodley reiterates the founding principles of the Bodleian. As a student at Elizabethan Oxford, Bodley witnessed the devastating effects of the Reformation on the medieval library of Duke Humfrey; as a result of this experience, Bodley recalls in an often-cited passage from his autobiography, he determined to "set up my Staffe at the Library doore in *Oxford*," concluding, "I could not busy my self to better purpose, then by reducing that place (which then in every part lay ruined and wast) to the publique use of Students."[84] Bodley's endowment of the library reiterates his aim to build anew "vpon the ruines of the olde decaied Library"; phoenix-like, the Bodleian was conceived from the start as an edifice reborn from the ashes of the past.[85]

For Bodley's project of building from ruins, the project of intellectual renewal was contingent upon the material project of restoration. Where Bodley complains that Bacon's reform would "leave us . . . unprovided of theoreticall furniture," he recalls his own outfitting of the Bodleian itself, which began with the furniture. As Bodley lamented in a letter to Oxford's vice-chancellor, by 1597 nothing survived of old Duke Humfrey's Library but "the rome itself remayning," the books and finally the desks having long since disappeared; his proposal to "reduce [the library] again to his former vse" began with the promise to fit it "with seates, and shelfes, and Deskes."[86] As Heidi Brayman Hackel notes, "from the beginning of the project, it seems, the space itself was central to Bodley's conception of a great library," an impression that is confirmed by Bodley's constant attention to the library's furnishings, as he directed the material contributions of "carpenters, joiners, glasiers," and all those concerned with the "mechanicall workes" of book storage, down to the "barres, lockes, hasps, grates, cheines, and other gimmoes or iron, belonging to the fastning, and riveting of the bookes."[87] Bodley's library was built according to the stall system that was then prevalent in the Oxford colleges, with books chained for safekeeping to book presses that were placed at right angles to the windows and equipped with narrow desks to accommodate several readers at once.[88] Like the "theoreticall furniture" of the mind whose importance Bodley defends against Bacon's attack, the Bodleian's material furniture was dedicated foremost to the work of storage and preservation. Following suit, the *Statutes* of the library, reflecting their author Bodley's own experience of the bibliographical trauma and loss inflicted by the Reformation, stress the importance of safeguarding books from future trauma: "to prevent by all good means, what hereafter may befall to the abusing, impairing, or perhaps (which God forbid) to the utter subverting of our Store of Books."[89]

When Bacon declares the history of thought, like the library, to be no more than "a granary and storehouse of things," he lifts terms that were routinely used to describe the Bodleian itself by its founder and first users. In 1601 Samuel Daniel praised the new Bodleian Library as a "storehouse of the choicest furniture" and "an everlasting Granery."[90] Bodley himself described the library in similar terms; as he writes to his librarian, Thomas James, "the general conceit as well of other nations as of our owne at home of the Librarie stoare, is so great, that they imagine in a manner, there is nothing wanting in it."[91] In soliciting donations for his library, Bodley echoes the same terms, inviting potential benefactors "to furnishe their stoarehouse with bookes."[92] Bodley's dream of a capacious "Librarie stoare" was the opposite of the library that he had witnessed as an undergraduate, "ruined and wast" by the Reformation, with only "the rome itself remayning."

In his letter praising Bodley for "having built an Ark to save learning from deluge," I have argued, Bacon both repeats terms that were routinely used to describe the dissolution's devastating effects on monastic libraries and acknowledges the differences between the two men's projects. Where Bodley attempts to reverse the "deluge" of the dissolution, by preserving fragile written knowledge in "an Ark," Bacon's sympathies align more closely with the purificatory aims of the deluge itself; translated into historical terms, where Bodley sees his library as a reparation of Reformation era damages, Bacon harnesses the Reformation's iconoclastic fervor in his intellectual project to break free from the accumulated knowledge of the past. As he asserts in the *Cogitata et visa*, with typical bravura: "the safest oracle for the future lies in the rejection of the past."[93]

In light of Bacon's connection with Bodley, many of the critiques of libraries that recur throughout Bacon's work can be read as direct responses to the Bodleian. Where Bacon imagines an experimental science that advances knowledge beyond tradition, Bodley defends "tradition" as the source of all knowledge worth preserving. And the religious valences of Bacon's attacks on the "superstition" and "idolatry" that continue to tenant human thought have a material referent in Bodley's acquisitions policy and practice. Bacon comments that books and libraries "are the shrines where the saint is," and the Bodleian, like the Cotton Library, made hagiographical texts a staple of its collection from the start. But whereas the Cotton librarian Thomas Smith insisted that these medieval religious texts were collected only as historical sources, Bodley promised—at least to a significant body of Catholic donors—to respect their religious origins. Of the eight hundred manuscripts that Bodley acquired for the library during his lifetime, Ian Philip estimates that 80 percent "were donations, mainly of medieval theology, and of English origin" that represented "the relics of monastic libraries," including large numbers of manuscripts from St. Augustine's Canterbury, Newark Priory, Reading Abbey, and Exeter Cathedral Library.[94] Among the collectors who helped to stock the library shelves were Catholic sympathizers like Thomas Allen, fellow of Gloucester Hall (known to be hospitable to recusants), who was named to the university committee established to oversee the library's foundation.[95] Allen's own numerous gifts include scientific and philosophical works, reflecting his academic background as a mathematician, as well as books of medieval theology, patristics, liturgy, and hagiography; they include the Glastonbury manuscript known as "St. Dunstan's Classbook," which features a tenth-century sketch of Dunstan at Christ's feet in Dunstan's own hand, manuscripts of *Piers Plowman*, Lydgate's *Troy Book* and *Siege of Thebes*, Richard Rolle's *De emendatio vitae* and *Form of Living*, and multiple manuscripts of Ailred of Rievaulx.[96] Allen made gifts of nineteen books to the library in 1601 and two more in 1608, but the bulk of his books came to the Bodleian through the bequest of Sir Kenelm Digby, the prominent Catholic nobleman who inherited Allen's library and, like Allen, also collected medieval devotional manuscripts formerly owned by Oxford-area monasteries and religious houses; two hundred manuscripts from the Digby collection came to the Bodleian in 1634.[97]

Bodley also encouraged benefactions from numerous other known Catholics, including Anthony, second Viscount Montague, "one of the most staunch and open Catholics of his rank in the country," and the Catholic bibliophile John, sixth Baron Lumley.[98] To recusant book collectors, preserving medieval manuscripts was more than an antiquarian impulse; Andrew

Watson is surely right when he speculates that Thomas Allen's interest in medieval manuscripts was motivated by "reverence for the past" arising from his religious sympathies.[99] In a similar fashion, Alan Coates traces the post-Reformation collection of books from Reading Abbey by Catholics who acquired them "out of *pietas* and a concern to preserve the monuments of the old religion."[100] A number of medieval religious books gathered by Catholics Sir Francis Englefield and the family of Clement, Humphrey, and William Burdett made their way into the Bodleian through a bequest in 1608, establishing the library as a suitable repository for medieval books collected by Catholics.[101] Bodley's promise to rebuild the library as a way of reversing the destructive effects of the dissolution would have been cultur-ally, as well as politically, appealing to Catholics; in the Bodleian they could see not only the return of Duke Humfrey's Library but the restoration of the pre-Reformation literary culture whose products they donated to Bodley in large number. Bodley's close relationships with Catholic collectors shaped the character of the Bodleian's collection, contributing to the richness of its holdings in medieval literary and liturgical texts, which are notably in short supply in contemporary collections like Cotton's.[102] Bacon's charge that libraries serve as shrines for the ancient saints, then, finds a specific target in the Bodleian's collection of medieval manuscripts, many of which owe their survival to their collectors' reverence for the lost past of medieval Catholicism.

Bodley's encouragement of donations from Catholic collectors did not arise from any covert Catholic sympathies on his own part; like Bacon, Bodley came from a family of Marian exiles with unimpeachable Protestant credentials. As he himself assured Thomas James, his "decidedly antipapist" librarian, "my hope was and is that the greatest part of our Protestant writ-ers will be giuen."[103] But instead of assembling his collection selectively, as did the Reformation era Matthew Parker when he distinguished the "monu-ments of antiquity" worthy of preservation from unworthy "monuments of superstition," Bodley envisioned his library in unusually ecumenical terms, directing it broadly toward "the benefit of posteritie" and "the studies of good learning," as he wrote to the vice-chancellor at Oxford, rather than the polemical aims that had driven Parker.[104]

This mission informs the Bodleian's then much-heralded status as a "publick library," indicating not its admissions policy—by statute, the library was effectively closed to all but the best-connected graduates (one notable exception being donors)—but its dedication to the "public" good.[105] Bodley conceived his "Librarie stoare" as a capacious receptacle that included texts both offensive and sacred, illicit and licit. As he wrote James, he wanted readers to perceive that "there is nothing wanting in it," thus aiming for an ideal of universality that was novel for the English library, though not for its seventeenth-century Continental counterparts. In his *Advis pour dresser une Bibliothèque* (1627), Gabriel Naudé counsels the Parisian bibliophile Henri de Mesmes, in words translated into English by John Evelyn in 1661, that "a Library which is erected for the publick benefit ought to be universal, but which it can never be, unlesse it comprehend all the principal Authors that have written upon the great diversity of particular Subjects." This goal of universality can be justified on the grounds of public relations, Naudé explains: "that every man who seeks for a Book, judges it to be good; ... so that coming at last to encounter it in some Library, he easily thinks, that the Owner of it knew it as well as himself: and that he bought it upon the same account that excited him to search after it; and in pursuit of this, conceives an incomparable esteem ... of the Owner."[106]

Bodley, who owed his collection's growth to voluntary contributions (rather than personal acquisition, like Cotton), had an interest in cultivating a reputation for inclusiveness, as it encouraged Catholic contributors to believe that their books would find a haven in his library. But the ideal of universal inclusion could also be justified to partisan objectors on intellectual grounds, as Naudé further explains: those who engage in "conflicts ... are so linkt together, that it were as great an error to read them separately, as to judge and understand one party without the other, or one Contrary without his Antagonist." Moreover, including the works on all sides of the religious controversies is advisable, Naudé insists, "since it is necessary that our Doctors should finde them in some places to refute them." Therefore, he concludes, "we make it no Scruple to have a *Thalmud* or an *Alcoran*, which belch a thousand Blasphemies against Jesus Christ, and our Religion" (33), and even "all the Works of the most learned and famous *Hereticks*."[107] Naudé qualifies his own goal of universality by excluding works on the basis of their quality, leading Roger Chartier to observe that his *Advis* exhibits a "tension between comprehensiveness and essence."[108] Yet Naudé is scrupulously comprehensive in the charged arena of religious controversy, a characteristic he shares with *La Bibliothèque d'Antione du Verdier* (1585), a massive catalogue that lists the holdings of an idealized "universal library of French books" and includes even Lutheran and Calvinist authors, with the understanding that their inclusion will benefit Catholics, who are "warned which books are reproved and censured so that they will flee them."[109]

Like Naudé, Bodley also draws distinctions of quality in his well-known (and widely reviled) decision to exclude "riffe raffe bookes," contemporary printed works that he judged to be ephemera, insisting that "such will but proue a discredit to our Librarie."[110] Yet Bodley allows the Bodleian to include the works of Edward Weston, a Catholic controversialist whose works Bodley calls "riffe raffe wordes without discretion," and instructs his librarian, Thomas James: "I haue sent you Weston by the cariar, which I pray you cause to be bound, upon my reckning, and place in the Librarie."[111] Like Naudé and du Verdier, Bodley goes out of his way to include religious and political tracts that were considered objectionable and even treasonous. Thus, like Naudé's library, the Bodleian's 1605 catalogue lists several editions of the *"Alcoran"* as well as an *"Alcorani* confutatio."[112] Closer to home, it includes, predictably, the *Opera* of John Jewel, translated by Bacon's mother, under the heading "Libri Theologici"; but it also includes responses to Jewel's works by the Catholic controversialist Thomas Harding and Jewel's responses to those responses, listing Harding's "confutation of the Apologie" (1565), "Iewels replie vnto M. Harding" (1565), "Thomas Hardings Reioynder to Mr Iewels reply" (1566), and "Iewels defence of the Apologie" (1571).[113]

In a sign of his willingness to include controversial works, Bodley instructs his librarian to accept two books into the library that James I had specifically prohibited, George Buchanan's *Rerum Scoticarum historia* and *De iure regni,* telling him, if need be, to "plead ignorance of any suche interdiction."[114] But even the king himself acknowledged the library's right to include offensive materials. In 1605 James I visited the library on its opening; discovering a copy of Robert Gaguin's *De puritate conceptionis Mariae Virginis* (1498), the king is reported to have "said it had often been his desire that such objectionable writings (especially on religious subjects) could be altogether suppressed rather than tolerated to the corruption of minds and manners. He admitted, however, that probably there was no disadvantage from their being stored up in collections of this kind."[115] We cannot be certain of the reasons for James's leniency here. He may have been mindful of the great restrictions placed on the Bodleian's early readership, which made potentially dangerous texts like this all but inaccessible to the general reader. Yet in the judgment of Robert Burton, the king shared Bodley's dream of the universal library; as Burton recounts in an anecdote in *The Anatomy of Melancholy:*

> King JAMES 1605, when he came to see our University of Oxford, and amongst other Aedifices, now went to view that famous Library, renued by Sr Thomas Bodley, in imitation of Alexander, at his departure brake out into that noble speech, If I were not a King, I would be an University man; And if it were so that I must be a Prisoner, if I might have my wish, I would desire to have no other Prison then that Library, and to be chained together with so many good Authors, et mortuis magistris.[116]

If James I shares with Thomas More the fantasy of being imprisoned in a library, his fantasy arises, according to Burton, not from a desire for ascetic withdrawal, but from a fantasy of the library as *thesaurus*, a capacious store of bountiful treasure; as Burton concludes from the anecdote: "So sweet is the delight of study, the more learning they have (as he that hath a dropsie, the more hee drinkes the thirstier he is) the more they covet to learne." The same line of thinking leads Burton to speculate on the vertiginous scope of the universal library: "you may contemplate the variation of the 23 letters, which may be so infinitely varied that the words complicated and deduced thence will not be contained within the compasse of the firmament."[117] In this, Burton, an avid user of the Bodleian, invokes an impossible ideal of bibliographical totality like that of the universal library, "edifices capable of welcoming the world's memory," that Roger Chartier traces to the Renaissance.[118] The Bodleian, built on the illusion that "there is nothing wanting in it," belongs to this idealized tradition. But where Chartier claims that the dream of the universal library is a historical constant ("the dream of a library . . . that would bring together all accumulated knowledge and all the books ever written can be found throughout the history of Western civilization," he argues), for the Bodleian, it arises out of a historically specific circumstance.[119] Bodley's dream of a library from which "there is nothing wanting" emerges in response to an equally affecting vision of bibliographical oblivion, symbolized by the empty room that was all that remained of Oxford's library after the Oxford visitations and accompanying dissolution. Where Bacon looks at libraries and observes that "the numberless host of opinions, tenets, and speculations goes on forever," Bodley imagines the necessity of preserving "all our Aximes and Maximes, and generall assertions that are left by tradition from our Elders to us," as a fragile wall between civilization and the threat of "Barbarism" that he has already seen breached.

The disagreement between the two men, rather than reflecting Bodley's misunderstanding of Bacon's project, shows that the two are speaking the same language, albeit from two opposing perspectives. Bodley, I have argued, reads Bacon's revisionary *Cogitata et visa* as a restaging of the dissolution, to the extent that, like that bibliographical catastrophe, Bacon's intellectual project would, Bodley holds, empty the shelves of tradition's library. However different their orientations, Bodley's reading accurately notices the reformist sources of Bacon's rhetoric, as when he attacks "blind superstition" as the enemy of reason and calls for bold correction of "error."[120] Ironically, however, Bacon's reformist rhetoric does not set him outside libraries so much as it borrows and adapts their formative discourse from founding figures such as John Bale and Matthew Parker. Similarly, Bacon's call for new forms of learning to correct the old, which he embodies in libraries, expropriates a debate then developing within the Bodleian itself concerning its ultimate purpose and goal: was the library to be a place for the storage of the written knowledge of the past or for the active production of new knowledge?

Thomas James: The Librarian Factor

Bodley developed his plans for his library in close consultation with his indefatigable librarian, Thomas James. James, a fellow at New College, secured Bodley's attention in 1599 by publishing an edition of Richard de Bury's *Philobiblon*, with a dedication to Bodley and a catalogue of Oxford manuscripts, printed in an "Appendix de manuscriptis Oxoniensibus," that James compiled himself.[121] The work, subtitled *De amore librorum, et institutione bibliothecae,* could have been expected to appeal to Bodley's ambition to recuperate Oxford's lost medieval library. In his choice of de Bury's *Philobiblon,* James published a medieval work that gave bibliophilia a new name and identity. Originally written in 1345 by the bishop of Durham, whose library was said to be without peer in fourteenth-century England, the work expresses and defends a love of books that borders on the obsessive: "this ecstatic love has carried us away so powerfully," de Bury writes, "that we have resigned all thoughts of other earthly things, and have given ourselves up to a possession for acquiring books."[122] In his dedication, James compares Bodley with de Bury on the basis of "the love which you have for books and literature" ("Epistle," my translation). In so doing, he also implies a parallel between Bodley and de Bury as founders of great Oxford libraries; like Bodley, de Bury planned to establish a library at Oxford by bequeathing his own large book collection to Durham College (the site of the current Trinity College, Oxford), a plan that might have established an Oxford library to rival Duke Humfrey's if de Bury's debts at his death in 1345 had not forced his library's sale and dispersal.[123] Without anticipating this fate, de Bury's *Philobiblon* concludes with a set of rules for the imagined library that resembles those of the Bodleian in their stipulations restricting the books' circulation and use.[124] By tracing a line of continuity between de Bury and Bodley, James's edition of the *Philobiblon* could be imagined to appeal to Bodley's own view of his library as an effort to restore the medieval library by repairing the damage inflicted on it by the Reformation. Nevertheless, James's own views aligned him more closely with the Reformation library breakers than with medieval library makers like de Bury.

James sharpened his ambitions as an editor and a librarian in response to the Counter-Reformation Vatican and its agents, who made bibliography into a powerful religio-political weapon. In 1562, the eighteenth session of the Council of Trent announced its intention to produce an *Index generalis librorum prohibitorum* that would list "suspected and pernicious books" in order to show the faithful how to "separate the various and strange doctrines as cockle from the wheat of Christian truth," and thereby "restore to its purity and splendor the doctrine of the Catholic faith, which in many places has become defiled and obscured by the opinions of many differing among themselves, and to bring back to a better mode of life morals which have deviated from ancient uses."[125] Strikingly, the edict cites Matthew 13.30, on the separation of the wheat from the tares ("Let both grow together vntil the haruest: and in the time of haruest, I will say to the reapers, Gather ye together first the tares, and binde them in bundels to burne them: but gather the wheat into my barne"), as an authority for the separation of good texts from bad—in a model that recalls but redirects Stephen Batman's use of the same parable as an image of Protestant reading, when he insists that "there be meanes and wayes to presarve the good corne by gathering oute the wedes."[126]

James, like his employer Bodley, rejected the selective collecting methods of the earlier Protestants as soundly as he did the calls for textual purification that drove the Counter-Reformation *Index*. Instead, he took a stand against censorship while also attempting to establish the Bodleian as a haven for censored Protestant books. In a gesture calculated to enrage and confound his Vatican counterparts, James prepared his own edition of the *Index*, but with the intention of using it to guide the Bodleian's acquisitions; as he wrote to Archbishop Ussher in 1624, "I have in the Press at the present . . . an Index librorum prohiborum . . . chiefly for the use of our publick Library, that we may know what Books, and what Editions to buy; their prohibition being a good direction to guide us therein."[127] The result was James's edition, *Index generalis librorum prohibitorum a pontificiis . . . In usum Bibliothecae Bodleiaanae, & curatoribus eiusdem specialiter designatus per Tho. Iames* (Oxford, 1627), which collates six editions of the Council of Trent's *Index* from 1582 to 1612.[128] James's *Index* offers itself as a general catalogue not only of antipapist books but also of the Bodleian's holdings, as James helpfully cross-references prohibited books that can be found in the library by marking them with an asterisk.[129] As well as Protestant books like Jewel's "Apologia" (sig. A5v), these include numerous non-Protestant works, such as an "Alchoranus Mahometis" (sig. A3v), that were censored by the *Index* but housed in the Bodleian. James may have been especially gratified to be able to print, and asterisk, listings of two of his own works that were included in the *Index:* "Tho. James, Bellum Papale" and "Ecloga Oxoniocantabrigiens. Lond. 1600" (sig. F2).

As James's *Index* reveals, the list of prohibited books can create its own imaginary antilibrary—such was the case with du Verdier's all-inclusive *Bibliothèque*, which justified its inclusion of prohibited titles as a warning to Catholics "so that they will flee them."[130] For James, the *Index*'s antilibrary is embodied by the Bodleian, whose catalogue announces the preservation of the very books that the *Index* would prohibit. As James recognized, the catalogue was a tool of immense ideological power, a fact that is confirmed by the inclusion of James's own *Ecloga Oxonio-Cantabrigiensis* (London, 1600) among the *Index*'s prohibited books. A massive listing of books from the Oxford and Cambridge college libraries, James's *Ecloga* has been called "the first union catalogue," and it went on to provide a standard model for subsequent college library catalogues.[131] But James's catalogue, like its model, John Bale's *Scriptorum illustrium maioris Britanniae... catalogus* (1557), had a distinctly Protestant religio-political function, offering the manuscripts it lists as weapons against "Papist corruptions."[132]

James's catalogues engage in a heated dialectic with the *Index.* Not only did James attempt to acquire censored books for the Bodleian, but he aimed to publicize those works widely, ordering "the places forbidden to be transcribed" and enlisting the printing press as his ally, as he remarks, "the reprinting of that which they commanded to be left out, will keepe one Presse going a yeere." This goal spurred James to call for a revival of medieval authors: "that the *Authors of the middle age,* that wrote in the defence of that Religion, which is now (thankes be to God) publikely established in the Church of England, for the substance thereof, may bee faithfully transcribed, diligently collated, & distributed into volumes" (emphasis in original). Among these medieval authors, James expresses the hope (in a statement that echoes Bacon's praise of Martin Luther) "to see *Wicleph* and *Peacocke* revived againe out of the dust of their graues, and our Libraries, and to write in defence an Apologie of our Religion."[133]

Such a desire led James to print extracts from the works of John Wyclif, collected from manuscripts in the Bodleian, as *An Apologie for John Wickliffe, shewing his conformitie, with the now church of England;... Collected chiefly out of diuerse workes of his in written hand, by Gods especiall providence remaining in the Publike Library at Oxford, of the Honorable foundation of Sr. Thomas Bodley Knight: by Thomas James keeper of the same* (1608). Convinced that papists were plotting "how either to abolish all ancient written [i.e., manuscript] books out of our Libraries, or els to banish al

ancient truth out of their books, by their new invented Purgatory of books,"
James frames Wyclif as "a most ancie[n]t, Catholike, and learned Deuine"
who "maintained the same doctrine then, which the Church of England
now (being guided by the Holy Ghost and sacred writings of Scripture and
Fathers) doth professe."[134]

In James's account of his recovery of Wyclif, he represents the library
as both a place of burial (Wyclif and Peacock lie buried in "the dust of
their graues, and our Libraries") and an arsenal of truth, as James seeks to
awake the dormant medieval authors before the papists can "abolish all
ancient written books out of our Libraries." In those medieval manuscripts
(i.e., "ancient written books"), James insisted, could be found the textual
"proofs" of papist corruptions: "The proofes which I shal alleadge shalbe
cleere, euident, apparent, authentical, for they shalbe produced out of his
own words and works, as they are extant in sundry good Manuscripts, in our
renowned publike Librarie, as the[m]selues may see or cause to bee seene
by others." James's *Apologie* cites Wyclif as an authority not only for key
Protestant doctrinal positions such as the centrality of scripture ("all truth
is contained in holy Scripture") but for the centrality of textual editing to
the Protestant cause; thus, James cites Wyclif's argument that "a continual
collation and comparing of Scripture, with Scripture, is required," a passage
that James gleans from Wyclif's *De veritate sacre scripture* (On the Truth of
Holy Scripture), which the Bodleian owned in manuscript (and still does).[135]
In so doing, James takes Wyclif as not only the subject but the model of, and
authority for, his own textual practice as an editor.[136]

In editions such as the *Apologie,* James attempted to recover "the Authors of the middle age" by not only preserving medieval texts but also
reissuing them in print. James's editorial practice aligns him with a tradition of activist librarianship fostered in Archbishop Parker's library, which
issued printed works of medieval texts such as Parker's editions of Aelfric,
A Testimonie of Antiquitie (1566), and of Matthew Paris, *Historia Major*
(1570), as evidence of (in the words of the *Testimonie*'s subtitle) "the auncient fayth in the Church of England."[137] Selected for their utility to the
cause of reform, these texts established an alliance between the library and
the press, making the library a center not just of textual preservation but
of textual production. By extension, in the model established by Parker and
John Joscelyn and followed by James, the librarian was not simply a custo-
dian of old manuscripts but an active textual critic and a producer of new
knowledge. Like the members of Archbishop Parker's circle, James turned
these productive energies to a polemical religious agenda. As well as bringing out editions of proto-Protestant religious authors like Wyclif, he also

heeded Wyclif's injunction that "a continual collation and comparing of Scripture, with Scripture, is required" by attempting to produce textually accurate editions of the church fathers. In corrected editions of St. Gregory, St. Cyprian, and St. Ambrose, he establishes the foundation of this project, which aimed to purge Christianity's founding texts from corruptions introduced in transmission.[138]

James's explication of his editorial method, the 1611 *Treatise of the Corruption of Scripture*, has been called "the first English manual in textual criticism" because of its innovation in the method of collation. "The best remedie for a diseased booke," James explains, "Is 4. or 5. Old *Manuscripts* ... compounded togither, and the best of them distilled through the Limbeck [alembic] of a good Diuines braine, that is of a sound iudgement, and unpartial temper."[139] James's collation method draws from those of humanists following Petrarch, as refined by the comparative method of Angelo Poliziano, which was based on comparing manuscripts, privileging the authority of the oldest ones, and using them as models to root out textual errors introduced in transmission. As Anthony Grafton observes, Poliziano applied his textual method to address the problem of "ancient sources that contradicted one another about historical or mythological details."[140] As James insists, "It is a role in criticisme, that *caeteris paribus*, the older the copy is, the better it is," an insight that led James to develop protocols for dating manuscripts paleographically.[141] James shared the humanists' desire to root out textual error, but his project was also driven by a religious motive, since he held that textual error was the root of doctrinal error. Thus, he insists that "a diligent collation of all the Fathers works, with all the best written [i.e., manuscript] coppies that can be gotten" would correct errors of doctrine that began as textual corruptions: "those places which seeme to be of least account, as the altering of a small comma, the difference of a letter, or the change of a word, ... have great consequence in case of Religion."[142]

The corruptions of the fathers result not only from mistransmission but by what James calls "wilfull corruptions" that his papist adversaries "haue thrust into the Text violently," in the form of sometimes-minute textual variants, in order to falsify the origins of doctrine such as papal supremacy, relics, and transubstantiation.[143] Declaring his intent to purify the authoritative texts of these errors, James repeats the Catholic *Index*'s scriptural rhetoric even while insisting that he will reverse its textual and doctrinal effects: "If the Diuel be so readie to sow tares in our bookes, shal not we bee as readie to purge them out of our writings? Should not we, be as diligent, to restore, as they are to take away, from the the [*sic*] workes of the ancient

Fathers?"[144] If the *Index* suppresses the truth by condemning books, James calls for a bibliographical practice that will suppress no books; instead, it projects its purificatory focus into the books themselves, seeking to root out textual error and redeem them for the Protestant cause. James's "tares" are not "suspected and pernicious books" but pernicious mistranscriptions that must be cleansed from otherwise-sound books. The library is to be the center for this cleansing practice, which James calls "the libration of bookes," employing a word whose obsolete meaning is "weighing"; thus, he discusses the variables that are to be "weighed in the libration of bookes."[145] This painstaking practice of critical judgment, of weighing alternate readings in search of accurate ones, defines the work of the librarian.

Following Parker's associate Joscelyn, James conflates the office of the librarian with that of the textual critic, whose chief function is to exercise his trained judgment on the books in his keeping. Thus, he defines the work of the "criticke" as "an Art of inquiring into the truth, and faith as such as haue written and put foorth bookes, according to certaine rules, examining and reading all maner of bookes, in what facultie soeuer," and basing readings "critically, upon Conjecture, or upon Iudgement." "*Iudgement* proceeds from the MSS, and is for the most part solide and certaine," James insists; but where readings derive from conjecture, the critic must make "choise of some good readings rather than other, but noting both unto the Reader; for a false reading many times, hath some footsteps of a truer lection, and what one cannot, another may observe."[146] And in the *Treatise of Corruptions*, he states that "this is the iudgement of the best cricks: whose precept it is, that we should note all the different readings in the margent of the printed books, although they seeme never so small, and chuse the best."[147]

If, as I have argued above, Bacon aspires to replace the library with a data-processing center, James works in a library tradition (which he develops into a full-blown method) already dedicated to the selection of evidence based on critical judgment and to the active production of knowledge, rather than the passive storage of documents. In these operations, James's project continues the work of monastic libraries like that of Bury St. Edmunds, with its dedication to the production of commentary and the collation of authorities as enabled by the great *Catalogus de libris autenticis et apocrifis* by Kirkestede, while appropriating such library-based practices to the rooting out of doctrinal and textual error. James imagines the monastic buildings themselves transformed into editorial factories: "I would to God, that this had been on K Henry the eights minde, when he pulled downe the Monasteries, either to have turned them into colledges, & nurseries for learning and religion . . . or . . . to the maintenance of a Colledge of writers, collators, comparers."[148] James's method of criticism accomplishes the ends of Henrician reform while cleansing, rather than destroying, its objects; just as he would preserve, but transform, the monastic buildings, James's reformed *lectio* would preserve and cleanse, rather than destroy, the monastic texts that are its objects.

James details his plans for such a neo-scriptorium in a broadsheet of 1610, which calls for "sixe discreete and sober students in Diuinity" to collate works "truly relating to and reporting the differences of the written copies of or from the printed Bookes." James was explicit about his expectations for the project: "Amongst so many written copies, they shall chuse out foure of the most auncient and approued Bookes, which shall be exactly compared with the . . . printed copies. The diverse readings shall be noted in the margents of the printed Bookes," with the end of producing "an index . . . which shall shew the corruptions of the printed copies."[149]

The project had the early approval of the archbishop of Canterbury, Richard Bancroft, who praised James's "very laudable purpose and intention" and offered his sponsorship: "Your industrie in your course there hath beene very profitable, and I dowbt not but in short time you shall receave a due recompense for the same, wherein (as I have sayd) my assistance shall not be wanting."[150] To assist with the project, Bancroft directed the vicechancellor of Oxford to supply adequate personnel, books, and "due reward," along with "what else Mr James shall commend to your wisedomes to be deliberated" in support of a work he deemed for "the good of the Churche" and "honour of our Vniversitie."[151] Given Bancroft's active uses of his own library in response to theological controversy, he may have seen in Thomas James a kindred spirit deserving of his beneficence.[152] But in 1612 James's collation project faltered, its chief patron, Bancroft, having died two years previously; as James reports, "they left off (which I shame to speake of) for want of paiment."[153]

While James's ambitious project would have been at home in the Parker Library or, one suspects, in Bancroft's Lambeth Palace Library, it failed to win the crucial support of Bodley himself. In a letter of 19 June 1610, possibly in response to James's broadsheet, Bodley complains that James's collation project distracts from, rather than advancing, what should be his chief aims as librarian: "Howe yow may be spared out of the Librarie, for that collation of the fathers, which you have undertaken, I can not readily tell, in regard it is a libertie, that must be vsed many yeres, which will also diuert your chief cogitations, from intending the good & bettering of the Librarie."[154]

Bodley's *Statutes* for the library define the librarian's chief offices otherwise:

> In writing the Register of Contributors, and the Alphabetical Tables affixed to the Standerds and Heads of every Desk: In digesting the Authors in their proper Partitions, as the Tables give Direction: In delivering those by hand, that are kept under Locks, and wholly left to his Custody: In speedy bringing in, and present placing of such Books, as shall from time to time be given: In observing his Hours of opening, and shutting, and tarrying in the Library: In excluding all kind of Persons, that are no Freemen of that Place; and in providing for the Books and Buildings, with all the Furniture of the Room, that it may be always freed from Dust and uncleanness: and That it goe not to decay, by Reason of Wind and Rain coming in at the Casements, or otherwise for want of timely Reparations.[155]

As these directions indicate, Bodley regarded his librarian as a human extension of the library "furniture" that the librarian is charged with dusting: like the presses, chains, and locks whose arrangement Bodley had so carefully overseen, the librarian's office is primarily to store and safeguard the books. Accordingly, Bodley frames what is perhaps the librarian's most formidable task, the production and constant updating of the catalogue, as a rote transcription of the "Alphabetical Tables affixed to the Standerds and Heads of every Desk" that are meant to secure "the Authors in their proper Partitions, as the Tables give Direction" ("tables" were the lists of titles in square wooden frames affixed to the ends of the library stalls; the Bodleian's remain in situ).[156] The diminution of the librarian's more active intellectual roles envisioned by James is palpable in Bodley's *Statutes*.[157] Bodley's expectations of the librarian's office clashed with those of the activist James, who complained that his cataloguing and custodial chores were keeping him from his critical pursuits.[158] Yet James submitted; the result of his efforts, the Bodleian's first printed catalogue, published in 1605, organizes the library's vast holdings by recording their placement on the Bodleian's shelves.[159] Following Bodley's directions to transcribe the "Tables," James's 1605 catalogue classifies books by pressmark, which Bodley determined would follow the order of the traditional faculties: Theology, Jurisprudence, Medicine, and Arts, with the books shelved alphabetically (by author) in each faculty.[160] The order of the faculties themselves followed a hierarchy of value: the preeminence of Theology was a given, as was the inferiority of the Arts, but Bodley instructed James to reverse the order of Jurisprudence and Medicine to reflect the superiority of the former over the latter, since "I doe

finde it agreed on by most men that Lawe in most places hath the prece-
dence."[161] Thus, the order of the books in the Bodleian—and the catalogue
that records it—follows the order of knowledge in the *universitas scientiarum*. To recall once again Bodley's comments to Bacon on the *Cogitata et
visa*: in the Bodleian, the library "Furniture" ("the Furniture of the Room")
establishes the "theoreticall furniture"—that is, the general categories, or
traditional faculties—by which books and knowledge are organized.

James produced the catalogue that Bodley ordered, following the arrangement of the book presses by faculties. But he also introduced an innovation;
in addition to listing the library holdings, James included a substantial addendum listing commentaries on the Bible, on Aristotle, and on civil and
canon law by author, leading Ian Philip to observe that "the 1605 catalogue
as finally published was in reality two catalogues."[162] The scope of James's
addendum also necessitated an "Index Auctorum," which fills sixty-four
pages.[163] If James's main catalogue produces a traditional shelflist, James's
addendum and index approach the more abstract ordering of the subject catalogue. The relationship between the two parts of James's 1605 catalogue
recalls that of Conrad Gesner's two catalogues, the *Bibliotheca universalis*
(1545), with its "catalogus omnium scriptorum locupletissimus," and the
Pandectae (1548), with its author index subdivided according to subject categories (indeed, the Bodleian 1605 catalogue records a copy of "Bibliotheca
Conr. *Gesneri* cum Appendice," which would have supplied James with
Gesner as a model); if the first records and preserves books, the other facilitates cross-referencing and comparison among them.[164] So too James's list of
"Intrepretes librorum Aristotelis" (Commentators on the Books of Aristotle) groups authors according to the works of Aristotle on which they write
and thus encourages readers to compare their interpretations, an arrangement repeated in his list of commentators on scripture.[165] The catalogue
shares this comparative function with the larger critical project that drove
James's call for a "Colledge of writers, collators, comparers." As a tool for
collation and comparison, James's subsequent subject catalogue to the Arts,
undertaken in 1607, further developed this goal, by classifying books under
an extensive range of headings and then subdividing them "in minutissimas
portiones vel sectiones."[166] Thus, the "Arts" are subdivided into "Astrono-
mia," "Architectura," "Arithmeticae," "Opticorum," "Musicae," and so on,
with each category also subdivided extensively, culminating in a voluminous "synopsis Historicorum," which makes up 117 of the catalogue's 258
pages and includes more than seventy subdivisions.[167]

James's descriptions of his collation method, and the innovations that
he introduced to subject cataloguing to enable it, show that the broad revision

of knowledge that Bacon situated outside the library was already being pursued within it. The similarities in the very terms in which James and Bacon
conceived their projects reflect unexpected parallels in their thinking. In
Cogitata et visa Bacon describes his inductive method: "which by slow and
faithful toil gathers information from things and brings it to the understanding," after which "the material collected should be sorted into orderly
Tables, so that the understanding may work upon it and thus accomplish
its appropriate task"—that is, a broad reevaluation and classification of all
human knowledge.[168] Bacon's description of the "orderly Tables" in which
information is arranged appropriates the basic terminology of library organization, recalling the "tables" that listed book titles at the ends of the
library stalls. Bacon further invokes the library as a precedent when he calls
the result of this imagined sorting of information into "orderly Tables" a
"catalogue," since both James and Bodley describe the action of compiling
the library catalogue as "printing the Tables." Where Bacon's "Catalogue of
Titles of Particular Histories" attempts to embrace the entirety of human
knowledge, from the "History of the Heavens" to the "History of Man," it
has a direct analogue in James's 1607 subject catalogue, with its vast "synopsis Historicorum" occupying the bulk of its contents. Furthermore, James
and Bacon share a vision of the indexing systems their catalogues would
produce: when Bacon calls for a notation system that would "note the origin of this or that piece of nonsense or gullibility" (NO 469) by means of an
index in which "note or advice" would enable false beliefs to be dismantled
(NO 469), he recaps the method and aims of James's own proposed system
of notation, in which "diverse readings shall be noted in the margents of the
printed Bookes," and "an index . . . shall shew the corruptions of the printed
copies."

The intellectual affinities between James and Bacon extend from the
forms of their efforts to the broader aims that govern them. Bacon's project
of "gather[ing] information" and "bring[ing] it to the understanding" envisions a reformation of human memory itself: thus, also in *Cogitata et
visa*, Bacon describes the goal of "true philosophy," which "takes the matter furnished by natural history and mechanical experience and stores it
in its memory, but not before it has been transformed and wrought upon
by the understanding."[169] Where Bacon aspires to submit the history of
knowledge to critical judgment—and thus to bring the faculty of reason to
bear on that of memory—James gives this aspiration an institutional and
bibliographical form. In his essay "Of Studies," Bacon urges the reader to
"read not to contradict, nor to believe, but to waigh and consider."[170] James
invokes a similar model of "weighing" reading when he insists that the

library is a place of active judgment, where evidence is "weighed in the libration of bookes." James's term "libration" translates literally as "weighing" (from the Latin verb *libro -are*, "to balance"; cf. *libra*, "scales"); it also obliquely puns on the library itself, which James directs at "weighing" textual evidence. For James, the ideal Bodleian reader actively compares and combines the texts of the past, handling old books not as "shrines" but as "proofs" in order to arrive at correct readings. Where Bacon's *Gesta Grayorum* juxtaposes the "library" with the "still-house...furnished with mills, instruments, furnaces and vessels," James invokes the operations of these very instruments to describe a judging process that takes place within libraries, where "old manuscripts" are "compounded together, and the best of them distilled through the limbeck of a good Diuines braine, that is of a sound iudgement, and unpartial temper." Comparing the reader's "braine," in which manuscripts are "distilled," to a "limbeck"—that is, an alembic, an apparatus used for distillation—James makes the library itself into an experimental site like Bacon's "still-house" or the laboratory of their contemporary Tycho Brahe, which was equipped with "distillation flasks," an observer reports, "in which unusual things are distilled."[171] James's library is a space in which the analytical processes of reading books and those of investigating natural phenomena mirror one another. Bacon would have had reason to sense an affinity with James. Indeed, if in 1608 Bacon believed that Richard Bancroft, archbishop of Canterbury, might "beleev[e] the sense" of his own project and extend it his sponsorship, it may be because the archbishop was already sponsoring another broadly analytical program with similarly ambitious aims—Thomas James's.[172]

In imagining the library as a place dedicated to the active investigation and production of knowledge, Thomas James, I am arguing, followed in the path of English library makers and librarians such as Parker's John Joscelyn, for whom the library was never a merely retentive institution, and Richard Bancroft, whose theological library was ordered and taxonomized in order to enable his active use of it in refuting religious controversy. But as James's own struggles with Bodley manifest, libraries and librarians were subject to redefinition in the early seventeenth century; thus, Bodley redefines the librarian from the institution's chief textual critic, in the model of Joscelyn, to its chief guardian, whose custodial tasks removed him ever further from interacting as an active reader with the books themselves. Years later, John Dury, deputy keeper of the King's Library, laments a similar development in *The Reformed Librarie-Keeper* (1650), when he writes "of Librarie-Keepers, in most Universities that I know; nay indeed in all, their places are but Mercenarie, and their employment of little or no use further, then to look to the Books committed to their custodie, that they may not bee lost; or embezeled by those that use them: and this is all." Against this sorry state of affairs, Dury argues that librarians should be empowered to play a more active role, not only in selecting books but also in promoting their use to the greatest benefit to learning: "The proper charge then of the Honorarie Librarie-Keeper in an Universitie ... is to keep the publick stock of Learning, which is in Books and Manuscripts to increase it, and to propose it to others in the waie which may bee most useful unto all; his work then is to bee a Factor and Trader for helps to Learning, and a Treasurer to keep them, and a dispenser to applie them to use, or to see them well used, or at least not abused." Yet the imperatives of storage have been allowed to outweigh use, Dury charges; the library "is no more then a dead Bodie as now it is constituted, in comparison of what it might bee, if it were animated with a publick Spirit to keep and use it, and ordered as it might bee for publick service."[173]

Dury's *Reformed Librarie-Keeper* develops from an earlier description of the "librarie keeper" in a letter that Dury wrote to his friend and collaborator Samuel Hartlib in August 1646.[174] That letter's immediate reference is the Bodleian, where Dury was attempting to promote Hartlib for the position of head librarian.[175] In revising for publication, Dury generalized his critique, but underlying it is a comment on the history of the Bodleian. While Dury's call for librarians to serve as active and creative "factors" for learning laments their degradation into mere conservators, it also looks back to an earlier age of activist Protestant librarianship in which the library was a knowledge factory, exemplified by Thomas James.

Dury's *Reformed Librarie-Keeper* articulates a conflict that played out within the Bodleian between Bodley and James in the early part of the century: was the librarian primarily an agent of conservation or of active investigation and knowledge production? Recalling the time of this conflict forces a reconsideration of the history of the library as it is refracted through Bacon's many representations of libraries throughout his work. One accomplished library historian, Paul Nelles, insists that, inspired by Bacon, the French librarian Gabriel Naudé "supplanted the dominant bibliographical conception of the library as a static repository of existing knowledge with a recognition of the library as an institution actively engaged in the production of new knowledge."[176] Yet I would argue that this formulation captures the history in reverse: rather than reflecting a "dominant bibliographical conception," the model of "static repository of existing knowledge" was one that Bacon imposed on libraries, even as he appropriated from them the very forms, rhetorics, and textual practices that he put into practice in his intellectual project and located outside libraries. The dismissive representation of libraries as mere conservators of knowledge—in contrast to experimental science, which produces it—is the legacy of Bacon's paradoxical engagement with the history of the English post-Reformation library. As I have argued in this chapter, by setting up an opposition between the active, productive site of science and the retentive site of libraries, Bacon was appropriating and externalizing a debate that was conducted within libraries themselves about their proper function, rather than reflecting accurately on libraries' contemporary forms or those of their recent past. When Bacon insists that libraries exercise a merely retentive function, as opposed to an active and creative one, he is in fact aligning himself with the more modern of the two sides, as manifested in Bodley's vision of the librarian-custodian. Yet in his critique of such retentive libraries—as well as the critiques that he specifically directed against Bodley's own library—Bacon occludes the alternative model of libraries that persisted even within the Bodleian, in the figure of Thomas James, whose very presence shows that the office of the librarian, like the identity of the library itself, remained a matter of active contention.

Thomas James, as I have argued, was an heir to post-Reformation library practices, with his determination to use the library as a place not simply for retaining and conserving received wisdom but for judicious weighing of textual evidence in order to arrive at truth—the process he calls "libration." This goal also made James, paradoxically, a more Baconian figure than Bacon himself would recognize when he portrays libraries and their practices as foils to his own intellectual project of reform. In calling for an alternative to the library that enshrines the past—and imagining that alternative as a center of contrastingly critical judgment and reasoned assessment—Bacon derives the very terms of his project by reaching into the library's recent history and recalling a moment in which librarians like James defined their work as an active practice of knowledge making. Bacon's advancement of learning comes about not by abandoning the modes of knowledge embodied in libraries—as he so often claims to do—but by actively adapting libraries' critical, active, and truth-seeking practices to new objects. Rather than rejecting the library in favor of nature, Bacon makes nature his library.

CODA

Memories of Libraries

This reading of the library's premodern past began as a reflection on its digital future. Scholars of medieval and early modern literature have a stake in, and stand to benefit greatly from, digital libraries—indeed, though researching this book involved many hours in old libraries, it could not have been written without these new ones.[1] But in the burgeoning literature addressing the future of the library there has been a strikingly widespread tendency to misrepresent the library's past, as if the very promise of the new must be purchased at the cost of understanding the old, which is repeatedly archaized and disowned. In a gesture that is continually replayed, the new library is set against, and made to vanquish, the old, a gesture that borrows from the paradigmatic break with the past that divides "medieval" from "Renaissance."[2] Just as the medieval/Renaissance divide rests on a language of darkness versus light, this imaginary division in library history pivots on a set of similar oppositions: closing versus opening, imprisoning versus liberating, and hoarding versus sharing. The library spaces of the past are paradigmatically places of dust and disorder; borrowing the moral valences that inflect the medieval/Renaissance divide, they are dark spaces awaiting illumination.

Such metaphors have framed the digital library from its earliest imaginings. In 1993 the premier issue of *Wired* magazine ran an article by John Browning entitled "Libraries without Walls for Books without Pages," which pronounces the obsolescence of the traditional library and offers these prognostications: "Books once hoarded in subterranean stacks will be scanned into computers and made available to anyone, anywhere, almost instantly." "Instead of fortresses of knowledge, there will be an ocean of information"; and "realizing this vision will transform libraries from guardians of tradition to catalysts of a vast change."[3] Despite the acuity of the article's comments about the library's digital future, it elicits a particularly medievalized vision of the library's past. Readers who have made it through *Memory's Library* may recognize echoes of the polemic that drove Reformation era library history. For example, the predicted opening of the "subterranean stacks" recalls John Bale's description of John Leland's Reformation era effort "to searche all the lybraryes of Monasteryes and Colleges" and to "redeme" their books "from dust and byrdfylynges, or pryuate use to no profyte, and so brynge them fourth to a commo[n] wealth of godly knowledge and lernynge."[4] In proclaiming the end of "fortresses of knowledge" the article recalls Wycliffite critiques of monks who hoard books in their cloisters "Þat ben as castellis or paleicis," together with John Foxe's critique of "begging friars" who "heaped up all the books that could be gotten, into their own libraries" and "kept them from such as more fruitfully would have perused them."[5] Its call for "an ocean of information" invokes the Baconian image of the open seas of experimental sciences, just as its description of libraries as "guardians of tradition" awaiting transformation into "catalysts of a vast change" further recalls Bacon's association of libraries with received wisdom "preserued in Bookes [and] Traditions," as opposed to the "discovering" that will drive his *Advancement of Learning*.[6] If this rhetoric casts *Wired*'s Browning as a latter-day Bale, Foxe, or Bacon, however, it also implicates him in their misrepresentation of library history and, by extension, of the phenomenon of, and implications of, historical change.

Turning explicitly to the medieval library, Browning cites the example of chained books as an antitype to the digital library: "The monks guarded their work jealously. In England's Hereford Cathedral, books were chained to the shelves." His source for this point is Daniel J. Boorstin's influential 1983 book *The Discoverers*, which asserts that "the symbol of the old library was the chained book. Hundreds of such captive volumes, called *catenati*, can still be seen neatly arrayed on the shelves of the library of Hereford Cathedral."[7] By identifying the chained book with captivity, this argument again echoes John Bale's attacks on monks and friars, whose books are "tyed up in cheanes, and hydden undre dust in the monkes and fryres libraryes."[8] But this argument misrepresents the history of chaining—first by overlooking its historical rationale, which was to make books available to readers rather than to "hoard" them (the modern analogue is the telephone book, which is "chained" to its booth precisely because it is shared property). Thus, Bishop William Rede of Chichester (d. 1385) bequeathed a hundred books to several Oxford colleges, with the stipulation that they be "securely chained" in communal collections.[9] Sir Thomas Bodley personally oversaw the installation of "barres, lockes, hasps, grates, cheines, and other gimmoes or iron, belonging to the fastning, and riveting of the bookes" when he opened his "public" library, Oxford's Bodleian, in 1605.[10] This point counters another assumption implicit in Bale's critique no less than in Browning's and Boorstin's: chaining books did not end with the Middle Ages but continued well through the early modern period and, in some cases, up to the nineteenth century. Indeed, the chained library at Hereford Cathedral—which Browning, following Boorstin, considers emblematic of monastic practice— was not installed until the seventeenth century, following the example of the Bodleian.[11] Chaining books persisted, in other words, well beyond the onset of print and Protestantism, a point illustrated by that monument of post-Reformation print culture, Foxe's *Acts and Monuments*, which, as John N. King observes, "was frequently chained alongside the Bible for reading by ordinary people at many public places including cathedrals, churches, schools, libraries, guildhalls, and at least one inn."[12]

By associating chained books like those of Hereford Cathedral with "monks" as "the symbol of the old library," Browning and Boorstin do more than confuse arcana relating to historical dating or the institutional differences between monasteries and secular cathedrals—which would make their correction a matter of mere pedantry. Instead, they rewrite the history of the medieval library in the service of a larger historical argument, which draws an implicit parallel between the onset of the digital library of today and the dissolution of the monasteries in the English Reformation. It is a comparison made explicit by Harold Billings, who likewise compares the library of the future with the monastic libraries of the past when he observes: "In . . . the English Reformation, there was a great plunder and dissolution of the cloisters, and the monastery libraries that had guarded what little there was of the written heart of learning for a thousand dark years were almost completely scattered," concluding that the digital library "represents as significant an opportunity for a new orderliness in libraries as when knowledge was cast out of the monasteries to begin a journey toward different types of storage."[13] Asserting that the dissolution resulted in "a new orderliness in libraries" and "different types of storage," Billings makes a point that is repeated in the *Wired* article with which I began, which asserts that, along with their propensity for "hoarding," "monks lacked a system for organizing books that could be found later." The implication is that cataloguing and organization, like the dissolution itself, liberated books from their earlier bondage of monastic disorder; but as we have learned, monastic libraries in fact pioneered sophisticated forms of organizing libraries as well as indexing and compiling texts. As Mary A. Rouse and Richard H. Rouse have found, the thirteenth-century development of such bibliographical tools as biblical concordances, alphabetical indexes, arabic numbering, and chapter divisions "represent efforts to search written authority afresh, to get at, to locate, to retrieve information," which they ascribe to "the attitude of the age toward its written heritage—practical, utilitarian, active rather than passive."[14] If works like Higden's *Polychronicon* and Lydgate's *Fall of Princes* attest to monks' abilities to manage large numbers of written sources, they also reveal the medieval library to have been a place designed and arranged for use. In works like the *Polychronicon*, moreover, monks produced models of compilation and bibliographical organization that continued to exert an influence well beyond the Reformation, as I have shown of Cotton's use of Higden in the Cotton Library.

By setting up the dark and disorderly monastic past of the library as a foil for a more open and enlightened future, these discussions ultimately owe the Baconian strain of their rhetoric—as did Bacon himself—to the iconoclastic Reformation era polemics of John Bale and John Foxe. By extension, their attempt to break from the monastic past does not depart from, but rather repeats—and thereby reveals their, and our, continued conceptual indebtedness to—a particularly English history of libraries. Even in the act of rejecting the past, we depend on it to establish the foundation and basic outline for the stories we still tell ourselves about who we are. And furthermore, Browning and Boorstin show that we continue to follow Bale, Foxe, Parker, and their later successors—who must include us—in rewriting the present, and the possibilities that are symbolized by our libraries, by rewriting the medieval library of the past.

Replacing these misrepresentations of medieval and Reformation era libraries with more nuanced models of the past, however, opens the possibility of considering our present moment as an outgrowth of history that is both more complex and more multilayered than its own self-authorizing stories would allow. Recent thinking on libraries in our own age has reassessed earlier pronouncements of their certain obsolescence and has sought rather to understand the distinctiveness of "the library as place," the title of a recent collection of essays that repeats a common catchphrase.[15] This work, much of it conducted by library architects and librarians, finds that the library as material place is not just a warehouse but a "dynamic learning environment," a setting for the production of knowledge rather than the simple storage of information.[16] While even the most insightful explorations of "library as place" persist in the habit of misrepresenting monastic libraries as foils for the present situation, their revisionary analyses of libraries' spaces and functions approach a better understanding premodern ideas about libraries as a place of active making.[17]

There is a striking convergence between these current reassessments of libraries as dynamic spaces and recent advances in the study of memory. In the twentieth century, models of computer memory were developed in a dialectic with the emergent field of cognitive science, making human memory a touchstone, if not a model, for digital information storage.[18] But such comparisons often imputed a static quality to each: "Just like a library, a computer directory, or any other knowledge store, our memory requires an internal organization that allows for economic storage and efficient memory search and retrieval."[19] More recent descriptions of a digital "memory library" move beyond search and retrieval to emphasize more dynamic, experimental, and transactional processes; in so doing, they allow for broadened understandings of both terms, "memory" and "library," which they bind together in their central metaphor.[20]

As I argued in my introduction, such conceptual models of digital memory share insights with recent advances in neuroscience, which show memory to be, not a warehouse, but a dynamic and active system, a process rather than a receptacle. Thus, Antonio Damasio observes, "The hippocampus does not store memories. It has been likened to an intelligent collating machine, which filters new associations, decides what is important and what to ignore or compress, sorts the results, and then sends various packets of information to other parts of the brain."[21] This insight draws nearer to the picture I have attempted to draw of premodern libraries, which were theorized and experienced by their contemporaries not as mere repositories but as dynamic and creative spaces dedicated to the production of knowledge. Damasio's description of the hippocampus recalls us to the sixteenth-century polymath Stephen Batman, who describes Archbishop Matthew Parker's Reformation era book collecting as a highly selective process: presented with "six thousand seauen hundred Bookes," Batman observes, Parker exercises a "choyse" of only two.[22] Turning from libraries to the brain, Batman employs strikingly similar terms to describe the faculty of memory: "For what the vertue imaginatiue shapeth & imagineth, she sendeth it to the iudgement of reason. And what that reason taketh of the imagination, as a Judge, iudgeth & defineth it sending to the memory."[23] In both cases, memory and the library work through selection and filtering, the active production of knowledge rather than the passive storage of information.

I have suggested that nuancing prevailing accounts of premodern libraries will enable us to recognize that our own age is an outgrowth of a rich and complex past. Thus, I find that current understandings about memory and libraries prepare us to appreciate the dynamism of medieval and early modern understandings of both. But understanding that past can further nuance the models of historical change that we attempt to uphold when we invoke the history of libraries as a move from darkness into light. If the dissolution caused books to be "cast out of the monasteries to begin a journey toward different types of storage," it did not necessarily make them more openly available to readers than the monastic libraries had (indeed, in the vast majority of cases, those "different types of storage" were wastebins, as N. R. Ker reminds us).[24] Our kinship with the agents of the dissolution may consist less in our common identity as liberators of knowledge than in our common tendency to rewrite the medieval past.

The message of this book is not that the past repeats itself but that ideas about libraries always bear an especially rich and complex relationship with the past, which consists—today no less than in the Reformation—of one part preservation, one part invention, and one part disavowal. Literary scholars, for this reason, have a particularly strong stake in libraries and their history: as I have argued throughout this book, not only are libraries repositories of written narratives, but they are also narrative-producing institutions. Furthermore, as places of reading and writing, libraries symbolize the complex "place" of reading and writing in relation to a culture's other institutions. To return to a point I made in my introduction, libraries are central to who we are because they are central to who we were, organizing the individual and collective memories that make up the stories of our lives as individuals, peoples, and nations. If figures from Duke Humfrey to Robert Cotton show that those who make libraries make history—a task that took on special urgency in the years preceding and following the English Reformation—they equally show that our libraries make us. Memory is a library.

NOTES

INTRODUCTION

1. M. Aurelius Cassiodorus, *Institutiones*, ed. R.A.B. Mynors (Oxford: Oxford University Press, 1937), I.5.2. Jerome, *Epistolae*, 60.10; cited by Mary Carruthers, *The Book of Memory: A Study of Memory in Medieval Culture* (Cambridge: Cambridge University Press, 1990), 33. The analogy remains resonant today; see, e.g., Francis X. Blouin Jr. and William G. Rosenberg, eds., *Archives, Documentation, and Institutions of Social Memory: Essays from the Sawyer Seminar* (Ann Arbor: University of Michigan Press, 2006), whose titles indicate ways in which the analogy between archives and memory continues to be employed: for example, Patrick Geary, "Medieval Archivists as Authors: Social Memory and Archival Memory"; Joan van Albada, "Archives: Particles of Memory or More?"; Rebecca J. Scott, "The Provincial Archive as a Place of Memory: Confronting Oral and Written Sources on the Role of Former Slaves in the Cuban War of Independence (1895–98)."

2. For Spenser, see chap. 3 below. Elizabeth Heale, *The Faerie Queene: A Reader's Guide* (Cambridge: Cambridge University Press, 1999), describes Spenser's representation of "Memory's Library," from which this book derives its title, on p. 64. See also Thomas Adams, *Five Sermons Preached Upon Sundry Especial Occasions* (London, 1626), 75.

3. See Carruthers, *Book of Memory*, 120–21; John Evelyn, "Method for a Library According to the Intellectual Powers," British Library, MS Add. 7863.

4. See, for example, Peter Grun, Nikil D. Dutt, and Alexandru Nicolau, *Memory Architecture Exploration for Programmable Embedded Systems* (New York: Springer, 2002), 79. Googling the term will also yield the recent site www.memorylibrary.com (accessed 13 May 2007), an online yearbook from Livermore High School, 1973–77, which opens with the following quotation from the television series *The Wonder Years:* "Memory is a way of holding onto the things you love, the things you are, the things you never want to lose."

5. For a consideration of "the situation of medieval manuscripts in the modern archive," see Siân Echard, "House Arrest: Modern Archives, Medieval Manuscripts," *Journal of Medieval and Early Modern Studies* 30 (2000): 185–210, quotation on 185; Stephanie H. Jed, *Chaste Thinking: The Rape of Lucretia and the Birth of Humanism* (Bloomington: University of Indiana Press, 1989), esp. 121–31.

6. C. J. Wright, "Editor's Foreword," in *Sir Robert Cotton as Collector: Essays on an Early Stuart Courtier and His Legacy* (London: British Library, 1997), n.p.

7. On this point, see Sears Jayne, *Library Catalogues of the English Renaissance* (Berkeley and Los Angeles: University of California Press, 1956), 39. For an invaluable resource on the history of libraries during this period, see the essays collected in *The Cambridge History of Libraries in Britain and Ireland*, vol. 1, *To 1640*, ed. Elisabeth Leedham-Green and Teresa Webber (Cambridge: Cambridge University Press, 2006). Of further relevance to this topic are the notes that follow.

8. On early modern annotating practices—which are much in evidence in the libraries I examine here—see William Sherman, *Used Books: Marking Readers in Renaissance England* (Philadelphia: University of Pennsylvania Press, 2007).

9. Felicity Heal, *Reformation in Britain and Ireland* (Oxford: Oxford University Press, 2003), offers a magisterial overview of the events of the English Reformation. Tom Betteridge, *Literature and Politics in the English Reformation* (Manchester: Manchester University Press, 2004); Cathy Shrank, *Writing the Nation in Reformation England, 1530–1580* (Oxford: Oxford University Press, 2004); and Brian Cummings, *The Literary Culture of the Reformation: Grammar and Grace* (Oxford: Oxford University Press, 2002), examine the cultural ramifications of those events. See as well references in chaps. 2 and 3 below.

10. John Speed, *History of Great Britaine* (London, 1611), 17–18.

11. Thus, the historian Daniel Woolf observes, "their use of techniques of conservation and cataloguing, wherein manuscripts were frequently rearranged or interfered with to produce what to their minds were neater and more useful volumes, offers us less an Olympian summit of antiquarianism than a chamber of codicological horrors." See his *The Social Circulation of the Past: English Historical Culture, 1500–1730* (Oxford: Oxford University Press, 2003), 170. See also my references in chap. 3 about the Parker Library and those in chap. 4 about the Cotton Library.

12. See James P. Carley, "The Dispersal of the Monastic Libraries and the Salvaging of the Spoils," in *Cambridge History of Libraries in Britain and Ireland*, ed. Leedham-Green and Webber, 1.270–74, 291.

13. See N. R. Ker, *Medieval Libraries of Great Britain: A List of Surviving Books* (London: Royal Historical Society, 1964), x–xv; Nigel Ramsay, "'The Manuscripts Flew about Like Butterflies': The Break-up of English Libraries in the Sixteenth Century," in *Lost Libraries: The Destruction of Great Book Collections since Antiquity*, ed. James Raven (New York: Palgrave Macmillan, 2004), 125–44.

14. Brian Stock, "The Middle Ages as Subject and Object," *New Literary History* 5 (1974): 527–47, quotation on 543. James Simpson cites and discusses Stock's observation in a work that traces its implications for English literary history: see *Reform and Cultural Reformation: The Oxford English Literary History*, vol. 2, *1350–1547* (Oxford: Oxford University Press, 2002), 7.

15. On such "standards of coherence," see Paul Van den Brock, Robert F. Lorch Jr., Tracy Linderholm, and Mary Gustafson, "The Effects of Readers' Goals on Inference Generation and Memory for Texts," *Memory and Cognition* 29 (2001): 1081–87.

16. Carruthers, *Book of Memory*; Mary Carruthers, *The Craft of Thought: Meditation, Rhetoric, and the Making of Images, 400–1200* (Cambridge: Cambridge University Press, 1998). See also Patrick J. Geary, *Phantoms of Remembrance: Memory and Oblivion at*

the End of the First Millennium (Princeton, NJ: Princeton University Press, 1994); Janet Coleman, *Ancient and Medieval Memories: Studies in the Reconstruction of the Past* (Cambridge: Cambridge University Press, 1992).

17. Alcuin, *De animae ratione*, in *Patrologia Latina*, ed. J. P. Migne, vol. 101 (Paris, 1855), 639–47, quotation on 642; translated in Mary Carruthers, "Imaginatif, Memoria, and 'The Need for Critical Theory' in *Piers Plowman* Studies," *Yearbook of Langland Studies* 9 (1995): 103–14, quotation from Alcuin on 105.

18. John Doddridge, *The English Lawyer* (London, 1631), 12. As Garrett A. Sullivan Jr. establishes, memory in the English Renaissance was an active force; building on early modern psychology, which made memory the ground of rational and prudent action, Shakespeare and his contemporaries saw memory as the means by which individual subjects established their place within the social collectivity. See Sullivan, *Memory and Forgetting in English Renaissance Drama: Shakespeare, Marlowe, Webster* (Cambridge: Cambridge University Press, 2005), 2–12. See also Lina Bolzoni, *The Gallery of Memory: Literary and Iconographical Models in the Age of the Printing Press*, trans. Jeremy Parzen (Toronto: University of Toronto Press, 2001); Paulo Rossi, *Logic and the Art of Memory: The Quest for a Universal Language*, trans. Stephen Clucas (Chicago: University of Chicago Press, 2000). Frances Yates, *The Art of Memory* (Chicago: University of Chicago Press, 1966), remains the classic exploration of memory and its Renaissance meanings.

19. Gerald M. Edelman and Giulio Tononi, *A Universe of Consciousness: How Matter Becomes Imagination* (New York: Basic Books, 2000), 93. See also Eric R. Kandel, *In Search of Memory: The Emergence of a New Science of Mind* (New York: Norton, 2006). Kandel finds that memory is not stored in cells but is created in the dynamic exchanges between them. Oliver Sacks, *An Anthropologist from Mars: Seven Paradoxical Tales* (New York: Knopf, 1996), substantiates similar insights with case studies involving memory and memory loss.

20. This point deserves to be cited within the broader context of its discussion, which includes a use of the term "memory-library" that bears striking relevance to my discussion of early modern ideas of "memory's library": "A revisionist historian of sorts, in the brain's memory-library receiving station, notices that the unvarnished history of [an] incident doesn't make enough sense, so he 'interprets' the brute events . . . by making up a narrative," and thus, "the record you rely on, sorted in the library of memory, is already contaminated." See Daniel C. Dennett and Marcel Kinsbourne, "Time and the Observer: The Where and When of Consciousness and the Brain," *Behavioral and Brain Sciences* 15 (1992): 183–247, reprinted in *The Nature of Consciousness: Philosophical Debates*, ed. Ned Joel Block, Owen J. Flanagan, and Güven Güzeldae (Cambridge, MA: MIT Press, 1997), quotation on 156.

21. Tobias Wolff, "War and Memory," *New York Times*, op-ed, 28 April 2001.

22. See Roger Chartier, "Libraries without Walls," in *The Order of Books: Readers, Authors, and Libraries in Europe between the Fourteenth and Eighteenth Centuries*, trans. Lydia G. Cochrane (Stanford, CA: Stanford University Press, 1994), 61–88.

23. The passage in which Foucault advances this argument is worth repeating in its entirety: "the idea of accumulating everything, of establishing a sort of general archive, the will to enclose in one place all times, all epochs, all forms, all tastes, the idea of constituting a place of all times that is itself outside of time and inaccessible to its ravages, the

project of organizing in this way a sort of perpetual and indefinite accumulation of time in an immobile place, this whole idea belongs to our modernity"; Foucault, "Of Other Spaces," trans. Jay Miskowiec, *Diacritics* 16 (1986): 22–27, quotation on 26.

24. The classic and still-invaluable statement of this project is D. F. McKenzie's *Bibliography and the Sociology of Texts* (1984; repr., Cambridge: Cambridge University Press, 1999).

25. Roger Chartier, "Laborers and Voyagers: From the Text to the Reader," *Diacritics* 22 (1992): 49–61, quotation on 50 and 54.

26. As well as *Cambridge History of Libraries in Britain and Ireland*, ed. Leedham-Green and Webber, see, for example, the microfilm collection *Renaissance Man: The Reconstructed Libraries of European Scholars, 1450–1608* (Marlborough, Wiltshire: Adam Matthew Publications, 1993); R. Sharpe, general ed., Corpus of British Medieval Library Catalogues, 13 vols. to date (London: British Library, 1990–); R. J. Fehrenbach and E. S. Leedham-Green, eds., *Private Libraries in Renaissance England: A Collection and Catalogue of Tudor and Early Stuart Book-Lists*, 6 vols. to date (Binghamton, NY: Medieval and Renaissance Texts and Studies, 1992–); as well as exemplary individual studies such as William H. Sherman, *John Dee: The Politics of Reading and Writing in the English Renaissance* (Amherst: University of Massachusetts Press, 1995); Colin G. C. Tite, *The Manuscript Library of Sir Robert Cotton*, Panizzi Lectures, 1993 (London: British Library, 1994); Andrew Watson, *Medieval Manuscripts in Post-medieval England* (Aldershot, Hants.: Ashgate, 2004).

27. My project reflects assertions by bibliographers in the last century—for example, Fredson Bowers's contention that "true bibliography is the bridge to textual, which is to say literary, criticism"; see his *Principles of Bibliographical Description* (Princeton, NJ: Princeton University Press, 1949), 9. Similarly W. W. Greg explores the assertion that bibliography is "the grammar of literary investigation," in "Bibliography—an Apologia," *The Library*, 4th ser., 13 (1932): 113–38, quotation on 113–14. While Greg's ensuing discussion insists "that bibliography has nothing to do with the subject-matter of books" (114)—a problematic point that the history of the book continues to struggle both with and against—I still take as salutary this foundational effort to consider bibliography and literary criticism as allied projects.

28. For a reflection on the early modern origins of disciplinarity that is relevant to the history of libraries in this period, see the essays collected in Donald R. Kelley, ed., *History and the Disciplines: The Reclassification of Knowledge in Early Modern Europe* (Rochester, NY: University of Rochester Press, 1997).

29. Diana Fuss, *The Sense of an Interior: Four Writers and the Rooms That Shaped Them* (New York: Routledge, 2004), 1. This point follows on Roger Chartier's observation that "reading is not only an abstract operation of the intellect: it puts the body into play and is inscribed within a particular space, in relation to the self and others"; Chartier, "Laborers and Voyagers," *Diacritics* 22 (1992): 53.

30. I discuss the adaptation of these terms in the following chapters: *allegoresis*, in chaps. 1 and 3; *lectio divina*, in chaps. 2 and 3; and *compilatio*, in chap. 4. For a discussion of medieval reading practices, see the essays collected in Sarah Rees Jones, ed., *Learning and Literacy in Medieval England and Abroad* (Turnhout, Belgium: Brepols Publishers, 2003).

31. The term "hermeneutics of suspicion" comes from Paul Ricoeur, *Freud and Philosophy: An Essay on Interpretation*, trans. Denis Savage (New Haven, CT: Yale University Press, 1970), 32–33, quotation on 27. It is worth considering the project of the post-Reformation library makers in light of Ricoeur's comments on modern hermeneutics, which aims to "clear the horizon for a more authentic word, for a new reign of Truth, not only by means of a 'destructive' critique, but by the invention of an art of *interpreting*" (33), and which counters "illusion and the fable-making function" (35), terms that could be taken from several of the writers I consider in chap. 3.

32. Thus, the libraries and reading practices I examine were conceived in their own age in terms that differ fundamentally from those discussed by Helen Freshwater, who identifies the rise of "archival research" with "forms of positivistic authentication and pseudo-scientific legitimization." See her "The Allure of the Archive," *Poetics Today* 24 (2003): 729–58, quotation on 730. The long-held assumption that modern protocols of objectivity were ushered in in the seventeenth century has come under critique in ways that are consistent with my readings here: see Patrick Collinson, "One of Us? William Camden and the Making of History," *Transactions of the Royal Historical Society*, 6th ser., 8 (1998): 139–64.

33. See M. B. Pranger, *The Artificiality of Christianity: Essays on the Poetics of Monasticism* (Stanford, CA: Stanford University Press, 2003). The term "textual communities" belongs to Brian Stock, *The Implications of Literacy: Written Language and Models of Interpretation in the Eleventh and Twelfth Centuries* (Princeton, NJ: Princeton University Press, 1983).

34. Catherine Gallagher and Stephen Greenblatt, *Practicing New Historicism* (Chicago: University of Chicago Press, 2000), 9. Compare their point to Paul Hamilton's assertion about the "double focus" of historicism: "Firstly, it is concerned to situate any statement—philosophical, historical, aesthetic or whatever—in its historical context. Secondly, it typically doubles back on itself to explore the extent to which any historical enterprise inevitably reflects the interests and bias of the period in which it was written"— a description that fits Gallagher and Greenblatt's view as well as the methodology of the early modern users of the Cotton Library. See Hamilton, *Historicism* (London: Routledge, 1996), 3. David Aers develops a critique of Gallagher and Greenblatt's uses of medieval religious iconography and doctrine in "New Historicism and the Eucharist," *Journal of Medieval and Early Modern Studies* 33 (2003): 241–59. For a critique of historicism in medieval literary studies, see the essays collected in Elizabeth Scala, ed., "The Ends of Historicism: Medieval English Literary Study in the New Century," special issue, *Texas Studies in Literature and Language* 44 (2002).

35. Michael Warner, "Uncritical Reading," in *Polemic: Critical and Uncritical*, ed. Jane Gallop (New York: Routledge, 2004), 13–38, quotations on 14 and 17.

36. Gallagher and Greenblatt, *Practicing New Historicism*, 12–13, 14.

37. "The touch of the real" is from a memorable chapter title in ibid., 20–48, which represents "access to the everyday, the place where things are actually done, the sphere of practice that even in its most awkward and inept articulations makes a claim on the truth that is denied to the most eloquent of literary texts" (48). For a critique of such uses of the archive, see Karen Newman, "Sundry Letters, Worldly Goods: The Lisle Letters and Renaissance Studies," *Journal of Medieval and Early Modern Studies* 26 (1996): 139–52.

Frank Grady critiques "the whiff of the archive" as a "credentializing device" in "Gower's Boat, Richard's Barge, and the True Story of the Confessio Amantis, Text and Gloss," in "The Ends of Historicism," ed. Scala, special issue, *Texas Studies in Literature and Language* 44 (2002): 1–15, quotation on 2.

38. Libraries can thus be seen to manifest a "spatializing urge" that underlies our desires to make the past visible as literary history; for a relevant discussion (and critique), see Marshall Brown, "Rethinking the Scale of Literary History," in *Rethinking Literary History: A Dialogue on Theory*, ed. Linda Hutcheon and Mario J. Valdés (Oxford: Oxford University Press, 2002), 116–54, quotation on 121.

39. Andrew G. Watson, *Medieval Manuscripts in Post-medieval England* (Aldershot, Hants.: Ashgate, 2004), xvi. See also Philip Schwyzer, *Literature, Nationalism and Memory in Early Modern England and Wales* (Cambridge: Cambridge University Press, 2004), 66, on Reformation periodization.

40. A. G. Dickens, ed., *Tudor Treatises*, Yorkshire Archaeological Society, Records Series 125 (Wakefield: printed for the Society, 1959), 38.

41. Margaret Aston, "English Ruins and English History: The Dissolution and the Sense of the Past," *Journal of the Warburg and Courtauld Institutes* 36 (1973): 231–55.

42. See the special issue, *Journal of Medieval and Early Modern Studies* 37 (2007): "Medieval/Renaissance: After Periodization," ed. Jennifer Summit and David Wallace; and in David Matthews and Gordon McMullan, eds., *Reading the Medieval in Early Modern England* (Cambridge: Cambridge University Press, 2007), Kathleen Davis, *Periodization and Sovereignty* (Philadelphia: University of Pennsylvania Press, 2008).

43. Stephanie Trigg, "The New Medievalization of Chaucer," *Studies in the Age of Chaucer* 24 (2002): 347–54, quotation on 352.

44. See J. N. L. Myers, "Thomas James and the Painted Frieze," *Bodleian Library Record* 4 (1952–53): 30–51.

45. For records of these and other users of the Cotton Library, see Colin G. C. Tite's invaluable *Early Records of Sir Robert Cotton's Library: Formation, Cataloguing, Use* (London: British Library, 2003).

46. On the Reformation's production of new cultural forms within a paradigm of conversion, see Andrew Pettegree, *Reformation and the Culture of Persuasion* (New York: Cambridge University Press, 2005).

47. Helen Cooper, *The English Romance in Time: Transforming Motifs from Geoffrey of Monmouth to the Death of Shakespeare* (Oxford: Oxford University Press, 2004); Andrew King, *"The Faerie Queene" and Middle English Romance: The Matter of Just Memory* (Oxford: Clarendon Press, 2000).

48. Robert S. Gottfried, *Bury St. Edmunds and the Urban Crisis: 1290–1539* (Princeton, NJ: Princeton University Press, 1982), 222–34. On fourteenth-century attacks against monastic literacy, see Susan Crane, "The Writing Lesson of 1381," in *Chaucer's England: Literature in Historical Context*, ed. Barbara Hanawalt (Minneapolis: University of Minnesota Press, 1992), 201–21; Steven Justice, *Writing and Rebellion: England in 1381* (Berkeley and Los Angeles: University of California Press, 1994).

49. Richard de Bury, *The Love of Books*, trans. E. C. Thomas (London: De La More Press, 1902), 57.

50. See my discussion of this event in chap. 1.

51. "There is no political power without control of the archive," asserts Jacques Derrida in *Archive Fever: A Freudian Impression* (Chicago: University of Chicago Press, 1996), 7.

52. See Barton Lodge, ed., *Palladius on Husbondrie*, Early English Text Society 52 and 72 (London: N. Trübner, 1873, 1879).

53. William Shakespeare, *The Tempest*, ed. Stephen Orgel (Oxford: Oxford University Press, 1987), 1.2.109–10.

54. On official "appropriation" in the fifteenth century "of the heretics' literary tools," see Anne Hudson, *"Laicus Litteratus:* The Paradox of Lollardy," in *Heresy and Literacy, 1000–1530*, ed. Peter Biller and Anne Hudson (New York: Cambridge University Press, 1994), 234.

55. "The fifteenth century was an age of libraries," writes C. L. Kingsford in *Prejudice and Promise in Fifteenth Century England* (Oxford: Clarendon Press, 1925), 42.

56. On Cotton's collecting practices, see Tite, *Manuscript Library of Sir Robert Cotton*, as well as the references in chap. 4.

57. Cotton upholds the authority of the "originall" record in the frontispiece that he attaches to his compilation of sources in British Library, Cotton MS Cleopatra E. i.

58. Francis Bacon, *The Advancement of Learning*, ed. Michael Kiernan, vol. 4 of *The Oxford Francis Bacon* (Oxford: Clarendon Press, 2000), 56.

59. One of the anonymous readers of this book for the University of Chicago Press evocatively called James's project "the philological equivalent of the evangelical stripping of the altars."

60. Thomas James, *An explanation or enlarging of the ten articles in the supplication of doctor James, lately exhibited to the clergy of England* (Oxford, 1626), 24.

61. As Lorraine Daston observes, "We often habitually oppose the humanities to the sciences along the axis of tradition versus progress: the humanities are portrayed as conservers of texts in editions or objects in museums, guardians of living cultural memory; the sciences as endlessly overthrowing old theories by new, deliberate amnesiacs about any disciplinary past older than yesterday's issue of *Science* or *Nature*"; see her "Type Specimens and Scientific Memory," in "The Arts of Transmission," special issue, *Critical Inquiry* 31 (2004): 153–82, quotation on 155.

62. For an overview of this line of argument, see Thomas Mann, *Library Research Models: A Guide to Classification, Cataloging, and Computers* (Oxford: Oxford University Press, 1993), 103–7.

63. The very concept of the "working memory" supports this; for the classic formulation of this term, see A. D. Baddeley and G. J. Hitch, "Working Memory," in *The Psychology of Learning and Motivation*, ed. G. A. Bower (New York: Academic Press, 1974), 47–89.

CHAPTER ONE

1. C. L. Kingsford, *Prejudice and Promise in Fifteenth Century England: The Ford Lectures, 1923–4* (Oxford: Clarendon Press, 1925), 42.

2. Richard Gameson, "The Medieval Library (to c. 1450)," in *The Cambridge History of Libraries in Britain and Ireland*, vol. 1, *To 1640*, ed. Elisabeth Leedham-Green

and Teresa Webber (Cambridge: Cambridge University Press, 2006), 13–50, esp. 13–14.
On the pre-fifteenth-century forms and definitions of libraries, see Michael Lapidge,
The Anglo-Saxon Library (Oxford: Oxford University Press, 2006). Lapidge asserts, "A
library is simply a collection of books. In the sense in which I shall use the word, however, a library is a collection of books acquired and arranged for the purposes of study and
the pursuit of knowledge" (1). On the other hand, J. C. T. Oates argues, "A library may
be defined as a room or building in which books are assembled (and such an assemblage
of books will itself, by extension, be called a library) and arranged in some way that will
enable them to be the more conveniently studied." See Oates, *Cambridge University
Library: A History* (Cambridge: Cambridge University Press, 1986), 1.1. David N. Bell asserts, "A medieval library was not a place so much as a process," a definition that allows
him to examine the institution's responsiveness to cultural, religious, and educational
change. See Bell, "The Libraries of Religious Houses in the Late Middle Ages," in *Cambridge History of Libraries in Britain and Ireland*, ed. Leedham-Green and Webber, 1.126.
See also David N. Bell, "Monastic Libraries: 1400–1557," in *Cambridge History of the
Book in Britain*, vol. 3, *1400–1557*, ed. Lotte Hellinga and J. B. Trapp (Cambridge: Cambridge University Press, 1999), 229–54. On Anglo-Saxon monastic book collections, see,
in addition to Lapidge, David Ganz, "Anglo-Saxon England," in *Cambridge History of Libraries in Britain and Ireland*, ed. Leedham-Green and Webber, 1.91–108; Karl Christ, *The
Handbook of Medieval Library History*, trans. Theophil M. Otto (Metuchen, NJ: Scarecrow Press, 1984); Helmut Gneuss, *Books and Libraries in Early England* (Brookfield, VT:
Variorum, 1996); Teresa Webber, "Monastic and Cathedral Book Collections in the Late
Eleventh and Twelfth Centuries," in *Cambridge History of Libraries in Britain and Ireland*, ed. Leedham-Green and Webber, 1.109–25.

3. In addition to these three main places, Francis Wormald finds evidence of books
stored in monastic infirmaries; see his "The Monastic Library," in *The English Library
before 1700*, ed. Francis Wormald and C. E. Wright (London: Athlone Press, 1958), 16–
17. On the Benedictine provision for books and its implications for monastic collections
and their storage, see Jean Leclerq, *The Love of Learning and the Desire for God: A Study
of Monastic Culture*, trans. Catharine Misrahi (New York: Fordham University Press,
1960), 17; Alan Coates, *English Medieval Books: The Reading Abbey Collections from
Foundation to Dispersal* (Oxford: Clarendon Press, 1999), 118. Despite its age, one of the
best treatments of medieval library furniture and settings is John Willis Clark, *The Care
of Books* (Cambridge: Cambridge University Press, 1909); on the development of library
rooms, see 97–103.

4. The mid-fifteenth-century upsurge of the term "library" is reflected in the date
chart in the *Oxford English Dictionary* (hereafter *OED*), s.v. "library"; see also *Middle
English Dictionary* (hereafter *MED*), s.v. "librari(e)," whose entries likewise cluster around
the mid–fifteenth century. See Bell, "Libraries of Religious Houses in the Late Middle
Ages," in *Cambridge History of Libraries in Britain and Ireland*, ed. Leedham-Green and
Webber, 1.147; E. A. Savage, *Old English Libraries* (Chicago: University of Chicago Press,
1912), 156.

5. Wormald, "Monastic Library," in *English Library before 1700*, ed. Wormald and
Wright, 20. The centralization of libraries into distinct locations can be illustrated by
the records of Durham. See *Catalogi veteres librorum Ecclesiae cathedralis dunelm;*

Catalogues of the Library of Durham Cathedral, at Various Periods, from the Conquest to the Dissolution, Surtees Society, vol. 7 (London: J. B. Nichols and Son, 1838). See also A. J. Piper, "The Libraries of the Monks of Durham," in *Medieval Scribes, Manuscripts, and Libraries: Essays Presented to N. R. Ker* (London: Scolar, 1978), 213–49. Stacey Gee traces a parallel development in parish churches; see Gee, "Parochial Libraries in Pre-Reformation England," in *Learning and Literacy in Medieval England and Abroad,* ed. Sarah Rees Jones (Turnhout, Belgium: Brepols Publishers, 2003), 199–222, esp. 202–3.

6. Gameson, "Medieval Library," in *Cambridge History of Libraries in Britain and Ireland,* ed. Leedham-Green and Webber, 1.29–32; Roger Lovatt, "College and University Book Collections and Libraries," in *Cambridge History of Libraries in Britain and Ireland,* ed. Leedham-Green and Webber, 1.152–77, esp. 164–66; Robert Willis and John Willis Clark, *The Architectural History of the University of Cambridge* (Cambridge: Cambridge University Press, 1886), 3.408–11; Oates, *Cambridge University Library,* vol. 1; N. R. Ker, "The Provision of Books," in *History of the University of Oxford,* vol. 3, *The Collegiate Library,* ed. J. McConica (Oxford: Clarendon Press, 1987), 441–77; M. B. Parkes, "The Provision of Books," in *The History of the University of Oxford,* vol. 2, *Late Medieval Oxford,* ed. J. I. Catto and Ralph Evans (Oxford: Clarendon Press, 1992), 459–62.

7. Henry Anstey, ed., *Epistolae academicae Oxon. (registrum F): A Collection of Letters and Other Miscellaneous Documents Illustrative of Academical Life and Studies at Oxford in the Fifteenth Century,* Oxford Historical Society 35–36 (Oxford: printed for the Oxford Historical Society, 1898), 1.244, 246. Oxford's letter to Duke Humfrey is cited and discussed by Stanley Gillam, *The Divinity School and Duke Humfrey's Library at Oxford* (Oxford: Clarendon Press, 1988), 11; Lovatt, "College and University Book Collections," in *Cambridge History of Libraries in Britain and Ireland,* ed. Leedham-Green and Webber, 1.155–56; James Westfall Thompson, *The Medieval Library* (New York: Hafner, 1965), 391–92.

8. Henry Noble MacCracken, ed., "Magnificencia ecclesie," *Publications of the Modern Language Association* 24 (1909): 687–98, quotation on 698.

9. On the expanded field of literacy in fourteenth- and fifteenth-century England, see the essays collected in Sarah Rees Jones, *Learning and Literacy in Medieval England and Abroad,* as well as Jo Ann Hoeppner Moran, *Growth of English Schooling, 1340–1548: Learning, Literacy, and Laicization in a Pre-Reformation York Diocese* (Princeton, NJ: Princeton University Press, 1985); Bell, "Libraries of Religious Houses in the Late Middle Ages," in *Cambridge History of Libraries in Britain and Ireland,* ed. Leedham-Green and Webber, 1.126. The classic study of literacy in this period is M. B. Parkes, "The Literacy of the Laity," in *The Medieval World,* ed. D. Daiches and Al Thorlby (London: Aldus Books, 1973), 555–77; see also H. S. Bennett, *English Books and Readers, 1475–1557* (Cambridge: Cambridge University Press, 1952), chap. 2.

10. Kingsford, *Prejudice and Promise,* 43.

11. K. W. Humphreys, *The Book Provisions of the Mediaeval Friars, 1215–1400* (Amsterdam: Erasmus Booksellers, 1964), 18–19; M. T. Clanchy, *From Memory to Written Record: England, 1066–1307,* 2d ed. (Oxford: Blackwell, 1993), 160.

12. See C. H. Talbot, "The Universities and the Mediaeval Library," in *English Library before 1700,* ed. Wormald and Wright, 74–80; Parkes, "Provision of Books," in *History of*

the University of Oxford, ed. Catto and Evans, 2.437; Humphreys, *Book Provisions of the Mediaeval Friars*.

13. Clanchy, *From Memory to Written Record*, 2d ed., 180–82, quotation on 160.

14. *Jack Upland*, lines 373–76; P. L. Heyworth, ed., *Jack Upland, Friar Daw's Reply, and Upland's Rejoinder* (Oxford: Oxford University Press, 1968), 70. Attacks against friars for hoarding books in their libraries, including this and passages cited below, are discussed by Mary A. Rouse and Richard H. Rouse in their *Authentic Witnesses: Approaches to Medieval Texts and Manuscripts* (Notre Dame, IN: University of Notre Dame Press, 1991), 412–21. For another discussion of these texts, see Margaret Aston, *Lollards and Reformers: Images and Literacy in Late Medieval Religion* (London: Hambledon Press, 1984), 200–201. Fiona Somerset discusses *Jack Upland*, its date and context, at length in *Clerical Discourse and Lay Audience in Late Medieval England* (Cambridge: Cambridge University Press, 1998), 135–78, 216–20.

15. For Corpus Christi College, Cambridge, MS 296, see M. R. James, *A Descriptive Catalogue of the Manuscripts in the Library of Corpus Christi College, Cambridge*, 2 vols. (Cambridge: Cambridge University Press, 1912), 2.74–75. These tracts are collected in F. D. Matthew, ed., *The English Works of Wyclif Hitherto Unprinted*, Early English Text Society, O.S. 74 (London, 1880). Thomas Arnold declares that these tracts are not the work of Wyclif himself, and Arnold dates them between 1390 and 1420; see Arnold, ed., *Select English Works of John Wyclif*, 3 vols. (Oxford: Oxford University Press, 1869–71), 3.vi–vii, xix, xx.

16. Matthew, *English Works of Wyclif*, 49.

17. Ibid., 221.

18. Ibid., 128.

19. Rouse and Rouse, *Authentic Witnesses*, 420.

20. See H. S. Bennett, "The Production and Dissemination of Vernacular Manuscripts in the Fifteenth Century," *The Library*, 5th ser., 1 (1946/47): 167–79; Jo Ann Hoeppner Moran, "A 'Common Profit' Library in the Fifteenth Century and Other Books for Chaplains," *Manuscripta* 28 (1984): 17–25; Wendy Scase, "Reginald Pecock, John Carpenter, and John Colop's 'Common-Profit' Books: Aspects of Book Ownership and Circulation in Fifteenth Century London," *Medium aevum* 61 (1992): 261–74; Gee, "Parochial Libraries in Pre-Reformation England," in *Learning and Literacy in Medieval England and Abroad*, ed. Jones, 203–4. In addition, see Anne Hudson, *The Premature Reformation: Wycliffite Texts and Lollard History* (Oxford: Clarendon Press, 1988); she finds evidence that Lollards owned books communally (206).

21. Rouse and Rouse, *Authentic Witnesses*, 416–17. On Franciscans' restrictions on their libraries and their Lollard critics, see also Peter J. Lucas, "Borrowing and Reference: Access to Libraries in the Late Middle Ages," in *Cambridge History of Libraries in Britain and Ireland*, ed. Leedham-Green and Webber, 1.242–62, esp. 248–53.

22. Willis and Clark, *Architectural History of the University of Cambridge*, 3.397 (my emphasis). Gameson additionally cites "numerous references to locks and keys" in college library records, which "reflect a preoccupation with security" ("Medieval Library," in *Cambridge History of Libraries in Britain and Ireland*, ed. Leedham-Green and Webber, 1.37).

23. British Library, MS Add. 7096, fol. 206v; on this regulation and other library regulations that were instituted by Curteys, see John William Elston, "William Curteys, Abbot of Bury St. Edmunds, 1429–1446" (PhD diss., University of California, Berkeley, 1979), 168.

24. Robert S. Gottfried, *Bury St. Edmunds and the Urban Crisis: 1290–1539* (Princeton, NJ: Princeton University Press, 1982), 212.

25. Willis and Clark, *Architectural History of the University of Cambridge*, 3.397; Roger Lovatt, "College and University Book Collections," in *Cambridge History of Libraries in Britain and Ireland*, ed. Leedham-Green and Webber, 1.171, 167.

26. On this point, see Richard Sharpe, "The Medieval Librarian," in *Cambridge History of Libraries in Britain and Ireland*, ed. Leedham-Green and Webber, 1.237. See also Savage, *Old English Libraries*, 157, on the deaccessioning of "useless" books.

27. Willis and Clark, *Architectural History of the University of Cambridge*, 3.394; *Statutes of Corpus Christi College, Oxford*, in *Documents Relating to the University and Colleges of Cambridge* (London: Longman, Brown, Green, and Longmans, 1852), 2.90. This development expands to the level of the library a practice that had earlier been observed in catalogues and bibliographies, which played a similar role in distinguishing "books that are to be accepted and those that are not" (de libris recipiendis et non recipiendis), to cite a book list compiled in sixth-century southern Gaul; as Mary A. Rouse and Richard H. Rouse observe, "Christian bibliography of this era was concerned not merely with who wrote a book, but with the question of whether or not the work itself was acceptable" (*Authentic Witnesses*, 475–76).

28. On the meanings of *"clericus"* and *"litteratus,"* the classic discussion is by Clanchy, *From Memory to Written Record*, 2d ed., 226–30. See also Anne Hudson, *"Laicus Litteratus:* The Paradox of Lollardy," in *Heresy and Literacy, 1000–1530*, ed. Peter Biller and Anne Hudson (Cambridge: Cambridge University Press, 1994), 222–36; Moran, *Growth of English Schooling*, 49–53.

29. Yet for a productive critique of the opposition between humanism and modernism—along with a discussion of the phenomenon of "ecclesiastical humanism"— see Andrew Cole, "Heresy and Humanism," in *Oxford Twenty-first Century Approaches to Literature: Middle English*, ed. Paul Strohm (Oxford: Oxford University Press, 2007), 421–38.

30. Henry Bergen, ed., *Lydgate's "Fall of Princes,"* 4 vols., Early English Text Society, E.S. 121–24 (Oxford: Oxford University Press, 1924–27), 2:3.3807–8. Subsequent quotations from *The Fall of Princes* will be from this edition, with the book and line numbers (in the case of Lydgate's text) noted parenthetically in the text.

31. On the role of the Bury library, see Rodney M. Thomson, *Archives of the Abbey of Bury St. Edmunds*, Suffolk Records Society, vol. 21 (Woodbridge, Suffolk: Boydell Press, 1980), 38–39; M. R. James, *On the Abbey of St. Edmund at Bury*, vol. 1, *The Library*, Cambridge Antiquarian Society, Octavo Publications, no. 28 (Cambridge, 1895); Elizabeth Parker McLachlan, *The Scriptorium of Bury St. Edmunds in the Twelfth Century* (New York: Garland, 1986), 16–24.

32. R. H. Rouse, "Bostonus Buriensis and the Author of the *Catalogus scriptorum ecclesiae,"* *Speculum* 41 (1966): 489.

33. Thomson, *Archives of the Abbey of Bury St. Edmunds*, 38–39; Elston, "William Curteys, Abbot of Bury St. Edmunds, 1429–1446" (PhD diss., University of California, Berkeley, 1979), 166–69.

34. "Depredatio abbatie Sancti Edmundi," reprinted in *Memorials of St. Edmund's Abbey*, ed. Thomas Arnold, *Rerum Britannicarum Medii Aevi scriptores*, Rolls Series 96 (Nendeln: Kraus Reprint, 1967), 2.330. For an overview of these events, see Mary D. Lobel, "A Detailed Account of the 1327 Rising at Bury St. Edmund's and the Subsequent Trial," *Proceedings of the Suffolk Institute of Archaeology and Natural History* 21 (1933): 215–31.

35. Cambridge University Library, MS Ee.60, fol. 65r, cited by James, *On the Abbey of S. Edmund at Bury*, 1.163. See Henry of Kirkestede, *Catalogus de libris autenticis et apocrifis*, ed. Richard H. Rouse and Mary A. Rouse (London: British Library, 2004), xlii–xliii, for a discussion of these events and their impact on the Bury library.

36. The charter of 1327 is reprinted in Arnold, *Memorials of St. Edmund's Abbey*, 3.302–18; for a discussion of its contents and contexts, see Gottfried, *Bury St. Edmunds and the Urban Crisis*, 222–31, esp. 224.

37. Henry of Kirkestede, *Catalogus*, ed. Rouse and Rouse; Raymond Irwin, *The Heritage of the English Library* (New York: Hafner, 1964), 108; Rouse, "Bostonus Buriensis," *Speculum* 41 (1966): 489–90. See also Richard Sharpe, "The Medieval Librarian," in *Cambridge History of Libraries in Britain and Ireland*, ed. Leedham-Green and Webber, 1.218–41, esp. 229–31.

38. Rouse and Rouse argue that the riots of 1327–31 "provided the necessary impetus to deal with a problem that had been growing for more than a century"—that is, disorganized books; see their introduction to Henry of Kirkestede, *Catalogus*, ed. Rouse and Rouse, xliii.

39. Lakenheath's prologue to his register is reprinted in Thomson, *Archives of the Abbey of Bury St. Edmunds*, 23–24. As Thomson points out, "these words have a pathetic ring when it is recalled that in 1381, when the Peasants' Revolt broke out in Suffolk, the rebels at Bury deliberately sought out John Lakenheath and, doubtless for the administrative efficiency displayed in this very book, beheaded him" (24).

40. Gottfried, *Bury St. Edmunds and the Urban Crisis*, 234.

41. See Thomas Walsingham, *Chronicon Angliae*, ed. Edward Maunde Thompson, Rolls Series 64 (London, 1874), 308; passage cited and translated in Steven Justice, *Writing and Rebellion: England in 1381* (Berkeley and Los Angeles: University of California Press, 1994), 18.

42. Thus, the library catalogue drawn up by the Premonstratensian canon of Tichfield in 1400 lists the expected theological and patristic works alongside records of statutes, privileges, and surveys of estates and rents owed to the house; see D. N. Bell, ed., *The Libraries of the Cistercians, Gilbertines and Premonstratensians*, Corpus of British Medieval Library Catalogues 3 (London: British Academy, 1992), 254, 257, 248. As Willis and Clark note in their *Architectural History of the University of Cambridge*, books are classified with charters and muniments in the statutes of Peterhouse, Cambridge, 1344, as well as in those of St. Catherine's Hall, Cambridge, 1475 (3.474, 3.394). On the medieval classification of books with muniments and documents, see also Clanchy, *From Memory to Written Record*, 2d ed., 153–55.

43. New College (1400), All Souls College (1443), and Magdalen College (1479) in Oxford had separate collections of books and muniments; see Willis and Clark, *Architectural History of the University of Cambridge*, 3.475–77.

44. Thomson, *Archives of the Abbey of Bury St. Edmunds*, 34. This overlap of archival and library practices leads Thomson to observe that "at Bury the periods of greatest intellectual activity and interest in the library coincided with the periods of maximum administrative efficiency and of new developments in the archives" (3). For comparison, consider the example of Ely Cathedral, which shows evidence of a similarly congruent organization of its library and archive: see Dorothy Owen, *The Library and Muniments of Ely Cathedral* (Ely: published by the Dean and Chapter of Ely, 1973), 3–4.

45. Rouse and Rouse, *Authentic Witnesses*, 8–9.

46. In the manuscript that preserves them, British Library, MS Add. 14848, Lydgate's *Cartae versificatae* is bound with a series of documents detailing disputes involving the abbey's privileges and are prefaced with a note explaining that Curteys ordered the cartularies redrawn in response to these disputes. See Thomson, *Archives of the Abbey of Bury St. Edmunds*, 35, 137.

47. On the "Vita et passio S. Edmundi abbreviata," see Arnold, *Memorials of St. Edmund's Abbey*, vol. 1; on the uses of hagiography for the founding myths of Bury St. Edmunds, see Antonia Gransden, "The Legends and Traditions concerning the Origins of the Abbey of Bury St. Edmunds," *English Historical Review* 394 (1985): 1–24.

48. See Thomson, *Archives of the Abbey of Bury St. Edmunds*, 137; Elston, "William Curteys, Abbot of Bury St. Edmunds, 1429–1446" (PhD diss., University of California, Berkeley, 1979), 165. Alfred Hiatt points out that "the eleventh-century documents" contained in Lydgate's *Cartae* "are all of questionable authenticity, although their substance may be genuine enough"; see Hiatt, *The Making of Medieval Forgeries: False Documents in Fifteenth-Century England* (London: British Library, 2004), 57. For the original charters, see P. H. Sawyer, *Anglo-Saxon Charters: An Annotated List and Bibliography* (London: Royal Historical Society, 1968), 293, 297, 311–12, 323.

49. See Emily Steiner, *Documentary Culture and the Making of Medieval English Literature* (Cambridge: Cambridge University Press, 2003), 17. See also Brigitte Bedox-Rezak, "Diplomatic Sources and Medieval Documentary Practice: An Essay in Interpretive Methodology," in *The Past and Future of Medieval Studies*, ed. John Van Engen (Notre Dame, IN: University of Notre Dame Press, 1994), 313–43. And for a broader discussion of the interpenetration of poetic and administrative modes in the late Middle Ages, see Ethan Knapp, *The Bureaucratic Muse: Thomas Hoccleve and the Literature of Late Medieval England* (University Park: Pennsylvania State University Press, 2001).

50. See Rosamond McKitterick, *The Carolingians and the Written Word* (Cambridge: Cambridge University Press, 1989), esp. chap. 3, for a consideration of earlier uses of charters.

51. See D. Vance Smith's discussion of "Charters and Beginnings" in relation to *Piers Plowman* in *The Book of the Incipit: Beginnings in the Fourteenth Century* (Minneapolis: University of Minnesota Press, 2001), 142–49. See also Patrick Geary, "Medieval Archivists as Authors: Social Memory and Archival Memory," in *Archives, Documentation, and Institutions of Social Memory: Essays from the Sawyer Seminar*, ed. Francix X. Blouin Jr. and William G. Rosenberg (Ann Arbor: University of Michigan Press, 2006).

52. On the uses of literary topoi in cartularies, see Pascale Bourgain and Marie-Clotilde Hubert, "Latin et rhétoric dans les prefaces de cartulaire," in *Les cartulaires: Actes de table ronde organisée par l'École nationale des cartes et le G. D. R. 121 du C.N.R.S.*, ed. Olivier Guyokjeannin, Laurent Morelle, and Micher Parisse (Paris: École des Chartres, 1993), 115–36.

53. P. J. Geary, *Phantoms of Remembrance: Memory and Oblivion at the End of the First Millennium* (Princeton, NJ: Princeton University Press, 1994), 117; see also Georges Declercq, "Originals and Cartularies: The Organization of Archival Memory (Ninth–Eleventh Centuries)," in *Charters and the Use of the Written Word in Medieval Society*, ed. Karl Heidecker (Turnhout, Belgium: Brepols, 2000), 147–70. On the uses of cartularies, see also the essays collected in Adam J. Kosto and Anders Winroth, eds., *Charters, Cartularies and Archives: The Preservation and Transmission of Documents in the Medieval West* (Toronto: Pontifical Institute of Medieval Studies, 2002). Kathryn A. Lowe examines Bury's cartularies in "Two Thirteenth-Century Cartularies from Bury St. Edmunds: A Study in Textual Transmission," *Neuphilologische Mitteilungen* 93 (1992): 293–301.

54. British Library, MS Add. 14848, fol. 243r.

55. Ibid., fol. 243. See Thomson, *Archives of the Abbey of Bury St. Edmunds*, 137; Hiatt, *Making of Medieval Forgeries*, 57–58.

56. On this dispute, see V. H. Galbraith, "The East Anglian See and the Abbey of Bury St. Edmunds," *English Historical Review* 40 (1925): 222–28; David Knowles, "Essays in Monastic History, IV: The Growth of Exemption," *Downside Review* 50 (1932): 201–31, esp. 209–11.

57. *Cartae versificatae*, reprinted in Arnold, *Memorials of St. Edmund's Abbey*, 3.233; subsequent quotations from the *Cartae* will be from this edition, with the page numbers noted parenthetically in the text.

58. Charters became acceptable as material evidence; on this development, see Clanchy, *From Memory to Written Record*, 2d ed., 254–55, 294–98.

59. The *Cartae versificatae* might therefore be read as an example of a phenomenon that Maura Nolan observes in Lydgate's occasional poetry, which issues simultaneous demands "to be read in topical terms" while also "resist[ing] topicality by asserting its status as a distinctly literary object." Indeed, this might explain why Curteys turned to Lydgate with his request to versify the abbey's charters. See Maura Nolan, *John Lydgate and the Making of Public Culture* (Cambridge: Cambridge University Press, 2005), 2.

60. Hiatt makes a similar point: see his *Making of Medieval Forgeries*, 57–62.

61. Stephen G. Nichols argues that "the concept of surrogacy, of copy in the stead of a fixed original, ruled the manuscript culture of the Middle Ages"; Nichols, "An Artifact by Any Other Name: Digital Surrogates of Medieval Manuscripts," in *Archives, Documentation, and Institutions of Social Memory*, ed. Blouin and Rosenberg, 140. Yet as we shall see, similar concepts were in evidence in the later libraries of Matthew Parker and Sir Robert Cotton.

62. Clanchy, *From Memory to Written Record*, 2d ed., 314–15.

63. Related to this point is Geary's comment that, in the archives, "not everything was to be preserved, only that which was useful," and "the result was a winnowing and restructuring process" (*Phantoms of Remembrance*, 114).

64. See Fiona Somerset, "'Hard is with seyntis for to make affray': Lydgate the 'Poet-Propagandist' as Hagiographer," in *John Lydgate: Poetry, Culture, and Lancastrian England*, ed. Larry Scanlon and James Simpson (Notre Dame, IN: University of Notre Dame Press, 2006), 258–78.

65. In a study of Bury's exemptions, David Knowles points out that Bury "depended for [its] economic and religious freedom on royal protection past and present"; Knowles, "Essays in Monastic History, IV: The Growth of Exemption," *Downside Review* 50 (1932): 204.

66. On the monastic genres of history writing, see Andrew Galloway, "Writing History in England," in *The Cambridge History of Medieval English Literature*, ed. David Wallace (Cambridge: Cambridge University Press, 1999), 255–83.

67. St. Augustine, *On Christian Doctrine*, trans. D. W. Robertson (Indianapolis, IN: Bobbs-Merrill Educational Publishing, 1958), 3.5.9.

68. Norman P. Tanner, ed., *Heresy Trials in the Diocese of Norwich, 1428–31*, Camden Fourth Series, vol. 20 (London: Royal Historical Society, 1977).

69. Nicholas Watson, "Censorship and Cultural Change in Late-Medieval England: Vernacular Theology, the Oxford Translation Debate, and Arundel's Constitutions of 1409," *Speculum* 70 (1995): 822–64. See also Hudson, *"Laicus Litteratus,"* in *Heresy and Literacy, 1000–1530*, ed. Biller and Hudson.

70. British Library, MS Add. 14848, fol. 109r. For a discussion of this document, see R. N. Swanson, *Catholic England: Faith, Religion, and Observance before the Reformation* (Manchester: Manchester University Press, 1993), 267.

71. See Tanner, *Heresy Trials in the Diocese of Norwich*, 99; Priscilla Heath Barnum, ed., *Dives et Pauper*, Early English Text Society, O.S. 275 (London: Oxford University Press, 1976); N. P. Tanner, *The Church in Late Medieval Norwich, 1370–1532* (Toronto: University of Toronto Press, 1984), 99. This episode is discussed in Hudson, *Premature Reformation*, 417–19. See also Watson, "Censorship and Cultural Change," *Speculum* 70 (1995): 849, 854–56.

72. Hudson, *Premature Reformation*, 417–18. The transcript of this examination is extracted and translated in A. R. Myers, ed., *English Historical Documents, 1327–1485* (New York: Oxford University Press, 1969), 866–68.

73. Tanner, *Heresy Trials in the Diocese of Norwich*, 28. On the "scoles of heresie," see also Ruth Nisse, "Grace under Pressure: Conduct and Representation in the Norwich Heresy Trials," in *Medieval Conduct*, ed. K. Ashley and L. A. Clark (Minneapolis: University of Minnesota Press, 2001), 207–23.

74. Barnum, *Dives et Pauper*, 53, lines 22–23; Hudson, *Premature Reformation*, 418–19.

75. See David R. Carlson, "Whethamstede on Lollardy: Latin Styles and Vernacular Cultures in Early Fifteenth-Century England," *Journal of English and Germanic Philology*, 2003, 21–41, quotation on 40–41.

76. On this point, see Hudson, *Premature Reformation*, 418: "The core of the issue was the legitimacy of enquiry into theological or ecclesiastical ideas within the strictly controllable environment of a Benedictine monastery as opposed to that allowable in the lay world of an unbeneficed chaplain in a country market town."

77. British Library, MS Add. 14848, fol. 84; edited and transcribed by John Gage, "Letters from King Henry VI to the Abbot of St. Edmundsbury, and to the Alderman and Bailiffs of the Town, for the Suppression of the Lollards," *Archaeologia* 23 (1831): 341–43; but see also J. A. F. Thomson, "A Lollard Rising in Kent: 1431 or 1438?" *Bulletin of the Institute of Historical Research* 37 (1964): 100–102, which revises the date of the letter preserved in fol. 328r–328v.

78. British Library, MS Add. 14848, fol. 102r–102v.

79. Roberto Weiss, *Humanism in England during the Fifteenth Century*, 2d ed. (Oxford: Basil Blackwell, 1957), 69; J. B. Trapp, "The Humanist Book," in *The Cambridge History of the Book in Britain*, ed. Hellinga and Trapp, 3.295. On the "prestigious heritage of the domestic book collections of the seignorial aristocracy" developing in fifteenth-century Italy, see Armando Petrucci, *Writers and Readers in Medieval Italy: Studies in the History of Written Culture*, ed. and trans. Charles M. Radding (New Haven, CT: Yale University Press, 1995), 225. Weiss's work, especially its interpretation of Humfrey's humanism, has been criticized by David Rundle: see "On the Difference between Virtue and Weiss: Humanist Texts in England during the Fifteenth Century," in *Courts, Counties, and the Capital in the Later Middle Ages*, ed. D. E. S. Dunn (New York: St. Martin's Press, 1996), 181–203; "Humanism before the Tudors: On Nobility and the Reception of *Studia Humanitatis* in Fifteenth-Century England," in *Reassessing Tudor Humanism*, ed. J. Woolfson (Basingstoke: Palgrave Macmillan, 2002), 22–42; "Habits of Manuscript-Collecting: The Dispersals of the Library of Humfrey, Duke of Gloucester," in *Lost Libraries: The Destruction of Great Book Collections since Antiquity*, ed. James Raven (London: Palgrave Macmillan, 2004), 106–23. For an overview of Humfrey's political career, see William Kuskin, "Duke Humfrey," in *The Historical Dictionary of Late Medieval England, 1272–1485*, ed. Ronald H. Fritze and William B. Robinson (Westport, CT: Greenwood Press, 2002), 264–65; see also Alessandra Petrina, *Cultural Politics in Fifteenth-Century England: The Case of Humfrey, Duke of Gloucester* (Leiden: Brill, 2004), 98–127.

80. This point is made forcefully and convincingly in Petrina, *Cultural Politics in Fifteenth-Century England*, 157, 174–258. See also David Rundle, "Two Unnoticed Manuscripts from the Collection of Humfrey, Duke of Gloucester," *Bodleian Library Record* 16 (1998): 211–24, 299–313.

81. Richard Firth Green puts Humfrey's patronage of Lydgate in the larger perspective of royal patronage practices; see his *Poets and Princepleasers: Literature and the English Court in the Late Middle Ages* (Toronto: University of Toronto Press, 1980).

82. Thus, Derek Pearsall argues that "Humfrey was touched . . . by the spirit of the Italian Renaissance and the reawakening of interest in classical literature, and his commissioning of a translation of the *De Casibus* is part of his admiration for anything that came out of Italy, but Lydgate responds only fitfully to the stimulus, and at almost every point reasserts . . . the medieval commonplaces upon which Boccaccio's work is so largely based"; Pearsall, *John Lydgate* (Charlottesville: University Press of Virginia, 1970), 224. For a general discussion of the opposition between Humfrey's "progressive" humanist interests versus the "backward[ness]" of his "contacts with English authors such as John Lydgate," see Susanne Saygin, *Humfrey, Duke of Gloucester (1390–1447), and the Italian Humanists* (Leiden: Brill, 2002), 10–17, 64–68, quotations on 10. Alain Renoir, *The Poetry*

of John Lydgate (Cambridge, MA: Harvard University Press, 1967), and Walter Schirmer, John Lydgate: A Study of the Culture of the XVth Century, trans. Ann E. Keep (1952; repr., Berkeley and Los Angeles: University of California Press, 1961), are virtually alone in seeing Lydgate as a proto-Renaissance figure. James Simpson takes issue with the assumption that Lydgate is a representative "medieval" poet in "'Dysemol daies and fatal houres': Lydgate's Destruction of Thebes and Chaucer's Knight's Tale," in The Long Fifteenth Century: Essays for Douglas Gray, ed. Helen Cooper and Sally Mapstone (Oxford: Clarendon Press, 1997), 15–33.

83. See E. P. Hammond, "Poet and Patron in The Fall of Princes," Anglia 38 (1914): 121–36.

84. See Nolan, John Lydgate and the Making of Public Culture, as well as the essays collected in Scanlon and Simpson, John Lydgate: Poetry, Culture, and Lancastrian England. For further reconsiderations of Lydgate's engagement with his patron, see also Nigel Mortimer, John Lydgate's "Fall of Princes": Narrative Tragedy in Its Literary and Political Contexts (Oxford: Clarendon Press, 2005), esp. chap. 3; Paul Strohm, Politique: Languages of Statecraft between Chaucer and Shakespeare (Notre Dame, IN: University of Notre Dame Press, 2005), 89–104.

85. My approach to Lydgate's mediation of Bury's and Humfrey's libraries is in accord with that of several essays in Scanlon and Simpson, John Lydgate: Poetry, Culture, and Lancastrian England, that stress Lydgate's translatio between two cultures, whether religious and secular or aristocratic and civic: see in particular C. David Benson, "Civic Lydgate: The Poet and London," 147–68; Maura B. Nolan, "The Performance of the Literary: Lydgate's Mummings," 169–206; Ruth Nisse, "'Was it not Route to Se?' Lydgate and the Styles of Martyrdom," 279–98; Somerset, "'Hard is With Seyntis for to make Affray.'" The term "cultural translatio" is Nolan's (171).

86. Petrucci, Writers and Readers, 211; Pearl Kibre, "The Intellectual Interests Reflected in Libraries of the Fourteenth and Fifteenth Centuries," Journal of the History of Ideas 7 (1946): 257–97.

87. M. R. James, "Bury St. Edmunds Manuscripts," English Historical Review 41 (1926): 251–60; R. A. B. Mynors, "The Latin Classics Known to Boston of Bury," in Fritz Saxl, a Volume of Memorial Essays, ed. D. J. Gordon (London: Thomas Nelson and Sons, 1957), 199–217.

88. Pearsall, John Lydgate, 37.

89. Beryl Smalley, English Friars and Antiquity in the Early Fourteenth Century (Oxford: Blackwell, 1960); Judson Boyce Allen, The Friar as Critic: Literary Attitudes in the Later Middle Ages (Nashville, TN: Vanderbilt University Press, 1971).

90. Smalley, English Friars and Antiquity, 35.

91. See John V. Fleming, "The Friars and Medieval English Literature," in Cambridge History of Medieval English Literature, ed. Wallace, 349–75, esp. 365. Anthony Grafton critiques this assumption in "The Humanist as Reader," in A History of Reading in the West, ed. Guglielmo Cavallo and Roger Chartier (Amherst: University of Massachusetts Press, 1999), 182.

92. Weiss, Humanism in England, 2d ed., 68; see also Roberto Weiss, "Portrait of a Bibliophile xi: Humfrey, Duke of Gloucester, d. 1447," Book Collector 13 (1964): 161–70, esp. 168–69.

93. A complementary line of argument is pursued by David R. Carlson when he observes that, while "dominant scholasticism and emergent humanism . . . have long been represented as antithetical," the work of John Whethamstede, who was abbot of St. Albans and maintained close relations with both Curteys and Humfrey, reveals that "in England the two Latin styles could work together in opposing the dissident tradition of vernacular theology, as represented in the Lollard movement." See his article "Whethamstede on Lollardy," *Journal of English and Germanic Philology*, 2003, 21–22.

94. For a general overview of the Jack Sharp rebellion, see K. H. Vickers, *Humphry, Duke of Gloucester: A Biography* (London: Archibald Constable, 1907), 222–24; K. B. McFarlane, *John Wycliffe and the Beginnings of English Nonconformity* (London: English Universities Press, 1952), 182; Aston, *Lollards and Reformers*, 31–38.

95. Vickers, *Humphry*, 223; Aston, *Lollards and Reformers*, 33.

96. Edward Hall, *Chronicle* (London, 1543), fol. 120v. Cited in Gage, "Letters from King Henry VI," *Archaeologia* 23 (1831): 340.

97. Gage, "Letters from King Henry VI," *Archaeologia* 23 (1831): 342; Aston, *Lollards and Reformers*, 34. See also Thomson, "A Lollard Rising in Kent: 1431 or 1438?" *Bulletin of the Institute of Historical Research* 37 (1964): 100–102.

98. Aston, *Lollards and Reformers*, 35.

99. For a discussion of the rebellion and its contexts, see Ralph A. Griffiths, *The Reign of King Henry VI: The Exercise of Royal Authority, 1422–1461* (London: Ernest Benn, 1981), 138–44.

100. Gage, "Letters from King Henry VI," *Archaeologia* 23 (1831): 342.

101. I. M. W. Harvey, "Was There Popular Politics in Fifteenth-Century England?" in *The McFarlane Legacy: Studies in Late Medieval Politics and Society*, ed. R. H. Britness and A. J. Pollard (New York: St. Martin's Press, 1995). For an analysis of an earlier history of the "communes," see also Emily Steiner, "Commonality and Literary Form in the 1370s and 1380s," *New Medieval Literatures* 6 (2003): 199–221.

102. On bill casting such as the 1431 rebels practiced, see Wendy Scase, "'Strange and Wonderful Bills': Bill-Casting and Political Discourse in Late Medieval England," *New Medieval Literatures* 2 (1998): 225–47. One of the Jack Sharp bills "presented by John Sharpe to Humfrey duke of Gloucester" survives in British Library, MS Harley 3375, fol. 120, and is edited by Henry Thomas Riley in *Annales monasterii S. Albani a Johanne Amundesham conscripti (A.D. 1421–1440); quibus praefigitur Chronicon rerum gestarum in monasterio S. Albani (A.D. 1422–1431) a quodam auctore ignoto compilatum*, Rolls Series 28 (London: Longmans, Green, and Co., 1870–71), 1.453–56. As John Watts argues, "the bill-caster" and "the heretic" were "bogeys of the official mind, reactions to a world where more people knew more things and more information circulated more freely"; see his "The Pressure of the Public on Later Medieval Politics," in *The Fifteenth Century*, vol. 4, *Political Culture in Late Medieval Britain*, ed. Linda Clark and Christine Carpenter (Woodbridge, Suffolk: Boydell Press, 2004), 164.

103. Justice, *Writing and Rebellion*, 24, 36.

104. *Calendar of the Close Rolls Preserved in the Public Record Office, Henry VI*, vol. 2, *A.D. 1429–1435* (London: His Majesty's Stationery Office, 1933), 123.

105. Aston quotes Bishop from Cambridge University Library, MS Dd.14.2, in *Lollards and Reformers*, 45; see also Gage, "Letters from King Henry VI," *Archaeologia* 23 (1831): 343.

106. Riley, *Annales monasterii S. Albani*, vol. 5, part 1, liv–v. See the Latin: "Quidam ganeo, Lollardia conspersus . . . motionem quamdam commovit in populo, jaciendo et spargendo billas in Londoniis, Coventria, Oxonia, et aliis villis," "qui, Deo mediante, captus fuit circa Festum Pentecostes in Oxoniis, cum billarum suarum scriptoribus" (63).

107. N. H. Nicolas and Edward Tyrrell, eds., *A Chronicle of London, from 1089 to 1483; Written in the Fifteenth Century, and for the First Time Printed from Mss. in the British Museum* (London: Longman, Rees, [etc.], 1827), 119.

108. Vickers, *Humphry*, 226.

109. Ibid., 227. *The Fall of Princes* is generally dated between the rebellion in May 1431 and Henry's return from France in January 1432, on the strength of its present-tense references to Humfrey's lieutenancy and suppression of the Lollards. See Hammond, "Poet and Patron in *The Fall of Princes*," *Anglia* 38 (1914): 121–36.

110. See Saygin, *Humfrey*, 48–56, for an account of Humfrey's actions during this time.

111. For other examples of official "appropriation . . . of the heretics' literary tools," see Hudson, "*Laicus Litteratus*," in *Heresy and Literacy, 1000–1530*, ed. Biller and Hudson, 234.

112. Weiss, *Humanism in England*, 2d ed., 58.

113. Petrucci, *Writers and Readers in Medieval Italy*, 225.

114. Vespasiano da Bisticci, *The Vespasiano Memoirs: Lives of Illustrious Men of the XVth Century*, trans. William George and Emily Waters (Toronto: University of Toronto Press, 1997), 102.

115. Ibid., 221.

116. Anthony Grafton, *Commerce with the Classics: Ancient Books and Renaissance Readers* (Ann Arbor: University of Michigan Press, 1997), 21.

117. Rundle, "On the Difference between Virtue and Weiss," in *Courts, Counties, and the Capital in the Later Middle Ages*, ed. Dunn, 197.

118. Mario Borso, ed., "Correspondence of Humfrey Duke of Gloucester and Pier Candido Decembrio," *English Historical Review* 19 (1904): 513–14. Humfrey's response is translated by Vickers (*Humphry*, 360).

119. Plato, *The Republic*, trans. Richard W. Sterling and William C. Scott (New York: W. W. Norton, 1985), 5.473d.

120. Vickers, *Humphry*, 370, 373.

121. Rev. Henry Anstey, ed., *Epistolae academicae Oxon.: Part I (1421–1457)* (Oxford: Clarendon Press, 1898), 177–79.

122. Pearsall, *John Lydgate*, 224.

123. See Stephanie H. Jed, *Chaste Thinking: The Rape of Lucretia and the Birth of Humanism* (Bloomington: University of Indiana Press, 1989), 8–11 and passim.

124. Michel Foucault, "Fantasia of the Library," in *Language, Counter-memory, Practice: Selected Essays and Interviews*, ed. and trans. Donald F. Bouchard (Ithaca, NY: Cornell University Press, 1977), 91.

125. Giovanni Boccaccio, *The Fates of Illustrious Men*, trans. Louis Brewer Hall (New York: Frederick Ungar, 1965), 137.

126. In another prologue, in which Bochas falls asleep from weariness, Lydgate adds the gratuitous detail that he "Fill in a slombre lenyng on a cheste" (7.4), which locates

him among the book chests that were the library's chief pieces of furniture. As Bergen notes, "Laurent does not mention a chest" (*Lydgate's "Fall of Princes*," 4:273). See Victoria Kirkham, "Decoration and Iconography of Lydgate's *Fall of Princes* (*De casibus virorum illustrium*) at the Philadelphia Rosenbach," *Studi sul Boccaccio* 25 (1997): 297–310, esp. fig. 3.

127. See Bergen, *Lydgate's "Fall of Princes*," 4:196.

128. Francis Petrarch, *The Life of Solitude*, trans. Jacob Zeitlin (Urbana: University of Illinois Press, 1924), 291. See also Douglas Radcliffe-Umstead, "Petrarch and the Freedom to Be Alone," in *Francis Petrarch, Six Centuries Later: A Symposium*, ed. Aldo Scaglione (Chicago: Newberry Library, 1975), 236–48.

129. Petrarch, *Life of Solitude*, trans. Zeitlin, 282.

130. See *OED* and *MED*, s.v. "common." See also I. M. W. Harvey, "Was There Popular Politics in Fifteenth-Century England?" in *The McFarlane Legacy: Studies in Late Medieval Politics and Society*, ed. R. H. Britness and A. J. Pollard (New York: St. Martin's Press, 1995). On the late medieval uses of the "communes," see Watts, "Pressure of the Public on Later Medieval Politics," in *Fifteenth Century*, vol. 4, ed. Clark and Carpenter; Emily Steiner, "Commonality and Literary Form in the 1370s and 1380s," *New Medieval Literatures* 6 (2003): 199–221; Jean E. Howard and Paul Strohm, "The Imaginary 'Commons,'" *Journal of Medieval and Early Modern Studies* 37 (2007) 549–77.

131. "Supplicatio pessima, porrecta per Johannem Scharpe Domino Humfredo, Duci Glovernae, regni protectori, in subversionem ecclesiae," British Library, MS Harley 3375, fol. 120; transcribed in Riley, *Annales monasterii S. Albani*, 1.453–56, quotation on 456. See Hall, *Chronicle* (1543), fol. 120v.

132. This example of how Lydgate elevates the community of clerks ("with clerkis to commune"; 1.387) while debasing that of the "comouns" is consistent with a paradoxical process of broadening and narrowing of "the public" that Maura Nolan diagnoses in Lancastrian culture: see Nolan, *John Lydgate and the Making of Public Culture*, 6.

133. It is noteworthy that this very example is cited in Wycliffite objections to "fabulation," as in the *Rosarium theologiae*, which charges "a prechor forso[th] ow not in his prechyng for to expoune to [th]e puple gramer or fables of Iupiter [or siche]"; Christine von Nolcken, ed., *The Middle English Translation of the "Rosarium rheogogie"* (Heidelberg: Carl Winter, 1979), 73.

134. Larry Scanlon, *Narrative, Authority, and Power: The Medieval Exemplum and the Chaucerian Tradition* (Cambridge: Cambridge University Press, 1994), 330.

135. Boccaccio, *Fates of Illustrious Men*, trans. Hall, 2.

136. See Maura Nolan, "'Now Wo, Now Gladnesse': Ovidianism in *The Fall of Princes*," *English Literary History* 71 (2004): 531–58, on Lydgate's response to Humfrey's "dictatorial consumption" (553).

137. See Jonathan Woolfson, "Between Bruni and Hobbes: Aristotle's *Politics* in Tudor Intellectual Culture," in *Reassessing Tudor Humanism*, ed. Woolfson, 197–222, on another book from Humfrey's library that would shift in the opposite direction, from being "a text fit for a royal duke into something resembling a republican manifesto" (197).

138. For a reading of this passage and how "Premierfait and Lydgate shared an external incentive to 'make it new' around the wishes of powerful aristocratic patrons," see Strohm, *Politique*, 93–94.

139. Boccaccio, *Fates of Illustrious Men*, trans. Hall, 2; see Bergen, *Lydgate's "Fall of Princes,"* 4:172, for the original Latin.

140. See Ian Donaldson, *The Rapes of Lucretia: A Myth and Its Transformations* (Oxford: Clarendon Press, 1982), 8–10, 106.

141. Wallace goes on to make the point that Boccaccio's retelling of the Virginia story "sacrifices all interest in family pathos (father stabs daughter with a butcher's knife) in order to concentrate on the political struggle of the plebeians against Claudius, an overweening *decemvir*." See David Wallace, *Chaucerian Polity: Absolutist Lineages and Associational Forms in England and Italy* (Stanford, CA: Stanford University Press, 1997), 303.

142. Bergen, *Lydgate's "Fall of Princes,"* 4:174.

143. Ibid., 174–75.

144. See the book list of Humfrey's library that has been reconstructed by Alfonso Sammut, *Unfredo duca de Gloucester et gli umanisti italiani* (Padua: Editrice Antenore, 1980), 64. On Lydgate's use of John of Salisbury in this episode, see also Pearsall, *John Lydgate*, 249; Wallace, *Chaucerian Polity*, 333; Petrina, *Cultural Politics*, 306; Strohm, *Politique*, 98. The borrowing is made explicit in Bergen, *Lydgate's "Fall of Princes,"* 4:172–75.

145. *Policraticus*, 5.2, from *The Statesman's Book of John of Salisbury*, trans. John Dickinson (New York: Alfred A. Knopf, 1927), 64–65.

146. As Scanlon observes of John of Salisbury's use of the figure, "the corporate fiction was always articulated from a position of social superiority" (*Narrative, Authority, and Power*, 98).

147. Nolan, *John Lydgate and the Making of Public Culture*, 6; Watts, "Pressure of the Public in Later Medieval Politics," in *Fifteenth Century*, vol. 4, ed. Clark and Carpenter.

148. For a somewhat-different reading of this episode, which stresses Lydgate's role as a moralizer, see Mortimer, *John Lydgate's "Fall of Princes,"* 61–78.

149. The book is now in Chetham's Library, Manchester, Mun. A. 3. 131 (27929); see Sammut, *Unfredo duca de Gloucester*, 111–12. On this episode, Petrina suggests that we understand line 1109, "Folwyng the tracis of Collucyus," as a continuation of the preceding stanza and thus "as part of a single sentence: his lord bade Lydgate not only to tell the story of Lucretia, but to follow 'Collucyus' rather than Chaucer or Boccaccio" (*Cultural Politics*, 303).

150. For the Latin version and a translation of Salutati's *Declamatio Lucretiae*, see the appendix to Jed, *Chaste Thinking*. For a close comparison between Salutati's and Lydgate's versions of the Lucrece story, see Eleanor Prescott Hammond, "Lydgate and Colluccio Salutati," *Modern Philology* 25 (1927): 49–57.

151. Jed, *Chaste Thinking*, 51; see also Donaldson, *Rapes of Lucretia*.

152. This manuscript is Bibliothèque de Ste. Genevieve, MS Francais, 777; see Vickers, *Humphry*, 438.

153. Bersuire is cited in Jacques Monfrin, "Humanisme et traductions au Moyen Age," *Journal des savants*, July–September 1963, 161–90, quotation on 173. On Bersuire's use of Livy as a source of exempla for rulers, see M. J. Rychner, "Observations sur la traduction de Tite-Live par Pierre Bersuire," *Journal des savants*, October–December 1963,

242–67; Marie-Helene Tesniere, "Un remaniement du 'Tite-Live' de Pierre Bersuire par Laurent de Premierfait," *Romania* 107 (1986): 231–81.

154. Rita Copeland's discussion of "vernacular exegetical translation" is relevant here: see her *Rhetoric, Hermeneutics, and Translation in the Middle Ages: Academic Traditions and Vernacular Texts* (Cambridge: Cambridge University Press, 1991), esp. 179–220. On the importance of edifying commentary to clerical literary production, see Leclerq, *Love of Learning*, 188; Smalley, *English Friars and Antiquity*, 299.

155. Petrus Berchorius, *De formis figurisque deorum. Reductorium morale, liber XV: Ovidius moralizatus*, ed. J. Engels (Utrecht: Rijksuniversiteit, Instituut voor Laat Latijn, 1962).

156. Pierre Bersuire, "*The Moral Reduction*, Book XV: *Ovid Moralized*, Prologue and Extracts," in *Medieval Literary Theory and Criticism, c. 1100-c. 1375: The Commentary Tradition*, ed. A. J. Minnis et al. (Oxford: Clarendon Press, 1988), 367.

157. Gage, "Letters from King Henry VI," *Archaeologia* 23 (1831): 342.

158. Lois Ebin notes that the "change in point of view" that Lydgate makes "is seen most dramatically in a conspicuous category of additions which he weaves into his source—the story of the churl rising to power"; see Ebin, *John Lydgate* (Boston: Twayne, 1985), 67.

159. Vickers, *Humphry*, 396–407. For an overview of Humfrey's donations to Oxford and the founding of the library, see Gillam, *Divinity School and Duke Humfrey's Library at Oxford*.

160. A. S. G. Edwards, "Duke Humfrey's Middle English Palladius Manuscript," in *The Lancastrian Court: Proceedings of the 2001 Harlaxton Symposium*, ed. Jenny Stratford (Donington, Lincolnshire: Shaun Tyas, 2003), 68–77.

161. Mark Liddell, ed., *The Middle English Translation of Palladius, "De re rustica"* (Berlin: E. Ebering, 1896), 22.

162. For lists of Humfrey's donations, see Sammut, *Unfredo duca de Gloucester*, 60–84. The contents of these lists are discussed extensively by Petrina, *Cultural Politics*, 243–54.

163. Vickers, *Humphry*, 422. Petrina critiques the claim that Humfrey's donations constitute a humanist program in *Cultural Politics*, 246, 250, 253–54.

164. Sammut, *Unfredo duca de Gloucester*, 62, 64, 68, 70. Similarly, Paul Oskar Kristeller notes that in Italy "some Northern monastic libraries that otherwise show no interest in secular Renaissance literature may contain an occasional manuscript of one of Petrarch's moral treatises"; see Kristeller, *Medieval Aspects of Renaissance Learning*, ed. and trans. Edward P. Mahoney (Durham, NC: Duke University Press, 1974), 101.

165. On Humfrey's involvement in the construction of the library, see Gillam, *Divinity School and Duke Humfrey's Library at Oxford*, 10–11.

166. Giles Barber, *Arks for Learning: A Short History of Oxford Library Buildings* (Oxford: Oxford Bibliographical Society, 1995), 6.

167. Norton's emphasis on the mobility of the library experience contrasts with the experience in the facility that preceded Duke Humfrey's, in which readers are said to have continuously crowded one another—at least so alleges the complaint meant to win Humfrey's support for the new library. See Gameson, "Medieval Library," in *Cambridge History of Libraries in Britain and Ireland*, ed. Leedham-Green and Webber, 1.47.

168. Anstey, *Epistolae academicae*, 296.

169. Ibid., 281.

170. Ibid., 168–69.

171. Anne Hudson, "Wycliffism in Oxford, 1381–1411," in *Wyclif in His Times*, ed. Anthony Kenny (Oxford: Clarendon Press, 1986), 67–84; Jeremy Catto, "Thomas Moston and the Teaching of Wyclif's Logic in Oxford, c. 1410," in *Text and Controversy from Wyclif to Bale: Essays in Honor of Anne Hudson* (Turnhout, Belgium: Brepols, 2005), 119–30.

172. J. I. Catto, "Wyclif and Wycliffism at Oxford, 1356–1430," in *History of the University of Oxford*, ed. Catto and Evans, 2.247–53. See also Ker, "Provision of Books," in *History of the University of Oxford*, ed. McConica, 3.466.

173. Henry Anstey, the nineteenth-century editor of *Epistolae academicae*, suggests as much himself: "The fifteenth century may be considered as the period of the commencement of what we should call the public buildings of the University; which now witnessed a great effort to restore learning, and especially the study of theology; stimulated, no doubt, by the rapid growth of heretical doctrines, and aided by the munificence of sympathizers" (vii).

CHAPTER TWO

1. See Ruth Mortimer, "The Author's Image: Italian Sixteenth-Century Printed Portraits," *Harvard Library Bulletin* 7 (1996): 7–87, especially the examples printed on 8–9; Dora Thornton, *The Scholar in His Study: Ownership and Experience in Renaissance Italy* (New Haven, CT: Yale University Press, 1997).

2. On these portraits, see J. B. Trapp, *Erasmus, Colet and More: The Early Tudor Humanists and Their Books*, Panizzi Lectures, 1990 (London: British Library, 1991), 64–73; Lisa Jardine, *Erasmus, Man of Letters: The Construction of Charisma in Print* (Princeton, NJ: Princeton University Press, 1993), 27–55; Kevin Sharpe and Steven N. Zwicker, "Introduction: Discovering the Renaissance Reader," in *Reading, Society and Politics in Early Modern England*, ed. Sharpe and Zwicker (Cambridge: Cambridge University Press, 2003), 16–17.

3. On the development of private libraries, see Thornton, *Scholar in His Study*; Armando Petrucci, *Writers and Readers in Medieval Italy: Studies in the History of Written Culture*, ed. and trans. Charles M. Radding (New Haven, CT: Yale University Press, 1995), 221. For this development in an English context, see Simon Jervis, "The English Country House Library," in *Treasures from the Libraries of National Trust Country Houses*, ed. N. Barker (New York: The Royal Oak Foundation and The Grolier Club, 1999).

4. As William H. Sherman observes: "the private library and the solitary scholarly reader are less representations of early modern reality than rhetorical strategies by which early modern subjects negotiated their place in society." See his *John Dee: The Politics of Reading and Writing in the English Renaissance* (Amherst: University of Massachusetts Press, 1995), 50. George Hoffman, in an analysis of Montaigne that applies equally well to other European humanist contexts, similarly points out, "not only did personal libraries often afford little refuge from one's business . . . but they played a significant role in the ongoing evaluation of rank that characterized many professional lives." See his *Montaigne's Career* (Oxford: Clarendon Press, 1998), 149.

5. This point paraphrases a historical argument by Sears Jayne, *Library Catalogues of the English Renaissance*, 2d ed. (Godalming, Surrey: St. Paul's Bibliographies, 1983), 24, 29. For a broad assessment of humanist libraries, see the essays collected in Rudolf De Smet, ed., *Les humanists et leur bibliothèque*, Travaux de l'Institut interuniversitaire pour l'étude de la Renaissance et de l'humanisme 13 (Brussels: Peeters, 2002). Elisabeth Leedham-Green presents invaluable insight into the organization and contents of early Tudor private libraries; see her *Books in Cambridge Inventories: Book-Lists from Vice-Chancellor's Court Probate Inventories in the Tudor and Stuart Periods*, 2 vols. (Cambridge: Cambridge University Press, 1986).

6. David Carlson argues that by around 1500 "the demand for humanist training became the common prerogative of England's dominant groups, the 'political class' of persons engaged immediately in running the country or in a position to employ others to administer their affairs." See his *English Humanist Books: Writers and Patrons, Manuscript and Print, 1475–1525* (Toronto: University of Toronto Press, 1993), 17. See also Fritz Caspari, *Humanism and the Social Order in Tudor England* (Chicago: University of Chicago Press, 1954), 5–10; M. B. Parkes, "The Literacy of the Laity," in *Literature and Western Civilization: The Mediaeval World*, ed. David Daiches and Anthony Thorlby (London: Aldus Books, 1973), 555–77.

7. Raymond Irwin, *The English Library before 1700*, ed. Francis Wormald and C. E. Wright (London: Athlone Press, 1958), 6. On More's library, see also R. J. Schoeck, "Sir Thomas More, Humanist and Lawyer," in *Essential Articles for the Study of Thomas More*, ed. R. S. Sylvester and G. P. Marc'hadour (Hamden, CT: Archon Books, 1977), esp. 575.

8. Elizabeth Frances Rogers, *The Correspondence of Sir Thomas More* (Princeton, NJ: Princeton University Press, 1947), 71.

9. On the Renaissance culture of collection in which Busleiden's library participates, see Paula Findlen, "Possessing the Past: The Material World of the Italian Renaissance," *American Historical Review* 103 (1998): 83–114. Leedham-Green's Cambridge inventories show that private libraries contained many objects other than books, including maps, instruments, pictures, clocks, and games; see her *Books in Cambridge Inventories*, 2.821–27.

10. See also Jardine, *Erasmus, Man of Letters*, esp. 30–38; Alan Stewart, *Close Readers: Humanism and Sodomy in Early Modern England* (Princeton, NJ: Princeton University Press, 1997), xlv.

11. William Roper, *The Life of Sir Thomas More*, in *Two Early Tudor Lives*, ed. Richard S. Sylvester and Davis P. Harding (New Haven, CT: Yale University Press, 1962), 211. On Roper's biography of More, see Judith Anderson, *Biographical Truth: The Representation of Historical Persons in Tudor-Stuart Writing* (New Haven, CT: Yale University Press, 1984), 40–51.

12. Mortimer, "Author's Image," *Harvard Library Bulletin* 7 (1996): 17.

13. Erasmus, *Life of Jerome*, in *Collected Works of Erasmus*, vol. 61, *Patristic Scholarship; The Edition of St. Jerome*, ed. and trans. James F. Brady and John C. Olin (Toronto: University of Toronto Press, 1992), 33.

14. On St. Jerome as an icon for such study-portraiture, see Mortimer, "Author's Image," *Harvard Library Bulletin* 7 (1996): 19; E. F. Rice, *Saint Jerome in the Renaissance*

(Baltimore, MD: Johns Hopkins University Press, 1985); Brian Cummings, *The Literary Culture of the Reformation: Grammar and Grace* (Oxford: Oxford University Press, 2002), 3–5.

15. Jardine, *Erasmus, Man of Letters*, 43–44 and, for a detailed consideration of Erasmus's identification with Jerome, her chap. 2.

16. Erasmus, *Life of Jerome*, 35.

17. Ibid., 35, 33. Similarly, in Erasmus's colloquy "The Soldier and the Carthusian," Erasmus "suggests a life given more to quiet study than to devotional exercises," as its editor remarks; see *Collected Works of Erasmus*, vol. 39, *Colloquies*, ed. and trans. Craig R. Thompson (Toronto: University of Toronto Press, 1997), 329.

18. Erasmus, letter to Paul Volz, in *Opus epistolarum Erasmi Roterdami*, ed. P. S. Allen (Oxford: Clarendon, 1906–58), epistle 858.

19. By opening up this gap between sacred and secular reading, More distances himself not only from contemporary humanists like Erasmus but also from those who later followed in the Erasmian tradition of seeing religious and scientific knowledge as allied to the larger aims of active humanism; see, e.g., Sherman, *John Dee*, 135.

20. Walter Hilton, *Scala perfectionis* (Westminster: Wynkyn de Worde, 1494), (London: Julian Notary, 1507), (London: Wynkyn de Worde, 1533). I bring up the best-seller status of works like Hilton's to counter the long-held assumption that medieval religious institutions had declined to the point where their eclipse was inevitable. This argument about the continuing influence of religious institutions is forcefully made by Eamon Duffy, *The Stripping of the Altars: Traditional Religion in England, 1400–1580* (New Haven, CT: Yale University Press, 1992).

21. Jayne, *Library Catalogues of the English Renaissance*, 2d ed., 24, 29.

22. This episode in More's life is treated in Theodore Maynard, *Humanist as Hero: The Life of Sir Thomas More* (New York: Macmillan, 1947), 30–32; R. J. Schoeck, "On the Spiritual Life of St. Thomas More," *Thought* 52 (1977): 231–48; G. R. Elton, "The Real Thomas More?" in *Reformation Principle and Practice: Essays in Honour of Arthur Geoffrey Dickens* (London: Scolar Press, 1980).

23. On the architecture of Carthusian devotion, see Roberta Gilchrest, *Contemplation and Action: The Other Monasticism* (London: Leicester University Press, 1995), 197–213.

24. *Consuetudines Cartusiae*, edited and translated "by a Carthusian" (Paris: Editions du Cerf, 1984), 224.

25. See Michael Sargent, "The Transmission by the English Carthusians of Some Late Medieval Spiritual Writings," *Journal of Ecclesiastical History* 27 (1976): 225–40; Vincent Gillespie, "Vernacular Books of Devotion," in *Book Production and Publishing in Britain, 1375–1475*, ed. Jeremy Griffiths and Derek Pearsall (Cambridge: Cambridge University Press, 1989), 317–44, esp. 323–24; Germain Marc'hadour, "Saint Thomas More et les auteurs spirituals," *Moreana* 34 (1997): 27–66; A. I. Doyle, ed., "The Libraries of the Carthusians," in *Syon Abbey*, ed. Vincent Gillespie, Corpus of British Medieval Library Catalogues 9 (London: British Library, 2001), which includes a list of books and manuscripts associated with the Smithfield (London) Charterhouse (614–29). On the literary practices of the Carthusians, see also E. Margaret Thompson, *The Carthusian Order in England* (London: Society for Promoting Christian Knowledge, 1930), 313–34; Dom David Knowles,

The Religious Orders in England, vol. 2, *The End of the Middle Ages* (Cambridge: Cambridge University Press, 1957), 343.

26. "Of whyche kynde is Bonauenture of the lyfe of Chryste, Gerson of the folowynge of Christe, and the deuoute contemplatyue booke of scala perfectionis wyth such other lyke." Thomas More, *The Confutation of Tyndale's Answer*, in *Complete Works of St. Thomas More*, vol. 8, ed. L. A. Schuster (New Haven, CT: Yale University Press, 1973), 37.

27. Nicholas Watson, "Censorship and Cultural Change in Late-Medieval England: Vernacular Theology, the Oxford Translation Debate, and Arundel's Constitutions of 1409," *Speculum* 70 (1995): 822-64; Nicholas Watson, "The Middle English Mystics," in *The Cambridge History of Middle English Literature*, ed. David Wallace (Cambridge: Cambridge University Press, 1999), 539-65.

28. Elizabeth Salter, "Nicholas Love's *Myrrour of the Blesed Lyf of Jesu Christ*," *Analecta Cartusiana* 10 (1974): 1-2.

29. Thomas à Kempis, *The Imitation of Christ*, ed. B. J. H. Biggs (Oxford: Oxford University Press, 1997), 3.48.117-18.

30. Salter, "Nicholas Love's *Myrrour*," *Analecta Cartusiana* 10 (1974): 228; Watson, "Censorship and Cultural Change," *Speculum* 70 (1995): 853.

31. S. J. Ogilvie-Thomson, ed., *Walter Hilton's Mixed Life edited from Lambeth Palace MS 472* (Salzburg, Austria: Institut für Anglistik und Amerikanistik, Universität Salzburg, 1986), 14.

32. See Andrew Taylor, "Into His Secret Chamber: Reading and Privacy in Late Medieval England," in *The Practice and Representation of Reading in England*, ed. James Raven (Cambridge: Cambridge University Press, 1996), 41-61. Mark Girouard, in *Life in the English Country House: A Social and Architectural History* (New Haven, CT: Yale University Press, 1978), 156-57, traces the emergence of the "closet" in late medieval and early modern houses.

33. Kempis, *Imitation of Christ*, ed. Biggs, 26; William Abel Pantin, "Instructions for a Devout and Literate Layman," in *Medieval Learning and Literature: Essays Presented to Richard William Hunt*, ed. J. J. G. Alexander and M. T. Gibson (Oxford: Clarendon Press, 1976), 398-422; the English text is on 399, the Latin, on 421. As Pantin notes, this cell "would contain such books and papers as the man possessed" and suited the need "for reading, meditation, and prayer" (398).

34. Thomas More, *A Dialogue of Comfort against Tribulation*, in *Complete Works of St. Thomas More*, vol. 12, ed. Louis L. Martz and Frank Manley (New Haven, CT: Yale University Press, 1976), 13, 164.

35. Christopher Cannon refers to "an ingenious attempt by monastic writers to externalize the very principles on which their own religious life was founded—withdrawal from the world, regular programmes of devotion and devotional reading, contemplation—and offer them to readers who were not necessarily professed monks or nuns themselves but who wanted to emulate the monastic ideal in their personal observance." See Christopher Cannon, "Monastic Productions," in *The Cambridge History of Medieval English Literature*, ed. David Wallace (Cambridge: Cambridge University Press, 1995), 336. See also Gillespie, "Vernacular Books of Devotion," in *Book Production and Publishing in Britain*, ed. Griffiths and Pearsall, esp. 317-19; Fiona Somerset, *Clerical Discourse and Lay Audience in Late Medieval England* (Cambridge: Cambridge University Press, 1998).

36. Denys Hay, "England and the Humanities in the Fifteenth Century," in *Itinerarium Italicum: The Profile of the Italian Renaissance in the Mirror of Its European Transformations*, ed. Heiko A. Oberman and Thomas A. Brady Jr. (Leiden: Brill, 1975), 331.

37. As Peter Burke has persuasively argued, terms describing the rise of humanism frequently suggest an organic process—implied in words like "spread," "growth," or "flow"— that masks the degree of selective appropriation, uneven distribution, and contestation that humanism actually engendered. See Peter Burke, "The Spread of Italian Humanism," in *The Impact of Humanism on Western Europe*, ed. Anthony Goodman and Angus Mackay (London: Longman, 1990), 2–3. Similarly, Cummings stresses the need, against "the formidable propaganda of humanism" in narrating its own "rise," "to pay attention to a longer historical process rather than slip into the charismatic rhetoric of new learning or *Zeitgeist*" (*Literary Culture of the Reformation*, 26, 20).

38. Anthony Grafton and Lisa Jardine, *From Humanism to the Humanities: Education and the Liberal Arts in Fifteenth- and Sixteenth-Century Europe* (Cambridge, MA: Harvard University Press, 1986), 144.

39. Interestingly, some evidence from contemporary private libraries supports a parallel division between Carthusian-tinged vernacular devotion and Erasmian-tinged humanism, with More's own works collected in the former. See Margery H. Smith, "Some Humanist Libraries in Early Tudor Cambridge," *Sixteenth Century Journal* 5 (1974): 15–34, which offers examples of libraries like that of William Davye (d. 1545), which included "revelations sancta brigitte" and "vita sermons bonaventuram" alongside "Sir T. More dyalogges" (25–26), and that of John Cheswryght (d. 1537), which included "the crafte to lyve well et to dye well" (27) and "de contemptu mundi" along with "a dyaloge of Sr Thomas More (29). In contrast to these are the humanist library of William Framyngham (d. 1537), which included Plutarch, Theophrastus, and "Erasmus de ratio studii" (30), and that of Thomas Ocley (d. 1539), which included four copies of Cicero's *De officiis* (33). Although Smith rightly cautions that book lists alone cannot tell us how the books were read, she still finds these diverse contents significant. Yet Leedham-Green's inventories of Cambridge libraries from the same time also show that contemplative and humanist books were occasionally held in the same collections; for example, Roger Soresby (d. 1546) owned Hilton's *Scala perfectionis* as well as works by Pliny, Ovid, Horace, and Erasmus; see Leedham-Green, *Books in Cambridge Inventories*, 1.74. Similarly, the Bridgettine House of Syon, which shows many parallels with the Carthusian houses, owned editions of Cicero, Virgil, Horace, Pliny, and Lucian and other humanist works, indicating that More's division between humanist and contemplative literacies was not uniformly observed when it came to actual libraries. See Vincent Gillespie, ed., *Syon Abbey*, Corpus of British Medieval Library Catalogues (London: British Library, 2001), lvi–lvii.

40. The term *translatio studii*, despite its medieval origins, has become associated with the humanist project and cultural transmission: see Karlheinz Stierle, "*Translatio Studii* and Renaissance: From Vertical to Horizontal Translation," in *The Translatability of Cultures: Figurations of the Space Between*, ed. Sanford Budick and Wolfgang Iser (Stanford, CA: Stanford University Press, 1996), 55–67; R. J. Schoeck, "Erasmus in England, 1499–1517: *Translatio Studii* and the *Studia Humanitatis*," *Classical and Modern Literature: A Quarterly* 7 (1987): 269–83. See also Gerald C. Bruns, "What Is Tradition?" *New Literary History* 22 (1991): 1–21, esp. 4.

41. James McConica, "The Patrimony of Thomas More," in *History and Imagination: Essays in Honour of H. R. Trevor-Roper*, ed. Hugh Lloyd-Jones, Valerie Pearl, and Blair Worden (London: Gerald Duckworth, 1981), 58. Catherine Jarrott articulates a long-prevailing view of this apparent conflict in More's "vocation" thus: "Is More the last of the great medievalists, forced by political circumstances to play a secular role which he really did not want? Or is he the first offspring of the English Renaissance, asserting the value of secular and temporal concerns against the sterile otherworldliness of an outlook no longer capable of comprehending the needs of an expanding age?" See her "The Vocation of St. Thomas More," *American Benedictine Review* 12 (1961): 298–309, quotation on 298.

42. Stephen Greenblatt, *Renaissance Self-Fashioning: From More to Shakespeare* (Chicago: University of Chicago Press, 1980), 32.

43. "It is, in effect, easy to see what attracted More to Pico," observes Alistair Fox. "The young Pico was an image of one side of himself: the humanist prodigy." See Alistair Fox, *Thomas More: History and Providence* (Oxford: Basil Blackwell, 1982), 30. The classic study responsible for linking Pico and More in a genealogy of humanism is R. W. Chambers, *Thomas More* (New York: Harcourt, Brace, 1935). For the same point, see also P. O. Kristeller, "Thomas More as a Renaissance Humanist," *Moreana* 65–66 (1980): 5–22, esp. 12.

44. Thomas Stapleton, *The Life and Illustrious Martyrdom of Sir Thomas More*, ed. E. E. Reynolds, trans. Philip E. Hallett (London: Burns and Oates, 1966), 9.

45. See A. S. G. Edwards, introduction to *Life of Pico*, in *Complete Works of St. Thomas More*, vol. 1, *English Poems, "Life of Pico," "The Last Things,"* ed. Anthony S. Edwards, Katherine G. Rodgers, and Clarence H. Miller (New Haven, CT: Yale University Press, 1997), 65. On the dedication to Joyce Leigh, see also M. P. Gilmore, "More's Translation of Gianfrancesco Pico's Biography," in *L'opera e il pensiero di Giovanni Pico della Mirandola nella storia dell'umanesimo*, 2 vols. (Florence: Nella sede dell'Istituto, 1965), 1.301–4.

46. For the "occulta concatenatio" in Pico's thought, see Ernst Cassirer, "Giovanni Pico della Mirandola: A Study in the History of Renaissance Ideas," *Journal of the History of Ideas* 3 (1942): 123–44, esp. 131.

47. See Pearl Kibre, *The Library of Pico della Mirandola* (New York: Columbia University Press, 1936). On Pico's pursuit of the "occulta concatenatio" linking the world's ideas, see E. H. Harbison, *The Christian Scholar in the Age of the Reformation* (New York: Charles Scribner's Sons, 1956), 52–53; Cassirer, "Giovanni Pico della Mirandola," *Journal of the History of Ideas* 3 (1942): 123–44.

48. Anthony Grafton, *Commerce with the Classics: Ancient Books and Renaissance Readers* (Ann Arbor: University of Michigan Press, 1997), 104.

49. Jardine, *Erasmus, Man of Letters*, 43–44.

50. Kibre, *Library of Pico della Mirandola*, 15.

51. *Complete Works of St. Thomas More*, ed. Edwards, Rodgers, and Miller, 1.87. Subsequent quotations from More's translation of the *Life of Pico* will be from this edition, with the page numbers given parenthetically in the text.

52. Edwards comments that More's largest excision to his source text "removes Gianfranco's account of Pico's works and the extent of his library. The effect is clearly to reduce Gianfrancesco's emphasis on the range of Pico's intellectual interests, particularly those

that concerned the occult and esoteric, which More seemingly saw as deflecting attention from the devotional focus he wished to impose on his work" (introduction to *Life of Pico*, in *Complete Works of St. Thomas More*, ed. Edwards, Rodgers, and Miller, 1.xlvi). Gianfrancesco's original is supplied as appendix A to this edition; the passages describing Pico's "Bibliothecas amplas" appear on 304–15.

53. Grafton, *Commerce with the Classics*, 93–94.

54. Cited by Charles B. Schmitt, "Gianfrancesco Pico's Attitude toward His Uncle," in *L'opera e il pensiero di Giovanni Pico della Mirandola nella storia dell'umanesimo*, 2.309.

55. Giovanni Pico della Mirandola, *Oration on the Dignity of Man*, trans. A. Robert Caponigri (Chicago: Gateway Editions, 1956), 21.

56. "Quin sunt nonnulli qui cognitionem rerum naturalium, velut viam sibi, qua transcendant in supernarum contemplationem, praestruunt, iterque per philosophiam, et liberal artes"; Thomas More, "Letter to the University of Oxford," in *Complete Works of St. Thomas More*, vol. 15, *In Defense of Humanism*, ed. Daniel Kinney (New Haven, CT: Yale University Press, 1986), 138–39.

57. Pantin, "Instructions for a Devout and Literate Layman," in *Medieval Learning and Literature*, ed. Alexander and Gibson, 406.

58. Andrew Taylor, "Authors, Scribes, Patrons and Books," in *The Idea of the Vernacular: An Anthology of Middle English Literary Theory, 1280–1520*, ed. Jocelyn Wogan-Browne et al. (University Park, PA: Pennsylvania State University Press, 1999), 363.

59. Edwards, introduction to *Life of Pico*, in *Complete Works of St. Thomas More*, ed. Edwards, Rodgers, and Miller, 1.lvi. For examples and similar woodcuts used as contemplative objects, see Martha W. Driver, *The Image in Print: Book Illustration in Late Medieval England and Its Sources* (London: British Library, 2004).

60. Thomas More, *The Complete Works of St. Thomas More*, vol. 8, *The Confutation of Tyndale's Answer*, ed. Louis A. Schuster et al. (New Haven, CT: Yale University Press, 1973), 37.

61. Richard Whitford, *Werke of Preparation unto Communion* (London, 1537), sig. Fiiii r–v.

62. See Mary Carruthers, *The Book of Memory: A Study of Memory in Medieval Culture* (Cambridge: Cambridge University Press, 1990), 33–35. For further devotional references to Christ as book, see Vincent Gillespie, "Strange Images of Death: The Passion in Later Medieval English Devotional and Mystical Writing," in *Zeit, Tod und Ewigkeit in der Renaissance Literature*, vol. 3, ed. James Hogg, Analecta Carthusiana 117 (Salzburg, Austria: Institut für Anglistik und Amerikanistik, Universität Salzburg, 1987), 111–59.

63. Trapp, *Erasmus, Colet and More*, 58, 127–31.

64. Thomas More, *Utopia*, in *The Complete Works of St. Thomas More*, vol. 4, ed. Edward Surtz, S.J., and J. H. Hexter (New Haven, CT: Yale University Press, 1965), 57. Subsequent references to *Utopia* will be to this edition, with page numbers given parenthetically in the text.

65. For an assessment of English humanism and More's role within it, see the two essays by Alistair Fox, "Facts and Fallacies: Interpreting English Humanism" and "English Humanism and the Body Politic," in *Reassessing the Henrician Age: Humanism, Politics, and Reform, 1500–1550*, by Alistair Fox and John Guy (New York: Blackwell, 1986), 9–51.

66. Fox, *Thomas More*, 4.

67. Erasmus, *Correspondence* (Sherbrooke, QC: Centre d'Études de la Renaissance, 1985), 90. See also Walter M. Gordon, "The Monastic Achievement and More's Utopian Dream," *Medievalia et humanistica*, n.s., 9 (1979): 200, 201. D. B. Fenlon, in "England and Europe: *Utopia* and Its Aftermath," *Transactions of the Royal Historical Society*, 5th ser., 25 (1975): 115–35, argues that More's *Utopia* is "a book about the infusion of monastic virtues onto the body politic" (126).

68. This reading engages a question that has been a focal point of recent criticism on the *Utopia:* what are the contemporary analogues of Utopian society, and to what extent does More's work endorse them? Like David Wootton, I find that Utopia "pays homage to Erasmian principles," while like Hanan Yoran, I also find that More's work contains "a hidden level of meaning which contradicts central notions of Erasmian humanism and subverts the ontological and epistemological presuppositions of humanist discourse." See Wootton, "Friendship Portrayed: A New Account of Utopia," *History Workshop Journal* 45 (1998): 29–47, quotation on 30; Hanan Yoran, "More's Utopia and Erasmus's No-place," *English Literary Renaissance*, 2005, 3–30, quotation on 4. Where Alistair Fox finds that *Utopia* "serves simultaneously to advertise More's enthusiastic commitment to Erasmian humanism, and his sceptical reservations about it," I find the former seriously outweighed by the latter; see Fox, "Paradoxical Equivocation: The Self-Subversiveness of Thomas More's *Utopia*," in his *Politics and Literature in the Reigns of Henry VII and Henry VIII* (Oxford: Blackwell, 1989), 92–107, quotation on 105.

69. On the "Hellenism" of the Utopians, which aligns them against the Ciceronian ideals of Italian "civic humanism," see Eric Nelson, "Utopia through Italian Eyes: Thomas More and the Critics of Italian Humanism," *Renaissance Quarterly* 59 (2006): 1029–57.

70. Louis Marin, *Utopics: Spatial Play*, trans. Robert A. Vollrath (London: Macmillan, 1984), 177.

71. *Complete Works of St. Thomas More*, vol. 4, *Utopia*, ed. Surtz and Hexter, 183.

72. Frances A. Yates suggests that the Utopians' hermeticism reflects Pico's influence; see her *Giordano Bruno and the Hermetic Tradition* (1964; repr., Chicago: University of Chicago Press, 1979), 185–87. For a catalogue of Pico's library, see Kibre, *Library of Pico della Mirandola*.

73. Erasmus, *De ratione studii (On the Method of Study)*, trans. Brian McGregor, in *Collected Works of Erasmus: Literary and Educational Writings 2*, ed. Craig R. Thompson (Toronto: University of Toronto Press, 1978), 669, 673.

74. Among other studies on the topic, see Jardine, *Erasmus, Man of Letters;* James K. Cameron, "Humanism in the Low Countries," in *Impact of Humanism on Western Europe*, ed. Goodman and Mackay, esp. 143–47; J. B. Trapp, "The Humanist Book," in *The Cambridge History of the Book in Britain*, vol. 3, *1400–1557*, ed. Lotte Hellinga and J. B. Trapp (Cambridge: Cambridge University Press, 1999).

75. Carlson, *English Humanist Books*, 141.

76. See Nicolas Barker, "The Aldine Italic," in *A Millennium of the Book: Production, Design and Illustration in Manuscript and Print, 900–1900*, ed. Robin Myers and Michael Harris (Winchester: St. Paul's Bibliographies, 1994). On Aldus more broadly, see Martin Lowry, *The World of Aldus Manutius: Business and Scholarship in Renaissance Venice* (Oxford: Basil Blackwell, 1979).

77. Stanley Morison, *Four Centuries of Fine Printing* (New York: Barnes and Noble, 1960), 23; Nicolas Barker, "The Aldine Roman at Paris, 1530–1535," *The Library*, 5th ser., 29 (1974): 5–20.

78. On Aldus's "libri portatiles," see Luigi Balsamo, "A Note on the Aldine Italic Type and Octavo Format," trans. Jeremy Parzen, in *The 1501 Aldine Edition of Le cose volgari de Messer Francesco Petrarcha*, facs. repr. (Lower Woodford, UK: Alecto Historical Editions, 1997), 24; H. George Fletcher, "The Portable Library," in *In Praise of Aldus Manutius: A Quincentenary Exhibition, the Pierpont Morgan Library, New York* (Los Angeles: UCLA University Research Library, Department of Special Collections, 1995), 49–54.

79. In the *Adagia*, 2.1.1, Erasmus specifically praises the "library without walls" that Aldus creates with his portable books: see Grafton, *Commerce with the Classics*, 45.

80. See Jardine, *Erasmus, Man of Letters*, 43–44.

81. Martin Davies, *Aldus Manutius: Printer and Publisher of Renaissance Venice* (Tempe: Arizona Center for Medieval and Renaissance Studies, 1999), 13. See also Ralph Hexter, "Aldus, Greek, and the Shape of the 'Classical Corpus,'" in *Aldus Manutius and Renaissance Culture: Essays in Memory of Franklin D. Murphy; Acts of an International Conference, Venice and Florence, 14–17 June 1994*, ed. David S. Zeidberg and Fiorella Gioffredi Superbi (Florence: Olschki, 1998), 143–60.

82. Schoeck, "Erasmus in England," *Classical and Modern Literature: A Quarterly* 7 (1987).

83. See Charles Trinkaus, *The Scope of Renaissance Humanism* (Ann Arbor: University of Michigan Press, 1983), 141; Anthony Grafton and Ann Blair, "Reassessing Humanism and Science," introduction to special issue, *Journal of the History of Ideas* 53 (1992): 535–40; Karen M. Reeds, "Renaissance Humanism and Botany," *Annals of Science* 33 (1976): 519–42.

84. *Aristotelis et Theophrastes opera*, vol. 2 (Venice: Aldus Manutius, 1497); Erasmus's copy is now owned by Wells Cathedral. See C. B. L. Barr and David Selwyn, "Major Ecclesiastical Libraries: From Reformation to Civil War," in *The Cambridge History of Libraries in Britain and Ireland*, vol. 1, *To 1640*, ed. Elisabeth Leedham-Green and Teresa Webber (Cambridge: Cambridge University Press, 2006), 378–79.

85. Charles B. Schmitt, "Theophrastus in the Middle Ages," *Viator* 2 (1971): 251–70, esp. 253.

86. T. Keith Dix, "Aristotle's 'Peripatetic' Library," in *Lost Libraries: The Destruction of Great Book Collections since Antiquity*, ed. James Raven (New York: Palgrave Macmillan, 2004): 58–74.

87. Strabo, *Geography*, ed. and trans. H. C. Hamilton and W. Falconer, 3 vols. (London: G. Bell, 1903–6), 13.1.54.

88. Louis Marin, *Utopics: Spatial Play*, trans. Robert A. Vollrath (Atlantic Highlands, NJ: Humanities Press, 1984), 178. On this episode see also Richard Halpern, *The Poetics of Primitive Accumulation: English Renaissance Culture and the Genealogy of Capital* (Ithaca, NY: Cornell University Press, 1991), 150; Nicole S. Morgan, "Le petit singe cercopithèque mangeur de bibliothèque," *Moreana* 118–19 (1994): 141–54.

89. Marin, *Utopics*, 178–79. Marin's original French refers to the animal as *"le singe"*; see Marin, *Utopiques: Jeux d'espaces* (Paris: Editions de Minuit, 1973), 230. See also

H. W. Janson, *Apes and Ape Lore in the Middle Ages and the Renaissance* (London: War-burg Institute, 1952), 208–12; Kathleen Coyne Kelly, "If a Trope Looks Like a Trope: The Ape Metaphor in Middle English Texts," *Allegorica* 16 (1995): 3–16, on the medieval history of the *simia-similis* trope.

90. For More's Latin, see Thomas More, *L'Utopie*, ed. Marie Delcourt (Geneva: Li-brairie Droz, 1983), 156; Thomas Elyot, *Dictionary (1538)*, ed. R. C. Alston (Menston, UK: Scolar Press, 1970), xviib.

91. Ovid, *Metamorphoses*, ed. and trans. D. E. Hill (Warminster: Aris and Phillips, 2000), 14.91–94. For a discussion of the literary heritage of the Kerkopes, see P. M. C. Forbes Irving, *Metamorphosis in Greek Myths* (Oxford: Clarendon Press, 1990), 292; Catherine Connors, "Monkey Business: Imitation, Authenticity, and Identity from Pithek-oussai to Plautus," *Classical Antiquity* 23, no. 2 (2004): 179–207.

92. Janson, *Apes and Ape Lore*, 208–12. On the ways in which "simian behavior holds the mirror up to human folly," see Kenneth Gouwens, "Human Exceptionalism," in *The Renaissance World*, ed. John Jeffries Martin (Routledge, forthcoming); I am grateful to Professor Gouwens for sharing his unpublished work on Renaissance apes with me.

93. Leonardo da Vinci, *The Notebooks of Leonardo da Vinci*, ed. Irma A. Richter (Oxford: Oxford University Press, 1998), 282.

94. The name Tricius Apinatus is a reference to Martial's *Epigrams*, 14.1; see *Utopia by Sir Thomas More, translated by Ralph Robynson, 1556*, ed. David Harris Sacks (Boston: Bedford/St. Martin's, 1999), 166n161. On the meaning of Hythloday's name, see Geoffrey Elton, "Humanism in England," in *Impact of Humanism on Western Europe*, ed. Good-man and Mackay, 267.

95. *A fruteful, and pleasaunt worke of the beste state of a publyque weale, and the newe yle called Vtopia*, trans. Raphe Robynson (London, 1556), sig. Ni r. Robinson's pun and anagram are consistent with More's own encryption of his name throughout his work: see John M. Perlette, "Of Sites and Parasites: The Centrality of the Marginal Anecdote in Book 1 of More's *Utopia*," *English Literary History* 54 (1987): 231–52, esp. 243; Germain Marc'hadour, "A Name for All Seasons," in *Essential Articles for the Study of Thomas More*, ed. Sylvester and Marc'hadour, 539–62.

96. On More's monkeys, see Anne Lake Prescott, "The Ambivalent Heart: Thomas More's Merry Tales," *Criticism* 45 (2003): 417–33, esp. 419. On the monkey in the Holbein portrait, see David R. Smith, "Portrait and Counter-portrait in Holbein's *The Family of Sir Thomas More*," *Art Bulletin* 87, part 3 (September 2005): 484–506. Erasmus mentions "the distinguished Englishman, Thomas More," who "kept at home a large monkey," in "Amicitia," in *Collected Works of Erasmus*, vol. 40, *Colloquies*, ed. and trans. Craig R. Thompson (Toronto: University of Toronto Press, 1997), 1043, 1051–52, n. 72.

97. Arguing in favor of humanist-reformer synthesis, James McConica's *English Hu-manists and Reformation Politics under Henry VIII and Edward VI* (Oxford: Clarendon Press, 1965) continues to exert considerable influence. Maria Dowling offers a nuanced rereading of this synthesis in *Humanism in the Age of Henry VIII* (London: Croom Helm, 1986), as do Peter Matheson, "Humanism and Reform Movements," and Richard Tuck, "Humanism and Political Thought," both in *Impact of Humanism on Western Europe*, ed. Goodman and MacKay.

98. As Jonathan Woolfson observes, "We disregard the relationship between human-ism and the Reformation only by reducing both to monoliths"; introduction to *Reassess-ing Tudor Humanism*, ed. Woolfson (New York: Palgrave Macmillan, 2002), 9.

99. Ibid., 4, 9–11; Alistair Fox, "Interpreting English Humanism," in *Reassessing the Henrician Age*, by Fox and Guy.

100. McConica, *English Humanists and Reformation Politics*, 191–94. Cromwell's contributions to English humanism—particularly his adaptation of humanist learning to political ends—have been given visibility in the work of G. R. Elton: see especially *Reform and Renewal: Thomas Cromwell and the Common Weal* (Cambridge: Cambridge Uni-versity Press, 1973). See also Arthur B. Ferguson, *The Articulate Citizen and the English Renaissance* (Durham, NC: Duke University Press, 1965); Dowling, *Humanism in the Age of Henry VIII*. Cromwell's influence on Reformation English humanism has been reaf-firmed in the recent and influential work of Alistair Fox, especially "English Humanism and the Body Politic," in *Reassessing the Henrician Age*, where he argues that "for the real humanist contribution to English politics one must look to a radically different type of humanism, evident in the circle of scholars fostered by Thomas Cromwell" (47).

101. This letter is cited and discussed by Dowling, *Humanism in the Age of Henry VIII*, 96–97.

102. On Cromwell and the Henrician "new men," see A. G. Dickens, *The English Reformation* (New York: Schocken Books, 1964), 109–10.

103. *The Commendation of matrimony, made by Cornelius Agrippa, [et] translated into englysshe by Dauid Clapam* (London, 1540), epistle. On other English translations of humanist works dedicated to Cromwell, see A. G. Dickens and Whitney R. D. Jones, *Erasmus the Reformer* (London: Methuen, 1994), 198–200.

104. See *Two Renaissance Book Hunters: The Letters of Poggius Bracciolini to Nico-laus De Niccolis*, trans. Phyllis Walter Goodhart Gordan (1974; repr., New York: Columbia University Press, 1991).

105. John Sherren Brewer, Robert Henry Brodie, and James Gairdner, eds., *Letters and Papers, Foreign and Domestic, of the Reign of Henry VIII*, 21 vols. (1862; repr., London: Kraus Reprint, 1965), 5.1034. Subsequent references to this source will be abbreviated LP.

106. See James P. Carley, "The Dispersal of the Monastic Libraries and the Salvaging of the Spoils," in *Cambridge History of Libraries in Britain and Ireland*, ed. Leedham-Green and Webber, 1.270–274, 291.

107. LP 9.529.

108. James P. Carley, ed., *The Libraries of King Henry VIII*, Corpus of British Medieval Library Catalogues 7 (London: British Library, 2000), xxxv.

109. Ibid.

110. LP 9.134.

111. LP 9.42.

112. Leonard E. Whatmore, *The Carthusians under King Henry the Eighth*, Analecta Cartusiana 109 (Salzburg, Austria: Institut für Anglistik und Amerikanistik, Universität Salzburg, 1983).

113. Francis Aidan Gasquet, *Henry VIII and the English Monasteries* (London: J. Hodges, 1889), 1.232.

114. Ibid., 234.

115. See Watson, "Censorship and Cultural Change," *Speculum* 70 (1995): 822–64.

116. Gasquet, *Henry VIII and English Monasteries*, 1.226.

117. Roper, *Life of Sir Thomas More*, 239. G. W. Elton draws out this analogy when he observes that More "found the peace of the monk's cell in prison." See Elton, "Humanism in England," in *The Impact of Humanism*, ed. Goodman and MacKay, 266.

118. Louis L. Martz and Richard S. Sylvester, *Thomas More's Prayer Book: A Facsimile Reproduction of the Annotated Pages* (New Haven, CT: Yale University Press, 1969), 3, 5.

119. Mary C. Erler points out that More's notes in his psalter "reflect his anxieties and fears as he read meditatively through the psalms while in the top and bottom margins of the book of hours More wrote the phrases of his 'Godly Meditation'—each phrase a self-contained injunction to himself"; Erler, "Devotional Literature," in *Cambridge History of the Book in Britain*, vol. 3, *1400–1557*, ed. Lotte Hellinga and J. B. Trapp (Cambridge: Cambridge University Press, 1999), 511.

120. Roper, *Life of Sir Thomas More*, 244.

121. See Sir Richard Morison, *A Remedy for Sedition wherein are contained many things concerning the true and loyal obeisance that commons owe unto their prince and sovereign lord the King (1536)*, reprinted in David Sandler Berkowitz, ed., *Humanist Scholarship and Public Order: Two Tracts against the Pilgrimage of Grace by Sir Richard Morison* (Washington, DC: Folger Shakespeare Library Folger Books, 1984), which commends "a very good custom" among the ancient Locrians: "No man might there come to speak against a law that was constituted by such as had authority to make it except he came to the disputation thereof with a cord about his neck. If he proved the law to be naught, then he cast off the cord and was highly commended; but if he did attempt it and after failed of his purpose, he was forthwith trussed up" (118).

122. On More's library and the fate of More's books, see Trapp, *Erasmus, Colet and More*, 43–64; also Schoeck, "Sir Thomas More, Humanist and Lawyer," in *Essential Articles for the Study of Thomas More*, ed. Sylvester and Marc'hadour, 575.

123. "Ro:Ba.," *The Lyfe of Syr Thomas More* (1599), ed. E. V. Hitchcock and P. G. Hallet (1950; repr., Woodbridge: Boydell and Brewer, 1996), 119.

124. Raymond Irwin, *The English Library: Sources and History* (London: George Allen and Unwin, 1966), 188.

125. The best full-scale treatment of Starkey's career and humanism is also the most recent: Thomas F. Mayer, *Thomas Starkey and the Commonweal: Humanist Politics and Religion in the Reign of Henry VIII* (Cambridge: Cambridge University Press, 1989).

126. See Thomas F. Mayer, *Reginald Pole: Prince and Prophet* (Cambridge: Cambridge University Press, 2000), 56.

127. Mayer, *Thomas Starkey and the Commonweal*, 97.

128. On Starkey's pragmatic humanism, see Fox, "English Humanism and the Body Politic," in *Reassessing the Henrician Age*, by Fox and Guy, 47–50.

129. British Library, Cotton MS Nero B. vi, fol. 169r; cited in Mayer, *Thomas Starkey and the Commonweal*, 97.

130. Sidney J. Herrtage, ed., *England in the Reign of King Henry the Eighth*, part 1, *Starkey's Life and Letters*, Early English Text Society, O.S. 32 (London: N. Trübner, 1878), x.

131. Vincent Gillespie, "The Book and the Brotherhood: Reflections on the Lost Library of Syon Abbey," in *The English Medieval Book: Studies in Memory of Jeremy Griffiths*, ed. A. S. G. Edwards, Vincent Gillespie, and Ralph Hanna (London: British Library, 2000), 185–208; Christopher de Hamel, *Syon Abbey: The Library of the Bridgettine Nuns and Their Peregrinations after the Reformation* (London: Roxburghe Club, 1991); Mary Carpenter Erler, "Syon Abbey's Care for Books: Its Sacristan's Account Rolls 1506/7–1535/6," *Scriptorium* 2 (1985): 293–307; James Hogg, ed., *The Speculum Devotorum of an Anonymous Carthusian of Sheen, Edited from the Manuscripts Cambridge University Library Gg.I.6 and Foyle, with an Introduction and a Glossary, II and III. Text: Parts 1 and 2* (Salzburg, Austria: Institut für Anglistik und Amerikanistik, Universität Salzburg, 1973–74).

132. Thomas Starkey, *Dialogue between Cardinal Pole and Thomas Lupset*, in *England in the Reign of King Henry the Eighth*, part 2, ed. J. M. Cowper, Early English Text Society, O.S. 31 (London: N. Trübner, 1878), 2–3. Subsequent quotations will be from this edition, with the page numbers given parenthetically in the text.

133. See Joseph G. Dwyer's introduction to his edition of *Pole's Defense of the Unity of the Church* (Westminster, MD: Newman Press, 1965), xiv. Thomas Mayer examines the evidence of Pole's position on the Supremacy, finding that "a slight balance of the exceptionally difficult evidence suggests that Pole opposed that solution to the divorce from the beginning" (*Reginald Pole*, 101).

134. This letter is quoted at length in Herrtage, *England in the Reign of King Henry the Eighth*, part 1; for the quotation here see lvii.

135. Pearl Hogrefe aptly calls one of Elyot's letters to Cromwell "a masterpiece of evasion or of tact, depending on the point of view." See her *The Life and Times of Sir Thomas Elyot, Englishman* (Ames: Iowa State University Press, 1967), 218. Alistair Fox sees Elyot's deliberate obscurity in moments like this as an adaptation of "the Morean indirect approach"; see Fox, "Sir Thomas Elyot and the Humanist Dilemma," in *Reassessing the Henrician Age*, by Fox and Guy, 62.

136. K. J. Wilson, "The Letters of Sir Thomas Elyot," *Studies in Philology* 73 (1976): 31, 32n5. Subsequent quotations from Elyot's letters will be from this edition, with the page numbers given parenthetically in the text. For the meaning of "usque ad aras," see Dom David Knowles, *The Religious Orders in England*, vol. 3, *The Tudor Age* (Cambridge: Cambridge University Press, 1961), 293n2. Elyot's definition of the proverb is cited and discussed by John M. Major, *Sir Thomas Elyot and Renaissance Humanism* (Lincoln: University of Nebraska Press, 1964), 91.

137. Greg Walker, *Writing under Tyranny: English Literature and the Henrician Reformation* (Oxford: Oxford University Press, 2005), 131.

138. Walker critiques a position held by Stanford E. Lehmberg, *Sir Thomas Elyot, Tudor Humanist* (Austin: University of Texas Press, 1960), 150–51; see Walker, *Writing under Tyranny*, 130 and passim.

139. Walker, *Writing under Tyranny*, 227–29.

140. Ibid.; see also Hogrefe, *Life and Times*, 212–15.

141. Elyot's involvement in the dissolution is a fact that his modern biographers have recognized but downplayed; thus, Hogrefe acknowledges Elyot's employment by the commission but distances him from its actions, surmising, "Elyot would not have

approved of the [brutal] methods of the two prominent commissioners, Richard Leighton and Thomas Leigh," and suggesting that his acceptance of the post does not imply his agreement with its objectives, since "he could hardly have refused without grave risk"; see Hogrefe, *Life and Times*, 241, 243. On this episode in Elyot's biography, see also Lehmberg, *Sir Thomas Elyot*, 157–58.

142. J. S. Brewer et al., eds., *Letters and Papers, Foreign and Domestic, of the Reign of Henry VIII*, 36 vols. (London, 1862–1932), 8.149.52.

143. Lehmberg, *Sir Thomas Elyot*, 158.

144. On the Oxford visitation, see Dowling, *Humanism in the Age of Henry VIII*, 96–97.

145. See G. H. Cook, *Letters to Cromwell and Others on the Suppression of the Monasteries* (London: John Baker, 1965), 5–6; "The First Act of Suppression, 1536," is reprinted on 256.

146. See F. D. Logan, "The First Royal Visitation of the English Universities, 1535," *English Historical Review* 106 (1991): 861–88, esp. 863.

147. Dr. Layton to Cromwell, from British Library, Cotton MS Faustina C. vi, fol. 205, reprinted in Thomas Wright, ed., *Three Chapters of Letters Relating to the Suppression of Monasteries* (London: Camden Society, 1843), 71.

148. I owe this point to Peter Stallybrass.

149. Erasmus, "Letter to Dorp," trans. R. A. B. Mynors and D. F. S. Tomson, in *Collected Works of Erasmus*, vol. 71, *Controversies*, ed. J. K. Sowards (Toronto: University of Toronto Press, 1993), 15. On the targeting of Duns Scotus in the visitation, see Logan, "First Royal Visitation," *English Historical Review* 106 (1991): 866, 877. Andrew Watson considers the implications and accuracy of Layton's claim at length in *Medieval Manuscripts in Post-medieval England* (Aldershot, Hants.: Ashgate, 2004), 71.

150. Wright, *Three Chapters of Letters Relating to the Suppression of Monasteries*, 70.

151. Ibid., 71. On the centrality of Greek to the humanist program, see Eric Nelson, "Utopia through Italian Eyes: Thomas More and the Critics of Civic Humanism," *Renaissance Quarterly* 59 (2006): 1029–57.

152. Wright, *Three Chapters of Letters Relating to the Suppression of Monasteries*, 71.

153. Logan, "First Royal Visitation," *English Historical Review* 106 (1991): 867.

154. Mayer, *Thomas Starkey and the Commonweal*, 203; for a consideration of humanist legal reform, see Richard Helgerson, "Writing against Writing: Humanism and the Form of Coke's Institutes," *Modern Language Quarterly: A Journal of Literary History* 51 (June 1990): 224–48.

155. Sir Thomas Elyot, *Pasquil the Playne*, in *Four Political Treatises by Sir Thomas Elyot*, ed. Lillian Gottesman (Gainesville, FL: Scholars' Facsimiles and Reprints, 1967), 78, 79, 63–64, 65.

156. Paul L. Hughes and James F. Larkin, eds., *Tudor Royal Proclamations*, 3 vols. (New Haven, CT: Yale University Press, 1964), 1.235–37. As Tom Betteridge observes, "Elyot's letter [to Cromwell] reflects a world in which knowledge and texts are not only subject to control but can be subjected to retrospective prohibition"; *Literature and Politics in the English Reformation* (Manchester: Manchester University Press, 2004), 54.

157. On the textual conventions of the miscellany, see Stephen G. Nichols and Siegfried Wenzel, eds., *The Whole Book: Cultural Perspectives on the Medieval Miscellany* (Ann Arbor: University of Michigan Press, 1996); Julia Boffey and John Thompson, "Anthologies and Miscellanies: Production and Choice of Texts," in *Book Production and Publishing in Britain, 1375–1475*, ed. Jeremy Griffiths and Derek Pearsall (Cambridge: Cambridge University Press, 1989), 279–315; Christopher de Hamel, "Medieval Library Catalogues," in *Pioneers in Bibliography*, ed. Robin Myers and Michael Harris (London: St. Paul's Bibliographies, 1988), 11–23, esp. 17–18; Alexandra Gillespie, "Poets, Printers, and Early English Sammelbände," *Huntington Library Quarterly* 67 (2004): 189–214.

158. As Elyot states in the preface, "almost two yeres passed" between his visit to the king's library and the publication of his *Dictionary*, which would place his visit sometime in 1536/37. Unless otherwise noted, all references to Elyot's *Dictionary* are to Thomas Elyot, *Dictionary (1538)*, ed. R. C. Alston (Menston: Scolar Press, 1970), with page numbers given parenthetically in the text. On Elyot's *Dictionary*, see Stephen Merriam Foley, "Coming to Terms: Thomas Elyot's Definitions and the Particularity of Human Letters," *English Literary History* 61 (1994): 211–30; John Considine, "Narrative and Persuasion in Early Modern English Dictionaries and Phrasebooks," *Review of English Studies*, n.s., 52 (2001): 195–207; Seth Lerer, *Error and the Academic Self* (New York: Columbia University Press, 2002), 30–34.

159. Tyldesley was not only the royal librarian but also seems to have played a role in the visitations; hence, William Holleway, prior of Bath, reports to Cromwell on 25 September 1535, "I have send your maistershipp hereyn an old boke *Opera Anselmi* which one William Tildysley after scrutinye made here in my librarye willed me to send unto youe by the kynge ys grace and commawndment" (LP 9.426).

160. Carley, *Libraries of King Henry VIII*, lxvi, lxxii. See also Lloyd W. Daly, *Contributions to a History of Alphabetization in Antiquity and the Middle Ages*, Collection Latomus, vol. 90 (Brussels: Latomus, 1967); de Hamel, "Medieval Library Catalogues," in *Pioneers in Bibliography*, ed. Myers and Harris, 15–17.

161. See Norman L. Jones, "Matthew Parker, John Bale, and the Magdeburg Centuriators," *Sixteenth Century Journal* 12 (1981): 35–49; H. Fischer, "Conrad Gessner, 1516–1565, as Bibliographer and Encyclopedist," *The Library*, 5th ser., 21 (1966): 269–81. On book classifications, see Leedham-Green, *Books in Cambridge Inventories*, 1.xxiv.

162. Mark Liddell, ed., *The Middle English Translation of Palladius, "De Re Rustica"* (Berlin: E. Ebering, 1896), 22. See also chap. 1 above.

163. Foley, "Coming to Terms," *English Literary History* 61 (1994): 219.

164. Carley, "The Dispersal of the Monastic Libraries and the Salvaging of the Spoils," in *Cambridge History of Libraries in Britain and Ireland*, ed. Leedham-Green and Webber, 1.270.

165. See Jakob Ziegler, *Contra haereticos Valdenses*, cited in Carley, *Libraries of King Henry VIII*, 47.

166. Carley, *Libraries of King Henry VIII*, 47.

167. Thus, Layton promises Cromwell, "ye shalle receve a bowke of our lades miracles well able to mache the Canterberies Tailes. Such a bowke of dremes as ye never saw wich I fownde in the librarie." The royal library itself, however, contained such works as "L'assomption nostre Dame," "De dignitate et excellentia uirginis gloriosae," "Hymna de

beata uirgine," "Oratio de beata uirgine," and "Plainte de la vierge" (Carley, *Libraries of King Henry VIII*, 394).

168. G. F. Warner and J. P. Gilson, *British Museum: Catalogue of Western Manuscripts in the Old Royal and King's Collections*, 4 vols. (London: British Museum, 1921), 1.xv.

169. "The Additions," in *The Dictionary of Syr Thomas Eliot knyght* (London, 1538), sig. Ggiii.

170. Henry's copies of Pliny's *Historia naturalis* are catalogued in Carley, *Libraries of King Henry VIII*, 96, 152. On the "Anabula" as giraffe, see Charles D. Cuttler, "Exotics in Post-medieval European Art: Giraffes and Centaurs," *Artibus et historiae* 12 (1991): 161–79, esp. 165.

171. On the invention of the potter's wheel by "Anacharsis the Scythian," see Pliny, in Mary Beagon, *The Elder Pliny on the Human Animal: Natural History, Book 7* (Oxford: Oxford University Press, 2005), 103.

172. Desiderius Erasmus, *The Education of a Christian Prince (1516)*, trans. Lester K. Born (New York: Octagon Books, 1963), 231. See Walker, *Writing under Tyranny*, 26, on the copy of the work that Erasmus sent Henry VIII.

173. Sir Thomas Elyot, *The Book Named the Governor* (London: J. M. Dent, 1962), 164–66.

174. What I take to be Elyot's subtle effort to instruct—and, even more subtly, correct—Henry is consistent with Greg Walker's reading of Elyot's "continued concern with the need for plain speaking in the courts of princes" *(Writing under Tyranny*, 181).

175. Carley, *Libraries of King Henry VIII*, 170. The manuscript entered the Cotton Library and became Cotton MS Vitellius F. vii; see Thomas Smith, *Catalogue of the Manuscripts in the Cottonian Library (Catalogus librorum manuscriptorum bibliothecae Cottonianae, 1696)*, ed. C. G. C. Tite (Cambridge: D. S. Brewer, 1984), 97. Ker, *Medieval Libraries of Great Britain*, 6, 422, identifies the library of Bardney Abbey, Lincolnshire, as the book's origin. On Henry's acquisitions from Lincolnshire, see J. P. Carley, "John Leland and the Contents of English Pre-dissolution Libraries: Lincolnshire," *Transactions of the Cambridge Bibliographical Society* 9 (1989): 350-57; J. P. Carley, "The Royal Library as a Source for Sir Robert Cotton's Collection: A Preliminary List of Acquisitions," in *Sir Robert Cotton as Collector: Essays on an Early Stuart Courtier and His Legacy*, ed. C. J. Wright (London: British Library, 1997), 212.

176. See early-sixteenth-century annotations of the work like the one cited here in Magdalene College, Cambridge, MS C. 2498, fol. 89r (which will be discussed in the following chapter), and Bodleian, MS Bodley 416, fol. 144r.

177. For an account of Lambert's trial and the charges against him, see Walker, *Writing under Tyranny*, 158–59. The incident is also recounted by John Foxe, *Acts and Monuments*, ed. George Townsend (New York: AMS Press, 1965), 5.229–34.

178. Thomas Elyot, *Bibliotheca Eliotae = Eliotis librarie* (London, 1548), proem.

179. Ibid., sig. Eiv v.

180. Sir Thomas Elyot, *The Boke of the Governor* (London, 1531), proem. For the various meanings of the term "devulgate," see David Weil Baker, *Divulging Utopia: Radical Humanism in Sixteenth-Century England* (Amherst: University of Massachusetts Press, 1999), esp. chap. 3.

181. *The Image of Governance* is reprinted in Lillian Gottesman, ed., *Four Political Treatises by Sir Thomas Elyot* (Gainesville, FL: Scholars' Facsimiles and Reprints, 1967); all citations are to this edition, with page numbers given parenthetically in the text.

182. Walker reads *The Image of Governance* as Elyot's boldest critique of Henry and Cromwell; see *Writing under Tyranny*, 240–75.

183. For a relevant discussion of the changing shape of the reading room in the humanist library, see Anthony Grafton, "The Humanist as Reader," in *A History of Reading in the West*, ed. Guglielmo Carallo and Roger Chartier, trans. Lydia G. Cochrane (Amherst: University of Massachusetts Press, 1999), 179–212, esp. 184–85.

CHAPTER THREE

1. Matthew Parker, "A Preface into the Byble," *The Holie Bible* (1568), sig. ii r.

2. Ibid.

3. On the dissolution's effect on libraries, see James P. Carley, "The Dispersal of the Monastic Libraries and the Salvaging of the Spoils," in *The Cambridge History of Libraries in Britain and Ireland*, vol. 1, *To 1640*, ed. Elisabeth Leedham-Green and Teresa Webber (Cambridge: Cambridge University Press, 2006), 265–91; Andrew G. Watson, *Medieval Manuscripts in Post-medieval England* (Aldershot, Hants.: Ashgate, 2004); Nigel Ramsay, "'The Manuscripts flew about like Butterflies': The Break-up of English Libraries in the Sixteenth Century," in *Lost Libraries: The Destruction of Great Book Collections since Antiquity*, ed. James Raven (London: Palgrave Macmillan, 2004); and the references in n. 7 below. The dissolution and its effects on the monasteries have received renewed attention thanks to Eamon Duffy, *The Stripping of the Altars: Traditional Religion in England, 1400–1580* (New Haven, CT: Yale University Press, 1992). See also David Aers, "Altars of Power: Reflections on Eamon Duffy's *The Stripping of the Altars*," *Literature and History* 3 (1994): 90–104; Anne Hudson, review of Eamon Duffy, *The Stripping of the Altars*, *Notes and Queries* 238 (1993): 523–25.

4. John Bale famously excoriates those who, after the dissolution of the monasteries, "reserved of those lybrarye bokes . . . some to scoure theyr candelstyckes, & some to rubbe their bootes some they solde to the grossers and sope sellers." See Bale, *The Laboriouse Journey and Serche of Johan Leylande, for Englandes Antiquitees, geven of hym as a New Yeares Gyfte to Kyng Henry the viii* (London, 1546), sig. Bi r; signature references for subsequent quotations from this work will be given parenthetically in the text.

5. C. E. Wright, "The Dispersal of the Monastic Libraries and the Beginnings of Anglo-Saxon Studies: Matthew Parker and His Circle, a Preliminary Study," *Transactions of the Cambridge Bibliographical Society* 1 (1949–53): 208–32, quotation on 166.

6. N. R. Ker, *Medieval Libraries of Great Britain: A List of Surviving Books* (London: Royal Historical Society, 1941), xi–xii; Andrew G. Watson, *Catalogue of Dated and Datable Manuscripts, c. 435–1600, in Oxford Libraries*, 2 vols. (Oxford: Clarendon Press, 1984), 1.xi.

7. The bibliographical work of these figures has been amply documented. See, e.g., M. R. James, *The Sources of Archbishop Parker's Collection*, Cambridge Antiquarian Society Publications, 32 (1899); Wright, "Dispersal of Monastic Libraries," *Transactions of the Cambridge Bibliographical Society* 1 (1949–53); Bruce Dickins, "The Making of the

Parker Library," *Transactions of the Cambridge Bibliographical Society* 6 (1972): 19–34; Margaret Aston, "English Ruins and English History: The Dissolution and the Sense of the Past," *Journal of the Warburg and Courtauld Institutes* 36 (1973): 231–55; Ronald Harold Fritze, "'Truth Hath Lacked Witnesse, Tyme Wanted Light': The Dispersal of the English Monastic Libraries and Protestant Efforts at Preservation, ca. 1535–1625," *Journal of Library History* 18 (1983): 274–91; James P. Carley, "John Leland and the Foundations of the Royal Library: The Westminster Inventory of 1542," *Bulletin of the Society of Renaissance Studies* 7 (1989): 12–22; James P. Carley, "John Leland and the Contents of the English Pre-dissolution Libraries: Glastonbury Abbey," *Scriptorium* 40 (1986): 107–20; Allen J. Frantzen, *Desire for Origins: New Language, Old English, and Teaching the Tradition* (New Brunswick, NJ: Rutgers University Press, 1990), 35–50; Benedict Scott Robinson, "'Darke Speech': Matthew Parker and the Reforming of History," *Sixteenth Century Journal* 29 (1998): 1061–83; Timothy Graham and Andrew G. Watson, *The Recovery of the Past in Early Elizabethan England: Documents by John Bale and John Joscelyn from the Circle of Matthew Parker*, Cambridge Bibliographical Society Monograph 13 (Cambridge: Cambridge University Library, 1998); Timothy Graham, "Matthew Parker's Manuscripts: An Elizabethan Library and Its Use," in *Cambridge History of Libraries in Britain and Ireland*, ed. Leedham-Green and Webber, 1.322–41; Watson, *Medieval Manuscripts in Post-medieval England.*

8. See, as well as the other sources on Parker cited in this chapter, May McKisack's important account, *Medieval History in the Tudor Age* (Oxford: Oxford University Press, 1971), 26–49.

9. Bale is cited in Robinson, "Darke Speech," *Sixteenth Century Journal* 29 (1998): 1065. Joscelyn is cited by McKisack, *Medieval History in the Tudor Age,* 39. On Leland's enterprise of reimagining national identity by reconstructing the British past, see Cathy Shrank, *Writing the Nation in Reformation England, 1530–1580* (Oxford: Oxford University Press, 2004), esp. 65–103.

10. George F. Warner and Julius P. Gilson, *Catalogue of Western Manuscripts in the Old Royal and King's Collections in the British Museum* (London: British Museum, 1921), xvi, xviii–xix.

11. See Carley, "John Leland and the Foundations of the Royal Library," *Bulletin of the Society of Renaissance Studies* 7 (1989); and "John Leland and the Contents of the English Pre-dissolution Libraries," *Scriptorium* 40 (1986).

12. It is clear, as Bruce Dickins notes, that "Parker collected what seemed of interest to him"; Dickins, "Making of the Parker Library," *Transactions of the Cambridge Bibliographical Society* 6 (1972): 34.

13. Fritze, "Truth Hath Lacked Witnesse, Tyme Wanted Light," *Journal of Library History* 18 (1983): 274. Patrick Wright shows that terms like "preservation" and "heritage" are hardly neutral today but remain charged with political significance: see his *On Living in an Old Country: The National Past in Contemporary Britain* (London: Schocken Books, 1985).

14. Fritze, "Truth Hath Lacked Witnesse, Tyme Wanted Light," *Journal of Library History* 18 (1983): 280.

15. This point resonates with Brian Cummings's argument that "the Reformation was a pre-eminently literary event." See Cummings, "Reformed Literature and Literature

Reformed," in *The Cambridge History of Medieval English Literature*, ed. David Wallace (Cambridge: Cambridge University Press, 1999), 824. This thesis forms the basis of his book *The Literary Culture of the Reformation: Grammar and Grace* (Oxford: Oxford University Press, 2002).

16. Parker, "A Preface into the Byble," *Holie Bible* (1568), ii r.

17. John Bruce, ed., *The Correspondence of Matthew Parker* (Cambridge: Cambridge University Press, 1953), 327.

18. Mary Carruthers cites John of Salisbury on memory as "the mind's treasure-chest," and St. Jerome calls the trained memory "a library for Christ"; Carruthers, *The Book of Memory: A Study of Memory in Medieval Culture* (Cambridge: Cambridge University Press, 1990), 113, 33. Similarly, Thomas Wilson's *Arte of Rhetorique* calls memory "the threasurie of the minde," while Mulcaster's *Elementarie*, 1.vii, refers to "the threasurie of rememberance"; both examples are discussed by James Nohrnberg, *The Analogy of the "Faerie Queene"* (Princeton, NJ: Princeton University Press, 1976), 348.

19. Jack Upland, *Friar Daw's Reply and Upland's Rejoinder*, ed. P. L. Heyworth (London: Oxford University Press, 1968), 70; cited and discussed in Mary A. Rouse and Richard H. Rouse, *Authentic Witnesses: Approaches to Medieval Texts and Manuscripts* (Notre Dame, IN: University of Notre Dame Press, 1991), 410.

20. See Wright, "Dispersal of Monastic Libraries," *Transactions of the Cambridge Bibliographical Society* 1 (1949–53): 226.

21. James P. Carley, "Marks in Books and the Libraries of Henry VIII," *Papers of the Bibliographical Society of America* 91 (1997): 583–606; Wright, "Dispersal of Monastic Libraries," *Transactions of the Cambridge Bibliographical Society* 1 (1949–53): 161.

22. James P. Carley, ed., *The Libraries of King Henry VIII*, Corpus of British Medieval Library Catalogues 7 (London: British Library, 2000), xliii.

23. As N. R. Ker observes, "the kinds of books which had on the whole the best chance of surviving were historical, patristic, and biblical," while "the kinds of books which had the least chance of surviving were those containing the scholastic theology and philosophy of the later Middle Ages, and the law-books"; see Ker, "The Migration of Manuscripts from the English Medieval Libraries," in *Books, Collectors and Libraries: Studies in the Medieval Heritage*, ed. Andrew G. Watson (London: Hambledon Press, 1985), 464.

24. On Parker's habits of annotating and, on occasion, dismembering and reassembling his books, see R. I. Page, *Matthew Parker and His Books: Sandars Lectures in Bibliography* (Kalamazoo, MI: Medieval Institute Publications, 1993). Specific examples are discussed by Mildred Budney, *Insular, Anglo-Saxon, and Early Anglo-Norman Manuscript Art at Corpus Christi College, Cambridge: An Illustrated Catalogue* (Kalamazoo, MI: Medieval Institute Publications, 1997), 528. Further examples will be discussed below.

25. John King, Cathy Shrank, Tom Betteridge, and Brian Cummings are likewise exploring the literary ramifications of the wide-scale symbolic revisions that were produced by the Reformation.

26. The 1574 bequest to Cambridge University Library attracted immediate notice: see J. C. T. Oates, "The Restoration of the Library in 1574," in *Cambridge University Library, a History: From the Beginnings to the Copyright Act of Queen Anne* (Cambridge: Cambridge University Press, 1986), 89–118. As R. I. Page notes, it is difficult to determine

when the books bequeathed to Corpus Christi actually arrived there, though "the library accounts show vigorous activity at various dates between 1576 and 1584"; see Page, "Christopher Marlowe and the Library of Matthew Parker," *Notes and Queries* 24 (1977): 510–14, quotation on 513. Spenser spent at least some time in Cambridge between the receipt of his BA in 1573 and of his MA in 1576–how much, though, is a matter of some speculation. For accounts of what we know about Spenser's time in Cambridge, see Richard Rambuss, "Spenser's Life and Career," in *The Cambridge Companion to Spenser*, ed. Andrew Hadfield (Cambridge: Cambridge University Press, 2001), 13–36, 18–19; William Allan Oram, *Edmund Spenser* (New York: Twayne Publishers, 1997), 4–5; Jean R. Brink, "'All his minde on honour fixed': The Preferment of Edmund Spenser," in *Spenser's Life and the Subject of Biography*, ed. Judith H. Anderson, Donald Cheney, and David A. Richardson (Amherst: University of Massachusetts Press, 1996), 45–64, 53–55. Alexander C. Judson, *The Life of Edmund Spenser* (Baltimore, MD: Johns Hopkins University Press, 1945), remains a valuable survey of surviving evidence of Spenser's biography: see esp. 42–44.

27. Grant Williams calls Eumnestes' chamber "an early modern memory palace" and contextualizes it within contemporary discussions of memory and the *ars memoriae*; see Williams, "Phantastes's Flies: The Trauma of Amnesic Enjoyment in Spenser's Memory Palace," *Spenser Studies* 18 (2003): 231–52. Andrew King also considers Spenser's memorial investments in *The Faerie Queene*; see King, *"The Faerie Queene" and Middle English Romance: The Matter of Just Memory* (Oxford: Oxford University Press, 2000), viii. And for a reading of this scene as a treatment of "the textual materiality of early modern memory," see Alan Steward and Garrett A. Sullivan Jr., "'Worme-eaten, and full of canker holes': Materializing Memory in *The Faerie Queene* and Lingua," *Spenser Studies* 17 (2003): 215–38, quotation on 219.

28. Edmund Spenser, *The Faerie Queene*, ed. A. C. Hamilton (London: Longman, 1977); all quotations are from this edition.

29. Warner and Gilson, *Catalogue of Western Manuscripts in the Old Royal and King's Collections in the British Museum*, xvi, xviii–xix.

30. For an account of these two volumes in Eumnestes' library, see King, *"Faerie Queene" and Middle English Romance*, 180–88; King likewise situates Spenser's representation of Eumnestes within the antiquarian tradition that flourished after the Reformation (7–8).

31. Bruce, *Correspondence of Matthew Parker*, 327.

32. British Library, Cotton MS Vitellius C. vii, fols. 310r–311v.

33. On Dee's humanism, as well as his own humanist-inspired library, see William H. Sherman, *John Dee: The Politics of Reading and Writing in the English Renaissance* (Amherst: University of Massachusetts Press, 1995). Where Sherman stresses the continuities between the English library of John Dee and the humanist libraries that Anthony Grafton examines in *Commerce with the Classics: Ancient Books and Renaissance Readers* (Ann Arbor: University of Michigan Press, 1997), I am interested in the distinctness of the English model because of the ongoing influence of the Reformation in redefining the meanings and uses of the library as a social space.

34. British Library, Cotton MS Faustina E. v, fol. 89r.

35. *OED*, s.v. "monument" and "muniment." Similarly, John N. King observes that "Foxe's conception of *monument* plays upon the word's different senses of sepulcher,

written document, and funerary memorial"; King, "'The Light of Printing': William Tyndale, John Foxe, John Day, and Early Modern Print Culture," *Renaissance Quarterly* 54
(2001): 52–85, quotation on 64. For a discussion of the importance of the antiquarian understanding of the term "monument" to Spenser, see Andrew Escobedo, *Nationalism and
Historical Loss in Renaissance England: Foxe, Dee, Spenser, Milton* (Ithaca, NY: Cornell
University Press, 2004), 69–80; John N. King, *English Reformation Literature: The Tudor
Origins of the Protestant Tradition* (Princeton, NJ: Princeton University Press, 1982), 438.
I am grateful to Emily Steiner for drawing my attention to the legal implications of the
term.

36. John Strype, *The Life and Acts of Matthew Parker*, 4 vols. (London, 1716), "Observations Upon this Archbishop," 4.529.

37. N. R. Ker, *Fragments of Medieval Manuscripts Used as Pastedowns in Oxford
Bindings* (Oxford: Oxford Bibliographical Society Publications, 1954), x.

38. Bruce, *Correspondence of Matthew Parker*, 297.

39. As W. W. Greg observes, Parker "was responsible for the exclusion or suppression
of unorthodox writings" at the same time that he "was active in collecting manuscripts
scattered at the Dissolution of the religious houses"; Greg, "Books and Bookmen in the
Correspondence of Archbishop Parker," *The Library*, 4th ser., 16 (1935): 243.

40. James Simpson, "Ageism: Leland, Bale, and the Laborious Start of English Literary
History, 1350–1550," *New Medieval Literatures* 1 (1997): 213–35. As Simpson observes,
Leland was "himself an agent of the destruction of the very past he seeks to recuperate"
(222).

41. Ramsay, "The Manuscripts flew about like Butterflies," in *Lost Libraries*, ed.
Raven, 127; Dom David Knowles, *The Religious Orders in England*, vol. 3, *The Tudor Age*
(Cambridge: Cambridge University Press, 1961), 285.

42. British Library, Cotton MS Cleopatra E. iv, fol. 120v.

43. See N. R. Ker, "Sir John Prise," in *Books, Collectors and Libraries*, ed. Watson. For
a list of Prise's books, see R. J. Fehrenback and E. S. Leedham-Green, eds., *Private Libraries
in Renaissance England: A Collection and Catalogue of Tudor and Early Stuart Book-
Lists* (Binghamton, NY: Medieval and Renaissance Texts and Studies, 1992–), vol. 2.

44. On Batman, see M. B. Parkes, "Stephen Batman's Manuscripts," in *Medieval Heritage: Essays in Honour of Tadahiro Ikegami*, ed. Masahiko Kanno et al. (Tokyo: Yushodo
Press, 1997); A. S. G. Edwards, "Editing and Ideology: Stephen Batman and the Book of
Privy Counselling," in *Chaucer in Perspective: Middle English Essays in Honour of Norman Blake* (Sheffield, UK: Sheffield Academic Press, 1999).

45. Stephen Batman, *The Doome Warning all Men to the Iudgemente* (London,
1583), 393–94. This letter is also extracted in Strype, *Life and Acts of Matthew Parker*,
528.

46. Batman, *The Doome Warning all Men to the Iudgemente*, 393.

47. Of the two manuscripts in Parker's library contributed by Batman, one is the
famous *Troilus* manuscript; see E. C. Pearce, "Matthew Parker," *The Library*, 4th ser., 6
(1925): 220.

48. Ker, *Medieval Libraries of Great Britain*, xii.

49. The term "distinction" as I use it here needs to be differentiated from the term
as understood through Pierre Bourdieu's *Distinction: A Social Critique of the Judgement*

of Taste, trans. Richard Nice (Cambridge, MA: Harvard University Press, 1984). For Bourdieu, the process of distinction describes the emergence of bourgeois taste in the post-
Enlightenment period, which translates into the realm of culture what is at base a religious
sublimation: thus, Bourdieu can observe that "cultural consecration does indeed confer
on the objects, persons, and situations it touches, a sort of ontological promotion akin to
a transubstantiation" (6). In contrast, the acts of distinction practiced by Parker and other
post-Reformation book collectors aim to produce, not a "sacred sphere of culture" (7), but
a "monument of antiquity" that can be extracted from the "superstition" of the Catholic
past. For an illuminating discussion of the Reformation's effects on the meanings of cultural objects, see H. L. Weatherby, "Holy Things," *English Literary Renaissance* 29 (1999):
422–42.

50. See J. R. Liddell, "Leland's Lists of Manuscripts in Lincolnshire Monasteries,"
English Historical Review 54 (1939): 88–95; Wright, "Dispersal of the Monastic Libraries,"
Transactions of the Cambridge Bibliographical Society 1 (1949–53): 163; Ker, *Medieval
Libraries of Great Britain,* xii; James P. Carley, "John Leland and the Contents of English
Pre-Dissolution Libraries: Lincolnshire," *Transactions of the Cambridge Bibliographical
Society* 9 (1989): 331–33.

51. Carley, "Marks in Books," *Papers of the Bibliographical Society of America* 91
(1997): 590–91.

52. Ibid., 592.

53. "The shape of the royal collection as a whole—at least in terms of manuscript
acquisition—seems determined by the concerns of 1527–35," observes Carley (*Libraries of
King Henry VIII,* xliii).

54. Cited by Greg, "Books and Bookmen," *The Library,* 4th ser., 16 (1935): 267.

55. Graham and Watson, *Recovery of the Past,* 19.

56. On the porous boundaries between historical and devotional writing before the
Reformation, see Laviece C. Ward, "Historiography on the Eve of the Reformation in an
Early-Sixteenth-Century English Manuscript, e Museo 160," in *The Work of Dissimil-
itude,* ed. David G. Allen and Robert A. White (Newark: University of Delaware Press,
1992). See also King, *"Faerie Queene" and Middle English Romance,* 20–21, 41–77, on the
interpenetration of historical and romance genres in medieval texts.

57. St. Augustine, *On Christian Doctrine,* trans. D. W. Robertson (Indianapolis:
Bobbs-Merrill Educational Publishing, 1958), 3.5.9.

58. For a discussion of *allegoresis* and the *integumentum,* see D. W. Robertson, *A
Preface to Chaucer: Studies in Medieval Perspectives* (Princeton, NJ: Princeton University
Press, 1962), 316–17.

59. Rita Copeland, *Rhetoric, Hermeneutics, and Translation in the Middle Ages:
Academic Traditions and Vernacular Texts* (Cambridge: Cambridge University Press,
1991), 112.

60. Ibid., 81.

61. William Tyndale, *Obedience of a Christian Man,* in *Doctrinal Treatises and Introductions to Different Portions of the Holy Scriptures,* ed. Henry Walter (Cambridge:
Cambridge University Press, 1848), 307; of the invented term "chopological" (presumably
for "tropological"), the editor observes: "Tyndale had meant to jest at the pedantic terms
used by the schoolmen" (301n1).

62. Ibid., 308.

63. Ibid., 304.

64. George Puttenham, *The Arte of English Poesie (1589)*, ed. Baxter Hathaway (Kent, OH: Kent State University Press, 1970), 30.

65. Francis Bacon, *The Advancement of Learning (1605)*, in *The Works of Francis Bacon*, ed. James Spedding, Robert Leslie Ellis, and Douglas Denon Heath, 14 vols. (London: Longman, Green, Longman, and Roberts, 1857–74), 3.142.

66. M. R. James suggests that Corpus Christi College, Cambridge, MS 43 formerly belonged to Bale and notes its contemporary annotations; James, *A Descriptive Catalogue of the Manuscripts in the Library of Corpus Christi College* (Cambridge: Cambridge University Press, 1912), 1.87–88. See Honor McCusker, "Books and Manuscripts Formerly in the Possession of John Bale," *The Library*, 4th ser., 16 (1935–36): 144–65. Carley notes another copy of *De gestis pontificum Anglorum* (now British Library, MS Harley 2) with "marginal notes, some possibly by Henry himself, on councils, on the authority of bishops and popes," and on laws of marriage, establishing the book's importance to the Reformation cause; Carley, "Marks in Books," *Papers of the Bibliographical Society of America* 91 (1997): 590–91.

67. This identification is based on comparison with Bale's manuscript notebooks, now preserved as Cambridge University Library, MS Ff.6.28; Bodleian, MSS Selden Supra 41, 72, 73; and British Library, MSS Harley 3838 and 1819.

68. H. L. D. Ward, *Catalogue of Romances*, 2 vols. (1893; repr., London: British Museum, 1962), 2.495. For William de Michlinia's 1482 English translation, see *The Revelation to the Monk of Evesham*, ed. Edward Arber (London: English Reprints, 1869).

69. British Library, Cotton MS Cleopatra D. ix, fol. 137v.

70. On Batman's annotations, see Kate McLoughlin, "Magdalene College MS Pepys 2498 and Stephen Batman's Reading Practices," *Transactions of the Cambridge Bibliographical Society* 10 (1994): 525–34.

71. On the provenance of Batman's manuscripts, see Parkes, "Stephen Batman's Manuscripts," in *Medieval Heritage*, ed. Kanno et al., 132–33.

72. Trinity College, Cambridge, MS 205, fol. 67v.

73. Walter Hilton, *The Prickynge of Love*, ed. Harold Kane, 2 vols. (Salzburg, Austria: Institut für Anglistik und Amerikanistik, Universität Salzburg, 1983), 1.47.

74. Ibid.

75. Jean Leclerq, *The Love of Learning and the Desire for God: A Study of Monastic Culture*, trans. Catharine Misrahi (New York: Fordham University Press, 1982), 13–20, esp. 13.

76. See Vincent Gillespie, "Lukyng in Holy Bokes: *Lectio* in Some Late Medieval Spiritual Miscellanies," in *Spätmittelalterliche geistliche Literatur in der Nationalsprache*, ed. James Hogg, 2 vols., Analecta Cartusiana 106 (Salzburg, Austria: Institut für Anglistik und Amerikanistik, Universität Salzburg, 1983–84), 2.1–27; Phyllis Hodgson, "*A Ladder of Foure Ronges by the whiche Men Mowe Wele Clyme to Heven*: A Study of the Prose Style of a Middle English Translation," *Modern Language Review* 44 (1949): 465–75.

77. Phyllis Hodgson, ed., *Deonise hid Diuinite and other Treatises on Contemplative Prayer*, Early English Text Society 231 (London: Oxford University Press, 1955), 101; see also James Hogg, ed., "*The Rewyll of Saint Sauioure" and "A Ladder of Foure Ronges by*

the Which Men Mowe Clyme to Heven" (Salzburg, Austria: Institut für Anglistik und
Amerikanistic, Universität Salzburg, 2003), 307–8.

78. Bodleian, MS Bodley 480, fol. 64v.

79. Bodleian, MS Bodley 416, fol. 144r. For the *Psalterium sancti hieronymi,* see J. B.
Severs and A. E. Hartung, eds., *A Manual of Writings in Middle English* (New Haven, CT:
Connecticut Academy, 1967–), 2.387 (15); Magdalene College, Cambridge, MS C 2498, fol.
89r.

80. Magdalene College, Cambridge, MS C 2498, fol. 44r.

81. Bodleian, MS Digby 171, fol. 2r.

82. Anthony Grafton, "The Humanist as Reader," in *A History of Reading in the
West,* ed. Guglielmo Cavallo and Roger Chartier, trans. Lydia G. Cochrane (Amherst:
University of Massachusetts Press, 1999), 179–212, esp. 182, 187, quotation on 184. On hu-
manist glossing practices, see also Anthony Grafton, "Is the History of Reading a Marginal
Enterprise? Guillaume Budé and His Books," *Papers of the Bibliographical Society of
America* 91 (1997): 139–57; William Sherman, *Used Books: Marking Readers in Renais-
sance England* (Philadelphia: University of Pennsylvania Press, 2008).

83. Stephanie H. Jed, *Chaste Thinking: The Rape of Lucretia and the Birth of Humanism* (Bloomington: Indiana University Press, 1989), 24.

84. As Robinson observes, "For Parker, the damaged text becomes metonymic for the
damage done to England by Catholicism; the restoration of medieval manuscripts, the very
possibility that they can be restored, signals the possibility of reforming English doctrine
and English practice by reforming English history"; Robinson, "Darke Speech," *Sixteenth
Century Journal* 29 (1998): 1081.

85. This admission comes from the preface to *Historia brevis Thomae Walsingham*
(London, 1574), in which Parker describes his encounters with "antique histories, in which
were hiding some monastic fragments, or rather old wives' fables" (historias antiquissimas
ediderim, in quibus monastica quaedam fragmenta, aut potius aniles fabulae reperientur),
fol. ii v. For a discussion of this text, see Robinson, "Darke Speech," *Sixteenth Century
Journal* 29 (1998): 1082n93.

86. The problem of Arthur's status in British history has been recently treated by Pa-
tricia Clare Ingham, *Sovereign Fantasies: Arthurian Romance and the Making of Britain*
(Philadelphia: University of Pennsylvania Press, 2001); King, *"Faerie Queene" and Middle
English Romance,* 69–77, 173–80; Escobedo, *Nationalism and Historical Loss,* chap. 2;
Joseph Levine, *Humanism and History: Origins of Modern English Historiography* (Ithaca,
NY: Cornell University Press, 1987), 40–45, 48–49; Anthea Hume, *Edmund Spenser:
Protestant Poet* (Cambridge: Cambridge University Press, 1984), 156–57; McKisack, *Me-
dieval History in the Tudor Age.* James P. Carley discusses antiquarian interest in Arthur
in his "Arthur and the Antiquaries," in *The Arthur of Medieval Latin Literature,* ed. Sîan
Echard (Cardiff: University of Wales Press, forthcoming). I am grateful to Professor Carley
for sharing this work with me in manuscript.

87. N. F. Blake, ed., *Caxton's Own Prose* (London: Andre Deutsch, 1973), 107.

88. Ibid., 109.

89. *The Nun's Priest's Tale* (3441–43), in *The Riverside Chaucer,* 3d ed., ed. Larry D.
Benson (New York: Houghton Mifflin, 1987), 261.

90. For example, Corpus Christi College, MSS 43, fol. 39v, and 26, fol. 79r. On the Tudor uses of Arthurian history, see Ingham, *Sovereign Fantasies*, 227–30.

91. Henry Ellis, ed., *Polydore Vergil's "English History," from an Early Translation* [Royal 18 C. VIII.IX], Camden Society 36 (London, 1846), 29. On Leland's battle against Vergil, see James P. Carley, "Polydore Vergil and John Leland on King Arthur: The Battle of the Books," in *King Arthur: A Casebook*, ed. Edward Donald Kennedy (New York: Garland, 1996). For an argument in favor of the relevance of this debate to Spenser, see Edwin Greenlaw, *Studies in Spenser's Historical Allegory* (New York: Octagon Books, 1932), 53–57. See also Escobedo, *Nationalism and Historical Loss*, chap. 2; Carley, "Arthur and the Antiquaries," in *The Arthur of Medieval Latin Literature*, ed. Echard.

92. On Prise's *Defensio*, see McKisack, *Medieval History in the Tudor Age*, 23.

93. Sir John Prise, *Historiae Brytannicae Defensio* (London, 1573), 21.

94. John Leland, *A learned and true assertion of the original, life, actes, and death of the most noble, valiant, and renoumed Prince Arthure, King of great Brittaine* (London, 1582), trans. Richard Robinson, reprinted as an appendix to Christopher Middleton, *The Famous Historie of Chinon of England*, ed. William Edward Mead (London: Oxford University Press, 1925), 27.

95. Carruthers, *Book of Memory*, 162–63.

96. LeClerq, *Love of Learning and Desire for God*, 17.

97. As LeClerq observes, *lectio divina* meant that "one must, in the monastery, possess books, know how to write them and read them, and, therefore, if it be necessary, learn how to read" (ibid., 16–17).

98. Here, of course, I borrow Paul Ricoeur's term, "hermeneutics of suspicion," from *Freud and Philosophy: An Essay on Interpretation*, trans. Denis Savage (New Haven, CT: Yale University Press, 1970), 33.

99. On the significance of this dedication, see Carley, "Polydore Vergil and John Leland on King Arthur," in *King Arthur: A Casebook*, ed. Kennedy, 193–96; see also Laurie A. Finke, "Spenser for Hire: Arthurian History as Cultural Capital in *The Faerie Queene*," in *Culture and the King: The Social Implications of the Arthurian Legend*, ed. Martin B. Shichtman and James P. Carley (Albany: State University of New York Press, 1994), 211–33.

100. Leland, *Learned and true assertion of the original, life, actes, and death of the most noble, valiant, and renoumed Prince Arthure*, sig. B3r–v.

101. Ibid. Carley suggests that "Batman's source was presumably John of Glastonbury's *Cronica sive Antiquitates Glastoniensis*"; Carley, "Polydore Vergil and John Leland on King Arthur," in *King Arthur: A Casebook*, ed. Kennedy, 195. On the association of Robinson and Batman, see also Carley, "Arthur and the Antiquaries," in *The Arthur of Medieval Latin Literature*, ed. Echard.

102. Anne Lake Prescott, "Spenser's Chivalric Restoration: From Batman's *Travayled Pilgrime* to the Redcrosse Knight," *Studies in Philology* 86 (1989): 166–97, quotation on 169.

103. Stephen Batman, *The Travayled Pylgrime* (London, 1569), I1, I4; on the connection to book 2, see Kathrine Koller, "*The Travayled Pylgrime* by Stephen Batman and Book Two of *The Faerie Queene*," *Modern Language Quarterly* 3 (1942): 535–41.

104. Renaissance allegory departs in significant ways from medieval *allegoresis*. Maureen Quilligan differentiates the "verticalness, levels, [and] hidden meaning" upheld by the latter from Renaissance allegory's "horizontal surfaces" in a useful discussion of the two; see Quilligan, *The Language of Allegory: Defining the Genre* (Ithaca, NY: Cornell University Press, 1978), 33. On Protestant culture's valorization of "plain speaking," see Patrick Collinson, *The Birthpangs of Protestant England: Religious and Cultural Change in the Sixteenth and Seventeenth Centuries* (London: Macmillan, 1988), 94–126.

105. See Stephen Greenblatt, *Renaissance Self-Fashioning: From More to Shakespeare* (Chicago: University of Chicago Press, 1980), 189; Harry Berger Jr., *The Allegorical Temper: Vision and Reality in Book II of Spenser's "Faerie Queene"* (New Haven, CT: Yale University Press, 1957), 218; Alan Sinfield, *Literature of Protestant England, 1560–1660* (Totowa, NJ: Barnes and Noble Books, 1983), 37; Ernest Gilman, *Iconoclasm and Poetry in the English Reformation* (Chicago: University of Chicago Press, 1986).

106. On iconoclasm and "biblioclasm"—a term I borrow from him—see Brian Cummings, "Iconoclasm and Bibliophobia in the English Reformations, 1521–1558," in *Images, Idolatry and Iconoclasm in Late Medieval England*, ed. Jeremy Dimmock, James Simpson, and Nicolette Zeeman (Oxford: Oxford University Press, 2002), 185–200.

107. See Frances A. Yates, *The Art of Memory* (Chicago: University of Chicago Press, 1966), esp. 32–34, 256, fig. 9. On the theory of the division between memory, imagination, and reason in the later Renaissance, see Lisa Jardine, *Francis Bacon: Discovery and the Art of Discourse* (Cambridge: Cambridge University Press, 1974), 90–93.

108. For a discussion of *Faerie Queene*, 6.proem.5, in relation to Spenserian allegory, see Jonathan Goldberg, *Voice Terminal Echo: Postmodernism and English Renaissance Texts* (New York: Methuen, 1986), 29–31.

109. On the multiple meanings of "scrine," see Judith H. Anderson, "'Myn Auctour': Spenser's Enabling Fiction and Eumnestes' 'immortall scrine,'" in *Unfolded Tales: Essays on Renaissance Romance*, ed. George M. Logan and Gordon Teskey (Ithaca, NY: Cornell University Press, 1989), 16–31, esp. 16–22.

110. Armando Petrucci, *Writers and Readers in Medieval Italy: Studies in the History of Written Culture*, ed. and trans. Charles M. Radding (New Haven, CT: Yale University Press, 1995), 213–14.

111. Jonathan Goldberg, *Endlesse Worke: Spenser and the Structures of Discourse* (Baltimore, MD: Johns Hopkins University Press, 1981), 76n1. On the "seemingly incoherent form" of Renaissance allegory in general, see Quilligan, *Language of Allegory*, 235; and for the argument that "an allegory is an incoherent narrative," see Gordon Teskey, *Allegory and Violence* (Ithaca, NY: Cornell University Press, 1996), 5.

112. On this point, see John E. Curran Jr., "The History Never Written: Bards, Druids, and the Problem of Antiquarianism in 'Poly Olbion,'" *Renaissance Quarterly* 51 (1998): 498–526; Arthur B. Ferguson, "John Twyne: A Tudor Humanist and the Problem of Legend," *Journal of British Studies* 9 (1969): 24–44, esp. 27–28; J. H. Levy, *Tudor Historical Thought* (San Marino, CA: Huntington Library, 1967), 146; T. D. Kendrick, *British Antiquity* (London: Methuen, 1950), 89.

113. Cited by Denys Hay, *Polydore Vergil: Renaissance Historian and Man of Letters* (Oxford: Clarendon Press, 1952), 159; see also Carley, "Polydore Vergil and John Leland on King Arthur," in *King Arthur: A Casebook*, ed. Kennedy, 193.

114. Hilton, *Prickynge of Love*, 1.47.

115. On this point, see Escobedo, *Nationalism and Historical Loss*, 80 and passim.

116. Compare this point to John E. Curran Jr.'s argument that early modern antiquarians, in rejecting the mythology of Geoffrey of Monmouth, were forced to acknowledge and accept "the gaps in the nation's heritage"; Curran, "The History Never Written," *Renaissance Quarterly* 51 (1998): 498–525.

117. Caroline Walker Bynum, "Wonder," *American Historical Review* 102 (1997): 1–26. Compare Bynum's account with Stephen Greenblatt, "Resonance and Wonder," in *Exhibiting Cultures: The Poetics and Politics of Museum Display*, ed. Ivan Karp and Steven D. Lavine (Washington, DC: Smithsonian Institution Press, 1991), 42–56. On the early modern encyclopedia, see William N. West, *Theatres and Encyclopedias in Early Modern Europe* (Cambridge: Cambridge University Press, 2002).

118. Lorraine Daston and Katharine Park, *Wonders and the Order of Nature, 1150–1750* (New York: Zone Books, 1998), 20.

119. Bacon, *Advancement of Learning (1605)*, in *Works of Francis Bacon*, ed. Spedding, Ellis, and Heath, 3.266. Bacon's comment is cited and discussed by Daston and Park, *Wonders and the Order of Nature*, 11.

120. Goldberg, *Endlesse Worke*, 8.

121. Thus, book 1 sings the praises "Of *Gloriane* great Queene of glory bright, / Whose kingdomes seat *Cleopolis* is red" (1.7.46).

122. On the colonial contexts of the "marvelous," see Stephen Greenblatt, *Marvelous Possessions: The Wonder of the New World* (Chicago: University of Chicago Press, 1991).

123. Thus, A. Bartlett Giamatti insists that "Arthur reads history, Guyon fiction"; Giamatti, *Play of Double Senses: Spenser's "Faerie Queene"* (Englewood Cliffs, NJ: Prentice-Hall, 1975), 54. See also Hume, *Edmund Spenser: Protestant Poet*, 156–57; Berger, *Allegorical Temper*, 111.

124. Pierre Nora, "General Introduction: Between Memory and History," in *Realms of Memory*, trans. Arthur Goldhammer, 3 vols. (New York: Columbia University Press, 1996–98), 1.3. My understanding of memory as a critical category has been much aided by Sarah Beckwith, "The Present of Past Things: The York Corpus Christi Cycle as a Contemporary Theatre of Memory," *Journal of Medieval and Early Modern Studies* 26 (1996): 355–79.

125. Michel de Certeau, "Walking in the City," in *The Practice of Everyday Life*, trans. Steven Rendall (Berkeley and Los Angeles: University of California Press, 1984), 108.

126. See Kerwin Lee Klein, "On the Emergence of 'Memory' in Historical Discourse," *Representations* 69 (2000): 127–50, which issues a trenchant critique of the recent emergence, within historical writing, of "memory" as a category outside history. The point that "memory has a history, or more precisely, histories," is made by Natalie Zemon Davis and Randolph Starn in their introduction to "Memory and Counter-memory," special issue, *Representations* 26 (1989): 2.

127. Thomas Richards, *The Imperial Archive: Knowledge and the Fantasy of Empire* (London: Verso, 1993), 7.

128. Robert Burton, *The Anatomy of Melancholy*, ed. Thomas C. Faulkner et al., 4 vols. (Oxford: Clarendon, 1989), 1.251. For an analysis of post-Reformation periodization of the Middle Ages as a realm of imagination, see James Simpson, "The Rule of Medieval Imagination," in *Images, Idolatry, and Iconoclasm in Late Medieval England: Textuality*

and the Visual Image, ed. Jeremy Dimmick, James Simpson, and Nicolette Zeeman (Oxford: Oxford University Press, 2002), 4–24. The most brilliant discussion of the faculty of imagination in Spenser remains Isabel G. MacCaffrey, *Spenser's Allegory: The Anatomy of Imagination* (Princeton, NJ: Princeton University Press, 1976).

129. William Tyndale, *The Obedience of a Christian Man*, in *Doctrinal Treatises and Introductions to Different Portions of the Holy Scriptures*, ed. Henry Walter (Cambridge: Cambridge University Press, 1848), 292; this passage is discussed by Greenblatt, *Renaissance Self-Fashioning*, 112–13.

130. On these examples, see King, *English Reformation Literature*; John N. King, *Spenser's Poetry and the Reformation Tradition* (Princeton, NJ: Princeton University Press, 1990), 113. On the Royal Visitor's Injunctions and English iconoclasm in general, see Ernest B. Gilman, *Iconoclasm and Poetry in the English Reformation: Down Went Dagon* (Chicago: University of Chicago Press, 1986), esp. 7–8.

131. King, *Spenser's Poetry*, 78; see also King, *English Reformation Literature*, 146.

132. King, *English Reformation Literature*, 146.

133. *Batman uppon Bartholome, his Booke de Proprietatibus Rerum*, trans. Stephen Batman (London, 1583), fol. 17v. On Batman's translation as a source for Spenser's Castle of Alma, particularly Eumnestes' library, see Daniel Boughner, "The Psychology of Memory in Spenser's *Faerie Queene*," *Publications of the Modern Language Association* 47 (1932): 89–96; Edwin Greenlaw et al., eds., *The Works of Edmund Spenser: A Variorum Edition* (Baltimore, MD: Johns Hopkins University Press, 1933), 465.

134. John Doddridge, *The English Lawyer* (London, 1631), 12. See also Garrett A. Sullivan Jr., *Memory and Forgetting in English Renaissance Drama: Shakespeare, Marlowe, Webster* (Cambridge: Cambridge University Press, 2005), 2–12; Lina Bolzoni, *The Gallery of Memory: Literary and Iconographical Models in the Age of the Printing Press*, trans. Jeremy Parzen (Toronto: University of Toronto Press, 2001); Paulo Rossi, *Logic and the Art of Memory: The Quest for a Universal Language*, trans. Stephen Clucas (Chicago: University of Chicago Press, 2000). Frances Yates, *The Art of Memory* (Chicago: University of Chicago Press, 1966), remains the classic exploration of memory and its Renaissance meanings.

135. *OED*, s.v. "define."

136. Magdalene College, Cambridge, MS C 2498, fol. 44r.

137. Ibid., fol. 89r; Bodleian, MS Bodley 416, fol. 144r.

138. Batman, *The Doome Warning all Men to the Iudgemente*, 394.

139. David Lee Miller, *The Poem's Two Bodies: The Poetics of the 1590 "Faerie Queene"* (Princeton, NJ: Princeton University Press, 1988), 188. On meditation as a key route toward memory, see Mary Carruthers, *The Craft of Thought: Meditation, Rhetoric, and the Making of Images, 400–1200* (Cambridge: Cambridge University Press, 1998), esp. 60–63.

140. On the digestive processes in the Castle of Alma, see Michael Schoenfeldt, "The Construction of Inwardness in *The Faerie Queene*, Book 2," in *Worldmaking Spenser: Explorations in the Early Modern Age*, ed. Patrick Cheney and Lauren Silberman (Lexington: University Press of Kentucky, 2000).

141. Carruthers, *Book of Memory*, 165–66.

142. King similarly finds that the chamber of Phantastes is externalized to, and attacked in, the Bower of Bliss. King's reading corroborates this point by observing furthermore

that "the Bower's 'painted flowres' (II.xii.58), 'diuersitie' (II.xii.59), and above all its artificiality" are foreshadowed in the chamber of Phantastes, which "was dispainted all
within, / With sundry colours, in the which were writ / Infinite shapes of things dispersed
thin" (2.9.50). See King, *"The Faerie Queene" and Middle English Romance*, 165–72,
quotation on 166. A similar point is made by Stewart and Sullivan, who note that "issues
of memory are worked out throughout the remainder of Book II"; Stewart and Sullivan,
"Worme-eaten, and full of canker holes," *Spenser Studies* 17 (2003): 227.

143. On Genius as a figure of imagination, see James Simpson, *Sciences and the Self
in Medieval Poetry: Alan of Lille's "Anticlaudianus" and John Gower's "Confessio Amantis"* (Cambridge: Cambridge University Press, 1995), 167, 266–67.

144. Gilman, *Iconoclasm and Poetry in the English Reformation*, 77.

145. Greenblatt notes that the scene suggests a parodic pietà (*Renaissance Self-
Fashioning*, 189). Of relevance to my argument about the Bower of Bliss as a seat of forgetting is Roland Greene's observation that "within the Bower, of course, the boundaries
between self and other, immanence and embassy, can scarcely be discriminated"; Greene,
"A Primer of Spenser's Worldmaking: Alterity in the Bower of Bliss," in *Worldmaking
Spenser*, ed. Cheney and Silberman, 25. My reading would extend this boundary blurring to
the distinction of past and present.

146. Aelfric, *A Testimonie of Antiquitie (sermo de sacrificio in die Pascae)*, ed. John
Joscelyn and Matthew Parker (London, 1566), sig. Av r. On Joscelyn's method, see Robinson, "Darke Speech," *Sixteenth Century Journal* 29 (1998): 1061–83.

147. Maurice Evans, cited by A. C. Hamilton, in Spenser, *Faerie Queene*, 297n.

148. See Greenblatt, *Renaissance Self-Fashioning*, 189; Sinfield, *Literature of Protestant England*, 37; Berger, *Allegorical Temper*, 218.

149. On the forcefulness of these verbs, see Gilman, *Iconoclasm and Poetry in the
English Reformation*, 69–70.

150. Spenser, *Faerie Queene*, ed. Hamilton, 296n.

151. Aston argues that monastic ruins spurred sixteenth-century historical consciousness; Aston, "English Ruins and English History," *Journal of the Warburg and Courtauld
Institutes* 36 (1973). The ruins that preoccupied Spenser are usually understood as classical
ruins; see Judith Anderson, "The Antiquities of Rome and *The Faerie Queene*," *Journal
of English and Germanic Philology* (1987): 199–214; Margaret Ferguson, "'The Afflatus of
Ruin': Meditations on Rome by Du Bellay, Spenser, and Stevens," in *Roman Images*, ed.
Annabel Patterson (Baltimore, MD: Johns Hopkins University Press, 1984), 23–50. But see,
for a consideration of the importance of medieval ruins to Spenser, Maryclaire Moroney,
"Spenser's Dissolution: Monasticism and Ruins in *The Faerie Queene* and *The View of
the Present State of Ireland*," *Spenser Studies* 18 (1998): 105–32. See also Philip Schwyzer,
Literature, Nationalism, and Memory in Early Modern England and Wales (Cambridge:
Cambridge University Press, 2004), chap. 1.

CHAPTER FOUR

1. As C. E. Wright remarks, "the history of Middle English literature might be
largely written from the material supplied by the Cotton manuscripts." See "The Elizabethan Society of Antiquaries and the Formation of the Cotton Library," in *The English*

Library before 1700, ed. Francis Wormald and C. E. Wright (London: Athlone Press, 1958), 194.

2. On Cotton's library, see, in addition to ibid., Richard Ovenden, "The Libraries of the Antiquaries (c. 1580–1640) and the Idea of a National Collection," in *The Cambridge History of Libraries in Britain and Ireland*, vol. 1, *To 1640*, ed. Elisabeth Leedham-Green and Teresa Webber (Cambridge: Cambridge University Press, 2006), 550–57; Kevin Sharpe, *Sir Robert Cotton, 1586–1631: History and Politics in Early Modern England* (Oxford: Oxford University Press, 1979), 48–83; Graham Parry, *The Trophies of Time: English Antiquarians of the Seventeenth Century* (Oxford: Oxford University Press, 1995), 70–94; C. J. Wright, ed., *Sir Robert Cotton as Collector: Essays on an Early Stuart Courtier and His Legacy* (London: British Library, 1997). The work of Colin G. C. Tite has been an invaluable resource for the understanding of the Cotton Library, its formation, and its contemporary context: see Tite's *The Manuscript Library of Sir Robert Cotton*, Panizzi Lectures, 1993 (London: British Library, 1994); and his *The Early Records of Sir Robert Cotton's Library: Formation, Cataloguing, Use* (London: British Library, 2003).

3. On Bale, Parker, and other sixteenth-century collectors, see James P. Carley, "The Dispersal of the Monastic Libraries and the Salvaging of the Spoils," in *Cambridge History of Libraries in Britain and Ireland*, ed. Leedham-Green and Webber, 1.265–91; see also the references in chap. 3 above.

4. Cotton acquired collections from the libraries of John Leland, Francis Thynne, Robert Bowyer, Michael Heneage, John Joscelyn, William Lambarde, Laurence Nowell, and Thomas Talbot; see Wright, "Elizabethan Society of Antiquaries and the Formation of the Cotton Library," in *English Library before 1700*, ed. Wormald and Wright, 197–98. For Cotton's acquisition of materials from Joscelyn, see Timothy Graham and Andrew G. Watson, *The Recovery of the Past in Early Elizabethan England: Documents by John Bale and John Joscelyn from the Circle of Matthew Parker*, Cambridge Bibliographical Society, Monograph no. 13 (Cambridge: Cambridge University Library, 1998), 11, 104–5. On the development of the seventeenth-century secondhand-book trade, see Ovenden, "Libraries of the Antiquaries," in *Cambridge History of Libraries in Britain and Ireland*, ed. Leedham-Green and Webber, 1.538–39; Richard Beadle, "The Middle English Manuscripts," in *Catalogue of the Pepys Library at Magdalene College, Cambridge*, vol. 5, *Manuscripts; Medieval*, ed. Robert Latham (Woodbridge, Suffolk: D. S. Brewer, 1992), xxi–xxvii.

5. On the development of library catalogues in the seventeenth century, see Archer Taylor, *Renaissance Guides to Books: An Inventory and Some Conclusions* (Berkeley and Los Angeles: University of California Press, 1945); David McKitterick, "Bibliography, Bibliophily, and the Organization of Knowledge," in *The Foundations of Scholarship: Libraries and Collecting, 1650–1750; Papers Presented at a Clark Library Seminar 9 March 1985 by David Vaisey and David McKitterick* (Los Angeles: William Andrews Clark Memorial Library, University of California, 1992), 29–61; Anthony Grafton, *Commerce with the Classics: Ancient Books and Renaissance Readers* (Ann Arbor: University of Michigan Press, 1997), 199–200. See also C. G. C. Tite, "The Earliest Catalogues of the Cottonian Library," *British Library Journal* 6 (1980): 144–57. On seventeenth-century ordering of knowledge, see Amy Boesky, "'Outlandish-Fruits': Commissioning Nature for the Museum of Man," *English Literary History* 58 (1991): 312; see also the essays collected in *The Renaissance Computer: Knowledge Technology in the First Age of Print*,

ed. Neil Rhodes and Jonathan Sawday (New York: Routledge, 2000). If, as N. Katherine Hayles asserts, "electronic textuality makes inescapably clear" the point that "navigation functionalities are not merely ways to access the work but part of a work's signifying structure," the seventeenth century clearly anticipates this insight. See Hayles, "Translating Media: Why We Should Rethink Textuality," *Yale Journal of Criticism* 16 (2003): 263–90, quotation on 264.

6. Neil Rhodes, introduction to *English Renaissance Prose: History, Language, and Politics* (Tempe, AZ: Medieval and Renaissance Texts and Studies, 1997), 8. See also Wlad Godzich and Jeffrey Kittay, *The Emergence of Prose: An Essay in Prosaics* (Minneapolis: University of Minnesota Press, 1987), 175; Elizabeth Fowler and Roland Greene, eds., *The Project of Prose in Early Modern Europe and the New World* (Cambridge: Cambridge University Press, 1997).

7. Although this chapter is concerned with Cotton's role in the development of seventeenth-century prose, Cotton also lent works to poets; British Library, Cotton MS Julius C. iii, fol. 153, is a holograph letter from John Donne "from my Prison in my Chamber," 20 February 1601, addressing "my very honest and very assured frinde Robert Cotton, Esqe." and thanking Cotton for lending him books during the imprisonment he endured for his secret marriage.

8. On the meanings and uses of the "source," see Martha C. Howell and Walter Prevener, *From Reliable Sources: An Introduction to Historical Methods* (Ithaca, NY: Cornell University Press, 2001), esp. 148–49.

9. Sharpe, *Sir Robert Cotton*, 105–6.

10. On the Reformation impulse toward self-historicization, see Thomas Betteridge, *Tudor Histories of the English Reformations, 1530–83* (Aldershot, Hants.: Ashgate, 1999).

11. On Elizabeth Barton and Mrs. Amadas, see Ethan H. Shagan, *Popular Politics and the English Reformation* (Cambridge: Cambridge University Press, 2003), 33, 61–88; Diane Watt, *Secretaries of God: Women Prophets in Late Medieval and Early Modern England* (Woodbridge, Suffolk: D. S. Brewer, 1997).

12. See, as well as the sources cited later in this chapter, Lorraine Daston, "Baconian Facts, Academic Civility, and the Prehistory of Objectivity," *Annals of Scholarship* 8 (1991): 337–64.

13. Dom Justin McCann and Dom Hugh Connolly, eds., *Memorials of Father Augustine Baker, O.S.B.*, Catholic Record Society 33 (London: John Whitehead and Son, 1933), 112.

14. Cotton's other Catholic associates included Nicholas Roscarrock, whose hagiographical work will be discussed below, and Lord William Howard, whom William Camden called "an attentive and learned searcher into venerable antiquity": see Howard S. Reinmuth Jr., "Lord William Howard (1563–1646) and His Catholic Associates," *Recusant History* 12 (1974): 226–34, esp. 232, 234. On Baker and his relationship with Cotton, see David Rogers, "Some Early English Devotional Books from Cambray," *Downside Review* 57 (1939): 458–63; David Lunn, "Augustine Baker (1575–1641) and the English Mystical Tradition," *Journal of Ecclesiastical History* 26 (1975): 267–77; J. T. Rhodes, "Dom Augustine Baker's Reading Lists," *Downside Review* 111 (1993): 157–73.

15. British Library, Cotton MS Julius C. iii, fol. 187. See also Fr. Augustine Baker, *Secretum*, ed. John Clark (Salzburg, Austria: Institut für Anglistik und Americanistik, Universität Salzburg, 1997).

16. McCann and Connolly, *Memorials of Father Augustine Baker*, 112–13.

17. Graham Parry, *The Trophies of Time: English Antiquarians of the Seventeenth Century* (Oxford: Oxford University Press, 1995), 70; McCann and Connolly, *Memorials of Father Augustine Baker*, 112.

18. McCann and Connolly, *Memorials of Father Augustine Baker*, 113.

19. A full account of the library closure and the events leading up to it is supplied by Sharpe, *Sir Robert Cotton*, esp. chap. 4. See also Blair Worden, "Ben Jonson among the Historians," in *Culture and Politics in Early Stuart England*, ed. Kevin Sharpe and Peter Lake (Stanford, CA: Stanford University Press, 1993), 67–89, esp. 86.

20. The book is now Bodleian, MS Bodley 336; for a description, see Colin G. C. Tite, "'Lost or Stolen or Strayed': A Survey of Manuscripts Formerly in the Cotton Library," in *Sir Robert Cotton as Collector*, ed. Wright, 262–306, esp. 263, 293.

21. "In istis sordibus confusaque scoriae massa purioris mettalli venas passim sparsas delitescere, judicio & labore secernendas, & quam plurima, quae statum & historiam tam civilem quam ecclesiasticam illorum temporum"; Thomas Smith, *Catalogus librorum manuscriptorum Bibliothecae Cottonianae* (1696), XL. For the English translation, I have used Thomas Smith, "A History and Synopsis of the Cotton Library," trans. Godfrey E. Turton, in *Catalogue of the Manuscripts in the Cottonian Library (1696)*, ed. C. G. C. Tite (Cambridge: D. S. Brewer, 1984), 54; the page numbers for subsequent quotations from this work will be noted parenthetically in the text.

22. Tite, *Early Records of Sir Robert Cotton's Library*, records Camden's borrowing of "Vita Sancti Albani in vers et vita Sancti Vulfridi" (possibly Faustina B. iv), "The lyf of an Irish Saint called Santa Modwenna, foundress of Burton abbay upon trent" (Cleopatra A. ii), and "vita Sancti Gothlaci" (Vespasian D. xxi), fols. 38–39. The manuscript "Camden Collectanea pro Britania" contains copious notes on saints, especially British ones: see Titus F. vii, fol. 140.

23. "neque fabulis diversi generis ad alendam plebes ex vitio & ignorantia seculi nimium quam credulae superstitionem admistis, & non tam ad docendum quam ad fallendum compositis, assutisque figmentis è crasso ingenio prognatis veritatem corrupissent"; Smith, *Catalogus librorum manuscriptorum Bibliothecae Cottonianae*, XL.

24. On such authorial postures, see Alastair J. Minnis, "Late-Medieval Discussions of *Compilatio* and the Role of the *Compilator*," *Beiträge zur Geschichte der deutschen Sprache und Literatur* 101 (1979): 385–421; Malcolm Beckwith Parkes, "The Influence of *Ordinatio* and *Compilatio* on the Development of the Book," in *Medieval Learning and Literature: Essays Presented to Richard William Hunt*, ed. J. J. G. Alexander, M. T. Gibson, and R. W. Southern (Oxford: Clarendon Press, 1976), 115–41.

25. Manfred Görlach, ed., *The Kalendre of the Newe Legende of Englande* (Heidelberg: Universitätsverlag C. Winter, 1994), 46. On the *South English Legendary*, see Ralph Hanna III, "Miscellaneity and Vernacularity: Conditions of Literary Production in Late Medieval England," in *The Whole Book: Cultural Perspectives on the Medieval Miscellany*, ed. Stephen G. Nichols and Siegfried Wenzel (Ann Arbor: University of Michigan Press, 1996), 37–51.

26. On *compilatio* see Minnis, "Late-Medieval Discussions of *Compilatio*," *Beiträge zur Geschichte der deutschen Sprache und Literatur* 101 (1979); Parkes, "Influence of *Ordinatio* and *Compilatio*," in *Medieval Learning and Literature*, ed. Alexander, Gibson, and

Southern; Hanna, "Miscellaneity and Vernacularity," in *The Whole Book*, ed. Nichols and Wenzel; Ralph Hanna III, "Compilatio and the Wife of Bath: Latin Backgrounds, Ricardian Texts," in *Pursuing History: Middle English Manuscripts and Their Texts* (Stanford, CA: Stanford University Press, 1996), 247–57.

27. Andrew Galloway, "Writing History in England," in *The Cambridge History of Middle English Literature*, ed. David Wallace (Cambridge: Cambridge University Press, 1999), 276. See also Antonia Gransden, *Historical Writing in England*, vol. 2, *c. 1307 to the Early Sixteenth Century* (1982; repr., London: Routledge, 1996), 43–57.

28. Beryl Smalley calls it "a glorious jumble of fact, legend, and marvel"; *English Friars and Antiquity in the Early Fourteenth Century* (Oxford: Basil Blackwell, 1960), 21. On Higden's compilation of his sources, see Ronald Waldron, ed., *John Trevisa's Translation of the "Polychronicon" of Ranulph Higden, Book VI* (Heidelberg: Universitätsverlag, 2004), xv–xiv. On universal history, see John Taylor, *The Universal Chronicle of Ranulf Higden* (Oxford: Clarendon Press, 1966), 33–50.

29. Churchill Babington, ed., *Polychronicon Ranulphi Higden Monachi Cestrensis; together with the English translations of John Trevisa and of an unknown writer of the fifteenth century*, Rolls Series 41, 5 vols. (London: Longman, Green, Longman, Roberts and Green, 1865), 1.19. All Higden quotations are from this edition of Trevisa's translation, with the volume and page numbers given parenthetically in the text.

30. Minnis explores Vincent of Beauvais's similar assertion that "the compilator is not responsible for the truth or falsity of what the pagans say"; see "Late Medieval Discussions of *Compilatio*," *Beiträge zur Geschichte der deutschen Sprache und Literatur* 101 (1979): 399.

31. Similarly, Chris Given-Wilson observes that Gervase of Canterbury's assertion that the historian's task is to "instruct truthfully" measures truth as a didactic value; see Given-Wilson, *Chronicles: The Writing of History in Medieval England* (London: Hambledon Press, 2004), 2.

32. On the history of the "fact," see Mary Poovey, *The History of the Modern Fact: Problems of Knowledge in the Sciences of Wealth and Society* (Chicago: University of Chicago Press, 1998).

33. Thus, Emily Steiner calls it "a supra-history, as a massive collection of stories and subjects laid out chronologically"; see "Radical Historiography: Langland, Trevisa, and the *Polychronicon*," *Studies in the Age of Chaucer* 27 (2005): 171–211, quotation on 176. See also Taylor, *Universal Chronicle of Ranulf Higden*, 34.

34. As Anthony Grafton and Megan Williams show, Eusebius himself marks a new age of library-based historical writing; see their *Christianity and the Transformation of the Book: Origen, Eusebius, and the Library of Caesarea* (Cambridge, MA: Harvard University Press, 2006). See also Alden A. Mosshammer, *The "Chronicle" of Eusebius and Greek Chronographic Tradition* (Lewisburg: Bucknell University Press, 1979); Andrew James Carriker, *The Library of Eusebius of Caesarea* (Leiden: Brill, 2003).

35. James Simpson, *The Oxford English Literary History*, vol. 2, *Reform and Cultural Revolution, 1350–1547* (Oxford: Oxford University Press, 2002), 559–60.

36. As Jeanette M. A. Beer observes, according to medieval conventions of truth telling, "facts ('vera') contributed to the truth ('veritas') without being essential to it"; see Beer, *Narrative Conventions of Truth in the Middle Ages* (Geneva: Librairie Droz, 1981),

29, 63–71. See also Richard Firth Green, *A Crisis of Truth: Literature and Law in Ricardian England* (Philadelphia: University of Pennsylvania Press, 1999); Barbara Shapiro, *A Culture of Fact: England, 1550–1720* (Ithaca, NY: Cornell University Press, 2002); Mary Poovey, *A History of the Modern Fact: Problems of Knowledge in the Sciences of Wealth and Society* (Chicago: University of Chicago Press, 1998).

37. Tite, *Manuscript Library of Sir Robert Cotton*, 5.

38. A. S. G. Edwards points out that the Julius and Otho manuscripts were originally collected by Henry Savile of Banke, while another Cotton *Polychronicon* (this time an extract in Titus A. xiii) is the work of William Lambarde; see Edwards, "The Influence and Audience of the *Polychronicon*," *Proceedings of the Leeds Philosophical and Literary Society* 17 (1980): 113–19, esp. 116.

39. See ibid.; A. S. G. Edwards, "A Sixteenth-Century Version of Trevisa's *Polychron-icon*," *English Language Notes* 11 (1973): 34–38. On Parker's *Polychronicon*, see May McKisack, *Medieval History in the Tudor Age* (Oxford: Oxford University Press, 1971), 38–39.

40. William Caxton, "Prohemye," in *Polychronicon* (Westminster, 1482), sig. A3v. On Caxton's association of Trevisa with the Wycliffite Bible, see Margaret Deanesly, *The Lollard Bible and Other Medieval Biblical Versions* (Cambridge: Cambridge University Press, 1920), 298–302.

41. Ronald Waldron, "Trevisa's Original Prefaces on Translation: A Critical Edition," in *Medieval English Studies Presented to George Kane*, ed. Edward Donald Kennedy, Ronald Waldron, and Joseph S. Wittig (Cambridge: D. S. Brewer, 1988); Waldron, *John Trevisa's Translation of the "Polychronicon,"* xvi–xxxviii.

42. Although Tiberius D. vii was badly damaged in the Cotton Library fire, Thomas Smith offers a (pre-fire) description of "the dialogue between a patron and a cleric which [Trevisa] prefixes to his version of the Polychronicon of Ranulf Higden of Chester," which Tite identifies with the Tiberius manuscript; see Smith, "A History and Synopsis of the Cotton Library," in *Catalogue of the Manuscripts in the Cottonian Library*, ed. Tite, 50. See also Fiona Somerset, *Clerical Discourse and Lay Audience in Late Medieval England* (Cambridge: Cambridge University Press, 1998), 78–93; Steiner, "Radical Historiography," *Studies in the Age of Chaucer* 27 (2005).

43. D. R. Woolf, *Reading History in Early Modern England* (Cambridge: Cambridge University Press, 2000), esp. 8, 12.

44. This question was asked at two different occasions when I presented an ear-lier version of this work, at U.C. Davis and Stanford: I am grateful to Frances Dolan and my colleagues David Riggs, Seth Lerer, and Roland Greene for questioning the value of manuscripts within cultures of print in stimulating ways. The 1528 edition of the *Polychronicon* was published by Wynkyn de Worde as *The Cronycles of Englonde with the Dedes of Popes and Emperours, and Also the Descripcyon of Englonde* (London, 1528).

45. Similarly, Woolf observes that in the seventeenth century, "as old books, in print or manuscripts, chronicles were also becoming antiquities in their own right" (*Reading History in Early Modern England*, 50).

46. Gransden, *Historical Writing in England*, 2.43.

47. Taylor, *Universal Chronicle of Ranulf Higden*, 10.

48. For these examples, see Sharpe, *Sir Robert Cotton*, 68, who notes that Cotton "fragmented as well as rescued manuscripts."

49. Tite, *Manuscript Library of Sir Robert Cotton*, 45.

50. On the later practice of unbinding volumes, see Dorothy Anderson, "Reflections on Librarianship: Observations Arising from Examination of the Garrick Collection of Old Plays in the British Library," *British Library Journal* 6 (1980): 1–23, esp. 3.

51. As Sharpe remarks, "often it is hard to see any logic in the compilations" (*Sir Robert Cotton*, 69).

52. As Tite observes of the volumes, "these collections are very much [Cotton's] own, their individual articles and leaves assembled from many different sources, to be investigated by him and then arranged and ordered in categories and sequences which he himself decided upon" (*Manuscript Library of Sir Robert Cotton*, 55). In some cases, manuscript materials were arranged in bundles and were later bound by William Dugdale; see Tite, *Early Records of Sir Robert Cotton's Library*, 11n59. For insight into Cotton's methods, see James P. Carley and Colin G. C. Tite, "Sir Robert Cotton as Collector of Manuscripts and the Question of Dismemberment: British Library MSS Royal 13 D. I and Cotton Otho D. VIII," *The Library* 14 (1992): 94–99; Carley and Tite conclude that "it can be altogether misleading to see the volumes owned by Cotton and other 'modern' collectors as identical in all their aspects to their medieval forbears" (99).

53. Parkes, "Influence of *Ordinatio* and *Compilatio*," in *Medieval Learning and Literature*, ed. Alexander, Gibson, and Southern, 137.

54. See Joseph M. Levine, *Humanism and History: Origins of Modern English Historiography* (Ithaca, NY: Cornell University Press, 1987), 73. The continuity between monastic and antiquarian historians has been noted by R. W. Southern, who observes that "the researchers of the period after 1560 were the secular successors" of the monastic chroniclers, with whom they held a common devotion "to a systematic examination of records and chronicles over a wide area"; see Southern, "Aspects of the European Tradition of Historical Writing: The Sense of the Past," *Transactions of the Royal Historical Society*, 5th ser., 23 (1973): 246–56.

55. As Tite suggests, the way Cotton assembled his volumes indicates that he was "inspired maybe by the example of the medieval chronicles and annals on his shelves" (*Manuscript Library of Sir Robert Cotton*, 55). Cotton's chronological ordering of the materials in his volumes, such as the examples I will discuss, represents an afterlife of the chronicle form, a point that might be read against Woolf's assertion that the chronicle was the victim of "genrecide" in the seventeenth century; see Woolf, *Reading History in Early Modern England*, 26. While Woolf does survey the survival of medieval and Tudor chronicles in Stuart libraries, he holds that their cultural impact is restricted because of limited accessibility and selection (202). Yet I suggest that the persistence of the chronicle form in Cotton's library in fact extends its influence—in modified forms—by providing a narrative shape for the use of primary sources, a topic I explore below.

56. Betteridge, *Tudor Histories of the English Reformations*, 10.

57. John N. King, "'The Light of Printing': William Tyndale, John Foxe, John Day, and Early Modern Print Culture," *Renaissance Quarterly* 54 (2001): 52–85.

58. Indeed, Foxe compares himself to Eusebius in *Acts and Monuments*; Betteridge discusses this comparison and its implications in *Tudor Histories of the English Reformations*, 176, 181.

59. Anthony Grafton, *Joseph Scaliger: A Study in the History of Classical Scholarship*, esp. vol. 2, *Historical Chronology* (New York: Clarendon Press, 1983). See also Anthony Grafton, "Dating History: The Renaissance and the Reformation of Chronology," *Daedalus*, Spring 2003, 74–85.

60. On Harrison, see G. J. R. Parry, *A Protestant Vision: William Harrison and the Reformation of Elizabethan England* (Cambridge: Cambridge University Press, 1987); on Ussher, see Graham Parry, *The Trophies of Time: English Antiquarians of the Seventeenth Century* (Oxford: Oxford University Press, 1995), esp. 143–53.

61. On the uses of chronology in historiography, see Hayden White, *The Content of the Form: Narrative, Discourse, and Historical Representation* (Baltimore, MD: Johns Hopkins University Press, 1987), esp. 4–5. For a relevant discussion of history as narrative, see Christopher Cannon, *The Grounds of English Literature* (Oxford: Oxford University Press, 2004), 21–33. And on the early modern uses of chronology, see Daniel Rosenberg, "Joseph Priestly and the Graphic Invention of Modern Time," *Studies in Eighteenth Century Culture* 36 (2007): 55–103.

62. On Ussher's chronological method, see James Barr, "Why the World Was Created in 4004 B.C.: Archbishop Ussher and Biblical Chronology," *Bulletin of the John Rylands University Library* 67 (1985): 577–608.

63. Parry, *Trophies of Time*, 138.

64. On the development of subject indexes in early modern libraries, see Taylor, *Renaissance Guides to Books*, 45–64. On the emperor classifications and the history of their use in the Cotton Library, see Colin G. C. Tite, "The Early Catalogues of the Cottonian Library," *British Library Journal* 6 (1980): 144–57.

65. Tite, *Early Records of Sir Robert Cotton's Library*, 10, 15.

66. The letters in Cleopatra E. iv have been reprinted in such important collections as Thomas Wright, ed., *Letters Relating to the Suppression of Monasteries* (London: Camden Society, 1843); Joyce Youings, ed., *The Dissolution of the Monasteries* (London: George Allen and Unwin, 1971).

67. Tite, *Early Records of Sir Robert Cotton's Library*, 45.

68. On the *Collectanea satis copiosa*, see John Guy, "Thomas Cromwell and the Intellectual Origins of the Henrician Revolution," in *Reassessing the Henrician Age: Humanism, Politics, and Reform, 1500–1550*, ed. John Guy and Alistair Fox (Oxford: Basil Blackwell, 1986), 157–58; on the documents compiled in Cleopatra E. iv, see Nicholas Pocock, *Records of the Reformation*, 2 vols. (Oxford: Clarendon Press, 1870), 2.385–421.

69. Tite confirms the presence of "organizational notes by Cotton" throughout these "Collections relating to the church in England"; see *Early Records of Sir Robert Cotton's Library*, 215–17.

70. Ibid., 217.

71. See Betteridge, *Tudor Histories of the English Reformations*, esp. chap. 4.

72. See Julia Crick, "*Pristina Libertas*: Liberty and the Anglo-Saxons Revisited," *Transactions of the Royal Historical Society* 14 (2004): 47–71. On Parkerian Anglo-Saxon

studies, see Allen J. Frantzen, *Desire for Origins: New Language, Old English, and Teaching the Tradition* (New Brunswick, NJ: Rutgers University Press, 1990), 35–49; along with the sources cited in chap. 3 above.

73. On antiquarian meetings like this one, see Ovenden, "Libraries of the Antiquaries," in *Cambridge History of Libraries in Britain and Ireland*, ed. Leedham-Green and Webber, 1.529–30. See also Wright, "Elizabethan Society of Antiquaries and the Formation of the Cotton Library," in *English Library before 1700*, ed. Wormald and Wright.

74. Thus, Foxe insists, "If the papists would needs derive the faith and religion of this realm from Rome, then let them set us and leave us there where they had us; that is, let them suffer us to stand content with that faith and religion which then was taught and brought from Rome by Eleutherius (as now we differ nothing from the same), and we will desire no better"; John Foxe, *Acts and Monuments*, ed. George Townsend (New York: AMS Press, 1965), 1.308.

75. On the uses of this manuscript and the Lucius legend, see T. D. Kendrick, *British Antiquity* (London: Methuen, 1950), 113; Guy, "Thomas Cromwell and the Intellectual Origins of the Henrician Revolution," in *Reassessing the Henrician Age*, ed. Guy and Fox, 158–60; D. R. Woolf, *The Idea of History in Early Stuart England: Erudition, Ideology, and "The Light of Truth" from the Accession of James I to the Civil War* (Toronto: University of Toronto Press, 1990), 42; Felicity Heal, *Reformation in Britain and Ireland* (Oxford: Oxford University Press, 2003), 389–92.

76. These are printed in A. W. Haddan and W. Stubbs, *Councils and Ecclesiastical Documents Relating to Great Britain and Ireland*, 3 vols. (Oxford, 1869–73), 3.506–7, 525–26, 577–78; and, more recently, in Michael Richter, ed., *Canterbury Professions*, Canterbury and York Society, vol. 67 (Torquay: Devonshire Press, 1972–73), 1–2, 2–3, 9. Richter posits that the Eadulf profession "betrays features of a forgery" because it is falsely attributed to "Eadulf of York," who was in fact consecrated in 992; Richter concludes that "the profession should be attributed correctly to Eadulf, Bishop of Lindsey, who was consecrated in 796" (2; see also xli–xlii).

77. This history is traced by Richter, who suggests that "the disappearance of episcopal professions [in Anglo-Saxon England] in the second half of the ninth century" may have resulted from "an attempt to curtail the metropolitan position of the archbishop of Canterbury, and the papacy itself might have been responsible for that" (*Canterbury Professions*, liv). See also F. R. H. du Boulay, review of *Canterbury Professions* by Michael Richter, *English Historical Review* 90 (1975): 879–80, who considers the professions as the object of a three-way struggle between the archbishop of Canterbury, the Crown, and the pope.

78. On this dispute and its repercussions, see Richter, *Canterbury Professions*, lvii–lxvi.

79. See Foxe, *Acts and Monuments*, ed. Townsend, 2.109–33, quotations on 113.

80. J. Planta, *A Catalogue of the Manuscripts in the Cottonian Library Deposited in the British Museum* (London, 1802), art. 15. This letter is reprinted in David Wilkins, *Concilia magnae Britanniae et Hiberniae*, 4 vols. (London, 1737), 1.26–27.

81. H. Idris Bell, "A List of Original Papal Bulls and Briefs in the Department of Manuscripts, British Museum, Part II," *English Historical Review* 36 (1921), art. 136.

82. Ibid., art. 147.

83. Planta, *Catalogue*, art. 57.

84. Foxe's source for the story of Augustine and the monks at Bangor is John Bale, *The first two partes of the actes of the Englysh votaryes* (London, 1551), fol. 29r, whose own source is Bede. Foxe cites Edward's struggle with Pecham as an example of how, "in the days of King Edward, the church of Rome began daily more and more to rise up, and swell so high in pride and worldly dominion, that no king almost in his own country could do anything but as the pope pleased" (Foxe, *Acts and Monuments*, ed. Townsend, 2.579).

85. Cotton's intention to present a chronology of key documents in British ecclesiastical history is indicated by the fact that, when his collection lacked an original source, he commissioned scribes to produce copies of the documents he sought, which he inserted into the appropriate chronological place. Thus, Tite concludes that Cotton sought to "present a full chronology or account, supplying the gaps where originals were unavailable with copies intentionally acquired—and even bought—for the purpose" (*Manuscript Library of Sir Robert Cotton*, 52).

86. Given-Wilson, *Chronicles*, 33.

87. Ibid., 38.

88. On Ussher, Ware, Dugdale, and Wharton, see Parry, *Trophies of Time*, and the essays collected in Levi Fox, ed., *English Historical Scholarship in the Sixteenth and Seventeenth Centuries* (Oxford: Oxford University Press, 1956).

89. On Caesar Baronius, see Paul Nelles, "The Renaissance Ancient Library Tradition and Christian Antiquity," in *Les humanists et leur bibliothèque*, ed. Rudolf De Smet, Travaux de l'Institut interuniversitaire pour l'étude de la Renaissance et de l'humanisme 13 (Brussels: Peeters, 2002), 159–73; Cyriac K. Pullapilly, *Caesar Baronius, Counter-Reformation Historian* (Notre Dame, IN: University of Notre Dame Press, 1975), 37–42.

90. Hippolyte Delehaye, *The Work of the Bollandists through Three Centuries, 1615–1915* (Princeton, NJ: Princeton University Press, 1922); Dom David Knowles, "The Bollandists," in *Great Historical Enterprises: Problems in Monastic History* (London: Nelson, 1963), 3–32; Lucia Bergamasco, "Hagiographie et sainteté en Angleterre aux XVIe–XVIIIe siècles," *Annales* 48 (1993): 1053–85.

91. Wilson's work was anonymously published as the work of "I.W. A Catholicke Priest," *The English Martyrologe Conteyning a Summary of the Lives of the Glorious and Renowned Saintes of the Three Kingdomes, England, Scotland, and Ireland* (Saint-Omer, 1608). Roscarrock's work survives in a single manuscript, Cambridge University Library, MS Add. 3041. It has been partially edited by Nicholas Orme as *Nicholas Roscarrock's "Lives of the Saints": Cornwall and Devon*, in *Devon and Cornwall Record Society*, n.s., 35 (1992). On these works and their context, see J. T. Rhodes, "English Books of Martyrs and Saints of the Late Sixteenth and Early Seventeenth Centuries," *Recusant History* 22 (1994): 7–25.

92. Indeed, Tite records that Roscarrock borrowed Cotton's manuscript of John of Tynemouth's *Sanctalogium Angliae*, probably Tiberius E. i. See Tite, *Early Records of Sir Robert Cotton's Library*, 111–12.

93. Sir Robert Cotton, *Serious Considerations for Repressing of the Increase of Iesuites, Priests and Papists without Shedding Blood* (London, 1641), 15. On this tract and the date and contexts of its composition, see Marc L. Schwarz, "'Twenty-four Arguments': Sir Robert Cotton Confronts the Catholics and the Church of England," *Albion* 8 (1976): 35–49.

94. Cotton's quasi-juridical language compounds in the passage from which this citation is lifted: "I need not Envy the name of a Martyr to the Jesuite; for his cause if it be rightly vveighed, will blanch that title; but I desire to have all those Lineaments defaced, vvhich may compound that counterfeit Image; in prosecuting of vvhich purpose, if I have failed in my advice, and by confused handling, intricated the question, I humbly request, that a vvise mans verdict may mitigate the heavinesse of the censure" (*Serious Considerations*, 51).

95. Foxe, *Acts and Monuments*, ed. Townsend, 1.313; on Foxe's error, see note, 1.407.

96. John Bale, *The Examinations of Anne Askew*, ed. Elaine V. Beilin (Oxford: Oxford University Press, 1996), 77. See also Jennifer Summit, *Lost Property: The Woman Writer and English Literary History, 1380–1589* (Chicago: University of Chicago Press, 2000), 149–50, on Bale's uses of Blandina and other women.

97. T. H. [Thomas Fitzherbert], *A Defence of the Catholyke Cause* (1598), 17.

98. This aspect of Lucius's story appears to be the result of conflation with the story of the Swiss fifth- or sixth-century St. Luzius; on whom, see Bruno Krusch, ed., *Vita Lucii confessoris curiensis*, Monumenta Germaniae historica, Scriptores rerum Merovingicarum 3 (Hannover, 1896), 1–17.

99. Wilson, *English Martyrologe*, 331.

100. Foxe, *Acts and Monuments*, ed. Townsend, 1.311.

101. Wilson, *English Martyrologe*, 333–34.

102. On the St. Emerita reliquary in Chur, see Johann Schmucki, *Di Kathedrale von Chur* (Chur: Dr. Beeno Filser Verlag, 1928), 38.

103. Raphael Holinshed et al., *The first and second volumes of Chronicles comprising 1 The description and historie of England, 2 The description and historie of Ireland, 3 The description and historie of Scotland: first collected and published by Raphaell Holinshed, William Harrison, and others: now newlie augmented and continued (with manifold matters of singular note and worthie memorie) to the yeare 1586* (London, 1587), 25.

104. John Speed, *History of Great Britain* (London, 1611), 223.

105. Roscarrock, however, is typically more circumspect than Wilson: although he begins his entry "of St Emerita virgin and marter" by asserting that "Saint Emerita was the sister of one Lucius a Brittaine, which some would have to be our first Christened king of Brittaine," he concludes his review of the evidence concerning Emerita's relation by stating, "yet I think him not the right Lucius" (199r).

106. Wright, "The Elizabethan Society of Antiquaries and the Formation of the Cotton Library," in *English Library before 1700*, ed. Wormald and Wright, 196. On the Cotton Library as a source of precedents, see Sharpe, *Sir Robert Cotton*, esp. 76–77, 122–23, 145, 185.

107. *A Relation of Proceedings Against Ambassadors* is printed in James Howell, ed., *Cottoni posthuma divers choice pieces of that renowned antiquary, Sir Robert Cotton, Knight and Baronet, preserved from the injury of time, and exposed to publick light, for the benefit of posterity* (London, 1672), 6; Robert Cotton, *A Short View of the Long Life and Raigne of Henry the Third, King of England* (London, 1627). On the latter, see Sharpe, *Sir Robert Cotton*, 45.

108. Richard J. Ross, "The Memorial Culture of Early Modern Lawyers: Memory as Key Word, Shelter, and Identity, 1560–1640," *Yale Journal of Law and Humanities* 10

(1998): 229–326. The classic study on the topic is J. G. A. Pocock, *The Ancient Constitution and the Feudal Law: A Study of English Historical Thought in the Seventeenth Century; A Reissue with a Retrospect* (Cambridge: Cambridge University Press, 1987), which links the rise in antiquarianism with "the common-law mind" emerging between 1550 and 1600; see chaps. 2 and 5. See further Woolf, *Idea of History in Early Stuart England*, 24–29; Richard Helgerson, *Forms of Nationhood: The Elizabethan Writing of England* (Chicago: University of Chicago Press, 1992), 70–88; both focus on the work of Elizabethan legal scholar Sir Edward Coke.

109. John Selden, speech of 23 February 1629, in *Commons Debates for 1629*, ed. Wallace Notestein and Frances Hellen Relf (Minneapolis: University of Minnesota, 1921), 62. Ross discusses this speech and the Cotton Library's utility for lawyers: "Memorial Culture of Early Modern Lawyers," *Yale Journal of Law and Humanities* 10 (1998): 240, 248.

110. Ross, "Memorial Culture of Early Modern Lawyers," *Yale Journal of Law and Humanities* 10 (1998): 248.

111. Jacobus de Varagine, *The Golden Legend*, trans. William Granger Ryan, 2 vols. (Princeton, NJ: Princeton University Press, 1993), 2.158.

112. Robert Fabyan, *Fabyan's Chronicle* (London, 1533), 28. As the *Legend*'s modern editor, William Granger Ryan, observes, the confusions of chronology that beset the Ursula story "do not in the least diminish the main point of the story" for the teller or for its medieval readers (*Golden Legend*, 2.158n3).

113. Manfred Gorlach, ed., *The Kalendre of the Newe Legende of Englande* (1516) (Heidelberg: Universitatsverlag C. Winter, 1994), 183.

114. William Camden, *Britannia*, trans. Philemon Holland (1610), ed. Robert Mayhew, 2 vols. (Bristol: Thoemmes Press, 2003), 1.197.

115. The term "testimony" no doubt derived its weight for post-Reformation antiquarians from Parker and Joscelyn's edition of Aelfric, *A Testimonie of Antiquitie* (London, 1566). For a discussion of "testimony" and the problem of "the credibility of books," see Nick Jardine, "Books, Texts, and the Making of Knowledge," in *Books and the Sciences in History*, ed. Marina Frasca-Spada and Nick Jardine (Cambridge: Cambridge University Press, 2000), 393–407, esp. 396–99.

116. Barbara J. Shapiro observes of early-seventeenth-century historiography, "perhaps because so many historians were lawyers, documents were often viewed as testimonies, whether or not they were the report of an individual"; see Shapiro, *Probability and Certainty in Seventeenth-Century England: A Study of the Relationships between Natural Science, Religion, History, Law, and Literature* (Princeton, NJ: Princeton University Press, 1983), 145. On the influence of legal models of evidence on antiquarians, see further Shapiro, *Culture of Fact*.

117. On the legal turn of early modern historiography, see Woolf, *Idea of History in Early Stuart England*, 35–44, 200–242. Woolf's two more recent books on early modern historiography also trace a rise in the status of textual and material evidence, in which Cotton plays a role: see *Reading History in Early Modern England* (Cambridge: Cambridge University Press, 2001); *The Social Circulation of the Past: English Historical Consciousness, 1500–1700* (Oxford: Oxford University Press, 2003).

118. Donald R. Kelley, "Historia Integra: François Baudouin and His Conception of History," *Journal of the History of Ideas* 25 (1964): 35–57, quotation on 14. On Baudouin, see also Anthony Grafton, *The Footnote: A Curious History* (Cambridge, MA: Harvard University Press, 1997), 132–33. Baudouin's relevance to Cotton's project was suggested to me by a lecture given by Anthony Grafton, "The First Theorists of History," Harry Camp Memorial Lecture, Stanford Humanities Center, Stanford University, 30 January 2006.

119. This use of the document as eyewitness may reflect the growing importance of eyewitness historiography in the medieval sources favored by antiquarian collectors, such as William of Malmesbury; see Peter Damian-Grint, *The New Historians of the Twelfth-Century Renaissance: Inventing Vernacular Authority* (Woodbridge, Suffolk: Boydell Press, 1999), 68–84; Beer, *Narrative Conventions of Truth in the Middle Ages*, 23–34.

120. This early production of the medieval manuscript as witness to the past bears comparison to Christopher Cannon's discussion of the idea that historical forms "actually are the past, brought forward into our present, but not made here." See Cannon, *Grounds of English Literature*, 31.

121. Lorraine Daston, "Marvelous Facts and Miraculous Evidence in Early Modern Europe," *Critical Inquiry* 18 (1991): 93–124, quotation on 109.

122. On this *votiva ara*, see Tite, "Lost or Stolen or Strayed," in *Sir Robert Cotton as Collector*, ed. Wright, 262–306, esp. 263, 293.

123. As Camden continues, Cotton "is a lover of ancient literature, and most diligently preserveth these incriptions, which by others that are unskilfull and unlettered be streight waies defaced, broken, and converted to other vses to exceeding great prejudice and detriment of antiquity" (*Britannia*, ed. Mayhew, 2.769). Woolf includes an illustration of Cotton's sketch in a discussion of "the archaeological economy" of early modern collecting, in which he observes, in a spirit of analysis close to my own, that "the artefact, as a subject of scholarship, is constructed as such by the scholar" (*Social Circulation of the Past*, 222, 225).

124. Marie-Thérèse Raepsaet-Charlier, *Diis deabusque sacrum: Formulaire votif et datation dans les trois Gaules et les deux Germanies* (Paris: De Boccard, 1993); R. G. Collingwood and R. P. Wright, *The Roman Inscriptions of Britain* (Oxford: Clarendon Press, 1965).

125. Tite, "Lost or Stolen or Strayed," in *Sir Robert Cotton as Collector*, ed. Wright, 293. As Tite explains, the letters "LL.M.D.D." are an abbreviation for "Laetus Libens Merito Dono Dedit."

126. As David McKitterick points out, Cotton should be seen as a collector of objects as much as of books; see "From Camden to Cambridge: Sir Robert Cotton's Roman Inscriptions, and Their Subsequent Treatment," in *Sir Robert Cotton as Collector*, ed. Wright, 105–28. On the early modern cabinet of curiosities and the culture of collecting that supported it, see Paula Findlen, *Possessing Nature: Museums, Collecting, and Scientific Culture in Early Modern Italy* (Berkeley and Los Angeles: University of California Press, 1994); Woolf, *Social Circulation of the Past*, 164–76.

127. John Speed, *The History of Great Britaine* (London, 1611), praises Cotton for collecting not only "ancient records" but also "old monuments." See Sharpe, *Sir Robert Cotton*, 67.

128. Sharpe, *Sir Robert Cotton*, 66–68.

129. According to David Howarth, "Cotton also owned part of the cranium of Thomas à Becket, or at least thought he did," a holding that emerges in an account the papal envoy Gregorio Panzani left of a tour Cotton gave him of his cabinet and library; Gregorio Panzani to Cardinal Francesco Barberini, 25 May 1635, Vatican Library, Barberini Latina MS 8634, fol. 99. See Howarth, "Sir Robert Cotton and the Commemoration of Famous Men," in *Sir Robert Cotton as Collector*, ed. Wright, 62n5.

130. On the afterlife of Becket's relics and the debates surrounding them, see John Butler, *The Quest for Becket's Bones: The Mystery of the Relics of St. Thomas Becket of Canterbury* (New Haven, CT: Yale University Press, 1995); H. S. Milman, "The Vanished Memorials of St. Thomas of Canterbury," *Archeologia*, 2d ser., 53 (1892): 211–28.

131. John Stow, *Chronicles of England from Brute vnto this Present yeare of Christ* (London, 1580), 1013–14.

132. James Gairdner and R. H. Brodie, eds., *Letters and Papers, Foreign and Domestic, of the Reign of Henry VIII*, vol. 14, part 1 (London, 1894), 402. The record continues by suggesting that a false skull had been placed in Becket's shrine and that the true skull was "taken away." "And forasmuch as his head almost whole was found with the rest of the bones closed within the shrine, and that there was in that church a great skull of another head, but much greater by the three quarter parts than that part which was lacking in the head closed within the shrine, whereby it appeared that the same was but a feigned fiction; if this head was burnt, was therefore St. Thomas['s] burnt? Assuredly it concludeth not." This document is discussed at length in Butler, *Quest for Becket's Bones*, 126–33.

133. This point is consistent with one made by D. R. Woolf: that the post-Reformation fascination with historical artifacts represents an afterlife of relic veneration in the pre-Reformation period; see Woolf, *Social Circulation of the Past*, esp. 191–97.

134. Julia Boffey, "Middle English Lives," in *Cambridge History of Medieval English Literature*, ed. Wallace, 619.

135. Smith, *Catalogue of the Cottonian Library*, 143.

136. See William Stubbs, ed., *The Historical Works of Master Ralph de Diceto*, 2 vols., Rolls Series 68 (London, 1876). The "Collectanea" appears in Cleopatra E. i, fols. 105r–109r; the selections correspond to the following pages in Stubbs, *Historical Works of Master Ralph de Diceto*, vol. 1: 312, 313, 334, 335, 336, 372, 401, 410.

137. Bale, *Laboryous Journey*, conclusion (n.p.); Holinshed et al., *The first and second volumes of Chronicles*, 147.

138. Charles Duggan and Anne Duggan, "Ralph de Diceto, Henry II and Becket, with an Appendix on Decretal Letters," in *Authority and Power: Studies on Medieval Law and Government Presented to Walter Ullman on His Seventieth Birthday*, ed. Brian Tierney and Peter Linchan (Cambridge: Cambridge University Press, 1980), 59–82, quotation on 61.

139. For example, Cleopatra E. i transcribes one letter ostensibly written by Becket to Henry II in which Becket demands the return of churches "so that we may dispose of them as our own property according to our pleasure," where the letter ends. (The same is true of the letter that Ralph of Diss reproduces in his chronicle: "ut faciamus de eis sicut de nostris, prout nobis placuierit, similiter habitare permittat.") But the letter omits a closing line in which Becket pledges his reciprocal duty to the king: "and we shall do for him whatever an archbishop should do for his king and prince, saving the honour of God and our order" (et nos faciemus ei quicquid achiepiscopus debet regi et principi suo, salvo

honore Dei et ordine nostro). For the complete letter, see Anne J. Duggan, ed. and trans., *The Correspondence of Thomas Becket, Archbishop of Canterbury, 1162–1170* (Oxford: Clarendon Press, 2000), 2.1092–43. Ralph's version is to be found in Stubbs, *The Historical Works of Master Ralph de Diceto*, 1.336; and in the Cotton transcription, Cleopatra E. i, fol. 107v. On the divergent approaches among medieval Becket biographies, see Michael Staunton, *Thomas Becket and His Biographers* (Woodbridge, Suffolk: Boydell Press, 2006).

140. Holinshed et al., *The first and second volumes of Chronicles*, 133.

141. Ibid., 133–34.

142. John Foxe, *Actes and Monuments* (London, 1563), 452. The reference can be found in David Loades et al., *Foxe's Book of Martyrs Variorum Edition Online* (version 1.1, summer 2006), http://www.hrionline.ac.uk/johnfoxe/main/3_1563_0454.jsp.

143. Compare Prise's response to Becket with contemporary responses to Becket's cult, as described and discussed by Helen L. Parish, *Monks, Miracles and Magic: Reformation Representations of the Medieval Church* (New York: Routledge, 2005), 92–119. On Foxe's compulsion to separate true from false, see Thomas Betteridge, "Truth and History in Foxe's *Acts and Monuments*," in *John Foxe and His World*, ed. Christopher Highley and John N. King (Aldershot, Hants.: Ashgate, 2002), 145–59. And on Foxe's response to medieval hagiography, see Alec Ryrie, "The Unsteady Beginnings of English Protestant Martyrology," in *John Foxe: An Historical Perspective*, ed. David Loades (Aldershot, Hants.: Ashgate, 1999), 52–66. Ryrie also cites another example of the charge "stynkyng marter," leveled against the Protestant Robert Barnes (59).

144. See Tite, *Manuscript Library of Sir Robert Cotton*, 48; on the significance of Cotton's practice for a history of reading, see Kevin Sharpe, *Remapping Early Modern England: The Culture of Seventeenth-Century Politics* (Cambridge: Cambridge University Press, 2000), 305–6.

145. On Foxe's artful uses of primary sources, see Thomas S. Freeman, "Fate, Faction and Fiction in Foxe's *Book of Martyrs*," *Historical Journal* 43 (2000): 601–23.

146. Derrida uses the term "archivization" to describe a process that "produces as much as it records." See Jacques Derrida, *Archive Fever: A Freudian Impression*, trans. Eric Prenowitz (Chicago: University of Chicago Press, 1996), 17.

147. Cotton MS Otho C. xvi, fol. 27. This manuscript was badly damaged in the Cotton Library fire of 1731, but the original contents are listed in Smith's *Catalogue of the Manuscripts in the Cottonian Library*, ed. Tite, 74.

148. The "Sermon in Defense of Scripture" listed in Otho C. xvi has been identified with a work also owned by Parker (Corpus Christi College, Cambridge, MS 100 and MS 298) and Worcester Cathedral Library; see Ivor Atkins and Neil R. Ker, *Catalogus librorum manuscriptorum bibliothecae Wignoriensis* (Cambridge: Cambridge University Press, 1944), 11. Margaret Deanesly reprints it in *The Lollard Bible and Other Medieval Biblical Versions* (Cambridge: Cambridge University Press, 1920), 437–45; as does Curt F. Bühler, "A Lollard Tract: On Translating the Bible into English," *Medium aevum* 7 (1938): 167–83. Although Deanesly attributes the work to John Purvey, this attribution has been questioned; see Anne Hudson, "John Purvey: A Reconsideration of the Evidence for His Life and Writings," *Viator* 12 (1981): 355–80; Maureen Jurkowski, "New Light on John Purvey," *English Historical Review* 110 (1995): 1180–90. I am grateful to Colin Tite for helping me confirm the identification of this work with Otho C. xvi, art. 6.

149. Deanesly, *Lollard Bible and Other Medieval Biblical Versions*, 441.

150. As Tite notes, Cotton left annotations throughout the manuscript; see fols. 26, 29, 52v, 54, and passim (Tite, *Early Records of Sir Robert Cotton's Library*, 154).

151. Taylor observes, "A main contribution of Augustine to medieval historiography was the emphasis which he placed upon the periodization of history." Taylor argues suggestively that "the theory of the six ages" as upheld by Higden "held the field in Europe until it was replaced by the notion, held by the humanist historians, of a division between classical antiquity and the period which followed" (Taylor, *Universal Chronicle of Ranulf Higden*, 35–36n3). In other words, Higden's chronology of successive ages both set the stage for and would cede cultural authority to a succeeding periodization of medieval/Renaissance.

152. On Speed and his indebtedness to Cotton, see Woolf, *Idea of History in Early Stuart England*, 66–72.

153. Smith, "A History and Synopsis of the Cotton Library," in *Catalogue of the Manuscripts in the Cottonian Library*, ed. Tite, 53.

154. F. J. Levy, "The Making of Camden's *Britannia*," *Bibliothèque d'humanisme et Renaissance* 26 (1964): 70–97.

155. Sharpe, *Sir Robert Cotton*, 27–28 and passim.

156. Wright, "Elizabethan Society of Antiquaries and the Formation of the Cotton Library," in *English Library before 1700*, ed. Wormald and Wright, 177; see also Elisabeth M. C. van Houts, "Camden, Cotton, and the Chronicles of the Norman Conquest of England," in *Sir Robert Cotton as Collector*, ed. Wright, 238–52.

157. On early modern antiquarian and historiographical uses of such archeological artifacts, see Woolf, *Social Circulation of the Past*, 164–68, 173–82; and on coins especially, see 229–56.

158. See Suzanne Keen, *Romances of the Archive in Contemporary British Fiction* (Toronto: University of Toronto Press, 2001), for an exploration of more recent examples of the genre.

159. Hugh Trevor-Roper, "Queen Elizabeth's First Historian: William Camden," in *Renaissance Essays* (Chicago: University of Chicago Press, 1985), 121–48, quotation on 146. On Camden's contribution to the new historiography of evidence and fact, see F. Smith Fussner, *The Historical Revolution: English Historical Writing and Thought, 1580–1640* (New York: Columbia University Press, 1962); Arthur B. Ferguson, *Clio Unbound: Perception of the Social and Cultural Past in Renaissance England* (Durham, NC: Duke University Press, 1979); Joseph Levine, *Humanism and History: Origins of Modern English Historiography* (Ithaca, NY: Cornell University Press, 1987).

160. Patrick Collinson, "One of Us? William Camden and the Making of History," *Transactions of the Royal Historical Society* 8 (1988): 139–63, quotation on 141.

161. Karen Newman, "Sundry Letters, Worldly Goods: The Lisle Letters and Renaissance Studies," *Journal of Medieval and Renaissance Studies* 16 (1996): 139–52, quotation on 149.

162. Levine asserts that "the *Britannia* was . . . first and principally a commemoration of Roman Britain" (*Humanism and History*, 93).

163. Camden, *Britannia*, ed. Mayhew, 1.34. Subsequent quotations from Camden's *Britannia* will be from this edition, with the volume and page numbers given parenthetically in the text.

164. See Tite, *Early Records of Sir Robert Cotton's Library*, 39, 56. See also Thomas Smith, *V. cl. Gulielmi Camdeni, et illustrium virorum ad Camdenum epistolae* (London, 1691), 92, on Cotton's loans of saints' lives to Camden.

165. See, for example, the Cotton MS Titus F. vi, which includes Camden's own "History of some English saints" (10–16b) and Camden's notes of the "vita Guthlaci" that he borrowed from Cotton (55r); in Cotton MS Nero E. i, Felix's "Life of Saint Guthlac" is heavily annotated in what I take to be an early modern hand, reflecting antiquarian interest (see 185–96).

166. Bede, *The Ecclesiastical History of the English People*, ed. Judith McClure and Roger Collins, trans. Bertram Colgrave (Oxford: Oxford University Press, 1994), 16.

167. Ibid., 19.

168. On medieval excavations of Saint Albans, see Philip Schwyzer, *Archaeologies of English Renaissance Literature* (Oxford: Oxford University Press, 2007), 56–57.

169. Similarly, Weever, *Ancient Funerall Monuments* (1631), will call Verulam "a City in a grave" (718). In "The Ruines of Time" Spenser likewise mourns "Verlame," "Of which there now remaines no memorie / Nor anie little moniment to see" (4–5), but memorializes the antiquarian labors of his former teacher, Camden:

> *Cambden*, the nourice of antiquitie,
> And lanterne vnto late succeeding age,
> To see the light of simple veritie,
> Buried in ruines, through the great outrage
> Of her owne people, led with warlike rage.
> *Cambden*, though time all moniments obscure,
> Yet thy iust labours euer shall endure. (lines 169–75)

J. C. Smith and E. de Selincourt, eds., *Spenser: Poetical Works* (1912; repr., Oxford: Oxford University Press, 1985), 471–73.

170. Leonard Barkan, *Unearthing the Past: Archaeology and Aesthetics in the Making of Renaissance Culture* (New Haven, CT: Yale University Press, 1999), xxv. Compare the archeological "discoveries" described by D. R. Woolf, "Little Crosby and the Horizons of Early Modern Historical Culture," in *The Historical Imagination in Early Modern Britain: History, Rhetoric, and Fiction, 1500–1800*, ed. Donald R. Kelley and David Harris Sacks (Cambridge: Cambridge University Press, 1997), 93–132. And see further, Schwyzer, *Archaeologies of English Renaissance Literature*, on the literary significance of archeology.

171. Robert Plot writes in his *Natural History of Staffordshire* (1689) that he will "chiefly apply my self to things"; cited in Michael Hunter, "The Royal Society and the Origins of British Archaeology: 1," *Antiquity* 65 (1971): 116. In contrast, Hunter cites Camden and his fellow antiquarians, whose works "show no conception of the value of archaeological evidence as an autonomous province of historical enquiry" (114). An example of such conflation of the textual and the archeological object is William Lambarde, who describes himself "digging and raking together the antiquities of this realm which (as metal conteyned within the bowels of the earth) lie hidden in old books hoarded up in corners"; *Perambulation of Kent* (1596), 526–27.

172. Tite, *Early Records of Sir Robert Cotton's Library*, 167.

173. Camden's wording differs from that of the other surviving copy of Henry's Vita S. Guthlaci (Cambridge University Library, MS Dd.11.78); see Jane Roberts, "An Inventory

of Early Guthlac Materials," *Mediaeval Studies* 32 (1970): 207, on Camden's source. I am very grateful to David Townsend for sharing his edition in progress of Henry of Avranches's life of St. Guthlac, which enabled me to compare the two texts.

174. See Schwyzer, *Archaeologies of English Renaissance Literature*, for a discussion of early modern archeological metaphors for literary and historical analysis.

175. For an edition of Camden's source, see David Townsend, "The Vita Sancti Fredemundi of Henry of Avranches," *Journal of Medieval Latin* 4 (1994): 1–24.

176. See Tite, *Early Records of Sir Robert Cotton's Library*, 111–12; and *Nova Legenda Anglie*, ed. Carl Hostman, 2 vols. (Oxford: Clarendon Press, 1901), 1.45–56.

177. William Camden, *Remains concerning Britain*, ed. R. D. Dunn (Toronto: University of Toronto Press, 1984), 318.

178. Thomas Hearne, ed., *A Collection of Curious Discourses Written by Eminent Antiquaries*, 2 vols. (London, 1775), 1.23.

179. Ibid., 122.

180. Camden, *Remains*, ed. Dunn, 465.

181. Parry remarks that "Camden from time to time introduces lines of chronicle verse or of monkish Latin poetry to give imaginative color to his narrative" (*Trophies of Time*, 198).

182. Gabrielle Spiegel, *Romancing the Past: The Rise of Vernacular Prose Historiography in Thirteenth-Century France* (Berkeley and Los Angeles: University of California Press, 1993).

183. See Edward Donald Kennedy, "Romancing the Past: A Medieval English Perspective," in *The Medieval Chronicle*, ed. Erik Kooper (Amsterdam: Rodopi, 1999). See also Peter Damian-Grint, *The New Historians of the Twelfth-Century Renaissance: Inventing Vernacular Authority* (Woodbridge, Suffolk: Boydell Press, 1999), esp. 172–207.

184. Richard Helgerson reads Drayton in the context of contemporary antiquarian chorography: *Forms of Nationhood: The Elizabethan Writing of England* (Chicago: University of Chicago Press, 1994), 107–47.

185. For further comparison of Drayton and Camden along these lines, see Wyman H. Herendeen, "Wanton Discourse and the Engines of Time: William Camden—Historian among Poets-Historical," in *Renaissance Rereadings: Intertext and Context*, ed. Maryanne Cline Horowitz, Anne J. Cruz, and Wendy A. Furman (Urbana: University of Illinois Press, 1988), 142–56. On Camden's own poetry, see George Burke Johnston, "Poems by William Camden," *Studies in Philology* 5 (1975): 1–143; Johnston calls *Britannia* "a small library" in that it is "an anthology of poems and poetical fragments from many centuries" (21). Yet Camden's biographer (and Cotton librarian) Thomas Smith is quick to differentiate Camden's historical studies from the lighter pursuit of poetry: "For, neglecting the delights of poetry by which young minds are captivated, he applied himself to solid and genuine erudition." Thomas Smith, *Viri clarissimi Gulielmi Camdeni vita* (1691), trans. Dana F. Sutton (2002), http://www.philosophical.bham.ac.uk/Smith/trans.html, paragraph 64.

186. On the fragment in the Renaissance, see Barkan, *Unearthing the Past*, 119–208.

187. Parry, *Trophies of Time*, 216. On Weever's literary career, see E. A. J. Honigmann, *John Weever: A Biography of a Literary Associate of Shakespeare and Jonson, together*

with a Photograph Facsimile of Weever's Epigrams (1599) (Manchester: Manchester University Press, 1987).

188. John Weever, *The mirror of martyrs, or The life and death of that thrice valiant capitaine, and most godly martyre Sir Iohn Old-castle knight Lord Cobham* (London, 1601), sig. F2, F3.

189. On Weever's response to Reformation iconoclasm, see Schwyzer, *Archaeologies of English Renaissance Literature*, 76–78.

190. Clare Giddings, *Death, Burial, and the Individual in Early Modern England* (London: Croom Helm, 1984), 39–59; Christopher Daniell, *Death and Burial in Medieval England, 1066–1550* (London: Routledge, 1997), 175–202.

191. Anti-Laudian iconoclasm was growing in the 1620s and 1630s; it became officially sanctioned in a 1641 House of Commons order calling for the destruction of "superstitious inscriptions" in churches. See Keith Thomas, "Art and Iconoclasm in Early Modern England," in *Religious Politics in Post-Reformation England: Essays in Honour of Nicholas Tyacke*, ed. Kenneth Fincham and Peter Lake (Woodbridge, Suffolk: Boydell Press, 2006), 16–40, esp. 18–19.

192. Tite, *Early Records of Sir Robert Cotton's Library*, 130–31.

193. Ibid., 104; see also Graham and Watson, *Recovery of the Past*, 104. Weever may have consulted Caligula A. xi for *Piers Plowman*, which he cites frequently, but he almost certainly used another manuscript for Robert of Gloucester, whose chronicle Cotton bound also in the Caligula MS (this point *pace* Parry, *Trophies of Time*, 199). Although Caligula A. xi was used by Cotton contemporaries such as John Selden, Selden's annotations are concentrated on Robert of Gloucester. See Tite, *Early Records of Sir Robert Cotton's Library*, 114.

194. Parry, *Trophies of Time*, 198, 199–200.

195. See Tite, *Early Records of Sir Robert Cotton's Library*, 104; Graham and Watson, *Recovery of the Past*, J2.110.

196. Translation from Eric W. Stockton, *The Major Latin Works of John Gower* (Seattle: University of Washington Press, 1962), 325.

197. As Nigel Saul observes, "only a small number of formal obituaries were written" to commemorate Richard II after his death; Saul, *Richard II* (New Haven, CT: Yale University Press, 1997), 435. On the political circumstances and significance of Richard II's entombment, see Paul Strohm, "Reburying Richard: Ceremony and Symbolic Relegitimation," in *England's Empty Throne: Usurpation and the Language of Legitimation, 1399–1422* (New Haven, CT: Yale University Press, 1998), 101–27.

198. Stockton, *Major Latin Works of John Gower*, 326.

199. Helen Barr argues that Gower's *Cronica Tripertita* "unfixes" the modes of authority that Richard II fashioned for himself, including "one of the Latin hexameters which Richard commissioned for his tomb [which] reads: 'The king [i.e., Richard] laid low those who violated regalia'"; Barr, *Socioliterary Practice in Late Medieval England* (Oxford: Oxford University Press, 2001), 75. In light of this point it is significant that Weever substitutes Gower's own *Cronica* as an alternative epitaph. On Gower's *Cronica* and its modes of Ricardian critique, see also Frank Grady, "The Generation of 1399," in *The Letter of the Law: Legal Practice and Literary Production in Medieval England*, ed. Emily Steiner and

Candace Barrington (Ithaca, NY: Cornell University Press, 2002), 202–29; John Scatter-good, "Remembering Richard II: John Gower's *Cronica Tripartita, Richard the Redeles,* and *Mum and the Sothsegger*," in *The Lost Tradition: Essays on Middle English Alliterative Poetry* (Portland, OR: Four Courts Press, 2000), 200–225.

200. Sharpe, *Sir Robert Cotton,* 143–46.

201. Translated by R. F. Yeager, *John Gower: The Minor Latin Works with "In Praise of Peace"* (Kalamazoo, MI: Medieval Institute Publications, 2005).

202. For relevant discussion, see Eamon Duffy, *The Stripping of the Altars: Traditional Religion in England, 1400–1580* (New Haven, CT: Yale University Press, 1992), chap. 9. See also the essays collected in Allen J. Frantzen, ed., "Four Last Things: Death, Judgment, Heaven, and Hell in the Middle Ages," special issue, *Essays in Medieval Studies: Proceedings of the Illinois Medieval Association* 10 (1993); and in Carolyn Walker Bynum and Paul Freedman, eds., *Last Things: Death and the Apocalypse in the Middle Ages* (Philadelphia: University of Pennsylvania Press, 2000).

203. "The neglect complained of is of prayers for the soul of the departed," remarks the poem's editor, G. C. Macaulay, *The Complete Works of John Gower,* vol. 4, *The Latin Works* (Oxford: Clarendon Press, 1902), 420.

204. Siân Echard, "Last Words: Latin at the End of the *Confessio Amantis,*" in *Interstices: Studies in Late Middle English and Anglo-Latin in Honour of A. G. Rigg,* ed. Richard Firth Green and Linne Mooney (Toronto: University of Toronto Press, 2004), 99–121, esp. 99.

205. For more on the medieval graveside prayer, see Anne McGee Morganstern, "The Tomb as Prompter for the Chantry: Four Examples from Late Medieval England," in *Memory and the Medieval Tomb,* ed. Elizabeth Valdez del Alamo, with Carol Stamatis Pendergast (Aldershot, Hants.: Ashgate, 2000), 81–89. Stephen Greenblatt's analysis of the Reformation's abolishment of purgatory and the subsequent transformation of memorial practices is relevant to this discussion: see his *Hamlet in Purgatory* (Princeton, NJ: Princeton University Press, 2001).

206. Helen Cooper, "'This worthy olde writer': *Pericles* and Other Gowers, 1592–1640," in *A Companion to Gower,* ed. Siân Echard (Cambridge: D. S. Brewer, 2004), 106.

207. Derek Pearsall, "The Manuscripts and Illustrations of Gower's Works," in *Companion to Gower,* ed. Echard, 78.

208. See Karen Mills-Courts, *Poetry as Epitaph: Representation and Poetic Language* (Baton Rouge: Louisiana State University Press, 1990); Joshua Scodel, *The English Poetic Epitaph: Commemoration and Conflict from Jonson to Wordsworth* (Ithaca, NY: Cornell University Press, 1991).

209. On Speght's "archaeological" effort "to historicize Chaucer, to place him firmly in a medieval context, and to mark out the historical and cultural distance separating manuscript and print, and power and editor," see Stephanie Trigg, *Congenial Souls: Reading Chaucer from Medieval to Postmodern* (Minneapolis: University of Minnesota Press, 2002), 130. Derek Pearsall points out that the manuscript study on which Speght's edition depends is in fact the work of John Stow, which Speght fails to acknowledge; see Pearsall, "John Stow and Thomas Speght as Editors of Chaucer: A Question of Class," in *John Stow (1525–1605) and the Making of the English Past: Studies in Early Modern Culture and the*

History of the Book, ed. Ian Gadd and Alexandra Gillespie (London: British Library, 2004), 119–25.

210. *The workes of our ancient and learned English poet, Geffrey Chaucer, newly Printed*, ed. Thomas Speght (London, 1602), dedicatory epistle to Robert Cecil. On Speght's use of black letter, see Trigg, *Congenial Souls*, 130.

211. See Pearsall, "John Stow and Thomas Speght as Editors of Chaucer," in *John Stow (1525–1605)*, ed. Gadd and Gillespie.

212. I borrow this term from Stephanie Trigg, who discusses "Chaucer's progressive 'medievalization,' as he recedes further back into a historical era that must seem more and more alien" (an effect she diagnoses in connection to the loosening hold of "the canon to bestow timeless value"), in "The New Medievalization of Chaucer," *Studies in the Age of Chaucer* 24 (2002): 347–54, quotation on 352.

213. Edmund Bolton, letter to Robert Cotton, 22 January 1612, Cotton MS Julius C. iii, fol. 29.

214. Ibid., fol. 30.

215. See Tite, *Early Records of Sir Robert Cotton's Library*, 216; Smith, "A History and Synopsis of the Cotton Library," in *Catalogue of the Manuscripts in the Cottonian Library*, ed. Tite, 144. The letters themselves are in Cleopatra E. vi, fols. 217–19 and 226–29.

CHAPTER FIVE

1. Francis Bacon, *The Advancement of Learning*, ed. Michael Kiernan, vol. 4 of *The Oxford Francis Bacon* (Oxford: Clarendon Press, 2000), 56; subsequent references to this work will be noted parenthetically in the text with the abbreviation AL.

2. Compare to the "convertibility of matter" in Baconian metaphysics, as discussed by Angus Fletcher in "Francis Bacon's Forms and the Logic of Ramist Conversion," *Journal of the History of Philosophy* 43 (2005): 157–69, whereby "gold can be made from lead, food from waste, healthy limbs from sick, new species from old" (157).

3. On Bacon's parliamentary connections with Cotton, see Lisa Jardine and Alan Stewart, *Hostage to Fortune: The Troubled Life of Francis Bacon* (London: Victor Gollancz, 1998), 284–85. On Bacon's use of the Cotton Library, see Colin G. C. Tite, *The Early Records of Sir Robert Cotton's Library: Formation, Cataloguing, Use* (London: British Library, 2003), 10, 43. For Bacon's own library, see the fascinating auction record listing its contents: *Bibliotheca Baconia, or, A collection of choice English books: all in folio, curiously bound, gilt, and lettered on the back, consisting of various subjects but chiefly history, formerly belonging to Mr. Francis Bacon, lately deceased, will be exposed to sale . . . on Wednesday next being the 19th of May, 1686 . . .* (London?, 1686?).

4. Francis Bacon, "To Sir Thomas Bodley, Upon Sending him his Book of the Advancement of Learning," in *The Letters and Life of Francis Bacon*, ed. James Spedding, 7 vols. (London: Longmans, Green, Reader, and Dyer, 1861–74), 3.253. Edmund Bolton will repeat similar words in his 22 January 1612 letter to Cotton, in which he praises the Cotton Library as "the Arck [in] whiche all noble things which the diluges of impious vanitie, and sacrilegious furie have not deuourd are kept" (Cotton MS Julius C. iii, fol. 29).

5. John Speed, *History of Great Britaine* (London, 1611), 17–18.

6. Edmund Bolton, letter to Robert Cotton, 22 January 1612, Cotton MS Julius C. iii, fol. 29.

7. David McKitterick similarly notes the uncharacteristically "conservative view" that Bacon expresses in this passage in praise of libraries: "the notion of repose, of passive storage, was one that sat slightly oddly next to his arguments and proposals, both in *Of the proficience and advancement of learning* (1605) and in the *Instauratio magna* (1620), for a more active approach." McKitterick, "Libraries and the Organisation of Knowledge," in *The Cambridge History of Libraries in Britain and Ireland*, vol. 1, *To 1640*, ed. Elizabeth Leedham-Green and Teresa Webber (Cambridge: Cambridge University Press, 2006), 607.

8. For a discussion of this image, see Denise Albanese, "The *New Atlantis* and the Uses of *Utopia*," *English Literary History* 57 (1990): 503–28, esp. 506. See also Timothy J. Reiss, "'Seated between the Old World and the New': Geopolitics, Natural Philosophy, and Proficient Method," in *Francis Bacon and the Refiguring of Early Modern Thought: Essays to Commemorate "The Advancement of Learning" (1605–2005)*, ed. Julie Robin Solomon and Catherine Gimelli Martin (Aldershot, Hants.: Ashgate, 2005), 223–46, esp. 229.

9. The implied contrast between experimental learning and written tradition is explored and historicized by Lisa Jardine, "Experientia literata or Novum organum? The Dilemma of Bacon's Scientific Method," in *Francis Bacon's Legacy of Texts*, ed. William A. Sessions (New York: AMS Press, 1990), 60; John Hunter, "The Euphuistic Memory: Humanistic Culture and Bacon's *Advancement of Learning*," *Renaissance Papers*, 1995, 47–63; Andrew Barnaby and Lisa J. Schnell, *Literate Experience: The Work of Knowing in Seventeenth-Century English Writing* (London: Palgrave Macmillan, 2002), chap. 1.

10. Bacon plays a part in what Adi Ophir calls "the institutionalization of special places for the search for knowledge," as "a crucial stage in the historical process that constituted science as an established cultural system"; Ophir, "A Place of Knowledge Recreated: The Library of Michel de Montaigne," *Science in Context* 4 (1991): 163–89. On the early modern "association between knowledge and place," see Paula Findlen, "Building the House of Knowledge: The Structures of Thought in Late Renaissance Europe," in *The Structure of Knowledge: Classifications of Science and Learning since the Renaissance*, ed. Tore Frängsmyr (Berkeley: University of California, Office for History of Science and Technology, 2001), 5–51, quotation on 7.

11. The examples from *Gesta Grayorum, Novum organum,* and *New Atlantis* will be discussed below. In the *Commentarius solutus*, a private book of memoranda and loose notes compiled in 1608, Bacon draws up a plan for "Gyving pensions to 4 for search to compile the 2 Histories ut suprà. Foundac. of a college for Inventors. 2 Galeries wth statuas for Inventors past and spaces or Bases for Inventors to come And a Library and an Inginary" (Spedding, ed., *Letters and Life of Francis Bacon*, 4.66). The plan, minus the "Library," is realized in Salomon's House in *The New Atlantis*, discussed below.

12. See Anthony Grafton, *Commerce with the Classics: Ancient Books and Renaissance Readers* (Ann Arbor: University of Michigan Press, 1997), 224.

13. On this point, see Steven Shapin, "The House of Experiment in Seventeenth-Century England," in *The Scientific Enterprise in Early Modern Europe: Readings from Isis*, ed. Peter Dear (Chicago: University of Chicago Press, 1997), 277.

14. Howard Marchitello, "Science Studies and English Renaissance Literature," *Literature Compass* 3 (2006): 341–65, quotations on 345. On this point see also Richard Serjeantson, "Natural Knowledge in the *New Atlantis*," in *Francis Bacon's "New Atlantis": New Interdisciplinary Essays*, ed. Bronwen Price (Manchester: Manchester University Press, 2002), 83–105. Serjeantson argues that the notion of "science" as an autonomous discipline is anachronistic when applied to the seventeenth century.

15. For an overview of the emergence of seventeenth-century disciplinarity, see the essays collected in Donald R. Kelley, ed., *History and the Disciplines: The Reclassification of Knowledge in Early Modern Europe* (Rochester, NY: University of Rochester Press, 1997); William N. West, *Theatres and Encyclopedias in Early Modern Europe* (Cambridge: Cambridge University Press, 2002).

16. Lorraine Daston observes, "We often habitually oppose the humanities to the sciences along the axis of tradition versus progress: the humanities are portrayed as conservers of texts in editions or objects in museums, guardians of living cultural memory; the sciences as endlessly overthrowing old theories by new, deliberate amnesiacs about any disciplinary past older than yesterday's issue of *Science* or *Nature*"; Daston, "Type Specimens and Scientific Memory," in "The Arts of Transmission," special issue, *Critical Inquiry* 31 (2003): 155. On the emergence of the opposition between the studies of nature and words—or between science and rhetoric—see Mary Baine Campbell, *Wonder and Science: Imagining Worlds in Early Modern Europe* (Ithaca, NY: Cornell University Press, 1999), 77.

17. On this point, see Wilhelm Totok, "The Ordering of Knowledge and the Knowledge of Ordering between Renaissance and Enlightenment," *International Classification* 8 (1981): 2–9; as well as the references that follow.

18. Bacon sets out his "new form of Induction" in his work *Cogitata et visa de interpretatione naturae, sive de scientia operativa* (*Thoughts and Conclusions on the Interpretation of Nature, or A Science Productive of Works*), trans. Benjamin Farrington, in Farrington, *The Philosophy of Francis Bacon: An Essay on Its Development from 1603 to 1609, with New Translation of Fundamental Texts* (Chicago: University of Chicago Press, 1966), 99. Bacon describes the ordering of elements of knowledge "like an alphabet" in *Advancement of Learning*, 220, and *Abededarium novum naturae*, on which see Graham Rees, "Bacon's Philosophy: Some New Sources with Special Reference to the *Abededarium novum naturae*," in *Francis Bacon: Terminologia e Fortuna*, ed. Marta Fattori (Rome: Edizioni dell'Anteneo, 1984), 223–44. On the alphabet as an ordering system for Bacon, see Timothy J. Reiss, "The Masculine Birth of Time," in *The Discourse of Modernism* (Ithaca, NY: Cornell University Press, 1982), 198–225, esp. 209–10. On seventeenth-century bibliography, see Archer Taylor, *General Subject-Indexes since 1448* (Philadelphia: University of Pennsylvania Press, 1966), esp. 140; Theodore Besterman, *The Beginnings of Systematic Bibliography*, 2d ed. (London: Oxford University Press, 1936), 17, 20, 38–39, 48–58. David McKitterick calls the late seventeenth century "the golden age of subject indexes"; see his "Bibliography, Bibliophily, and the Organization of Knowledge," in *Foundations of Scholarship: Libraries and Collecting, 1650–1750; Papers Presented at a Clark Library Seminar 9 March 1985 by David Vaisey and David McKitterick* (Los Angeles: William Andrews Clark Memorial Library, University of California, 1992), 32.

19. Bacon's connection with Lambeth Palace Library will be more fully documented in a later section of this chapter; see especially, among those references, an invaluable

account by James P. Carley, "'A Great Gatherer Together of Books': Archbishop Bancroft's Library at Lambeth (1610) and Its Sources," *Lambeth Palace Library Annual Review*, 2001, 50–64. The Bancroft collection includes most of the manuscripts that survive from the priory of Augustinian canons at Lanthony; see James P. Carley, "The Dispersal of the Monastic Libraries and the Salvaging of the Spoils," in *Cambridge History of Libraries in Britain and Ireland*, ed. Leedham-Green and Webber, 1.265–91, esp. 287.

20. This account of Bacon's involvement with Lambeth Palace Library comes from George Abbot, Bancroft's successor, in 1612; Lambeth Palace Library, Library Records F.1. A transcription, edited by A. C. Ducarel, is in *History and Antiquities of the Archiepiscopal Palace of Lambeth*, Bibliotheca Topographica Britannica (1785; repr., New York: AMS Press, 1968), 2.48.

21. On seventeenth-century book catalogues, see Archer Taylor, *General Subject-Indexes since 1548* (Philadelphia: University of Pennsylvania Press, 1966), 140; Archer Taylor, *Book Catalogues: Their Varieties and Uses* (Chicago: Newberry Library, 1957), 49–53; Karl Schottenloher, "Concerning Seventeenth Century Libraries," in *Books and the Western World: A Cultural History*, trans. William D. Boyd and Irmgard H. Wolfe (London: McFarland and Co., 1989); David McKitterick, "La bibliothèque comme interaction: La lecture et le langage de la bibliographie," in *Le pouvoir des bibliothèques: La mémoire des livres en Occident*, ed. Marc Baratin and Christian Jacob (Paris: Albin Michel, 1996), 107–21. Sidney L. Jackson, in *Libraries and Librarianship in the West* (New York: McGraw-Hill, 1974), compares Bacon's "total classification scheme" to the catalogues of seventeenth-century libraries but concludes that his "classification of knowledge owes no recognition to" bibliographical classification (200; see also 172). Though Jackson's survey of early modern libraries is generally excellent, I disagree with this conclusion.

22. My understanding of Baconian induction has been greatly aided by Lisa Jardine, *Francis Bacon: Discovery and the Art of Discourse* (Cambridge: Cambridge University Press, 1974), esp. chap. 6. On the problem of particulars and universals in Bacon, see also Mary Poovey, *A History of the Modern Fact: Problems of Knowledge in the Sciences of Wealth and Society* (Chicago: University of Chicago Press, 1998), esp. chap. 1.

23. Campbell, in *Wonder and Science*, 78–85, compares Bacon's "Catalogue of Particular Histories" to the museum catalogue. On the uses and influences of catalogues and cataloguing, see also Elizabeth Spiller, *Science, Reading and Renaissance Literature* (Cambridge: Cambridge University Press, 2004), 10–11.

24. See Adrian Johns, "Reading and Experiment in the Early Royal Society," in *Reading, Society and Politics in Early Modern England*, ed. Kevin Sharpe and Steven N. Zwicker (Cambridge: Cambridge University Press, 2003). Johns cites Cowley's praise of Bacon on 247. See also Tara Nummedal and Paula Findlen, "Words of Nature: Scientific Books in the Seventeenth Century," in *Thornton and Tully's Scientific Books, Libraries, and Collectors: A Study of Bibliography and the Book Trade in Relation to the History of Science*, 4th ed., ed. Andrew Hunter (Aldershot, Hants.: Ashgate, 2000); Grafton, *Commerce with the Classics*. Bacon's pronouncement that "men study words and not matter," from *The Advancement of Learning*, is discussed by William T. Lynch, "A Society of Baconians? The Collective Development of Bacon's Method in the Royal Society of London," in *Francis Bacon and the Refiguring of Early Modern Thought*, ed. Solomon and Martin, 181.

On the ambiguity of Bacon's notion of *"experientia literata,"* see Reiss, "The Masculine Birth of Time," in *Discourse of Modernism*.

25. Francis Bacon, *Gesta Grayorum* (1594–95), in *Letters and Life of Francis Bacon*, ed. Spedding, 1.325–43, quotation on 334–35.

26. Ibid., 335.

27. Hans H. Wellisch, *Conrad Gessner: A Bio-Bibliography* (Zug, Switzerland: IDC AG, 1984), 10–11.

28. William H. Sherman, *John Dee: The Politics of Reading and Writing in the English Renaissance* (Amherst: University of Massachusetts Press, 1995), 35–36. On Dee's library, see also Julian Roberts and Andrew G. Watson, *John Dee's Library Catalogue* (London: Bibliographical Society, 1990). For a discussion of the relationship between libraries and laboratories, cabinets, and other collections, see Bruno Latour, "Ces réseaux que la raison ignore: Laboratoires, bibliothèques, collections," in *Le pouvoir des bibliothèques*, ed. Baratin and Jacob, 23–46.

29. Sherman, *John Dee*, 45. For an analysis of the Dee household as a reflection of "the practice of natural philosophy during the early modern period, at a time when sites of knowledge production were in transition," see also Deborah Harkness, "Managing an Experimental Household: The Dees of Mortlake and the Practice of Natural Philosophy," *Isis* 88 (1997): 247–62, quotation on 248.

30. Of Dee's library Sherman observes, "the interface between library and world is complicated and blurred" (*John Dee*, 50).

31. Cotton is typical in this regard: see David McKitterick, "From Camden to Cambridge: Sir Robert Cotton's Roman Inscriptions, and Their Subsequent Treatment," in *Sir Robert Cotton as Collector: Essays on an Early Stuart Courtier and His Legacy*, ed. C. J. Wright (London: British Library, 1997), 105–28. See also the inventories by Elisabeth Leedham-Green in *Private Libraries in Renaissance England: A Collection and Catalogue of Tudor and Early Stuart Book-Lists*, ed. R. J. Fehrenbach and E. S. Leedham-Green (Binghamton, NY: Medieval and Renaissance Texts and Studies, 1992–). A similar capaciousness is visible in the early modern museum, which, as Paula Findlen establishes, embraced a full range of objects—natural, human-made, and textual; see Findlen, *Possessing Nature: Museums, Collecting, and Scientific Culture in Early Modern Italy* (Berkeley and Los Angeles: University of California Press, 1994).

32. Donna Coffy, "As in a Theatre: Scientific Spectacle in Bacon's *New Atlantis*," *Science as Culture* 13 (2004): 259–90, quotation on 273.

33. Francis Bacon, *"The Great Instauration" and "New Atlantis,"* ed. J. Weinberger (Arlington Heights, IL: AHM Publishing, 1980), 70.

34. Bacon, *New Atlantis*, ed. Weinberger, 70.

35. Ibid., 79–80. On the taxonomy of knowledge workers in Salomon's House, see Serjeantson, "Natural Knowledge in the *New Atlantis*," in *Francis Bacon's "New Atlantis,"* ed. Price, 96–97.

36. On the relationship between More's *Utopia* and Bacon's *New Atlantis*, see Albanese, "The *New Atlantis* and the Uses of *Utopia*," *English Literary History* 57 (1990).

37. Neil Hathaway, "Compilatio: From Plagiarism to Compiling," *Viator* 20 (1989): 19–44. It is worth noting as well that "depraedatio" is a term that Bacon himself applies to his commonplace book, as when he describes his "Notae omnifarae tam ex depraedatione

Authoru[m] quam ex conceptu proprio per Titulos digestae et ordinatae. This is meerly a como[n] place book." See Spedding, ed., *Letters and Life of Francis Bacon*, 4.60. On such commonplace books and practices, see Ann Blair, *The Theater of Nature: Jean Bodin and Renaissance Science* (Princeton, NJ: Princeton University Press, 1997), 66–68; William Session, "Francis Bacon and the Classics: The Discovery of Discovery," in *Francis Bacon's Legacy of Texts*, ed. Sessions, 240–41; Mary Thomas Crane, *Framing Authority: Sayings, Self, and Society in Sixteenth-Century England* (Princeton, NJ: Princeton University Press, 1993); Ann Moss, *Printed Commonplace-Books and the Structuring of Renaissance Thought* (Oxford: Oxford University Press, 1996).

38. Bacon, *New Atlantis*, ed. Weinberger, 72, 75, 76–77. This is despite the fact that some readers have felt that Salomon's House *should* have a library, even if Bacon neglects to mention one; see Raymond Irwin, *The Origins of the English Library* (London: Allen and Unwin, 1958), 148.

39. Francis Bacon, *The Instauratio magna, Part II. Novum organum*, ed. and trans. Graham Rees with Maria Wakely, vol. 11 of *The Oxford Francis Bacon* (Oxford: Clarendon Press, 2004), 197. Subsequent quotations from this work will be noted parenthetically in the text with the abbreviation NO.

40. On the perceived problem of information overload in the Renaissance, see Ann Blair, "Reading Strategies for Coping with Information Overload, ca. 1550–1700," *Journal of the History of Ideas* 64 (2003): 11–28.

41. Robert Burton, "Democritus Junior to the Reader," in *The Anatomy of Melancholy*, ed. Thomas C. Faulkner, Nicolas K. Keissling, and Rhonda L. Blair (Oxford: Clarendon Press, 1989), 1.10–11. On Burton and libraries, see Grant Williams, "Resisting the Psychotic Library: Periphrasis and Paranoia in Burton's *Anatomy of Melancholy*," *Exemplaria* 15 (2003): 199–222. In *Religio Medici*, Thomas Browne refuses to "deplore the combustion of the Library of Alexandria," confessing that he believes that "there be too many [books] in the world" and condemning minor authors whose work serves only "to maintain the trade and mystery of Typographers." *Religio Medici*, in *The Prose of Sir Thomas Browne*, ed. Norman Endicott (New York: Anchor Books, 1967), 32. See Jon Thiem, "Humanism and Bibliomania: Transfigurations of King Ptolemy and His Library in Renaissance Literature," *Res publica litterarum: Studies in the Classical Tradition* 2 (1982): 227–46.

42. For an overview of the three faculties, see Jardine, *Francis Bacon*, 90–91, on memory. On Bacon's category of memory, see also Hunter, "Euphuistic Memory," *Renaissance Papers*, 1995.

43. Jardine, *Francis Bacon*, 93.

44. See Grazia Tonelli Olivieri, "Galen and Francis Bacon: Faculties of the Soul and the Classification of Knowledge," in *The Shapes of Knowledge from the Renaissance to the Enlightenment*, ed. Donald R. Kelley and Richard H. Popkin (Dordrecht, the Netherlands: Kluwer Academic Publishers, 1991), 61–81, esp. 71.

45. For this passage and a discussion of the voyaging-ship emblem, see Jardine and Stewart, *Hostage to Fortune*, 437; Sachiko Kusukawa, "Bacon's Classification of Knowledge," in *The Cambridge Companion to Bacon*, ed. Markku Peltonen (Cambridge: Cambridge University Press, 1996), 70; Michele le Doeuff, "Hope in Science," in *Francis Bacon's Legacy of Texts*, ed. Sessions, 12–13.

46. Le Doeuff, "Hope in Science," in *Francis Bacon's Legacy of Texts*, ed. Sessions, 13.

47. Devon L. Hodges, *Renaissance Fictions of Anatomy* (Amherst: University of Massachusetts Press, 1985), 93. While Bacon gives his idols a classical pedigree, they have an unmistakably (and, in the early seventeenth century, unavoidably) religious valence; on this point, see Charles Whitney, *Francis Bacon and Modernity* (New Haven, CT: Yale University Press, 1986), 38; Stephen A. McKnight, *The Religious Foundations of Francis Bacon's Thought* (Columbia: University of Missouri Press, 2006), 79.

48. John Jewel, *An Apologie or Answer in Defence of the Churche of England*, trans. Anne (Cooke) Bacon (London, 1564), sig. H3v; see Valerie Wayne, ed., *The Early Modern Englishwoman: A Facsimile Library of Essential Works*, vol. 1, *Anne Cooke Bacon* (Aldershot, Hants.: Ashgate, 2000), xii–xiv. On Anne's religious influence on her son, see also Sessions, "Francis Bacon and the Classics," in *Francis Bacon's Legacy of Texts*, ed. Sessions, 240.

49. Sessions, "Francis Bacon and the Classics," in *Francis Bacon's Legacy of Texts*, ed. Sessions, 239. On the same passage, see Morris W. Croll, "Attic Prose: Lipsius, Montaigne, Bacon," in *Style, Rhetoric, and Rhythm: Essays by Morris W. Croll*, ed. J. Max Patrick et al. (Princeton, NJ: Princeton University Press, 1966), 189; Judith Rice Henderson, "'Vain Affectations': Bacon on Ciceronianism in *The Advancement of Learning*," *English Literary Renaissance* 25 (1995): 209–34, esp. 222; Hunter, "Euphuistic Memory," *Renaissance Papers*, 1995, 59–61.

50. John Bale, *The laboryouse iourney and serche of Iohan Leylande* (London, 1549), preface (n.p.).

51. As Bernard Cohen asserts, Bacon means "revolution" in its astronomical sense, as a circular movement, rather than as a disruption or historical break; see Cohen, *Revolution in Science* (Cambridge, MA: Harvard University Press, 1985), 500–505.

52. See Timothy Graham, "Matthew Parker's Manuscripts: An Elizabethan Library and Its Use," in *Cambridge History of Libraries in Britain and Ireland*, ed. Leedham-Green and Webber, 1.332–41, esp. 337, 339.

53. Ann Cox-Johnson, "Lambeth Palace Library, 1610–1664," *Transactions of the Cambridge Bibliographical Society* 2 (1955): 105–26, esp. 105. See also Carley, "A Great Gatherer Together of Books," *Lambeth Palace Library Annual Review*, 2001, 50–64; Geoffrey Bill, "Lambeth Palace Library," *The Library*, 5th ser., 21 (1966): 192–206; M. R. James, "The History of Lambeth Palace Library," *Transactions of the Cambridge Bibliographical Society* 3 (1959): 1–31; Dorothy Gardiner, *The Story of Lambeth Palace: A Historic Survey* (London: Constable, 1930), 209–13; Thomas Allen, *The History and Antiquities of the Parish of Lambeth and the Archiepiscopal Palace* (London: J. Allen, 1826), 186–98.

54. Spedding, ed., *Letters and Life of Francis Bacon*, 4.23, 63.

55. Lambeth Palace Library, Library Records F.1, 1–2; reprinted in Ducarel, *History and Antiquities of the Archiepiscopal Palace at Lambeth*, 48.

56. C. B. L. Barr and David Selwyn, "Major Ecclesiastical Libraries: From Reformation to Civil War," *Cambridge History of Libraries in Britain and Ireland*, ed. Leedham-Green and Webber, 1.391.

57. Abbot's comment about Bancroft is preserved in Lambeth Palace Library, Library Records F.1, 1. Carley asserts that "the Royal Library must have been Bancroft's single largest source of loot, and a wonderfully rich one at that" ("A Great Gatherer Together of Books," *Lambeth Palace Library Annual Review*, 2001, 53); and he discusses a book of

sermons of Nicholas de Aquavilla that was rejected by the commissioners as "non perti-nentes" (60).

58. See Montague Rhodes James and Claude Jenkins, *A Descriptive Catalogue of the Manuscripts in the Library of Lambeth Palace* (Cambridge: Cambridge University Press, 1932); Henry John Todd, *A Catalogue of the Archiepiscopal Manuscripts in the Library at Lambeth Palace, with an Account of the Archiepiscopal Registers and Other Records There Preserved* (London: Law and Gilbert, 1812). For an overview of the collection and the provenance of its contents, see Carley, "A Great Gatherer Together of Books," *Lambeth Palace Library Annual Review*, 2001.

59. On contemporary religious conflicts and Bancroft's role in them, see Peter Lake, "Anti-Puritanism: The Structure of a Prejudice," in *Religious Politics in Post-Reformation England: Essays in Honour of Nicholas Tyacke*, ed. Kenneth Fincham and Peter Lake (Woodbridge: Boydell Press, 2006), 80–97; Peter Lake with Michael Questier, *The An-tichrist's Lewd Hat: Protestants, Papists, and Players in Post-Reformation England* (New Haven, CT: Yale University Press, 2002), 538–63; Charles W. A. Prior, *Defining the Ja-cobean Church: The Politics of Religious Controversy, 1603–1625* (Cambridge: Cambridge University Press, 2005), 206–13; Alexandra Walsham, *Charitable Hatred: Tolerance and Intolerance in England, 1500–1700* (Manchester: Manchester University Press, 2006), 56–73.

60. See Richard Palmer, "In the Steps of Sir Thomas Bodley: The Libraries of Lambeth Palace and Sion College in the Seventeenth Century," *Lambeth Palace Library Annual Review*, 2006, 53–67; D. Pearson, "The Libraries of English Bishops, 1600–1640," *The Library*, 6th ser., 14 (1992): 235; Tite, *Early Records of Sir Robert Cotton's Library*, 44–45, 215–16; Nicholas W. S. Cranfield, "Richard Bancroft," *Dictionary of National Biography*.

61. Lambeth Palace Library, Library Records F.1, 51; as well as Bacon's *Essays* (Lam-beth Palace 1597.11) and *Advancement of Learning* (Lambeth Palace 1605.1). Lambeth Palace Library also owns a magnificent copy of Bacon's *Novum organum* (1620) that Bacon presented to Abbot (Lambeth Palace 1620.45).

62. Bill, "Lambeth Palace Library," *The Library*, 5th ser., 21 (1966): 195. For similar arrangements of libraries by subject heading, see the essays collected in Robin Myers and Michael Harris, eds., *Property of a Gentleman: The Formation, Organisation, and Disper-sal of the Private Library, 1620–1920* (Winchester, UK: St. Paul's Bibliographies, 1996); and for contemporary examples, see T. A. Birrell, "Reading as Pastime: The Place of Light Liter-ature in Some Gentlemen's Libraries of the Seventeenth Century," in the same volume.

63. See Nicolas Barker, "Libraries of the Mind of Man," in *A Potencie of Life: Books in Society* (London: British Library, 1993), 179–201, esp. 190–91. See also William Clark, "On the Bureaucratic Plots of the Research Library," in *Books and the Sciences in History*, ed. Marina Frasca-Spada and Nick Jardine (Cambridge: Cambridge University Press, 2000), 190–206; Ann Cox-Johnson, "Lambeth Palace Library," *Transactions of the Cambridge Bibliographical Society* 2 (1955): 106–8.

64. Lambeth Palace Library, Library Records F.1, 47v. On the ordering of the books, see Cox-Johnson, "Lambeth Palace Library," *Transactions of the Cambridge Bibliographical Society* 2 (1955): 107–8.

65. For the works cited, see James and Jenkins, *Descriptive Catalogue of the Manuscripts in the Library of Lambeth Palace*: Polychronicon (48, 104, 112, 160, 181); Brut (84, 259); Legenda Aurea (222); Legendary in English (223).

66. David McKitterick, *Print, Manuscript and the Search for Order, 1450–1830* (Cambridge: Cambridge University Press, 2003), finds that, although the 1605 Bodleian catalogue does not separate manuscripts from printed books, the separation is in place in catalogues of the 1620s and 1630s (12–13). By separating manuscripts from printed books, the 1612 catalogue of the Bancroft Library is a forerunner of the later practice.

67. As Richard Palmer observes, "The books were arranged as if in battle order" ("In the Steps of Sir Thomas Bodley," *Lambeth Palace Library Annual Review*, 2006, 59). On conventional ordering of subjects in library catalogues, see Sears Jayne, *Library Catalogues of the English Renaissance*, 2d ed. (Godalming, Surrey: St. Paul's Bibliographies, 1983), 34.

68. Lambeth Palace Library, Library Records F.1, 1r–1v.

69. Campbell similarly compares Tradescant's catalogue of 1656 to "a merchant's inventory or a detailed will. It has reference to property rather than, or anyway more than, to knowledge" (*Wonder and Science*, 80).

70. On the wall system versus the stall system of shelving books, see John Willis Clark, *The Care of Books* (Cambridge: Cambridge University Press, 1909), esp. 274–75. See also Jackson, *Libraries and Librarianship in the West*, on shelf arrangement (169–72).

71. Cataloguing can thus be said to play a major role in Bacon's project of "disciplining" natural history, which Paula Findlen describes in "Francis Bacon and the Reform of Natural History in the Seventeenth Century," in *History and the Disciplines*, ed. Kelley, 239–60.

72. Bacon, *Cogitata et visa*, trans. Farrington, 75. On *Cogitata et visa* and the "Tables of Discovery," see David Colclough, "'Non canimus surdis, respondent omnia sylvae': Francis Bacon and the Transmission of Knowledge," in *Textures of Renaissance Knowledge*, ed. Philippa Berry and Margaret Tudeau-Clayton (Manchester: Manchester University Press, 2003), 81–97.

73. Bacon, *Cogitata et visa*, trans. Farrington, 75, 99.

74. For a comparison of Bacon and Gesner, see Sachiko Kusukawa, "Bacon's Classification of Knowledge," in *Cambridge Companion to Bacon*, ed. Peltonen, 70. See also Virgil K. Whitaker, *Francis Bacon's Intellectual Milieu*, William Andrews Clark Memorial Library Lecture (Los Angeles: William Andrews Clark Memorial Library, University of California, 1962), 2.

75. See Brian Vickers, "Francis Bacon and the Progress of Knowledge," *Journal of the History of Ideas* 53 (1992): 495–518, esp. 503. On Baconian history as "repository of matters of fact," see Robert Mayer, *History and the Early English Novel: Matters of Fact from Bacon to Dafoe* (Cambridge: Cambridge University Press, 1997), 26; Lorraine Daston, "Baconian Facts, Academic Civility, and the Prehistory of Objectivity," *Annals of Scholarship* 8 (1991): 337–64, esp. 339.

76. On the varieties of data processing in the Renaissance, see the essays collected in Jeffrey Masten, Peter Stallybrass, and Nancy Vickers, eds., *Language Machines: Technologies of Literary and Cultural Production* (New York: Routledge, 1997); Neil Rhodes and Jonathan Sawday, eds., *The Renaissance Computer: Knowledge Technology in the First Age of Print* (London: Routledge, 2000).

77. Compare to Ann Blair, "Note Taking as an Art of Transmission," *Critical Inquiry* 31 (Autumn 2004): 85–107, who stresses the historical emergence of the subject index as an

early modern locator aid. See also Ann Blair, "Annotating and Indexing Natural Philoso-phy," in *Books and the Sciences in History*, ed. Frasca-Spada and Jardine, 69–89.

78. The connection between Bodley and Bacon may have begun as early as 1576, the date of a letter that Bodley is sometimes held to have sent to the young Bacon; see Jardine and Stewart, *Hostage to Fortune*, 531n39. The authenticity of the letter's as-cription to Bodley has been called into question, however, most recently by Brian Vick-ers, "The Authenticity of Bacon's Earliest Writings," *Studies in Philology* 94 (1997): 248–96. The familiarity between the two men is clear, however, from Bacon's letter of 1607.

79. "A Letter to Sir Tho: Bodley, After he had imparted to Sir Tho. A writing entituled Cogitata et Visa," in *Letters and Life of Francis Bacon*, ed. Spedding, 3.366.

80. Bacon, *Cogitata et visa*, trans. Farrington, 75.

81. "Sir Thomas Bodleys Letter to Sir Francis Bacon, About his Cogita & visa, wherein he declareth his opinion freely touching the same," in *The Remaines of the Right Hon-orable Francis, Lord Verulam, Viscount of St. Albanes, sometimes Lord Chancellour of England* (London, 1648), 85.

82. On Bacon's critique of axioms, see Daston, "Baconian Facts," *Annals of Scholar-ship* 8 (1991): 343–44.

83. "Sir Thomas Bodleys Letter to Sir Francis Bacon, About his Cogita & visa, wherein he declareth his opinion freely touching the same," in *The Remaines of the Right Honor-able Francis*, 82.

84. *The Life of Sir Thomas Bodley, the Honourable Founder of the Publique Library in the University of Oxford, Written by Himselfe* (Oxford, 1647), 15.

85. William Dunn Macray, ed., *Annals of the Bodleian Library*, 2d ed. (Oxford: Clarendon Press, 1890), 413.

86. Thomas Bodley, letter of 23 February 1597, in *Letters of Sir Thomas Bodley to the University of Oxford, 1598–1611*, ed. G. W. Wheeler (Oxford: Oxford University Press, 1927), 4.

87. Heidi Brayman Hackel, "'Rowme' of Its Own: Printed Drama in Early Libraries," in *A New History of Early English Drama*, ed. John D. Cox and David Scott Kastan (New York: Columbia University Press, 1997), 127; G. W. Wheeler, ed., *Letters of Sir Thomas Bodley to Thomas James* (Oxford: Clarendon Press, 1926), 1; Wheeler, *Letters of Sir Thomas Bodley to the University of Oxford*, 7. On the physical furnishing of the Bodleian, see David Sturdy, "Bodley's Bookcases: 'This Goodly Magazine of Witte," *John Donne Journal* 5 (1986): 267–89.

88. On the stall system employed by Bodley, see Clark, *Care of Books*, chap. 5; J. N. L. Myres, "Oxford Libraries in the Seventeenth and Eighteenth Centuries," in *The English Library before 1700*, ed. Francis Wormald and C. E. Wright (London: University of London, Athlone Press, 1958).

89. "Sir Thomas Bodley's First Draught of the Statutes of the Publick Library at Oxon, Transcribed from the Original Copy, Written by his Own Hand, and Reposited in the Archives of the Said Library," reprinted in *Literature of Libraries in the Seventeenth and Eighteenth Centuries*, ed. John Cotton Dana and Henry W. Kent (1906; repr., Metuchen, NJ: Scarecrow Reprint, 1967), 64.

90. Samuel Daniel, "To the Librarie in Oxford erected by Sir Thomas Bodley Knight," in *The Complete Works in Verse and Prose of Samuel Daniel*, ed. Alexander B. Grossert, 5 vols. (London: Hazell, Watson, and Viney, 1885–96), 1.4, 6.

91. Letter of 26 October 1604, in *Letters of Sir Thomas Bodley to Thomas James*, ed. Wheeler, 114.

92. Bodley, "Letter read in Convocation, 13 April 1602," in *Letters of Sir Thomas Bodley to the University of Oxford*, ed. Wheeler, 12.

93. Bacon, *Cogitata et visa*, trans. Farrington, 99.

94. Ian Philip, *The Bodleian Library in the Seventeenth and Eighteenth Centuries: The Lyell Lectures, Oxford, 1980–1981* (Oxford: Clarendon Press, 1983), 18.

95. Michael Foster, "Thomas Allen, Gloucester Hall, and the Bodleian Library," *Downside Review* 100 (1982): 116–37, esp. 126.

96. Patrick J. Horner, *The Index of Middle English Prose*, Handlist 3, *A Handlist of Manuscripts Containing Middle English Prose in the Digby Collection, Bodleian Library, Oxford* (Cambridge: D. S. Brewer, 1986), x.

97. Ibid., ix–x; A. G. Watson, "Thomas Allen of Oxford and His Manuscripts," in *Medieval Scribes, Manuscripts, and Libraries: Essays Presented to N. R. Ker*, ed. M. B. Parkes and Andrew G. Watson (London: Scolar Press, 1978), 279–314, esp. 281; Philip, *Bodleian Library in the Seventeenth and Eighteenth Centuries*, 16–17.

98. A. Davidson, "Catholics and Bodley," *Bodleian Library Record* 8 (1971): 252–56, quotation on 252.

99. Watson, "Thomas Allen of Oxford," in *Medieval Scribes*, ed. Parkes and Watson, 288; Alan Coates, *English Medieval Books: The Reading Abbey Collections from Foundation to Dispersal* (Oxford: Clarendon Press, 1999), 125.

100. Coates, *English Medieval Books*, 140.

101. Ibid., 135–42.

102. Cotton also received books from Allen, but they reflect Cotton's interests: as Watson points out, they mostly "contain historical writings of one kind or another of the type that Cotton particularly sought out—cartularies, chronicles, saints' lives or materials in Anglo-Saxon—nearly all of which are related to England" (Watson, "Thomas Allen of Oxford," in *Medieval Scribes*, ed. Parkes and Watson, 300).

103. Letter of 22 July 1601, in *Letters of Sir Thomas Bodley to Thomas James*, ed. Wheeler, 11. For the entirely accurate reflection on James as "decidedly antipapist," see Archer Taylor, *Renaissance Guides to Books: An Inventory and Some Conclusions* (Berkeley and Los Angeles: University of California Press, 1945), 43.

104. Letter of 23 February 1597, in *Letters of Sir Thomas Bodley to the University of Oxford*, ed. Wheeler, 4.

105. The primary meaning of "publick" here is to designate the library's status as belonging to the whole university, not just the individual colleges, but the other contemporary meaning of "public"—benefiting the nation and people as a whole—also seems clearly to underlie Bodley's mission; see *OED*, s.v. "public." On the library's admissions policies, Bodley's *Statutes* are clear on the restriction of the readership, insisting, "We do utterly reject the Opinion of those, that would have no Exeption to no Man's Access"; "Sir Thomas Bodley's First Draught of the Statutes of the Publick Library at Oxon," in

Literature of Libraries in the Seventeenth and Eighteenth Centuries, ed. Dana and Kent,
93. On the meaning of "publick" library, see Jackson, *Libraries and Librarianship in the
West*, 151–52. For a relevant discussion of the emergence of a "public sphere" in the seventeenth century, see David Norbrook, "Aeropagitica, Censorship, and the Early Modern
Public Sphere," in *The Administration of Aesthetics*, ed. Richard Burt (Minneapolis: University of Minnesota Press, 1994), 3–33.

106. Gabriel Naudé, *Instructions Concerning the Erecting of a Library*, trans. John
Evelyn (London, 1661), 19, 21.

107. Ibid., 27, 33, 34.

108. Roger Chartier, *The Order of Books: Readers, Authors, and Libraries in Europe
between the Fourteenth and Eighteenth Centuries*, trans. Lydia G. Cochrane (Stanford,
CA: Stanford University Press, 1994), 69.

109. Ibid., 87.

110. Wheeler, *Letters of Sir Thomas Bodley to Thomas James*, 35. See Hackel,
"'Rowme' of Its Own," in *New History of Early English Drama*, ed. Cox and Kastan,
113.

111. Wheeler, *Letters of Sir Thomas Bodley to Thomas James*, 73.

112. *The First Printed Catalogue of the Bodleian Library (1605): A Facsimile* (Oxford:
Clarendon Press, 1986), 11.

113. Ibid., 75, 77.

114. Letter of 27 July 1604, in *Letters of Sir Thomas Bodley to Thomas James*, ed.
Wheeler, 104.

115. Macray, *Annals of the Bodleian Library*, 31–32.

116. Robert Burton, *The Anatomy of Melancholy*, ed. Nicolas K. Kiessling et al.,
6 vols. (Oxford: Clarendon Press, 1990), 2.88.

117. Ibid., 88, 92.

118. Chartier, *The Order of Books*, 62. This vision of bibliographical totality (as
Chartier observes) resembles that of Jorge Luis Borges's Library of Babel, whose

> shelves register all the possible combinations of the twenty-odd orthographical
> symbols (a number which, although vast, is not infinite): in other words, all
> that it is given to express, in all languages. Everything: the minutely detailed
> history of the future, the archangels' autobiographies, the faithful catalogue of
> the Library, thousands and thousands of false catalogues, the demonstration
> of the fallacy of those catalogues, the demonstration of the fallacy of the true
> catalogue, the Gnostic gospel of Basilides, the commentary on that gospel, the
> commentary on the commentary on that gospel, the true story of your death,
> the translation of all books in all languages, the interpolations of every book
> in all books. When it was proclaimed that the Library contained all books,
> the first impression was one of extravagant happiness. (*Labyrinths; Selected
> Stories and Other Writings*, ed. Donald A. Yates and James E. Irby [New York:
> New Directions, 1964], 54–55)

119. Chartier, *The Order of Books*, 62.

120. Bacon, *Cogitata et visa*, trans. Farrington, 79, 81. In a similarly, but even more
overtly, reformist framework, Bacon focuses the same attack against "the Scholastics and
their followers," who "have not only done their best to reduce Theology into the form

of a manual but have had the temerity to incorporate the disputations and contentious philosophy of Aristotle into the body of religion" (78).

121. *Philobiblon Richardi Dunelmensis sive De amore librorum, et institutione bibliothecæ, tractatus pulcherrimus: Ex collatione cum varijs manuscriptis editio jam secunda; cui accessit appendix de manuscriptis Oxoniensibus*, ed. Thomas James (Oxford, 1599).

122. *The Philobiblon of Richard de Bury*, trans. E. C. Thomas (London: De la More Press, 1902), 5.

123. On de Bury, see Michael Camille, "The Book as Flesh and Fetish in Richard de Bury," in *The Book and the Body*, ed. Dolores Warwick Frese and Katherine O'Brien O'Keeffe (Notre Dame, IN: University of Notre Dame Press, 1997), 34–77.

124. Thus, de Bury requires that "each keeper shall take an oath to observe all these regulations when they enter upon the charge of the books. And the recipients of any book or books shall thereupon swear that they will not use the book or books for any other purpose but that of inspection or study, and that they will not take or permit to be taken it or them beyond the town and suburbs of Oxford" (*Philobiblon*, trans. Thomas, 116).

125. H. J. Schroeder, ed., *Canons and Decrees of the Council of Trent* (London: B. Herder Book Co., 1940), 125.

126. Trinity College, Cambridge, MS B 1419, fol. 65v; see above, chap. 3.

127. R. Parr, *Life of James Usher* (London, 1686), 318.

128. *Index generalis librorum prohibitorum a pontificiis . . . In usum Bibliothecae Bodleiaanae, & curatoribus eiusdem specialiter designatus per Tho. Iames* (Oxford, 1627). James describes the project in *An Explanation or Enlarging of the Ten Articles in the Supplication of Doctor James* (Oxford, 1625), 7.

129. *Index generalis librorum prohibitorum . . . per Tho. Iames*, "Ad lectorum."

130. Chartier, *The Order of Books*, 87. See also Debora K. Shuger, *Censorship and Cultural Sensibility: The Regulation of Language in Tudor-Stuart England* (Philadelphia: University of Pennsylvania Press, 2006), 56–78.

131. Taylor, *Book Catalogues*, 54; R. W. Hunt, *A Summary Catalogue of Western Manuscripts in the Bodleian Library* (Oxford: Oxford University Press, 1953), 314.

132. Richard W. Clement, "Thomas James's *Ecloga Oxonio-Cantabrigiensis*: An Early Printed Union Catalog," *Journal of Library History* 22 (1987): 1–22, esp. 4, 19.

133. James, *Explanation*, 7–8, 14, 16.

134. Thomas James, *An Apologie for John Wickliffe, shewing his conformitie, with the now church of England; . . . Collected chiefly out of diuerse workes of his in written hand, by Gods especiall providence remaining in the Publike Library at Oxford, of the Honorable foundation of Sr. Thomas Bodley Knight: by Thomas James keeper of the same* (Oxford: Joseph Barnes, 1608), quotations from 73 and "Dedicatory Epistle."

135. Ibid., 2, 8, 11. For Wyclif's *De Veritate Sacre Scripture*, see *First Printed Catalogue of the Bodleian Library (1605): A Facsimile*, 159.

136. In addition to the *Apologie*, James edited *Two Short Treatises, against the orders of the Begging Friars, compiled by that Famous Doctour of the Church, and Preacher of Gods word, John Wickliffe . . . Faithfully Printed according to two ancient Manuscript copies, extant, the one in Benet Colege in Cambridge, the other Remaining in the Publike Librarie at Oxford* (Oxford, 1608).

137. On the Parker Library and its affiliation with the printer John Day, see Felicity Heal, "Appropriating History: Catholic and Protestant Polemics and the National Past," *Huntington Library Quarterly* 68 (2005): 109–32.

138. N. R. Ker, "Thomas James's Collation of Gregory, Cyprian, and Ambrose," *Bodleian Library Record* 4 (1952): 16–30, esp. 23.

139. Richard W. Clement, "Librarianship and Polemics: The Career of Thomas James (1572–1629)," *Libraries and Culture* 26 (1991): 269–82, quotation on 276. Thomas James, *A Treatise of the Corruption of Scripture* (London, 1611), 2.38.

140. Anthony Grafton, *Defenders of the Text: The Traditions of Scholarship in an Age of Science, 1450–1800* (Cambridge, MA: Harvard University Press, 1991), 55–64, quotation on 55.

141. James, *Explanation*, 22.

142. James, *Treatise of the Corruption of Scripture*, 5.20.

143. James, *Explanation*, 4.

144. James, *Apologie*, 46.

145. James, *Explanation*, 24. See *OED*, s.v. "libration."

146. James, *Explanation*, 22.

147. James, *Treatise of the Corruption of Scripture*, 5.10.

148. James, *Apologie*, 46.

149. *The humble supplication of Thomas James, student in Divinitie, and keeper of the publike Librarie of Oxford, for the Reformation of the ancient fathers workes* (London: John Windet, 1610).

150. Letters from Richard Bancroft to Thomas James, 4 December 1607 and 5 March 1609, in *Letters Addressed to Thomas James, First Keeper of Bodley's Library*, ed. G. W. Wheeler (Oxford: Oxford University Press, 1933), 8–9.

151. Archbishop Bancroft's chaplain, John Barcham, explains "how that my Lo. Grace hath beene sollicited to give way and furtherance to a project of Mr Tho. James for the revizing and repurging some of the Latine Fathers" and conveys the archbishop's "purpose and desire" in his letter to the vice-chancellor of Oxford, John King, 25 May 1610, in *Letters Addressed to Thomas James*, ed. Wheeler, 10. See also Ker, "Thomas James's Collation," *Bodleian Library Record* 4 (1952): 17–19.

152. James responded to Bancroft's support by sending him a handwritten catalogue of ecclesiastical, papal, and heretical authors, *Enchiridion theologium* (1610) (now Lambeth Palace, MS 524), which he followed up with similar gifts to Bancroft's successor, George Abbot, in 1610 and 1611.

153. James, *Explanation*, 5; for a discussion of this effort, see Philip, *Bodleian Library in the Seventeenth and Eighteenth Centuries*, 15.

154. Wheeler, *Letters of Sir Thomas Bodley to Thomas James*, 186.

155. *Sir Thomas Bodley's First Draught of the Statutes of the Publick Library at Oxon*, in *Literature of Libraries in the Seventeenth and Eighteenth Centuries*, ed. Dana and Kent, 104–5.

156. G. W. Wheeler, *The Earliest Catalogues of the Bodleian Library* (Oxford: Oxford University Press, 1928), confirms this impression in his description of Bodley's aim to "print the 'Tables'" (34–35). See also Philip, *Bodleian Library in the Seventeenth and Eighteenth Centuries*, 12, 117n54.

157. Jackson, *Libraries and Librarianship in the West*, 159.

158. Ibid., 157.

159. *First Printed Catalogue of the Bodleian Library (1605): A Facsimile.*

160. Ibid., ix–xiii. On the ordering of the shelves in the Bodleian, see Giles Barber, *Arks for Learning: A Short History of Oxford Library Buildings* (Oxford: Oxford Bibliographical Society, 1995), 8–10.

161. Wheeler, *Letters of Sir Thomas Bodley to Thomas James*, 96. This ordering of the disciplines follows Coluccio Salutati, who contends that medicine is inferior to law in *De nobilitate legum et medicine* (1399); the modern edition of this work is edited by Eugenio Garin (Florence: Vallecchi, 1947).

162. *First Printed Catalogue of the Bodleian Library (1605): A Facsimile*, 641–45. Z. Philip, *Bodleian Library in the Seventeenth and Eighteenth Centuries*, 14. Wheeler points out that initially "James, whose chief interest was in theological studies, had added a detailed list of commentaries on the various parts of the Bible, and also on the works of Aristotle, but had neglected to provide similar guides to 'the Expositours upon the Canon and Civil Laws,'" until Bodley "insisted that lists of commentators on the chief authorities in Law and Medicine should be prepared" as well. Wheeler, *Earliest Catalogues*, 42.

163. *First Printed Catalogue of the Bodleian Library (1605): A Facsimile*, 656; Wheeler, *Earliest Catalogues of the Bodleian Library*, 43; Philip, *Bodleian Library in the Seventeenth and Eighteenth Centuries*, 14.

164. *First Printed Catalogue of the Bodleian Library (1605): A Facsimile*, 327. For a comparison of James's bibliography with Gesner's, see Frederick N. Nash, "Enumerative Bibliography from Gesner to James," *Library History* 7 (1985): 10–20. On Gesner, see further Hans Fischer, "Conrad Gesner (1516–1565) as Bibliographer and Encyclopedist," *The Library*, 5th ser., 21 (1966): 269–81; Hans H. Wellisch, "How to Make an Index—16th Century Style: Conrad Gessner on Indexes and Catalogues," *International Classification* 8 (1981): 10–15; Archer Taylor, *General Subject-Indexes since 1548* (Philadelphia: University of Pennsylvania Press, 1966), 41–51; Theodore Besterman, *The Beginnings of Systematic Bibliography*, 2d ed. (London: Oxford University Press, 1936), 17–20.

165. For James's "Interpretes librorum Aristotelis," see *First Printed Catalogue of the Bodleian Library (1605): A Facsimile*, 417–25; and for James's collation of authorities on scripture, "Appendix ad expositores S. scripturae supra," see *First Printed Catalogue of the Bodleian Library (1605): A Facsimile*, 641–46.

166. Wheeler, *Earliest Catalogues of the Bodleian Library*, 109.

167. Bodleian, MS Rawlinson D984 is a transcript of the original Arts catalogue; the "synopsis Historicorum" begins on 142b. See Wheeler, *Earliest Catalogues of the Bodleian Library*, 108–9, 112.

168. Bacon, *Cogitata et visa*, trans. Farrington, 89, 99.

169. Ibid., 97.

170. Francis Bacon, "Of Studies," in *Essays or Counsels, Civil and Moral*, vol. 6, part 2, of *The Works of Francis Bacon*, ed. James Spedding, Robert Leslie Ellis, and Douglas Denon Heath (1878; repr., London: Routledge / Thoemes Press, 1996), 525.

171. Joel Shackelford, "Tycho Brahe, Laboratory Design, and the Aim of Science: Reading Plans in Context," *Isis* 84 (1993): 211–30, quotations on 215.

172. Spedding, *Letters and Life of Francis Bacon*, 4.23, 63.

173. John Dury, *The Reformed Librarie-Keeper* (1650), reprinted in *Literature of Libraries in the Seventeenth and Eighteenth Centuries*, ed. Dana and Kent, 40–41, 44–45, 43.

174. J. Crawford et al., eds., *The Hartlib Papers*, 2d ed. (Sheffield: HROnline, 2002), CD-ROM, 3/3/27A. I am grateful to Michael Leslie for pointing me to this valuable reference.

175. On the circumstances of the letter, see G. H. Turnbull, *Hartlib, Dury and Comenius: Gleanings from Hartlib's Papers* (London: University Press of Liverpool, 1947), 30–31. I am grateful to Carol Pal for this reference.

176. Paul Nelles, "The Library as an Instrument of Discovery: Gabriel Naudé and the Uses of History," in *History and the Disciplines*, ed. Kelley, 41.

CODA

1. On the digitization of medieval texts, see Sîan Echard, *Printing the Middle Ages* (Philadelphia: University of Pennsylvania Press, 2008).

2. See Margreta de Grazia, "The Modern Divide: From Either Side," *Journal of Medieval and Early Modern Studies* 37 (2007): 453–68.

3. John Browning, "Libraries without Walls for Books without Pages: Electronic Libraries and the Information Economy," *Wired* 1 (March/April 1993).

4. John Bale, *The Laboryouse Journey & Serche of Johan Leylande, for Englandes Antiquitees, geven of hym as a newe yeares gyfte to kynge Henry the viij* (London, 1549), Bviii r, Ciiii v.

5. The full passage, from "How Religious men should keep certain Articles," warns mendicant and monastic orders not to "drawen . . . noble bokis of holy writt & holy doctouris & opere needful sciences fro curates & clerkis in-to here owne cloistris, þat ben as castellis or paleicis of kyngis & emperouris, & suffre hem be closed Þer & waxe rotyn." F. D. Matthew, ed., *The English Works of Wyclif Hitherto Unprinted*, Early English Text Society, O.S. 74 (London, 1880), 221. See also John Foxe, *Acts and Monuments*, ed. George Townsend (New York: AMS Press, 1965), 3.721.

6. Francis Bacon, *The Advancement of Learning*, ed. Michael Kiernan, vol. 4 of *The Oxford Francis Bacon* (Oxford: Clarendon Press, 2000), 56.

7. Daniel Boorstin, *The Discoverers* (New York: Random House, 1983), 534.

8. Bale, *Laboryouse Journey & Serche*, Cv r–v.

9. Richard Gameson, "The Medieval Library (to c. 1450)," in *The Cambridge History of Libraries in Britain and Ireland*, vol. 1, *To 1640*, ed. Elisabeth Leedham-Green and Teresa Webber (Cambridge: Cambridge University Press, 2006), 13–50, quotation on 35.

10. Heidi Brayman Hackel, "'Rowme' of Its Own: Printed Drama in Early Libraries," in *A New History of Early English Drama*, ed. David Scott Kastan and John D. Cox (New York: Columbia University Press, 1997), 127; G. W. Wheeler, ed., *Letters of Sir Thomas Bodley to Thomas James* (Oxford: Clarendon Press, 1926), 1; G. W. Wheeler, ed., *Letters of Sir Thomas Bodley to the University of Oxford, 1598–1611* (Oxford: Oxford University Press, 1927), 7. On the physical furnishing of the Bodleian, see David Sturdy,

"Bodley's Bookcases: 'This Goodly Magazine of Witte,'" *John Donne Journal* 5 (1986): 267–89.

11. R. A. B. Mynors and R. M. Thomson, *Catalogue of the Manuscripts of Hereford Cathedral Library* (Cambridge: D. S. Brewer, 1993), xxi–xxii; Gameson, "Medieval Library," in *Cambridge History of Libraries in Britain and Ireland*, ed. Leedham-Green and Webber, 1.42.

12. John N. King, *Foxe's Book of Martyrs and Early Modern Print Culture* (Cambridge: Cambridge University Press, 2006), front matter.

13. Harold Billings, "Magic and Hypersystems: A New Orderliness for Libraries," *Library Journal*, 1 April 1990, 46–53, quotations on 52, 48; reprinted in *Magic and Hypersystems: Constructing the Information-Sharing Library* (Chicago: American Library Association, 2002), 9–22. This article draws interesting conclusions from early modern exempla, such as John Dee, despite its mistaken dating of the dissolution ("the 1550s" puts us squarely in the reign of the Catholic Queen Mary I, 1553–58).

14. Mary A. Rouse and Richard H. Rouse, *Authentic Witnesses: Approaches to Medieval Texts and Manuscripts* (Notre Dame, IN: University of Notre Dame Press, 1991), 221–55, quotations on 221, 222. In the same volume, see also 469–94.

15. *The Library as Place: Rethinking Roles, Rethinking Space* (Washington, DC: Council on Library and Information Resources, 2005). See also Sue Searing and Karla Stover Lucht, eds., "The Library as Place: The Changing Nature and Enduring Appeal of Library Buildings and Spaces" (Urbana: University of Illinois, 2006), http://clips.lis.uic.edu/2002-O9P2.html.

16. Geoffrey T. Freeman, "The Library as Place: Changes in Learning Patterns, Collections, Technology, and Use," in *The Library as Place*, 1–9, quotation on 3. On the distinction between "information" and "knowledge" that drives this discussion, see John Guillory, "The Memo and Modernity," *Critical Inquiry* 31 (2004): 108–32; John Seely Brown and Paul Duguid, *The Social Life of Information* (Boston: Harvard Business School Press, 2002), 119–22; Michael E. Hobart and Zachary S. Schiffman, *Information Ages: Literacy, Numeracy, and the Computer Revolution* (Baltimore, MD: Johns Hopkins University Press, 1998).

17. Freeman contrasts Enlightenment era "centers of learning" with "the medieval cloistered buildings that were frequented only by monks" ("The Library as Place," in *The Library as Place*, 1).

18. A. D. Baddeley, "Working Memory," *Philosophical Transactions of the Royal Society of London, Series B, Biological Sciences* 302 (1983): 311–24.

19. Herbert Bless, Klaus Fiedler, and Fritz Strack, *Social Cognition: How Individuals Construct Social Reality* (London: Psychology Press, 2004), 51–52.

20. I am reminded of the Bodleian Library of Thomas James by Sun Microsystem's description of its Dynamic Software Transactional Memory Library 2.0: "The Dynamic Software Transactional Memory Library is an experimental framework for building different software transactional memory implementations for comparison"; http://www.sun.com/download/products.xml?id=453fb28e (accessed 13 May 2007).

21. Antonio Damasio, *Descartes's Error: Emotion, Reason, and the Human Brain* (New York: G. P. Putnam, 1994), 23.

22. Stephen Batman, *The Doome Warning all Men to the Iudgemente* (London, 1583), 393.

23. Stephen Batman, trans., *Batman uppon Bartholome, his Booke de Proprietatibus Rerum* (London, 1582), 17v.

24. N. R. Ker, *Fragments of Medieval Manuscripts Used as Pastedowns in Oxford Bindings, with a Survey of Oxford Bindings, c. 1515–1620* (Oxford: Oxford University Press, 1954).

INDEX

Abbot, George (archbishop of Canterbury),
208, 210, 213, 314n20, 317n57, 318n61,
324n152
Adams, Thomas, 241n2
Aelfric, *A Testimonie of Antiquitie*, 132, 164,
224, 302n115
Aers, David, 245n34, 279n3
Agarde, Arthur, 152–53
Agrippa, *Commendation of Matrimony*, 79
Ailred of Rievaulx, 216
Alban, Saint, 164, 177–78, 197
Albanese, Denise, 312n8, 315n36
Alcuin, *De animae ratione*, 4
Aldus Manutius, 72–75, 77, 270n76, 271n78,
271n79
Alexander II (pope), 154
Alexander IV (pope), 154
allegoresis (exegesis), 7, 30, 40–41, 44, 47–48,
50, 112–13, 117, 119, 244n30, 284n58,
288n104
Allen, Judson Boyce, 257n89
Allen, Thomas, 216–17, 317n53, 321n102
Alnwick, William (bishop of Norwich), 24,
27–28
Amadas, Mrs. Robert, 138, 293n11
Ambrose, Saint, 50, 225
Anacharsis, 94–95, 278n171
Ancrene wisse, 95, 117, 130, 136
Anderson, Dorothy, 297n50
Anderson, Judith H., 264n11, 288n109,
291n151
Anglicus, Bartholomaeus, 49, 130
Anglo Saxon Chronicle, The, 136
Anselm of Canterbury, 50

Anstey, Henry, 263nn168–70, 263n173
Anthony, 2nd Viscount Montague, 216
Arfast (bishop of Elmham), 24
Aristophanes, 72
Aristotle, 50, 72, 74–75, 123, 203, 205–6, 229
Arnold, Thomas, 250n15, 253n47
Arthur (king of England), 119–27, 131, 286n86,
287n90
Arundel, Thomas (archbishop of Canterbury),
27, 52, 58–59, 99
Askew, Anne, 159
Aston, Margaret, 8, 250n14, 258n94, 258n95,
258n98, 279–80n7, 291n151
Atkins, Ivor, 305n148
Augustine, Saint, 26, 42, 50, 112, 117, 147,
153–55, 300n84, 306n151; *On Christian
Doctrine*, 112
Averroës, 49
Avicenna, 49

Bacon, Lady Anne Cook, 206, 219, 317n48
Bacon, Sir Francis, 6, 9, 13–14, 113, 197–237,
289n119, 311n3, 312nn10–11, 312n7,
313n19, 314nn20–24, 315n37, 316n42,
317n47, 317n51, 319n71, 319n74,
320n78, 320n82, 322–23n119; *The
Advancement of Learning*, 13, 197–200,
205, 207, 209, 212–13, 233, 235, 312n7,
312n18, 314n24; *Cogitata et visa*, 211,
213, 215, 220, 229–30, 313n18, 322n120;
Commentarius solutus, 198, 312n11;
Essays, 209; *Gesta Grayorum*, 198, 201–4,
231; *Great Instauration*, 198, 208; *New
Atlantis*, 198, 203–4, 312n8, 313n14,

Made in the USA
San Bernardino, CA
15 April 2013